I've travelled the world twice over,
Met the famous: saints and sinners,
Poets and artists, kings and queens,
Old stars and hopeful beginners,
I've been where no-one's been before,
Learned secrets from writers and cooks
All with one library ticket
To the wonderful world of books.

© Janice James.

The wisdom of the ages
Is there for you and me,
The wisdom of the ages,
In your local library.

There's large print books
And talking books,
For those who cannot see,
The wisdom of the ages,
It's fantastic, and it's free.

Written by Sam Wood, aged 92

DEAR DODIE

Frank and funny, unorthodox, liberated, quintessentially English, the writer Dodie Smith is the subject of this candid biography. Dodie Smith became an overnight sensation with her first play, AUTUMN CROCUS, in 1931. With the sell-out of DEAR OCTOPUS in 1938, she became the most successful female dramatist of her generation, but then left England to spend the war in California, with her pacifist husband, Alec Beesley. Back in postwar Britain, she wrote a children's book inspired by her own dogs. When Disney filmed THE HUNDRED AND ONE DALMATIANS, Dodie and Pongo, her Dalmatian, became household names the world over.

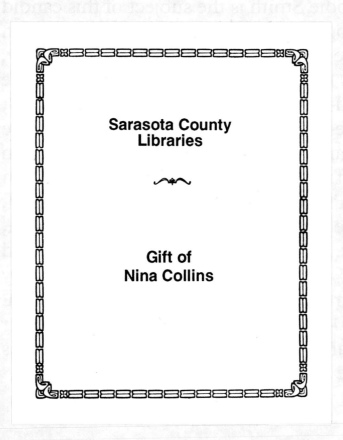

VALERIE GROVE

◆

DEAR DODIE

The Life of Dodie Smith

Complete and Unabridged

ULVERSCROFT
Leicester

First published in Great Britain in 1996 by
Chatto & Windus Limited, London

First Large Print Edition
published 1997
by arrangement with
Chatto & Windus Limited, a division of
Random House (UK) Limited, London

British Library CIP Data

Grove, Valerie, *1946 –*
    Dear Dodie: the life of Dodie Smith.
    —Large print ed.—
    Ulverscroft large print series: non-fiction
    1. Smith, Dodie, *1896 –* —Biography
    2. Women authors, English—20th century
    —Biography 3. Authors, English
    —20th century—Biography 4. Large type books
    I. Title
    828.9′12′09

    ISBN 0–7089–3774–8

Published by
F. A. Thorpe (Publishing) Ltd.
Anstey, Leicestershire

Set by Words & Graphics Ltd.
Anstey, Leicestershire
Printed and bound in Great Britain by
T. J. Press (Padstow) Ltd., Padstow, Cornwall

This book is printed on acid-free paper

TO MARGARET FORSTER

Foreword

My involvement with Dodie begins and ends with a spotted dog. Twenty years ago I became a Dalmatian owner by marriage: when I first met my husband, there was a Dalmatian named Gus always at his heels. Like every Dalmatian owner, I liked the idea of Dodie Smith who had made Pongo the Dalmatian a literary hero, and who was always photographed with a smiling dog beside her. On one occasion I almost went down to interview her, but I had too many prams in the hall at the time. Then, in the winter of 1991, I was interviewing the actress Gwen Ffrangcon-Davies for *The Times*, for Gwen's hundredth birthday, at her Essex cottage. As we drove away, I was told that we were passing Dodie Smith's home, The Barretts: it was dark and empty, since Dodie had recently died. 'What happened to her Dalmatian?' I asked, remembering a picture of her with Dalmatian number seven, Charley. I was told that Charley had died of a broken heart.

A year later, Dodie's literary executor, Julian Barnes, asked me to undertake her biography. I was familiar with only her most famous play, *Dear Octopus*, and two volumes of her four-volume autobiography. I had read *The Hundred and One Dalmatians* to my children, and had seen the Disney cartoon film; but I had not yet read the book I now regard as her masterpiece, *I Capture the Castle*. Like so many readers before me, I was captured from the opening sentence: 'I am writing this sitting in the kitchen sink.' Repeatedly, people of all ages the world over — from Antonia Fraser to Armistead Maupin — told me they regarded this as a seminal book of their youth.

Then there was Dodie's archive, which filled the spacious hall of Julian Barnes's house. There were boxes and trunks and suitcases and files of letters, diaries, journals, notebooks, which were all to be shipped to Boston University, to join the other 2000 authors comprising Dr Howard Gotlieb's Twentieth Century

Archive. In February 1994 I spent a month in Boston, buried in Dodie's papers while the street outside was three feet deep in snow.

What native flair, I wanted to find out, enabled her to strike gold three times, in three different genres in three different decades, with works that have each remained in print or performance (and still find new fans) after forty or fifty years? *Dear Octopus, I Capture the Castle* and *The Hundred and One Dalmatians* are utterly different works: but all have originality, some wit and irony, wrapped up in a technically skilful plot and a nicely judged skein of sentimentality that seemed to find public favour. And the only thing they had in common was their geographical location in the counties of Essex and Suffolk.

★ ★ ★

At the end of writing Dodie's life, I went one day for another look at Dodie's Essex cottage, and from there drove on to Suffolk to visit the Misses

Robertson, the Dalmatian breeders who had supplied Dodie's dog Disney; and to call on Anne Grahame-Johnstone, one of the twin artists who had illustrated the original *The Hundred and One Dalmatians*, capturing so perfectly the springing athleticism and beguiling nature of the breed. As I drove home to London, the appeal of Dalmatians lingered. In the course of Dodie's long life she had become more and more exclusively devoted to her dogs: they were a very close second to her husband Alec Beesley in her affections, while she grew less affectionate towards other human beings.

I began to feel, as Dodie did, that a house without a dog was incomplete. The moment I had finished my manuscript, one Sunday evening in November, I rang the British Dalmatian Club and asked whether there were any litters near London at the moment. There were three; the nearest was in Welwyn Garden City. I rang the breeder, who told me that from a litter of nine with the finest of pedigrees, four pups remained, but only one was still unspoken for, 'a dear little boy'. I drove there the next day, ignoring the huge posters on the hoardings that featured a spotted dog and 'A dog is for life . . . not just for Christmas'.

Five days later, my eldest daughter and I drove up in the December dawn to collect 'Mr Beesley'. He now occupies a central role in our household. Apart from being the handsomest dog in the world, he seems to me to embody the spirit and *joie de vivre* of the Dalmatian at its best. I think Dodie would have been vastly amused and pleased that her biographer — and she had often wondered whether her mountain of private papers would ever be read by some unknown person — would be blessed with a canine legacy of her own particular passion. The many pages of her journal devoted to her favourite Dalmatian, Buzzle, apply equally to Beezle (as we now call him) and for him, and for much else, I am forever grateful to have got to know Dodie.

Part One

1896 — 1934

1

Little Dodie Smith of Kingston House

OF the millions of words Dodie Smith wrote, most were about herself. Her plays and novels were, in length at least, mere trifles compared to the magnum opus of her journals that occupied her well into old age, when she continued to sit at her cottage window, much of the day and well into the night, by candlelight, writing on and on. She found it thrilling to sit there, alone, in the small hours, under a brilliant moon, with no other house in sight. 'But I often felt astonished — astonished that I should be allowed to live here, and sit up all night if I wanted to. Was I the only woman in the world who, at my age — and after a lifetime of quite rampant independence — still did not feel quite grown up?' At the age of eight, she would sit by her window and write. At eighty, she did the same. And at heart she still thought of herself as 'little Dodie Smith of Kingston House', a small girl who was unusually clever, fiercely ambitious, and always the centre of attention in the household.

Dorothy Gladys Smith, at first nicknamed 'Dodo', was born on 3 May 1896 at Whitefield in Lancashire in a Victorian redbrick semi-detached villa named Stonycroft. Her father, Ernest Walter Smith, was a bank manager. The name Ernest greatly impressed Dodie's mother, Ella Furber, when she met her future husband. Like Oscar Wilde's Cecily she thought Ernest a noble name, and a good antidote to Smith. Ella, known as Nell, the daughter of a licensed victualler of Cheadle, was married to Ernest in September 1892.

When Dodie was eighteen months old, Ernest died of cancer. He was only thirty. Her mother told her that he had been romantic-looking though short, and that on the day before Dodie was born he said he wished she was going to be a collie dog. Dodie, besotted by dogs, found this 'estimable' as collies were her favourite dog too. She remembered nothing of him. 'I have a coloured photograph of him wearing a pink tie with green spots,' she later wrote, 'but mother says the photographer made up the green spots.'

The relics left to her were few: a poem he had copied out in a beautiful hand, entitled 'If I should die tonight'; a sea-chest of letters, photographs and songs; his train set and his vintage *Boy's Own Papers*, which pleased Dodie who liked to slip back into the world of children of an earlier generation; and a book called *Afternoon Tea*, in which children wandered through gardens lit by afternoon sunlight, which filled her with a mysteriously satisfying sadness. She learned early to relish melancholy feelings.

The Furbers took in the widowed Ella and her baby daughter and they all went to live at Kingston House, Old Trafford, then a quiet and leafy semi-rural suburb of Manchester, where the corncrake could still be heard. The household consisted of Dodie's Furber grandparents, three bachelor uncles named Harold, Arthur and Eddie, two aunts, Madge (known as Nan) and Bertha, Dodie and her mother, and two maids, Maggie, who could do the splits, and Annie, who had lost a finger. So Dodie was surrounded by doting adults who liked nothing better than to entertain and be entertained by her, and who argued the whole time so she had to learn to speak out and hold her own. 'Must talk, want to talk, got to talk, going to talk,' was one of her first remembered utterances. To be an only child, with no threat of rivals, receiving the constant, adoring attention of ten uncritical and amusing adults, was fertile grounding for a writer. 'My family made a special climate all its own,' Dodie wrote. 'The talk I listened to perpetually (and took my part in) was about books, theatres, music, murder trials — the principle being that anything I could understand I was very welcome to overhear.' It was said that the Furbers would tear their best friends to pieces with the heartiest goodwill, a sport which Dodie early learned to enjoy.

Kingston House was detached, double-fronted and impressive, in Dodie's imagination old and romantic. It was built on two floors, on a hill above the Manchester Ship Canal, with sloping gardens and a high flight of steps which one of the maids scrubbed daily, while a washerwoman named Mrs Darbyshire slaved over the dolly tub. The rent was £50 a year.

The morning room had a sofa across the window; the enormous kitchen had two tall dressers, a row of iron bells, copper kettles and preserving pans gleaming on the shelf above the range. In front of the range and its glowing fire, Dodie had her bath, with the washing rack above, like Cassandra in *I Capture the Castle*. It was a firelit life; even the bathroom had a fireplace. Dodie's memories were always lit by a particular light — sunlight, twilight, candlelight, flickering firelight: lamplight conjured up 'contented middle-class families, nothing disturbing the golden peace' while candlelight 'always makes me feel that something wonderful is about to happen'. Whenever she saw a play of hers into production in later years, she would browbeat the director into getting the lighting exactly right.

The house had four sitting rooms and three pianos, one grand and two upright. It was filled with fine fittings:

marble wash-stands, painted doors with decorated china finger-plates, bronze gaseliers, green Venetian blinds; and a tiled hall hung with watercolours and a painting of Ellen Terry as Ophelia. The landing and stairs formed a natural stage for charades; there was a lifesize lady holding a gas globe lamp, and 'lighting the lady' was a ritual at dusk. Dodie shared a bedroom with her mother, but also had her own sitting room, the former day nursery, its walls covered in varnished scraps. Her toys included a toy theatre and a tin cooking stove operated by candle power — the first and last time Dodie ever took any interest in cooking.

Her mother was just five foot high in her rose-embroidered bonnet. She had a predilection for delicate, airy clothes and muslin petticoats with rows of lace and ribbon. She was not well-educated, but she was well-read and loved argument, and encouraged Dodie to argue back. She scorned conventional religion, and when she died, she said, she wanted no tombstone: if people wanted to think of her they could go into the country on a sunny day and feel as cheerful as possible. She was impulsively generous, once giving away a particularly fine black hat to an aunt who tried it on.

'Of all the women I have ever known,' Dodie wrote in *Look Back With Love*, 'I liked my mother best. Of course I loved her, but most children love their mothers, and it is no particular compliment. True liking implies a reasoned judgement, and I have come to believe it is more important than loving; it wears better.' Writing this fifty years after her mother's death in 1912, she said she no longer felt any emotional loss but she did still long to share things with her. She was the kind of person who would always understand: when Dodie described to her the peculiar feeling of liberation she had when upside down on a swing, Ella knew exactly what she meant. And Ella often said Dodie had been sent to her as a compensation for losing her husband. Yet mother-love remained Dodie's least favourite subject, and an emotion she never wished to sample in person; she found herself quite interesting enough without having to embellish herself with offspring.

Grandmother Margaret Furber, known as Grandima, would sleep sitting up, supported by many pillows, so to Dodie she seemed always to be awake in her high bed, under a mosquito net of Valenciennes lace. Here she would invent for Dodie a kind of soap opera fairytale called 'Golden Palace', continued each morning. She wore long pointed weskits, fine lace collars and cuffs, elaborate lace caps, and bonnets with ribbons. In 1885, when her husband had lost his job with the chemical company Brunner Mond, Grandima, mother of eight, had written a well-reviewed novel under the pen-name of George Challis, entitled *Britain's Slaves*. It was a polemic against 'the enforced education of the masses', a futile attempt to persuade people that the Education Act should be repealed. 'Mr Challis has performed his task well,' declared the *Birmingham Gazette*. 'We only hope that Mr Challis raises his voice against the absurd fads of our legislature outside the realm of fiction.' Dodie read it when she was herself starting to write novels, and found it hard going. Though the characters were vivid and the dialogue excellent, Grandima had a tendency to hammer her case — 'like me, Grandima puts in too much detail' — and after all, nobody could seriously make a case for child labour, and against education for the poor. Grandima's husband, Dodie's grandfather, died quietly one afternoon during a nap, when Dodie was still a small child. But she remembered his taking her at eleven each morning to feed the hens in his hen-feeding hat. Then they would go for their walk past the Old Trafford cricket ground.

The three bachelor uncles, known as 'the boys', would all come home for midday dinner. They were distinctive characters, who worked at Manchester's great Cotton Exchange, home of the Royal Exchange Theatre today. Uncle Harold was a talented amateur theatricals star, famous for his recitations from *Macbeth* and for his 'I'm going mad' mime. He had been a velvet buyer for a large textile firm, and was now an agent for Hanschin and Ronis (Hanro) the Swiss manufacturers of ladies' lacy underwear. His two brothers also freelanced as manufacturers' agents. Uncle Arthur had a luxuriant moustache and a fruity tenor voice, and kept rabbits and bees. For a while he worked as a milkman, until Grandima decided she could not have her milk delivered by her own son. He was a mine of unexpected information (from a book called *A Thousand Facts Worth Knowing*) and thrived on toasted cheese. Eddie, the youngest and handsomest brother, who prospered best of the three in the cotton business, was tall and lean and specialised in doing a 'wolf' act. Of the two aunts, Nan was the better educated and could work as a governess; Bertha had the more original personality, bordering on the eccentric. 'She could not, for instance, tell her right hand from her left unless she hopped. And she never ceased to be surprised when people liked her, as they invariably did.' Later both aunts married, which had them crocheting doilies like fiends during the months of their engagements. Grandima grimly iced three-tiered wedding cakes for them, dismayed (Dodie said) that any of her children should marry and leave the nest. None of the three boys ever even had a romance, let alone an engagement.

And why should they wish to leave? No other household could have been as animated. The Furbers were vociferous about their literary and dramatic tastes, thespian matters being central to their lives. Dodie knew all about plays long before she ever entered a theatre. The first play she ever saw, at the age of four, was a farce called *Jane*, starring Uncle Harold at the Urmston amateur dramatic society. They went in a private bus, Dodie tingling with excitement in her Red Riding Hood cloak. From that day on, the sound of an orchestra tuning up was to her the most thrilling in the world. She found the play dull and incomprehensible, but the seed was sown. She was determined on the stage. She was very soon involved in Uncle Harold's productions with his friend, the playwright Stanley Houghton, at the Athenaeum, one of Manchester's sixty-four amateur dramatic clubs at that time.[1] The Athenaeum literary and dramatic reading society was founded in 1835 'for the purpose of reading the works of Shakespeare and other authors, and . . . to be a source of mutual improvement and amusement to its members.' Christabel Pankhurst's

---

[1] Edwardian Manchester was a theatrical mecca. In just three central streets there were eight theatres, and the *Manchester Guardian* reviews were as influential as those of any London paper. Arnold Bennett wrote of Manchester in 1907: 'There is no place which can match its union of intellectual vigour, artistic perceptiveness and political sagacity.' The critic James Agate — who was at Manchester Grammar School with Stanley Houghton, later to write *Hindle Wakes*, and Harold Brighouse, later to write *Hobson's Choice* — celebrated Manchester's liberal culture, awareness and gaiety. In the world of the theatre, everyone came to Manchester: in 1909 alone, Lewis Casson, Harley Granville Barker, Henry Irving, Cyril Maude, Esmé Percy, Nigel Playfair, Fred Terry and H. Beerbohm Tree all signed the visitors' book at the Brasenose Club.

grandfather had been president in the 1850s. Uncle Harold became president in 1904, by which time the productions had become more elaborate; a technician called Willie Clemson would create realistic storms, sunrises, smoke that curled out of chimneys. In her playwright days Dodie rarely found a technician who could achieve such dramatic stage effects as Willie Clemson's.

Dodie was soon out of the audience and on stage herself. The earliest press clipping in her scrapbook is from the *Manchester Evening News* for 2 October 1909, when she was thirteen, and in the cast of the Athenaeum's production of *Le Courrier de Lyon* at the Schiller Institute in Nelson Street, Manchester. In the front row sits 'Dodo' Smith, playing the inn-keeper's boy Joliquet in knee-britches. (She often played boy parts: she was Derek in Pinero's *His House in Order* and Little Willie in *East Lynne* and was taken to a boys' outfitters for her corduroy trousers.) Behind her in the photograph is Uncle Harold; and in the middle row stands the handsome Norman L. Oddy with whom Dodie thought herself, at thirteen, desperately in love. (In her note-books she disguised his name rather unfortunately as 'Vincent Queer'.) After *Le Courrier de Lyon*, during which there were so many dries among the actors that Dodie had to ad-lib and prompt from on stage, Oddy had given her a sixpenny box of chocolates, and she would fervently kiss the empty box, and bicycle past his house just to gaze up at his lighted drawing room window.

★ ★ ★

When Dodie's mother was a girl, the Furbers had lived at Darley Old Hall near Farnworth, in the Lancashire moorland. Dodie was fascinated by the idea of eight children living in wild countryside, with animals. Like many only children, she sometimes imagined that life in a large family might have been more fun. In her twenties, she fancied she had a distant memory of living in a great house with chestnuts in the garden, and lots of brothers and sisters, 'luxurious children, with ponies and nurses galore . . . this is possibly a *réchauffée* of all the children's books I read about the Squire's children living at the Manor or the Grange. I always preferred to read about opulent children. Stories about poor children bored me.' And later in life, 'No book about childhoods that are different from mine can ever be really nostalgic for me,' she said.

Grandima called her The Discontented Elf (who, in the story, had to be taught what real suffering was). Dodie was prone to tears and already developing what she later called her masochistic tendencies — creating miseries out of unusually happy circumstances. It was therefore good for her to have teasing uncles who never minded how often they repeated their jokes. One joke was to pretend that the theatre they were going to had just burned down that afternoon. Or, when they arrived at the theatre, the uncle with the tickets would claim to have left them behind, and a charade would ensue about whether there was time to get home and fetch the tickets before the second act began — and so on, until the tickets were produced.

17

In the afternoons her mother read aloud to her — from *Alice*, or *Little Women* — but would then fall asleep, leaving Dodie to her imaginative life. 'Anything would get my imagination going, the pattern on wallpapers and carpets, cracks on the ceiling, flowers, leaves and even blades of grass, also intangible things like Christian names, which had colours and shapes for me.' Her first notebook, 'the one-shilling notebook', survives, black and shiny, containing her earliest creative efforts — at eight — in pencil. She made a series of observations entitled 'As I Sit By My Window', describing the people passing by: a man on crutches 'and in my heart I am sory for him because it must be dredful to be lame'; a crying child who has lost his companions: 'I wonder if he found them again. The church blocks my view now so I have to immagen.' One day she showed the notebook to her mother, who said it saddened her because it made her seem so lonely. 'I like being lonely,' Dodie replied.

The black one-shilling notebook also contains her earliest play, 'The Ghost of Gainsborough', packed with vivid drama:

FRITZ (*excitedly*): Someone must be approaching the castle, for the drawbridge has been put up, and the pixeys have arranged themselves as if for a battle . . .

HELENA: Look, look, can it be yes it is, Prince Max swimming through the water, now he has clambered on the banks of the island . . .

This notebook contains several Daisy Ashford-like beginnings to stories: 'It was a fine afternoon in October that Marjorie Gillford sat at her desk impaitently waiting for school to be dismist. To say she was doing her lesons would be sertenle not the truth, for although she was soposed to be she was doing nothing but thinking what her two cousins who were coming to live with her would be like . . . ' Since she had no siblings Dodie's own lively cousins played a large part in her life: Nan's children Esmé (and later also Ronnie) Reynolds-Jones, and the five Moore cousins, children of her father's well-off brother Tyrrel (he had changed his name from Smith) who emigrated to Texas. 'Aunt' Carrie,

19

a family friend, would sometimes bring her three daughters, who 'could make more noise than any three females I ever knew, and like the bells of Bredon it was "a happy noise to hear"'. All the sisters and Dodie would go to the swimming baths, shrieking and screaming in their stockinette costumes, Aunt Carrie smoking a Gold Flake the while — and none of them could swim a stroke.

High tea in Manchester, she later recalled, was quite a horrible meal really but being at six o'clock it did allow you a nice long evening afterwards. Its ritual spread of bread and butter, parkin, seedy loaf, Nan's Special Damp Cake, and stewed fruit with cold meat and pickles and sauces somehow went with the mayhem of voices, 'the shouting and talking and tin plates clattering, and haddock and milk and jelly and cake all getting mixed up together'. For Dodie this was followed by entertainment by Grandima, then bath and haircurling in rags, and firelit stories from Mother, with Dodie invariably as the heroine.

The Furbers were a family dedicated to amusement. They were mad about fairgrounds, seaside donkey-rides, afternoons on the pier, and newfangled roller-skating rinks — whatever was the latest fun going. They naturally took up dancing to gramophone records, and later went to the first movies, the brothers being particularly taken with Maurice Chevalier. At home, with the three pianos, a violin, a guitar, a mandolin and a banjo, there were musical evenings, with charades and singing round the Angelus piano-player (a form of pianola). Uncle Bertie would recite 'Casey at the Goal-Mouth' and bring the house down; Uncle Eddie made up doggerel verses about the family ('There's half an egg for Bertie,/ And I shall suck the shell,/ And if he doesn't stop his grumbling, he can go to . . . ') and Uncle Harold would recite something called 'Bejabers'. Dodie herself was allowed at least four recitations including 'a sickening song about a defunct linnet'. There were bridge parties every week at Auntie Nan's after her marriage — noisy occasions, as Frances Reynolds-Jones, who married Dodie's cousin Ronnie sixty years ago, confirms: 'They all talked together, and nobody listened to anyone. But they were a quite marvellous family, who all looked after each other.'

They had a dog known as Good Old Rover, and a cat called Kit Kennedy — a characterful tabby with a torn ear who later developed a cough like a bark: when Dodie had her tonsils out Kit Kennedy ate them. They did not tell Dodie that when old and ill he was drowned in the dolly tub. She already showed signs of being quite neurotic where animals were concerned. Most children are affected by the sufferings of small creatures but she took this sentiment to ferocious extremes: having once been prostrate with misery after killing one fly, she would allow no swatting thereafter. The family never could admit to Dodie that their chickens were killed for eating, so she would announce to dinner guests, 'This poor hen was found dead this morning.'

Every summer there were seaside holidays at St Anne's, or Blackpool, where Dodie saw her first car, an electric brougham belonging to Lillie Langtry. Once they went as far as Salcombe in Devon. They liked all amusement parks and attended the concerts at the Old Trafford Botanical Gardens, in an aroma of newly mown grass. Only Dodie disliked circuses, as acrobats made her feel sick and performing animals even sicker. Church played no part; indeed the Furbers scorned the Victorian gothic church opposite them; they disapproved of church, much as church-going families then disapproved of the theatre. Her mother and Aunt Nan were among the local ladies chosen for walk-on roles when Sarah Bernhardt and her company came to Manchester; and Uncle Harold was involved with Miss Horniman's company, founded by the tea heiress who had started the Abbey Theatre in Dublin. She put on the first Shaw and Ibsen plays at the Gaiety Theatre, to which Harold took Dodie. At home there was always music: Mendelssohn's 'Song Without Words', Tchaikovsky's 'June Barcarolle', 'Chanson Triste' and 'Chant Sans Paroles'; and home entertainment, with Dodie — of course — as the star.

They told Dodie she was pretty, with her winning combination of dark eyes and fair hair. Her mother once won a phonograph in a contest just by submitting Dodie's photograph. Who could have imagined she would grow up plain? Her looks had gone, Dodie always said, by the age of seven. But nobody ever told her she wasn't a born actress, and they encouraged her to perform at all times. She sang, she danced, she recited and the reception of the family was ecstatic. There was always someone to read aloud to her; Mother's various fiancés had to be readers-aloud, and Dodie later insisted that her 'inner ear', with which she instinctively heard all dialogue spoken aloud, stemmed from hearing her uncles read their parts for the local theatricals, over a glass of whisky and a cigar in the evening. She could also have screaming, kicking tantrums if not indulged, belabouring the uncles about their heads. Mother called this behaviour 'spirited'.

Even allowing for the afterglow of middle-aged hindsight, Dodie's charmed childhood has the authentic ring of the Edwardian middle-class idyll, with plenty of picnicking and boating and scrapes which involved cousins falling off roofs.

Having three uncles at home, as she later said, quite made up for having no father, and she liked to remember herself, pretty and beloved, bonneted and in best white doeskin shoes, walking hand in hand between two straw-hatted uncles. The age of eight she regarded, probably rightly, as the most enviable age in the world.

Her imagination was kindled by the Victorian illustrations in fairy-tale books: it was because of a particular picture in her Hans Andersen that she always loved red shoes. The stage directions for her first play, *Autumn Crocus*, set in a Tyrolean inn, drew on this memory: 'Sensitive newcomers to the inn are sometimes reminded of the illustrations to an old German storybook, loved in childhood, and, though memory steadfastly refuses to yield the name of the book, a sense of recaptured magic remains.' As soon as she could read for herself, the dining room bookcase was hers to range through: Shakespeare, Dickens, Trollope. In her books and plays, Dodie frequently created a dreamy young heroine with a passionate love of literature. Curiously, she read no Beatrix Potter as a child; and Jane Austen and the Brontës only much later. She went straight from *The Boy's Own Paper* to George Bernard Shaw at nine, instantly enchanted by the preface of *You Never Can Tell*. An old lady in Manchester had told Mother that Dodie ought not to read Shaw, but Mother replied that the parts she understood would do her good, and those she did not could do her no harm. Years later Dodie realised how great Shaw's influence had been, 'and I cannot think of a better one for a child of my period'.

When Kingston House was to be demolished to make a railway cutting in 1907, the family took up a new hobby of looking at houses on Saturday afternoons. No house was too large or too derelict for their taste. They found Thorncliffe, in Talbot Road, near the Old Trafford cricket ground; it was then stuccoed cream, with a capacious attic storey, where her mother skilfully fashioned Dodie a hideaway with bright curtains, rose-patterned lino, pictures on white walls. The cistern lid became a desk.

She was given a child-sized upholstered armchair, which she could still fit into at ninety. Her first school was the only private school in Old Trafford, 'Mrs North's Girls' School, Finishing School, Kindergarten and Preparatory for Boys'. Here Dodie was instantly popular, and discovered the elation of appearing on stage, and the need not to mind if her name was left off the programme. Any writer's story is incomplete without its affectionate memories of an English teacher, and in Dodie's life that teacher was the tiny, charmingly dressed Miss Emily Allen at Whalley Range High School, the secondary school where she went at eleven. Miss Allen could recreate the past with a swish of her stylish skirts or a stride across the platform. 'Everything she taught was worth remembering,' wrote Dodie, 'and is remembered by me to this day.'

Dodie at eight was already longing for romance, attracted to boys of fourteen. A boy called Jackie — who resembled the child star Jackie Coogan, held her hand on sofas, and followed her about doe-eyed, proposing marriage — was never forgotten, for introducing her to the feeling that it is better to be liked than not. She adored dancing, and the anticipation of parties: 'The drive there was the high spot of my evening for anticipation soared; the drive back was very different for never, never did I enjoy parties once I got to them.' And just as flat, stodgy Christmas Day never lived up to the shining anticipation of Christmas Eve, never did the tea on the party table fulfil the expectation raised by the first vision of it. 'I have retained a dislike for large numbers of people gathered together hellbent on enjoying themselves.' But she preeningly preferred her own parties, when mature boys asked her to dance, and older girls flirted with her uncles. 'There was an astonishing amount of juvenile lovemaking in that pleasant Manchester suburb.' She meant only flirting of course, an activity she enjoyed.

The pretty widowed Ella had her own admirers too. There was one suitor named Jack who put his head on the mantelpiece and sobbed when she refused him; Dodie was much harrowed by this. ('Harrowed', throughout her life, was her favourite word in response to anything disturbing, or even faintly irritating.) Another fiancé had to be placated and consoled by Dodie when he was dropped. A new fiancé named Uncle Ru was installed as a paying guest and came with a large Great Dane that died just as Dodie was growing fond of it. To console her he gave her a deerhound with 'Ten shillings reward to anyone returning this dog to Miss Dodie Smith at Kingston House' engraved on its collar — an invitation to wicked boys in the neighbourhood, who returned it thrice a week. Seven years later, her mother went back to the first fiancé, and agreed to marry him.

He was Alec Gerald Seton-Chisholm, an electrical engineer from London. He was good-looking with a clipped ginger moustache and a withered leg, and walked with a crutch. He said this was an asset in business, as nobody ever forgot him, and it did not prevent him from taking part in tennis, cricket and rowing.

Her mother's re-marriage would mean moving to London, the cause of much misery to both mother and daughter. Dodie at fourteen did not want to leave Manchester, her uncles, her amateur theatricals, her school friends, Miss Allen — and the adored Norman L. Oddy. Her mother said that if Dodie felt so strongly about it, she would break off her engagement: perhaps she was having her own doubts about Seton-Chisholm. After all, she had already broken off her earlier engagement to him; and though he affected an air of overwhelming jollity, none of the bachelor uncles liked or trusted him, especially over the matter of a financial settlement he was supposed to bestow on his bride. But Dodie was temporarily seduced by 'Uncle Gerald's' lavish gestures. It was he who bought her a bicycle, and he promised many visits to London theatres. Fate stepped in when Edward VII died in May 1910, and Aunt Blanche, her grandmother's cousin, widow of Dr Frederick Guthrie, the distinguished Victorian scientist, invited Dodie and her mother to London for the funeral, which Uncle Gerald said they could watch from his club.

While in London, Dodie, her mother

and Aunt Blanche went to see Fred Terry in *The Scarlet Pimpernel*, and Dodie decided she must live in the same thrilling city as Terry, to 'breathe the same air'. She convinced herself that it would be easier to get on the stage herself if she lived in London. So she waved goodbye to the old life, sang 'Forty Years On' at school, and did not see Miss Allen again for more than forty years. On a gloomy wet October day in 1910 her mother's wedding took place, the only occasion on which any of the Furbers attended Whalley Range Church. After their ten-day honeymoon in Belgium, her mother and new stepfather were to join Dodie, accompanied by Annie the maid, in a London flat. Dodie took flowers to her father's grave, thinking how strange it was that she had no mental picture of him; the sun shone on the cemetery and she felt oddly peaceful. Then she went home for one last tea with her uncles, 'the boys', trying to feel sad — 'Who would hear them read their parts now?' — but in fact elated about going to London, where there were no fewer than thirty theatres, and endless possibilities.

'I never cease,' wrote Dodie at seventy, 'to be grateful for my upbringing in Manchester. My family was more stimulating than most. Apart from their talent, they were so much more alive than most families. Even my grandfather Furber, who died when I was tiny, taught me Shakespeare before I could read. Why couldn't they all have had better luck? It saddens me to think of all the talent that got wasted — especially my mother's.'

She never tried to reproduce in a play or a novel the 'dear, dear family' she grew up with — though the Furbers were, as she said herself, as entertaining as the characters in any of her plays. But she did say, in a letter to a woman who admired her *Dear Octopus*, that she particularly wanted to depict a happy family. 'I was brought up in a large family of grown-up people, who quarrelled frequently in the shrillest of Lancashire voices, and yet all cared for each other so much that they didn't even like having outsiders in to family parties.'

Never in any of her journals and confidences in letters did she express regret for the early loss of her father, or for being an only child. She was cut out to be an only child: she liked her own company, and was enthralled by what went on in her own mind; siblings would have got in the way. The discovery that she had an 'inner world' was 'frightfully exciting', she remembered later: 'I never felt a bit lonely. Rather I resented the intrusion of other people into the little garden of inside my mind.' She was as self-absorbed as Cassandra, sitting with her feet in the kitchen sink, writing her journal in *I Capture the Castle*. She was also like Ann, who recited Rossetti's poems before school in *Call It A Day*. These two portraits were the closest to herself: 'my beautifully sensitive children,' as she self-mockingly said, 'little Dodie Smiths of Kingston House'. To the end of her long life, she loved the idea of her young self, with her 'vivid, eager face'. But she also wrote: 'I was not a happy child, and I was aware of that from a very early age. Nothing was ever as wonderful as I expected it to be — not even *Jane*, a farce.'

2

An Eye on Posterity

THE move to London was a retrogressive one for Dodie. Not only was her mother noticeably less cheerful, but Dodie was suddenly obliged to behave less precociously. Having been at the centre of the stage, and treated as an equal among adults for all her fourteen years, she now found herself treated as a tiresome child among disapproving strangers.

This period of Dodie's life is recorded in 'An Eye on Posterity', five notebooks of an autobiographical novel written, in pencil, when she was thirty in the form of an adolescent journal, often deliberately melancholy in tone: 'When I am enjoying myself I do not seem to write anything at all. It is only when I am lonely and dull that I want to write.' It ran to well over 100,000 words and took her life story only from the age of fourteen to twenty-three. 'It is, of course, a fake,' she wrote years later on the fly-leaf of book one, as a warning to the biographer. She was then, at the age of sixty-eight, reading through the five notebooks before starting to write her memoirs. The incidents described were all true, she added; she had merely given the characters fictitious names (like 'Vincent Queer'). It was never intended for publication, but the journal-keeping style of a fifteen-year-old girl was an effective literary device, blending ingenue knowingness, innocent candour and sly charm, which she later used for Cassandra in *I Capture the Castle*, where she divided the narrative girlishly into 'the sixpenny book', 'the shilling book', etc. The adolescent female personality reappears repeatedly in her plays in a series of precocious girl characters who, as the theatre critic Kenneth Hurren later said of Cassandra, seemed 'poised between childhood and adultery'.

'Posterity' begins in 1911 with a more disagreeable picture of her new stepfather than she paints in her published memoirs. 'He is a fairly nice man,' she writes at first, 'though he does not seem quite as nice as he did in Manchester when he used to come up for weekends with chocolates and magazines. He used to tell me he knew a lot of actors in London, which is one of the reasons I didn't object to my mother marrying him but, up to now, no actors have appeared. He does not rush round taking us to theatres as he used to when my mother was only engaged to him.'

They lived first in a top floor flat in Battersea, chosen by Gerald's mother Sybil, and installed themselves with Annie, their maid from Manchester. Gerald did not care for Annie's singing in the kitchen 'but nobody dares mention it as she is easily hurt. And we could not possibly go on without her. Besides, she is someone for my mother to talk to as we have no friends in London . . .

'I sometimes see nice children in the gardens but I don't know them because their mothers never call on my mother. Apparently in London nobody ever gets to know anyone. This certainly is one drawback of London. Annie thinks it is mostly drawbacks. She says the tradesmen are thieves and the maids are dirty.'

Uncle Gerald was a drinker and a gambler, Dodie gradually discovered. But his least appealing characteristic (as reported in 'Posterity') was that he and his family were disagreeable to his new stepdaughter. 'His mother, father and three sisters are without doubt the nastiest people I ever met. There is keen competition among them to be the nastiest and I think the mother wins. She has a dark stuffy flat in Kensington with gold cupids holding the lights and an inlaid cabinet worth £200. She says I have a Lancashire accent and ought to go to boarding school. My mother tries hard to say nice things about her but when I tell her they are not true, she does not argue with me.' Annie the maid, a shrewd young woman, agreed with Dodie.

Even allowing for the natural resentment towards a step-parent and the trauma of moving from north to south at the age of fourteen (I write as one who made that move at the same age, and can confirm that it was like moving into a race of alien beings), Dodie's memories of encounters with the stepfather's family have the ring of authenticity. One evening when the in-laws are invited to dinner, Dodie pats her mother's hand. 'That child is terribly demonstrative,' snorts the mother-in-law reprovingly. ('They never talk to me, only *about* me,' said Dodie.) 'Well, why not?' says Dodie, astonishing the old woman by speaking up for herself. Dodie, accustomed to fond attention for her every word, and admiration for her precocity, was horribly crushed by any criticism. The new family would lecture her mother about Dodie's hairstyle and her shortness, and told her it was wrong to let the child go to the theatre so much. Mother had to warn Dodie never to contradict Uncle Gerald 'as he gets so cross.'

'Well, there we have it,' Gerald used to say, addressing the company when Dodie argued with him. 'Sixteen dictating to thirty-six.' (She was fourteen, and he was rather more than thirty-six.) Then one night he was talking about the theatre; Dodie kept quiet, but Uncle Gerald exploded with rage because, he said, she was 'looking sarcastic'. 'I cannot help it if I have an expressive face,' said Dodie, flouncing off to the kitchen to take refuge with Annie.

Annie had soon managed to make friends by talking to the maids on the nearby balconies 'and the man who brings the meat and the one who brings the grocery have both asked her to walk out with them, so she is a success in London. But she would not demean herself by walking out with a Londoner as they are all sloppy.'

Dodie had, however, a white bedroom to herself with a rose frieze and three mirrors, important to a girl practising Shakespeare recitations every night, and dreaming up her stage name — Marguerite Vincent perhaps? Or Beryl Heather? She might have recited all night had not her mother knocked on the door at 9 p.m. and told her she must go to bed in order to grow taller to go on the stage. ('So I retire and stretch out as far as I can. It hurts rather but I keep telling myself that Ellen Terry is quite six foot and I am only four foot eleven and a quarter.') The photographs on her walls were of actors — Fred Terry and

Forbes-Robertson — and of the good-looking barrister F. E. Smith (later Lord Birkenhead) who had thrilled her during the general election of December 1910. She tried to write letters of equal length and interest to each of the three uncles: to Harold about acting, to Arthur about the awfulness of Uncle Gerald, because he disliked his new brother-in-law the most, and to Eddie about animals — though they had none in London. But soon she had a new distraction: they moved to Riverview Gardens, Barnes, and Dodie started at St Paul's Girls' School, a short walk across the river in Brook Green, Hammersmith. She sailed through the entrance exam: the questions included 'What comes first, the thunder or the lightning?' 'What does VC stand for?' and 'Describe your favourite sovereign, in 100 lines.' 'I couldn't describe an ear-ring in 100 lines,' wrote Dodie, 'let alone my heroine Elizabeth I.'

But St Paul's proved a disappointment. 'On the whole I think it is a horrible school,' she wrote later in the guise of her fourteen-year-old self. 'I am not shy, and have always been popular at school.

And it was a sort of law at my old school that everyone was nice to new girls until they got used to things, even if they were deadly. But London girls have disgraceful manners. The first words addressed to her were, 'What a funny way you talk, are you Scotch?' and when she replied, 'No, Lancashire,' the response was 'Oh, help!' and a group of girls stared and giggled. ('I have noticed in London that if you are Scotch or Irish you may be a lady too but if you are Lancashire you are supposed to be common.')

She had never encountered anything like this withering snootiness, this languid affectation of manner. It had to be countered with a robust Dodie-ism. When one girl said, 'What is your name again, I've forgotten it,' Dodie rejoined with, 'How rotten for you to have such a bad memory.' Nor did Dodie find herself able to enter into the school spirit of academic self-regard. The awe-inspiring and dignified headmistress, with her white coiled hair, struck her as merely uninteresting; and to stand up whenever she entered the room, Dodie thought, was quite idiotic.

She decided that while the sun had always shone during prayers at Whalley Range, it never did so during assembly at St Paul's. Gustav Holst the music-master did not introduce songs as interesting as Miss Allen's repertoire. Dodie was no good at games, felt chronically sick during the long playground afternoons and was terrified of losing her front teeth in hockey. She was rather proud of her white teeth, which protruded slightly. She had heard that women who had what Annie called 'out-of-door teeth' seemed to get husbands very easily. 'Mother says she has noticed it too. Perhaps it is because most men are fond of horses.' Within a year of their arrival in London the odious mother-in-law had decided Dodie had 'improved'; but added that 'she hoped I would get married early, because a girl with a mouth like mine would never have any strength of mind where men were concerned.' 'Anyhow,' added the 'Posterity' Dodie, 'I am going to practise shutting my mouth very firmly.'

A woman living in the flat opposite had the most out-of-door teeth Dodie had ever seen, and indeed, this woman had had three husbands; though 'Mother found out that they had not been all quite husbands'. One evening the woman came to dinner and outraged Dodie's mother by asking Uncle Gerald whether he wore pyjamas or a nightshirt, adding that she could not possibly go to bed with a man who wore a nightshirt. A disgusting remark, Mother later said, to have made in front of Dodie. 'I know it is vulgar to talk about men's underwear,' wrote Dodie ingenuously in 'Posterity', 'but I think Mrs Prike is right and I could not imagine going to bed with a man who wore a nightshirt. But then I cannot imagine going to bed with a man at all. It seems to me an extraordinary thing to do just because you are married. You are trained from when you are quite little that you must not let a man, even a relation, see you in your nightdress and then after the wedding, go and share a bed with one. I think it's beastly and it must be very uncomfortable because men are mostly large and bony.'(Though this was written in ingénue style, it reflected Dodie's later aversion to sharing a bed: she always told people that the secret of her own lasting marriage was 'separate bedrooms'.)

Meanwhile Dodie was learning about the facts of life from the other young girls in the Gardens, whom she calls Maisie and Phoebe. They had no difficulty in attracting boys as Dodie longed to. Maisie apprised Dodie of 'the facts' and 'I have never been so astonished in my life because I have known them for ages — these facts of life have been dogging me for years — and I never believed them.' At eight, while having her hair put in curlers, Dodie had asked her mother to tell her the facts. Mother had replied that she would if Dodie really wanted to know, but she thought Dodie would never feel the same again, and it might make her rather sad. So Dodie agreed to put it off for a bit.

During Maisie's re-telling of the astonishing facts, there had been a violent thunderstorm. Maisie had said that the facts happened to all married people, and to lots of people who weren't married, 'and then she told me about girls who have babies and no husbands. And rain was simply falling out of the sky and it got more and more depressing. So I thought I would go home, and got soaked.' She felt sad and disillusioned, with the sense of having found out something that 'ought to be exciting but is in fact horrid'.

Still, she was a girl with a sensuous nature, and when she went home to Manchester that summer to stay with the uncles, a boy put his arm around her, which she rather liked, and tried to kiss her, which she liked less. She confided to her journal: 'It is extraordinary how one can do things one hates oneself for afterwards. But it seems to make life more exciting if there is someone who admires you, even if you do not like them much.'

In London she had less luck with boys. Maisie kindly confided to her 'for her own good' that she would never attract men because she was so sarcastic and self-conscious. Dodie was naturally upset and told her mother, who declared it was nonsense and that Maisie and the others were precocious little horrors. 'Mother says I will be all right when I grow a bit. But I don't seem to manage it. I only get fatter. Mother got me some grown-up stays to make me a better shape but I felt faint when I wore them so I had to give them up. She says I will slim down in a year or two and that it is nice and womanly to have a figure.' Dodie had developed a pronounced bosom: Annie used to ask her, 'What you got in there Miss Dodie — cabbages?'

On 17 June 1910 during their first year in London, Dodie and her mother decided to accompany Aunt Blanche to the great suffragette procession to the Albert Hall. Uncle Gerald voiced his disapproval but her mother was determined. She did not in fact approve of militant suffragettes so this may have been in sheer defiance of Gerald. Dodie, who knew that the Pankhursts too came from Old Trafford, thought she might go to work for the suffragettes, 'but I am afraid it might interfere with going on the stage'. As they marched through Trafalgar Square a man shouted to Dodie, 'Hello, little'un, do you want a vote?' and Dodie shouted back, 'Yes, when I'm grown up,' and the crowd cheered. In fact she could hardly have developed into a less political animal. It was a splendid, proud occasion and Dodie never forgot hearing Dame Ethel Smyth's stirring tune, 'March of the Women'. But when they got home for their supper of cold salmon, Uncle Gerald was sulky and cross 'for making a laughing stock of him'. 'I am beginning to think,' wrote Dodie, again with hindsight in 'Posterity', 'he is an extraordinarily stupid man.'

He was selfish and inconsiderate, staying out late at night at 'business dinners', making her mother anxious, and often returning after midnight. This, Dodie said, was one of his more trivial faults. There were dreadful quarrels over his drinking, and the fact that he backed horses when he did not seem to make enough money to keep his family. Dodie hated him for hurting her mother. She suspected he was never actually drunk, but he would become excitable, and her mother's incipient illness, which was now becoming apparent, made her more nervous and excitable too. 'One night,' she records in 'Posterity', 'he wakened me up because he said she was threatening to throw herself out of the window. I said if she did it would be murder.

He and I have not been very friendly since.' So Dodie and her mother, who was looking increasingly thin and sad, began going to the theatre without him, paying for their tickets with the money sent by the generous uncles. They saw the scandalous, much-discussed *Hindle Wakes*, feeling proud of the author Stanley Houghton, their family friend from Manchester; they went to *The Merry Wives of Windsor*, and although Dodie found it dull ('you cannot get thrilled with a man like Falstaff') she managed to get Ellen Terry to sign her new autograph book on the first page with the words, 'Wishing you your heart's desire.'

The high spot of Dodie's year was returning to Manchester to stay with the uncles in the summer, accompanying them to the seaside, while her mother went to watch Gerald fishing. On one of her trips north, Dodie saw her former heart-throb Norman Oddy married, to a lady five years older than himself. 'I wonder if I will ever be happy again,' she wrote, remembering the tragic figure she cut on the sands at Prestatyn that summer, when she went into a church and allowed the tears to roll down her face as the organ played. Dodie went so far as to be confirmed, 'to give religion its chance', at sixteen, as the idea of confirmation in St Paul's Cathedral appealed to her; but in a later novel Dodie wrote about confirmation as a way of inducing instant atheism. Going into a church still made her mother feel faint; she and Dodie agreed that God was more likely to be found outdoors than in any church.

At Christmas in 1912, when Dodie and her mother went back to Manchester to stay with the uncles, Harold brought Stanley Houghton to share their Christmas dinner. Houghton was newly rich and famous and being lionised in London after the success of his plays. As they sat down to the turkey they realised they were thirteen, but Houghton very deliberately sat down last anyway. It was an unhappy augury. Early in the new year, in Paris, Houghton became ill, and that summer in Venice, where a friend had rented an old palazzo, Houghton was rushed to hospital, operated on without anaesthetic, and died a few months later. He was only thirty-two. 'I cannot think of any playwright,' wrote Dodie seventy-three years later, 'who had so much influence on the theatre as it then was, and the theatre has accepted his influence without mentioning where it came from.'[1]

For Dodie, schooldays at St Paul's began to improve. She still felt, as she crossed the bridge on her way home, a

---

[1] Stanley Houghton was, I think, an unacknowledged influence on Dodie's writing. He was a homosexual, as witty as Wilde or Coward, and burnt the candle at both ends, as his friend Harold Brighouse said: in 1911 alone he wrote five new plays, reviewed nine plays and seventeen novels including *The Phantom of the Opera* for the *Manchester Guardian*, and still kept his day job at the Cotton Exchange. In his mid-twenties Houghton had written a still performed one-act play, *The Dear Departed*, in which an old man is pronounced dead, but comes back downstairs just as his family is squabbling over who is to inherit what. Dodie had played Victoria in *The Dear Departed* at the Athenaeum, and the author

wild desire to throw her school books into the river. But although Dodie remained unimpressed with the calibre of the girls, who seemed to her ploddingly obedient, capable of 'good sound work' on their essays but without any spark of brilliance, she began to discover that the teaching was impressive. The 'moth-like lady' who taught literature inspired her to enjoy Jane Austen, the Brontës, Thackeray. An extraordinary

---

gave her a set of Lewis Carroll books in gratitude, signed 'To Victoria'. But the impact of his *Hindle Wakes*, written at the age of thirty, was huge. The revelation of Fanny, the mill-girl that she had gone away with the mill-owner's son just for a lark was truly shocking. ('Love you? Good heavens, of course not! Why on earth should I love you? You were just someone to have a bit of fun with. You were an amusement — a lark. I'm a woman, and you were my little fancy.') *Hindle Wakes* pre-figures not only H. G. Wells's *Ann Veronica*, and George Moore's *Esther Waters*, but Dodie's first (unperformed and unpublished) play *Pirate Ships*.

Frenchwoman, Mademoiselle Fouquet, read French classics aloud to them; her genius was to make the girls feel that they were all charming, intelligent and possessed of great individuality. Dodie went in for the William Watson essay contest in June 1913; the subject was a quotation from Shelley — 'Poetry redeems from decay the visitations of the Divinity in man'. This sent Dodie into rapturous flow ('Poetry is like a clear stream which rises in still fairer mountains') and, with liberal support from Wordsworth, Browning and Sir Philip Sidney, she won third prize.

Miss Gray told her she detected 'a spark of the real thing' in this essay, and mentioned the possibility of her going in for a university scholarship; but Dodie was fixed on the stage. Miss Gray had nothing against the stage, but saw that Dodie, lacking both height and beauty, and with 'deplorable breathing and false theatricalism' in her stage diction, would never be a raging success on it. Dodie hated games, but as she rose up the school she could ignore team sports and merely swim every day, which she loved; she was taught to play the piano excellently; she found she could shine in debate in the literary and history societies, and began contributing to a rakish typewritten magazine started by some intellectual Jewish girls.

In the library, she had a semi-mystical experience. 'It is a lovely room. There is a sort of ladder with a seat on top to get to the high shelves and one day I was sitting on it reading an eighteenth-century book when I suddenly had the most queer feeling that all the ages were muddled up and that then is now, really. I can't explain it, but it made me feel truly close to the past and the future too.

'I thought of all the girls who would sit and work in the library long after I am dead and imagined that I could almost see them. The library was quite empty and the late afternoon sun was shining right onto me so that I seemed to be in a golden haze. I had the most marvellous feeling of peace and knowledge, something that won't go into words.' Feeling differently about the school, she decided to stay on a term after the summer when she might have left, being sixteen. During her extra term she would rise at 6.30 to read Shelley and Rossetti before school. This was the young self she later re-created as Ann in *Call It A Day*, 'the closest self-portrait I ever attempted in a play'. Still, on her last day she gleefully jumped on her old straw boater before flinging it into the wastebasket.

In the new year of 1914, after another Christmas in Manchester, she took her entrance exam for the Academy, not yet Royal, of Dramatic Art (Dodie always called it The Academy; never RADA) in Gower Street. For the occasion she made herself a distinctive hat: a black velvet mob cap trimmed with swansdown and roses. She wore a short astrakhan-look coat and Aunt Bertha's shoes, which were two sizes too large, and was conscious of looking quite different from the carmine-lipped, marcel-waved, willowy creatures in the waiting room alongside her. After her renderings of the Shrew and Lady Teazle, there was a long pause from the director Kenneth Barnes's office. Had they been so *bouleversés* that they were about to offer her a scholarship on the spot? Later Kenneth Barnes confided that they had been discussing whether they could possibly let this extraordinary creature in to the Academy at all. ('All my life, my mind seems to have been a meeting place of modesty and conceit,' wrote Dodie.)

Dodie's two RADA years were not distinguished: but neither was it a particularly illustrious time for the Academy. Of her contemporaries only Kathleen Harrison and Miles Malleson, the character actor, met with any great success; the majority never again stood on a stage at all. Dodie's attempts at tragedy seemed to invoke hilarity in audiences: her lack of height was a notable disadvantage and made her look comical even before she opened her mouth. But she was distracted from acting and the Academy, because during her first term her mother had undergone an operation for cancer, a word Dodie could not even bring herself to write. She still looked young, but was increasingly wan and thin and had 'a desperate look in her eyes'. On the day her mother returned from an extended stay in Manchester at

Christmas 1913, soot had fallen down the dining room chimney: a sign Ella superstitiously believed presaged death.

Ella was soon undergoing her second breast cancer operation. She began to confide in Dodie about how unhappy her marriage was: she felt guilty about burdening her daughter with her misery, but was obviously relieved to have a confidante. Aunt Bertha came from Manchester to nurse her sister, but even though Dodie was distraught with misery, having decided she must leave the Academy for the term, she felt she could manage more peaceably without Bertha's restless busyness. So during the last weeks of her mother's life — still convinced that with treatment her mother would recover — Dodie nursed her mother alone, through talkative days and long, wakeful nights, while Annie ran the household and looked after her stepfather. For the first time since the re-marriage Dodie had an opportunity for intimate discussions with her mother. Ella told her, among other things, that Dodie was never to believe a woman could not expect physical pleasure from marriage — 'astonishing frankness, gratefully received by me, from a woman usually so reticent about sex'. Every day Dodie arranged flowers in silver vases for her; every night she would read poetry aloud to her, especially from the drowsily alliterative *Piers Plowman*. On Dodie's eighteenth birthday in May 1914, there was a box of luxurious presents including fine silk stockings, which her mother had not expected to live to see Dodie open. Ella would sit up in bed, pretending to be cheerful when Dodie knew very well she was filled with fear and dread; she would even play a small harp, saying she might as well get in some practice for heaven. She died a month after the birthday, in June 1914, at dawn, with Dodie at her bedside. As Dodie described it, her mother had taken a last dose of morphia, had listened as Dodie read Shelley's lines from *Adonais* ('He is made one with Nature . . . / He is a portion of the loveliness/ Which once he made more lovely . . . ') and had said, barely audibly, that Dodie was the best daughter any woman could want. At the moment of death she looked suddenly years younger, and 'an extraordinary look came into her eyes, as though she were seeing something wonderful for the first time.'

That the orphaned Dodie should feel bereft was inevitable. Although she had been so dutiful, she felt guilty about not having made her mother happier, guilty about having left her for a prolonged motoring holiday to Scotland and the Lake District the previous summer with the Manchester uncles, guilty about not having accompanied her on one of her few pleasures, window-shopping. Her mother's happiness had been so short-lived. She had had an impoverished childhood, a brief romantic girlhood, a few years of happiness with Ernest and Dodie and then, from her middle twenties, only the hope of building a second happiness, but it had turned out all wrong. On the other hand, Dodie could console herself that she had been, for a time, a real companion to her mother, whom she always admired and valued. She held imaginary conversations with her for decades afterwards.

One factor which had a lasting impact on Dodie's life was that during those last weeks she and her mother both became interested in Christian Science. A 'practitioner' came to the flat, bringing tulips of strange dark colours and leaving a copy of *Science and Health*, which Dodie decided was full of reason and good sense, and far more like a philosophy than any religion she had come across, even though she resisted some of its 'more ludicrous tenets'. She rejected the idea of attending services after one try, and although she never attended another service for the rest of her life, setting her mind utterly against all such mass rituals, she read from *Science and Health* every day, which gave spiritual sustenance though it never staved off her fiendish colds. She also persuaded herself to take the stoical view that her mother would not have been happy had she lived; after all, she would have had to live with her unhappy marriage, and Dodie knew, with a clear-sighted self-knowledge, that she would have become too preoccupied with her own life, and the Academy, to be much solace to her mother.

On the day after the funeral, and the scattering of her mother's ashes in Richmond Park, Dodie's bitterness towards her step-father erupted into a blistering row about her own and her mother's possessions. She managed to retain her mother's piano and her own dear little armchair, but lost almost all her books. The money left to her by her mother (in stocks and debentures) took ten years to recover, Dodie settling eventually for less than the full amount, a few hundred pounds. Once, in the coming years, Gerald called for her at a stage door and Dodie was told by a fellow company member that he was notorious for hanging round stage doors. Much later, when her first play was produced, he pressed her to meet him again, but she rebuffed him, unable to forgive the misery he had caused her mother.

'Attractive, talented, amusing, loving and very lovable, why did my mother not attract to herself more good fortune? I doubt if ever, after the end of her first few years of married life, she was really happy. But she was usually both cheerful and hopeful, ready to enjoy any party or outing, and always eager to provide little festivals for me.'

The Manchester uncles proceeded to fill Dodie's mourning months with excursions to theatres; family friends, the Wattses, took her to Stratford to cheer her up; in her hotel room she sobbed through the night, saying 'Never, never again' — the terrible fact of the finality of death which drums itself into the brain of everyone who is bereaved. She was surprised to find how little she cried, partly helped by a letter which her mother had written five years before in case she died, advising Dodie not to wallow in grief but to think only of their happiest memories and to fill her days with occupations. Dodie found this effective advice: thirty years later she wrote in condolence to a small boy of eleven whose mother had died, that treasuring all the best thoughts about her mother had kept them alive. 'But my dear mother's unhappiness and illness,' she wrote in her memoirs, 'cast a gloom over my early years in London, which took some time to pass away.'

The outbreak of the First World War had passed almost unnoticed by Dodie. She told herself she ought to feel more worried about it, but 'it seemed as unconnected with me as the dimly remembered Boer War.' She wrote a silent-movie screen-play, *Maisie Manages Things*, under the pseudonym of Charles Henry Percy, and sent it to a film company, Messrs Hepworths, who requested a different title (*Schoolgirl Rebels*) and sent Mr Percy £3 10s for it — the first and last money she was to earn from writing for sixteen years. And she returned to the Academy, the uncles lending her fees and expenses. She lodged at first in depressingly suburban, redbrick Hornsey, where she would look out of her bedroom onto 'little autumnal back gardens' of 'respectable, elderly houses' which felt more provincial than Manchester, and made her fear 'that life held nothing whatever for me'. But she soon moved to Shepherd's Bush, which at least felt more metropolitan, and began to make a new set of friends among the next intake at the Academy.

One of them was Barbara Noel, daughter of Conrad Noel the Socialist vicar of Thaxted in Essex. She and Barbara, who like Dodie was small and unbeautiful, had embarrassingly to perform a lament about the fatal burden of beauty: 'Our faces *madden* men!' Dodie had to cry, which had the audience convulsed. A weekend spent at the Noels' vicarage in 1915 — her first visit to Essex, and 'never before had I seen so much sky' — was a memory Dodie held dear for ever: the tiny toy-like railway, the walk across fields and stiles to Thaxted, with its windmill; the vicarage garden, where an annual summer festival was being held, with the village girls singing and waving white handkerchiefs on the lawn at twilight. She was clearly fascinated by Conrad Noel himself, and by his brothers: one a famous composer who did the music for the festival, one an actor-manager who acted in his own play. Gustav Holst, then living in Thaxted, was there too. The theme, and the scene, kept resurfacing in unperformed plays; it finally saw publication in her third novel, *The Town in Bloom*, and Thaxted was the setting for her own favourite, but never performed, play, *Esmeralda and the Cloth*.

But her best friend at the Academy was Phyllis Morris, whose wit was as sharp as Dodie's and whose taste in hats was as outrageous. She had one hat like a black cartwheel with a lifesize yellow leather chicken on top, and another exactly like a child's chamber pot, as Dodie told her. She promptly added a golden waterfall veil which compounded the resemblance. Phyllis had a handsome allowance of five pounds a week from her wealthy family, who had made their fortune from Ambrosia rice pudding. She was educated at Cheltenham Ladies' College, and had renounced her RADA scholarship so that a poorer girl could have one. She was fair-haired, pretty and gamine, and, like Dodie, deeply ambitious. She wrote poems — which was what first attracted Dodie to her — and later children's books and plays, but most importantly she was as strong and spirited a character as Dodie, witty and argumentative enough to satisfy Dodie's needs in a friend for life. They were to 'bicker more or less cheerfully for the next sixty years', as Dodie wrote; the evidence from her journals suggests that though the friendship with Phyllis was unusually steadfast — Phyllis kept resurfacing, wherever Dodie was — the bickering became less and less cheerful.

While Phyllis did establish herself as a useful character actress, Dodie seemed unlikely to prosper. When she played Mrs Arbuthnot in Wilde's *A Woman of No Importance* the director Fisher White uttered the crushing words: 'Miss Smith, I have been under the impression that you were as devoid of talent as it is possible for a human being to be. I now realise that a tremendous amount is going on inside your head; but nothing, nothing is coming over the footlights. What your acting needs is a little more oomph.'

She never acquired oomph; but she did manage, for the next few years, to scrape a precarious living in suburban Empires and Hippodromes, understudying and playing character ingénues in now forgotten comedies. She also discovered, through Phyllis, the Three Arts Club, a women's hostel opposite Madame Tussaud's in the Marylebone Road, which she instantly recognised as the perfect base from which to launch herself, in her 'worst actress' phase, at men.

3

Girls of Slender Means

THE Three Arts Club was perfect for girls of slender means. It stood on the corner of the Marylebone Road and was run exclusively for girls working as actresses, musicians and dancers. It was a five-storey house with a handsome portico and a high walled garden with tall plane trees, which gave the feeling of a leafy haven far from streets and buses. For as little as ten shillings a week you could rent a cubicle in a dormitory, including breakfast served in bed by a friendly maid known as Charlotte the Harlot. Hot baths cost twopence in a slot on the bathroom door. The cream-painted lounge had magenta silk curtains, cream wicker chairs and little red lacquer tables. The bedroom furniture was from Heal & Son, in the Tottenham Court Road (a shop Dodie had not heard of before), in the very latest weathered oak.

Here Dodie fell in with a gang of friendly, hard-up actresses and glorified chorus girls with such names as Nina, Owl, and Pixie. (Of Pixie Shackleton she wrote: 'Name and all, Pixie was a schoolgirl's dream of a heroine; flaming red hair and piercing blue eyes . . . ') Anyone named Dodie would fit in here at once. A dotty flavour lingers in women who never shake off such baby names as Bunty, Googie, Boo: it confers a perpetually skittish image and a certain period charm. The Three Arts girls initiated Dodie into their soulful conversations on the Club roof while the sun set over Baker Street station, and their shared midnight feasts of sticky brown Veda bread. They were aptly named flappers. Dodie and friends certainly flapped, fluttering their eyelashes under cloche hats, flicking their skirts and flouncing off on their heels, trainee *femmes fatales* hoping for tempestuous love affairs. Dodie's later novel *The Town in Bloom* reflected how intoxicating she found every detail of life in the Three Arts Club.

Her stage career, which had started unpromisingly in the role of the Useful Maid in Pinero's *Playgoers* at Tottenham Palace (with dead-white face and front teeth blacked out), tended to be on the hilarious side. In private, before her dressing table mirror, she convinced herself she could play Lady Macbeth, but in reality theatrical agents and managers found her a comical figure. She would arrive in her audition outfit of black turban with an eighteen-inch feather sticking up at the front, which she believed gave her height. As Evelyn ('Boo') Laye recalled, 'She was a funny little thing really, in the most peculiar clothes: a black coney fur coat, and a little hat with the longest feather I've ever seen in my life, it went right up to the sky. And the highest heels, and a little box handbag.' Dodie had a series of these dressing-box handbags, and named them all 'Anthony' — possibly after St Anthony of Padua, patron saint of lost property.

At just five feet, with strong features and the high, clipped voice RADA had failed to improve, she was never going to be Sybil Thorndike and would never play

Saint Joan. One agent, Captain Lestoq, and his theatre manager Tod Slaughter (who had played the Demon Barber in *Sweeney Todd*) were so helpless with laughter, watching her audition for a tour of *Kitty Grey*, they were hardly able to speak. Still, she landed a tour as the dashing American Sadie, wearing a dress that had belonged to the lofty Edwardian actress Irene Vanbrugh; it was almost a foot too long. She earned £2 a week and lived on baked beans (three-pence), Heinz spaghetti and a weekly egg: so began a hand-to-mouth existence of dim provincial theatres, theatrical landladies, dingy dining rooms, icy bedrooms and icier bathrooms, one of which contained heaps of old clothes, bits of broken furniture and 'large mysterious bundles that didn't look quite dead'. She was almost too preoccupied with her own life to notice when Zeppelin raids threatened — the only time she watched a Zeppelin overhead, 'silvered by searchlights', she was astonished to find she did not feel at all frightened — as she travelled to bleak suburban Walthamstow or Woolwich. She seemed endlessly to be standing on station platforms on Sundays at places called Sandy; 'I have sometimes feared that, after death, I may find myself on Sandy platform with no rooms booked for the night.'

This life is described in cheerful detail in *Look Back With Mixed Feelings*: tours of provincial cities where she would change her library books at Boots, light candles to St Anthony in cathedrals, and share dressing rooms with often tiresome fellow actresses including one named Dolly who, Dodie said, made her realise why some men murder their wives.

'I could always talk myself into a job,' Dodie used often to say, 'and act myself out of it.' Seedy agents would ask her to raise her skirts to her knickers, to see if her legs would do for the chorus; she would gratefully seize even the smallest part in *Peg o' My Heart*. She was a walk-on pageboy in pantomime; she played a circus girl on a donkey which carried her off into the wings, ruining the scene. After that little débâcle there was a Victorian farce named *Betsy* — 'a small, peaceful part independent of livestock'.

She even took a role in the farce called *Jane*, which she had found so boring on her first theatre outing at the age of four.

Once, she sat on the grass outside Salisbury Cathedral wondering whether she would not rather die peacefully than face the tap-dance she had to perform that evening. In the title role in a play called *Dick's Sister*, before an audience of soldiers, she had to say: 'Well, here I am, with no Dick.' Gales of laughter erupted. She had to change it to 'Well, here I am, but my brother has not yet arrived.' She had, she later suspected, an unrecognised talent for high comedy, but was never to be given the chance to prove it. High comedy was for beautiful leading ladies, not for 'rather large-headed shrimps'. In these juvenile and ingénue roles in largely forgotten farces, she said, 'I achieved my low as an actress.'

One day she fell asleep on the staircase of an agent named Mr Henry in Bow Street. Having tripped over her inert body as he returned to his office, he gave her a few lines as Low Sung, in *Mr Wu* at 35 shillings a week. She asked Mr

Henry, 'Would you like me to take my boots off?' 'I should hate it,' he replied. And it was on the tour of *Mr Wu* that she met the enchantingly beautiful Evelyn Laye, for whom dashing young officers would queue up with chocolates at the stage door. They shared a dressing room, where (as Boo aged ninety remembered) Dodie spent all her time with her nose in a book, or sewing. One night Dodie was reading Dumas' *The Queen's Necklace* and Boo, aged fifteen, asked what it was about. 'Marie Antoinette,' replied Dodie. 'Who were they?' asked Boo.

New Year's Eve — which Dodie, like her Cassandra in *I Capture the Castle*, always invested with a special magic, to which special rites were due — could be particularly melancholy. One was spent drinking whisky and water with Boo Laye and another actress, Lola Duncan, in a boarding house bedroom in Coventry. On this tour, Dodie revisited her Manchester family, and guiltily found she did not much enjoy it, nor did she wish to talk to them about her life.

And yet her acting life left happy memories: she developed a fondness for bedsitting rooms where one could go to sleep by firelight, and boil a kettle without getting out of bed. She retained a lingering nostalgia for the intimate camaraderie of theatrical tours, and for county towns with market squares, and cathedral cities: Salisbury, Canterbury, York, Bath, Exeter, Ely, Peterborough, Chesterfield, Norwich, Nottingham, Newcastle, Goole ('*where was Goole?*'), many of whose flourishing theatres were soon to be turned into cinemas. One night, in a theatre dressing room, Elsie Routledge's fiancé was teaching her to foxtrot when they heard the news of Lord Kitchener's death at sea. 'We paused long enough to say "how awful" then went on fox-trotting.'

Dodie took up smoking gold-tipped My Darling cigarettes, with sophisticated gestures. She let a half-French chorus girl named Gwendo cut her hair into a fringe. She made herself a black taffeta dress with a flowing sash, a hat with streamers and a long black scarf, and wearing this she flapped into a job playing a hysterical chambermaid in *Ye Gods* in the pier theatre at Colwyn Bay. Phyllis advised

Dodie that smart clothes were less her style than 'original' ones. (Phyllis and her friend Esmé Wynne-Tyson, who had been a child star with Noël Coward, liked to drape themselves in Isadora Duncan tunics and dance in the Sussex woods, calling one another 'Gnome' and 'Dryad' in amusing little gnomic verses.) So, Dodie too adopted *robes de style*, independent of the prevailing fashion, the shapeless tube dresses of the 1920s. She preferred tight bodices, full skirts and black buckled shoes. She had a series of 'looks': her Marie Antoinette look (taffeta dress with fichu); her Kate Greenaway look (high-waisted chintz); her Jane Eyre look (black cloak with coal-scuttle straw bonnet) and Dick Turpin look (same black cloak with tricorn hat). For both Dodie and Phyllis, clothes were an obsession and a consolation; when close to tears Dodie would rush off to Wardour Street and blow two weeks' salary on a frock. A Mr Davey gave them both parts in something called *Facing The Music*: Dodie was to play a young wife, and Phyllis the glamorous Miss Fotheringay, for which she made herself a stupefying hat fifteen inches high with wire, gold lace, and green plumes. When Mr Davey protested, Phyllis replied: 'In farce, one disregards the probabilities.'

But Dodie was now aged twenty and restless, convinced that unless something happened soon she would go mad. She was permanently undernourished, despite pawning her family jewellery; sometimes it was a choice of paying for rail fares or sandwiches, and her friend Gwendo once fainted in the dressing room. Dodie spent time in an isolation hospital at Norwich with chicken-pox, and she also developed alopecia nervosium — 'nervous, fox-mange'. 'God knows, foxes have cause to feel nervous', remarked Dodie, paying a Dr Ettie Sayers a guinea to have a stick waved at her head, which seemed to work because her hair did grow back.

Her Red Notebook, written sporadically between 1917 and 1921, is a classic study of the accidie that comes with chronic disappointment. What she really longed for was a man in her life. Her friends Vi and Flapper advised her to flutter her eyelashes at officers in the audience (she wished she had her mother's skill in eyelash-fluttering) and soon this paid off. Two Canadian officers turned up at the stage door, and followed Flapper and Dodie to Eastbourne. There is a detailed account of this weekend in her notebook, which evokes the two girls' coquettish behaviour, their resorting to sulks and ignoring the two swains on the station platform, then 'arranging themselves at the piano' at their boarding house in the hope that the officers would turn up and be suitably impressed.

Their spirits rose 'stupendously' when a messenger boy brought an invitation to lunch. They took a taxi ride from Eastbourne to Brighton ('which I felt was an enormous adventure, positively asking for seduction'), had tea at the deserted Metropole Hotel under the eyes of a supercilious waiter; and, shrieking with laughter, put pennies in slot machines on the pier. Dodie sulked when her 'cheery but stupid' lieutenant wanted to kiss her, but was pacified by his promise to hand her a box of chocolates on stage that night.

Alas, the chocolates went astray. Dodie chose to be bitingly sarcastic to the hapless officer ('Say, you're awful cross. Gee, you *are* ratty tonight'). Only the next day did she discover the chocolates, left by a programme girl on a radiator. So followed more days of aimless taxi rides, enormous meals, and roller-skating rinks, where the Canadian held her hand. Neither of the officers had any brains but they were 'the dearest, most generous things'. The sun shone; Dodie danced along the road with a spring in her step, realising that she was after all attractive to men. 'I felt that Life Had Begun.' But three days later she fancied herself heartbroken (no letter) and, while in Nottingham on tour, consulted four 'comforting' palmists. (As a character in one of her plays later said, 'Nobody ever consults a fortune-teller while they are happy. Happy people only want to hear: *No change.*'

Within days, fortune did change, when along came another Canadian who 'eclipsed the first Canadian in half an hour'. So begins Dodie's lengthy rollercoaster association with Leonard Paul Duvall who insisted, to Dodie's embarrassment, on being called Bud.

The name was horribly ill-matched to his intellectual pince-nez spectacles, to his civilian profession of drama critic in Toronto, and to Dodie's notions of romance. (Though Pixie had recently married a Canadian called Ern.) Bud was twenty-eight and English born; he told her he had made and lost two fortunes in Canada, and when the war was over he would make a third. He played the piano, was moved to tears by 'Dear Old Pal of Mine', and called Dodie his 'little Pal'.

It was Sunday 22 April 1917, a pale spring evening shortly before her twenty-first birthday. Dodie was sitting in Regent's Park, when she was told she had a gentlemen caller at the Three Arts Club. And there was Bud: over six feet tall, dark, and good-looking behind the pince-nez. 'Gee, aren't you tiny!' he said. She took him into the lounge. They sat at a table by the window, eyeing each other warily, so Dodie said, 'Let's both stare, shall we,' and they did. He stayed until midnight, when the club porter had to ask him to leave. Dodie was smitten. She was so ready to be smitten.

When the gang at the Club asked about him the next day Dodie froze them with a glance, and said in a faraway voice: 'This is different. This is not to be joked about. It is real.' What she enjoyed was being found attractive, and by a man in a handsome uniform, though he was only a sergeant-major. Yet she 'never liked him so much when he was there as when he wasn't'. He was an unscrupulous suitor: he proposed marriage at their first meeting, and gave her the idea he might invite her out to live in Canada. Only after several months did he confess that he had been married for some years, though he was now contemplating divorce.

Characteristically, Dodie persuaded herself that to be a married man's friend might be an appealingly unconventional and emotionally storm-tossed existence. Happily she joined the band of girls who wait for telephone calls from married men, encouraged by the fact that best friend Phyllis also 'had married man trouble' with an ageing South African major of distressingly high moral principles, who had confounded her plans for seduction. 'I did everything — I even tore my dress open,' reported Phyllis. How? asked Dodie, enthralled. 'With a dramatic gesture she tore at her shoulder. Three press-hooks popped open revealing two inches of collar-bone.'

When Dodie called on her Manchester family that summer, on their holiday at Blackpool, she felt quite aloof from them all, and made the mistake of confiding to Aunt Nan — who had guessed something was afoot — about her married man. Aunt Nan, dismayed, told her that 'a girl's purity was like a limb, one never knew how much one would miss it until one had lost it' — so that was the end of confidences. But Nan also said something very pertinent. 'Has he ever given you anything?' she asked. Dodie realised that Bud had given her nothing: no chocolates, no flowers, even on her twenty-first birthday in May. Nan said: 'You can take it from me, if a man really loves a girl he gives her presents, whatever the circumstances.' (And she was right, said Dodie. The only man who ever really loved her began giving her presents he could ill afford soon after

80

they met, and 'Reader, I married him.')

'I never did fully understand,' Dodie wrote about Bud, in distant retrospect, in *Mixed Feelings*, 'the goings-on of that infuriating man who so thoroughly muddled up my early twenties and erupted in frantic cables as long as ten years after.' It was a mysterious liaison, explicable only by Dodie's desperate longings, and her total immaturity in love affairs. Her notebooks show how she so yearned for romance she was doomed to mistake infatuation and arousal for love. Why did she persist in writing down every thought in her notebook? Who was it for? Why put it on paper? 'No one is going to read this,' she told the Red Notebook, 'so little red book, forgive me if I am sentimental . . . I'm convinced it's hopeless to start out as the heroine of everything one writes.' But she was always going to be her own heroine.

On the New Year's Eve that heralded 1918, Dodie was alone, in a restless mood, still waiting for something thrilling. But she did not envy the girls at dances that night, because the past year had brought her 'my little chapter of romance'. (She had only held Bud's hand.) Would she arrive at the next New Year's Eve 'in the same unkissed state'? 'It is too ridiculous to think of a female of twenty-one who is not actually hideous, who has never been kissed.' Bud had not answered her last letter. Where was he? Was he even alive?

She had also been out of work for months and was running out of capital (now down to about fifty pounds). She still received half a crown a week from her stocks, into which £300 had been put on her behalf in childhood. But this had dwindled to the point where her bank manager satirically said he might offer her a job: her funds were so low, and she had never, ever, paid any sums in. Only her Manchester uncles rescued her, promising £3 a week whenever she was out of work. Dodie was now paying 18 shillings a week for a room to herself in the Three Arts Club: its dormer window had a seat cushioned in black and mustard cotton from Heal's, which she had now discovered was *the* place for modern furnishings.

After six months of waiting, and

resorting to prayer ('I'm not sure what God I believe in but I do believe there is some force in the world that one can draw on, if one has faith and determination'), a letter arrived from Bud in Folkestone: cool, perfunctory, enclosing a snapshot. 'The poor darling was evidently afraid I might have forgotten him, for he signed his full name and rank.' Mad with joy, she went to an audition, failed to get the part, and did not care; it was far more important to spend hours searching for pretty writing paper on which to reply to Bud, on her window seat while a summer thunderstorm erupted outside. Still, she waited a whole week for an answer and by Sunday was in 'a blue fury of rage'. When he finally showed up he said he had had Spanish fever and a temperature of 104, 'poor darling'. Shaking with nerves, she finally met him at Charing Cross, and they went to the Trocadero for lunch, which grew cold as they talked about the high principles which had stopped him from writing to her, and argued about whether she had ever let him kiss her. He distinctly remembered kissing her one day on the river; she said she really ought to know, having spent a year regretting *not* letting him kiss her. He must have mixed her up, with someone else, said Dodie frostily. 'Dear heart,' she told the Red Notebook, 'any man in his senses could have seen that I was still head over heels in love with him, as I had declared in writing a year before.' He claimed to have feared Dodie would drop him once she knew he was married. 'And I was going through agonies and begging him not to leave me. He must be mad!' Hadn't she spent that summer reading a novel about Canada, 'discouragingly full of snow and bears'?

They sat in Green Park on that green-and-gold afternoon, among all the soldiers and their girls who were — enviably — blithely kissing and not caring who saw them. 'Of course, having refined instincts is all very well but I almost wished I was of the lower classes so that I could let him kiss me there. For it always seems a case of "Never the time and the place and the loved one together" with us.'

He warned her she was playing with fire; she replied that she was wearing asbestos gloves. They had tea in a little Belgian café; then went to the pictures, when all she wanted was to go on talking. Before they parted in Piccadilly she told him she longed to live in a Chelsea flat, and wished some rich old gentleman would leave her thousands of pounds. After all this banter Dodie (was she really so naive?) was convinced Bud might offer to keep her. 'But it would be the end of me. I should go right under. There's an awful lot of bad in me and if once I started on that road, God knows how it would end,' she told her Red Notebook. 'I know I'm really very highly sexed.'

So it went on. He would fail to ring as promised; she would wait in all day, inventing excuses for him. Gwendo had told her she must decide either to be a pure little English girl or a 'whatlet', her word for a mistress; and that the French proverb said a door must be either open or shut. It was time to open the door. 'I know I'm an awful prig,' she mused. 'Perhaps it would be better to have the priggishness and puritanism and provincialism knocked out of me.' Phyllis encouraged her. 'I shall! Even with all this misery, it's wonderful to love and be loved, even by a married man, with no money and an artistic temperament *and* a Canadian.' She would pursue him to his camp at Folkestone, leaving her asbestos gloves behind, and throw modesty and discretion to the winds. Phyllis remarked that she had never seen anyone embarking on a respectable weekend taking so much trouble with her underclothes. And so, in the bedroom of a boarding house in Folkestone, with high tea including tinned peaches waiting on the table downstairs, Dodie received, at twenty-one, her first kiss: prolonged, but not very thrilling.

Tea was followed by three hot, heavy hours on the sofa while the landlady was out. Dodie had read Marie Stopes, but she had no idea what 'the foothills of sex' entailed: was Bud abnormal? He assured her that between people who loved each other, nothing was wrong. They repeated this heavy foreplay the next night, which gave Dodie 'one authentic thrill' and nearly frightened her out of her wits. Seeing herself in the mirror afterwards, she thought she looked blowsy. ('In the present days,' wrote Dodie in 1978, 'when I hear of girls starting their sex lives in their middle-teens, I think they're lucky not to be troubled by soul-searchings. And yet . . . don't they find such a matter-of-fact acceptance of sex a bit *dull*?') She and Bud then quarrelled over supper; and Bud coldly suggested she go back to London, after an irritable walk on the sea-front when he discussed his future, which no longer seemed to include Dodie. He said love was only a very small part of his life and he had managed without it for years. They parted with a wooden kiss; she returned to the Club to tell Phyllis all about it, and to write a poem beginning 'Love lies dead at Folkestone /And perhaps it's just as well.'

★ ★ ★

In November of 1918, Dodie was in Dieppe. She had sailed there with a Lena Ashwell Concert Party — the only member of the cast not to be seasick — on the *Vera*, to entertain the troops with one-act plays. In fact the flu epidemic cancelled everything and all the actresses had to work in the canteen instead. On Armistice Day the town went wild in hysterical celebration, the air full of shouts and sirens. The troops in the canteen were in celebratory mood and would show Dodie their snaps of wives and babies they were returning to, while Dodie, though 'behaving like a perfect little lady', just wanted to shriek. The ending of the war, she guiltily realised, would afflict her far more than the war ever had: Bud would go back to Canada and out of her life. He had suggested she should meet other men, to be sure of her feelings — a classic way of saying goodbye. She joined the celebrating throngs, falling in with more Canadians, waving the Union Jack in the streets, and acquiring the first and last hangover of her life: an Awful Warning centred on Grand Marnier. But she and the other girls resolved to see the battlefields and to entertain the troops still stationed there, with scenes from *Peter Pan*.

Dodie was amazed by the sheer

emptiness of the battlefields: vast wastes of snow, with barely discernible trenches, and little crosses to indicate graves. Once, by moonlight, she clambered into a trench and looked into a dug-out, feeling only 'a superficial emotion and considerable pride at having achieved such an experience'. But afterwards, the memory depressed her: it was 'partly guilt, guilt because the war had meant so little to me. I had never even considered doing war-work (for that matter, few of my friends had). Surely I ought to have done?' Before she left Dieppe, she had a 'pacifism' dream. In it she was carrying a bayonet, and met a figure also carrying a bayonet, which said 'Kill or be killed': whereupon she flung down her bayonet thinking, 'Then I must die'. The bayonet went through her, and she died; then she woke up, no longer guilty not to have done any war work, but a committed pacifist instead. Her last memory of Dieppe was of an encounter with a rat. They had been warned of rats in the garden 'said to have eaten a German prisoner'. One night on the stairs, carrying her candlestick, she met a rat; they looked at each other for a while, the rat walked on, and she knew she would always be a friend to rats.

She joined another concert party at Le Havre and entertained dashing Australian soldiers who gave dances, where Dodie first heard jazz. She had a chaste fling with an elderly colonel, then sailed back to London in May 1919 and went at once to have her hair bobbed (two feet of hair was cut off), which lifted her spirits. Under a picture of herself at twenty-three in her volume of autobiography *Look Back With Mixed Feelings*, Dodie wrote the caption:

All alone, all by myself
Growing old and quite on the shelf.

She rejoined Phyllis at the Three Arts, and they took a short holiday in Sussex, where Phyllis began writing a children's book, *Peter's Pencil* about a magic pencil that drew things which came to life (it was published by John Lane) and Dodie wrote poems about not being in love, including one called 'The Inn of the Empty Heart'. Then they went on another army camp tour and shared rooms overlooking the Market Square in Ripon where the Wakeman still blew his horn at sunset.

On New Year's Eve 1920–21 she took up her Red Notebook again — in yet another rented room, in Aldershot this time, on yet another camp tour in a play called *French Leave*. Reading over her previous 'amazing sloppiness' made her toes curdle, as she put it. She was glad to realise she was no longer wretched; she must have been 'hardened'. She could not imagine feeling any tender flowering in the heart for any man now. During her six months in France, meeting thousands of soldiers, she had never let one kiss her: 'and now — well, I don't seem to be very particular. I seem to have been behaving badly lately. If one cuts the tenderness out of love it becomes an extremely low form of physical attraction.' (This notebook entry was, Dodie noted in 1965, at nearly seventy, 'a surprisingly shrewd assessment of myself'. But she also wondered, 'are any people today so bloody young at 23?')

Bud had written her sixty letters from

Canada in 1920, in green ink and sealed with gold sealing wax, vaguely promising to get divorced, yet she no longer had hysterics at the sight of his postmark. 'And I started this new year of 1921 by letting a young cub of an officer who brought me home from a dance at 3 a.m., kiss me as much as he liked. Nasty licking kisses and he had a horrid little moustache, all bristly. And his eyes seemed to get piggier and smaller with emotion. And yet I had to let him, because I'm so desperately starving for something. And all week I sat up till one a.m. seducing R.F. [Reginald Fry, business manager of the company]. What a comic code he has! You may put your arms round a girl. You may hold her in your arms. You may hold your cheek against her lips and take a great interest in the lace on her undies BUT you may not kiss her or you are on the road to ruin and disloyal to your wife! So says R. I do want him to kiss me. If it hadn't been for his strong-mindedness I should never have let that detestable little officer kiss me.'

Like her man-chasing heroines in

later plays, Dodie was still full of yearnings. In 'An Eye on Posterity' she wrote: 'Somehow I cannot write about lovemaking. It makes me feel embarrassed, even with myself.' But she had begun to enjoy the overtures of an agent called Rich, feeling 'rather absurdly pleased with herself' but resolved to go no further than kisses. When Rich went off to America, 'Life has gone flop. All my feelings of myself as a rather daring adventuress have dwindled and I see myself as a nasty silly creature. Apparently Rich has many affairs and the most beautiful actresses have been his mistresses. Unless he does something drastic for me, I may as well go home to Manchester. I shall never get work in my present state of mind, which is dowdy. I'm no beauty and the only work I am going to get is through my vitality. And I haven't the vitality of a tadpole at present.'

Out of work, out of funds, she did go back to Manchester, to The Croft — where the family were now living, a handsome and comfortable Edwardian house still standing in Harboro Road,

Sale, a pleasantly leafy enclave. Aunt Bertha told her one of the uncles had said: 'I'm afraid we've lost Dodie.' She stayed for several months, and rediscovered her rosy-cheeked cousin Ronnie Reynolds-Jones, now aged twelve and a good companion. When younger they had enjoyed sharing jokes, like pretending to peel the smiles off their faces and throwing them across the table at one another; she liked him because 'he responded to any kind of nonsense'. Now he walked with Dodie to see Zane Grey Westerns like *Riders of the Purple Sage* at the Sale Palace cinema, where he introduced her to the manager proudly as 'my cousin, the actress'. But it was Ronnie who also sighed and said astutely, 'Oh Dodie love, I wish you weren't on the stage. I'm afraid you've got such a frail chance.'

Among Dodie's Three Arts crowd, always known as 'The Gang' — including Madge Compton, Peggy Calthrop, Phyllis — was Gwen Ffrangcon-Davies, who was playing the fairy princess Etain in *The Immortal Hour* at the Old Vic; whenever the Gang asked her she would sing simple unaffected folk songs, to Cecil Sharp settings. Gwen was quite unlike any other actress; they found they censored their conversation slightly when she was around. Whenever Dodie felt particularly 'soiled' by an evening of heavy petting she would ask Gwen to sing 'Searching for Lambs' — which found its way later into the drama of *Autumn Crocus*.

Dodie started a new journal (the Black Notebook, entitled 'As It Happened'), a self-conscious writer's notebook that observed the slate-grey February sky, when 'the air seemed full of a kind of reserved vitality . . . I think Spring's first smile is the blue, blue sky seen through the still bare twigs'. Dodie later found this notebook horribly sentimental: 'Who (least of all me) wants to know I sat on the leas at Folkestone with a great hopeful longing?' She plots future fiction, and draws sharply observed vignettes. A woman and child emerge from a house. '"Let me look at your face, 'Erbert." 'Erbert's face was washed clean with a licked handkerchief. Nice dirty 'Erbert. Nice clean mother.' On the train down to Folkestone on 22 February

1921, she describes fellow passengers in the 'hateful' carriage: 'A loud, haw-haw voiced army officer, snooty with piggy eyes; a handsome girl of the common type in really good fur coat and an impossible hat, carrying a massive silver chain purse, which she informed us cost £9 as she "believed in having the best"; a child with a large handkerchief and a larger cold, eating an orange; a hopelessly tired looking mother, utterly washed out, with such a plain baby with great staring brown eyes, a pasty skin and a peevish expression... What an utterly miserable trio, exhausted mother, helpless father and peevish baby! What a ghastly life for the woman.' Dodie, who was trying to think and to read, could find no escape. 'One day I shall write about a girl who is going to her lover and travels a journey like mine. She will be wrapped in dreams of romance — and by the time she arrives she will have a sickening headache, be in a vile temper and see no fairy prince in her lover, only the potential father of a peevish baby . . . and will have a blazing row with the said lover.'

Back in Folkestone, haunted by

memories, irritated by life in general and by the scratchy bonnet strings she had to wear in the role of an old peasant woman in *French Leave*, she found herself staying in the same road where she had lodged when she pursued Bud to his camp. 'I can remember so well sitting in the twilight, waiting, waiting for him to come. And it got darker and darker and he never came.' At the street corner was the little post office where she had tried to telephone Bud, to the intense interest of all the people in the shop: 'But I was so desperate I was oblivious of them.' A thunderstorm had arrived (again) and she sheltered in the bandstand, watching the black clouds above and the torrential rain; out at sea the sun shone brightly. Would the sun ever shine on her again? And she had gone to Smith's the bookshop to buy a copy of Rupert Brooke, so she could send it to Bud with the sonnet 'Now that we've done our best and worst, and parted' marked — but nobody in the shop had even heard of Rupert Brooke.

Dodie covered pages about the dullness of her life. 'I want excitement. I want to be in London. I want to be in the country. I want an entire new outfit of clothes. I want to be independent of the stage, so that I can write. I want to play a big part to let off steam. I want Bud to come back so that I can marry him; and I also want to be entirely free. I am tired of moving about, living in a suitcase, ruining all my clothes with continuous packing. And I have to stick to this beastly part as long as it will stick to me because I've no money. Hell and ten thousand devils! Money, money, money. Oh, if only I could scream and kick and smash and curse. Why the blazes doesn't something nice happen?' She was bored. She was nearly twenty-five, and a virgin.

Suddenly she was overwhelmed by a sense of determination. She must get a new outfit that would bring both a mental lift and a new personality — something as flamboyant as her white fox fur and jade green hat with purple pansies; something as startling as the tubular chemise in green georgette she made for Peace Night, which had stopped a young officer in his tracks saying, 'My God, it's a caterpillar.'

She asked Aunt Nan to sell her mother's piano for forty pounds, quickly stifling any feelings of guilt when Nan agreed to buy it for cousin Ronnie, so it would stay in the family. Then she designed herself a suit and coat of soft pale grey, and bought a scarlet sweater in knitted silk with gold threads, and a matching hat of gold tinsel and knitted chenille edged in moleskin, one of her 'hats of a lifetime'. She had the outfit made to measure, at eight guineas the set, by Mr Faikosch, a proper Russian tailor, into whose window in Marylebone High Street she had often gazed. She added a pale grey raincape, a red umbrella and a red handbag. Her fashion-conscious friend Nadine said, 'That is real dressing: you could go anywhere,' and took her for her first lunch at the Ivy. Thus kitted out, she walked with determination into the office of the flirtatious agent, Rich, 'and there, instead of Rich, was Eric Arlington'. This was her pseudonym for Norman MacDermott, of the Everyman Theatre in Hampstead.

4

The Disreputable Undergrowth of Passion

NORMAN MACDERMOTT, aged thirty, recently arrived from Liverpool, was small and slight and pale with dark hair and striking, deep blue eyes. He had come to London without experience, influence or money, yet had managed to construct a repertory theatre, the Everyman in Hampstead (now a cinéastes' cinema), which had opened on 15 September 1920 with the blessing of George Bernard Shaw, who launched several of his plays there. MacDermott undoubtedly had a plausible manner, which Dodie describes as gently ingratiating, even wheedling: he could charm wealthy benefactors such as Emerald Cunard into donating funds. Some thought him a rather seedy dandy.

Dodie's friend Pixie had declared that if still unmarried by the age of twenty-five, a girl had the right to have an affair.

Dodie was now twenty-five, and fixed on MacDermott, alias 'Arlington', as eminently seducible. She had heard that he 'combined devotion to his wife with a determination to philander as often as he liked'. But at her first interview, she felt he was more attracted by her new clothes than by the inner Dodie. Afterwards she walked across Hampstead Heath on a February day, with melting frost seeping through her new soft pale grey suede shoes, no job having been offered. But she was prepared to wait, returning each week to see every play at the Everyman, hoping to remind MacDermott of her existence.

While she waited, she could earn a few pounds by making dresses and hats, and four guineas for one day's crowd work on a film called *The Glorious Adventure* directed by J. Stuart Blackton, 'a foolish fandangle' according to Philip Ziegler, set in the golden days of Good King Charles and starring Lady Diana Cooper (then Manners) and the former boxer Victor McLaglen. The shooting took place in a large garden at Chiddingfold in Surrey: Dodie merely had to 'stroll around in costume' outrageously out of period, but at sunset they all sat on the grass, while Lady Diana, whose first film appearance this was, walked around with the producer so that everyone could gaze upon her fabled patrician beauty, while she smiled down on them all 'like an angel of mercy upon a battlefield'.

Despite her shoestring existence Dodie regarded this summer of 1921 as one she would always like to live again, the summer of *The Town in Bloom*. She had seen little of her best friend Phyllis that year. Phyllis had published another children's book, seemed to have lost interest in the stage, and was living with her parents at the Garden House, Hove. Now she arrived at the Three Arts and invited the Gang to come *en masse* to her wedding: she was to marry a distinguished doctor named Lulham, thirty years older than herself, and her parents were giving a ball at their home. (Dodie decided that such weddings were a rather indecent public spectacle.) Peggy Calthrop made Phyllis a gold wedding gown, and after a brief honeymoon the newlyweds settled in Hurstpierpoint where Phyllis dwindled, briefly, into a wife. On another memorable evening at the club, the aged Lord Leverhulme invited Dodie and all the Gang to dine at his palatial Hampstead house. He wore full court dress with knee breeches and a box-shaped hearing-aid which emitted blue sparks, and danced after dinner with every lady in the room.

At last, in the new year of 1922, back in London after a final Christmas with the three uncles in Manchester, Dodie heard from MacDermott. He offered her a part-time job — not acting, but running the Everyman bookshop, which meant she could see him every day, and carry out her seduction. In *Look Back With Mixed Feelings*, she gives the public version of the event, a chapter called 'Seduction on Demand'. 'So there I was in early March 1922, just waiting until "Arlington" felt we could safely spend a night in his studio.' MacDermott seemed 'pleased, if startled' to be thus pursued. But this amorous adventure was to be used and re-used by Dodie: in *Call It A Day*, where Catherine visits a married man in his studio; and in more exact detail in *The Town in Bloom*, where 'Mouse' flings herself at an actor-manager, insisting on spending the night with him. 'And a green and gold studio is such an inducement,' as Dodie wrote in her Black Notebook. But she never wrote the details of her actual seduction in this diary. 'I funked recounting the events of 1922,' she wrote in her journal in 1965. 'One had more inhibitions in those days as regards writing about sex . . . I used to be discreet about such matters, but after 44 years it ceases to matter.' She wondered then if MacDermott might still be alive (he was, and over eighty). He used to tell her that he only had five years to live, a good ploy for making girls sorry for him.

Her first evening visit to MacDermott's studio was arranged with impurest intent: she wanted physical satisfaction or an acting job from him, and got neither. She returned home still *virgo intacta*: 'Although I had acquiesced without demur to every one of his requests, he had stopped short of asking for the final surrender.' She analysed her feelings of shame in 'Posterity' with a shrewdness which later impressed her. 'She had betrayed her innocence,' she wrote of herself, 'without getting one iota of physical pleasure, and without benefiting materially. If he had awakened her physically she would have felt that, at however great a cost, she had advanced in experience. If she had got a job from him, although she would have felt prostituted, there would have been a certain elation in her shame.' As it was, she had merely 'explored the disreputable undergrowth of passion, and sacrificed her modesty, all the more because she had retained her virginity, and become one of the vast army of *demi-vierges*'. She was now 'one of that detestable class of women that lacks purity but lacks also the courage of her desires. She had submitted to his lovemaking through a latent curiosity and nastiness in her nature: yes, that was it, there was some small streak of vice hidden in the conventionality and priggishness of her nature.'

Within a week she was convinced — despite no penetration having taken place — that she was going to have a baby. 'Surely anticipating the Russell case,' she later wrote (in which Christabel Russell claimed to be pregnant by her husband Lord Ampthill despite their marriage having been unconsummated). 'Girls in those days feared that spermatozoa could practically leap out at you out of thin air.' She went through the usual suspense followed by euphoric relief.

Three months later, the long-desired deflowering took place. 'I was dead set on a whole night. I couldn't feel that a snatched daylight meeting would be *right* for such a distinguished first occasion.' MacDermott was stricken with scruples at the last minute on the grounds of her virginity; Dodie retorted that this was a most old-fashioned view; she didn't wish to be seduced by anyone who made a favour of it. He said he did not wish to make love to anyone who considered it a seduction. But he handed her the key to his studio, and told her to go there that night and arrive ahead of him, in a cloak-and-dagger intrigue.

The studio was possibly in or near Arlington Road in Camden Town. She asked the taxi driver to take her round the Outer Circle of Regent's Park, where she gazed on the moonlit frieze of classical figures above Cambridge Terrace, to a tube station, possibly Chalk Farm. She saw herself as a worldly *femme galante*, tiptoeing to stop the clicking of her high heels, as she let herself into a Victorian house with a separate entrance to the garden flat. She had dressed 'as for a party' but took her yellow chiffon nightdress with green ribbons, having told her friends she was going to a raffish party in Hampstead that might last all night.

In her memoirs, and in several references to the occasion in her journals, she re-created the scene in intricate detail: the gold-painted gas stove, the jade-green floor cushions, the amber-shaded table lamps. As she waited for him, she thought happily, 'This is what I was made for.' Afterwards, she felt only discomfort and a lack of emotion or physical fulfilment; despite the patience and expertise of MacDermott, it had been *dull*. 'I was, as yet, one of the women who find the courtyard more interesting than the castle, both mentally and physically.' She also discovered how much she disliked sharing a bed. 'I lay awake for hours. And when I did eventually sleep I dreamt I was a small child lying beside my mother . . .' which affected her far more than the loss of her virginity. She awoke to perceive pale daylight through jade silk curtains that turned his and her skin a deathly pale green. They dressed in silence, and he left.

It now seems incredible, she wrote, that a woman of twenty-five who has just spent the night with a man could not bring herself to ask him where the lavatory was, but she couldn't, and nor could she find one. She tiptoed out into the street and it took her nearly an hour to reach Tottenham Court Road on foot, where she found a café, still closed (it was 8 a.m.), but a girl let her in. She studied her face in the glass in the ladies' room. Did she look any different, or feel any different, she wondered (reminiscent of Madame Bovary's '*J'ai un amant!*'). Into the café came a dwarf, who sat down; and then another dwarf came along outside, breathed onto the window and wrote a message on it for the first dwarf. 'The whole thing seemed a suitably grotesque climax to my nightmare walk.' She bought a bunch of daffodils from a flower-seller, and with her nightgown wrapped in a Chinese shawl in the crook of her arm (like an instant baby) all she needed, she said, was a snowstorm.

Back at the Three Arts Club, she bathed and dressed for work, and sat down for an early lunch with Madge Compton. What happened next would be unbelievable in a novel. Madge told her that she had met Norman MacDermott the previous evening, an hour before his assignation with Dodie (of which Madge was quite unaware), and 'he had made a dead set at her both verbally and physically'. Dodie's face fell; she was furious and stricken. Her reaction was to go straight to the Everyman and burst in on MacDermott's office — and having told herself not to make a scene, she instantly made one. He was furious: how dare women talk to each other like that? Hadn't they any decency? He explained that it was his habit to make overtures to practically every attractive woman he met, out of sheer curiosity. He seldom carried matters further; he simply liked the fun of finding out how the woman reacted. Eventually Dodie calmed down, and soon agreed to go back to MacDermott's studio.

In 'Posterity' there is an episode which vividly evokes Dodie at the beck and call of her lover. Half way through dinner one night at the club, after an exhausting dress rehearsal, 'Anne' (i.e. Dodie) is told by the hall porter she is wanted on the telephone.

'It was Arlington. His voice conveyed his personality so strongly that she felt he was with her in the small dark box. Her heart was beating a little wildly. "So you couldn't manage it tonight," said Arlington's voice.

'"Tonight!" exclaimed Anne. "But I thought it was tomorrow. Your letter wasn't dated, and it was postmarked today."

'"I posted it yesterday. I've been waiting for you twenty minutes. Is it too late for you to come now?"

'"I don't know," said Anne helplessly. "I'm very tired. I've just come from a dress rehearsal. I'm going on tour, you know."

'"Oh Lord! Look here, suppose you take a taxi all the way?"

'"Can't you manage tomorrow? I'm so cross and tired!"

'"In other words, you don't want to come."

'She could feel he was hurt and gave in instantly — as she had known all along she would. "Of course I'll come. I'll be at the station by ten. But I'll have to come back by one."

'She ran out of the box and down into the dining room to collect her things. Her half-finished meal lay on the table. She felt entirely dislocated from the cold fish.'

After that second night at the studio she walked all the way home through Regent's Park with the trees in blossom and felt happier than she was to feel for a number of years; although she did learn 'that it is possible to get along quite tolerably without happiness'. And she went off to have a passport photograph taken, as MacDermott had agreed to try her out in two parts: Anne in Galsworthy's *The Pigeon* and Dolly in Shaw's *You Never Can Tell*, which he was taking to the Zurich summer festival.

Galsworthy himself attended a rehearsal of *The Pigeon*, later commenting: 'Little Miss Smith's very quaint.' Shaw too sent a telegram, referring to Dodie as Dudu. But she knew she was 'catastrophically bad' in both plays, and when they got to Zurich MacDermott engaged Dodie's friend Nadine March to replace her; he also began to transfer his sexual interest to Nadine. 'I am 99 per cent certain that Nadine March had an affair with NM too,' says Dodie's journal. It was a blow; Dodie could not eat for misery; but worse was to come. One hot afternoon, in the dusty garden of the Zurich pension where the company were staying, MacDermott broke the news that a friend of his wife's was coming to take over the bookstall at the Everyman; wouldn't Dodie like to return to acting anyway? Although of course he could offer her no part at the moment. 'Oh, the miseries of Zurich!' She had saved nothing, though she had been earning seven pounds a week in *The Pigeon*. MacDermott explained that they could not go on meeting, since his wife suspected something, 'and when a ship is in danger of sinking, sometimes even the lifeboats must be thrown overboard'. (News to me, thought Dodie tartly, knowing very well that he had Nadine in the wings.)

'Having lost the theatre and now having lost him, I was down and out. And I was about to be downer and outer.' Uncle Harold wrote to tell her that he could no longer afford to keep on sending her the allowance, as business was so bad. Also, she had written only twice in the last six months, out of guilt about her affair, and the family resented this. They said she could still come home to live in Manchester, but she felt she would rather starve — a distinct possibility in those days when there was no unemployment pay for resting actors. (She did not go back to Manchester for nine years, by which time Uncles Arthur and Eddie were dead.) At this point a sudden cable arrived from the infuriating Bud offering her a life in Toronto; and he sent her his gold signet ring (a present at last), but when she replied that she had no money, silence fell again.

Rescue came in the form of another tour of *French Leave*, during which she sobbed a good deal, and wrote a poem ending:

And if the summer brings regrets, and autumn ends the spell, I shall have had the springtime and so — all's well.

In her Hastings boarding house, she records, there was a fellow lodger having a miscarriage; Dodie ran at midnight to fetch a rather reluctant doctor. The baby, three months premature, was born alive, and could have been saved had the mother wanted it; it was kept alive in a shoebox by the landlady overnight, while Dodie lay awake wondering if she could find a hospital with an incubator and take the baby there in a taxi. But the baby died before she could do anything. Dodie was appalled. 'I had never — and never have — longed to have a child,' she wrote in *Look Back With Mixed Feelings*. 'Indeed I consider myself curiously lacking in maternal instincts (all the more curious as I like writing both for and about children). And any feelings I had about

114

that baby were entirely on its behalf, not my own. I could not bear to think it was going to get no chance of life.'[1]

She decided to write a novel about MacDermott, his wife and 'Another Woman'. Knowing nothing about his marriage did not hold her back. But she later got to know Mrs MacDermott, who came to believe that she had wrongly suspected Dodie and did all she could to make it up to her. She bought an embroidered Chinese shawl of Dodie's mother's for £30, which enabled Dodie to furnish her first bedsitting room. 'At the end I was just an embarrassment to him, I don't think he wanted me to succumb — though a few years later

---

[1] This odd episode in Dodie's published memoirs aroused a brief suspicion that it might have been Dodie having that premature baby, six months after her brief fling with MacDermott. But there is no shred of evidence to support this possibility, and no reference to any such guilty secret in all the millions of words about her distant past that Dodie later wrote.

he was madly keen to reopen the affair, and I never would. Then he married his second wife, and we were all friendly, but his new wife was a crashing bore.'

That year, 1922, was the last of Dodie's acting career. She went briefly back to the Everyman at Christmas for the children's show, *Brer Rabbit*, but could no longer afford a room at the Club. 'I was on my own at last, and determined to earn money by writing.'

She took a room over a bakery, filled with the comforting smell of bread, and embraced life in a garret, sometimes earning £1 for stringing beads or addressing envelopes. The Gang brought her books and flowers, and took her out to dine, but her financial situation was parlous. Gwen's career was meanwhile flourishing; Dodie and Phyllis went to Birmingham to see her playing the lead in Rutland Broughton's *Bethlehem*, in which she was 'enchanting'.

Dodie read William Archer's book *Playmaking*, and wrote her first play, *Pirate Ships*, renamed *Portrait of the Artist's Wives*; '*Pirate Ships* refers to young women who see nothing against stealing other women's husbands,' she wrote, sixty years later, in a letter to a PhD student who inquired. 'Personally I only managed to *borrow* a few husbands, but all of them were quite used to being borrowed.' The husband in her play was called Eric Arlington, and the seduction scene occurs in Act I scene iii, drawing heavily on her own experience with MacDermott. The play opens in a studio, 'a cross between a thing of beauty and a dustbin'. Diana, her heroine, has a brother named Hillary who sprawls on a sofa as his sister packs her nightdress for her illicit weekend, offering brotherly advice as to how to make herself alluring. 'For God's sake don't take that yellow rag. It makes your complexion look like mud, especially in the grim light of morning . . . I've suffered it too often at breakfast to wish it on any man.'

Diana ponders: 'I wonder how I will feel. Wouldn't it be dreadful if I feel bedraggled and soiled and like a broken lily?'

Hillary replies: 'Not an earthly chance. The lower classes have a monopoly of all those fine feelings. You'll forget all about it in a couple of days and feel all the keener on your work.'

She sent the play to agents, and it was almost bought several times in the next few years. Dodie's grey seduction outfit became so faded she dyed it black. And it was in black that she went, with a heavy heart, in February 1923, to an interview at Heal & Son, the furniture emporium on Tottenham Court Road. She had heard on the Three Arts grapevine that Evelyn Herring had turned down a job there. Ambrose Heal, in his pin neat hand, duly offered Dodie the job of selling woodcuts, prints, decorative books and toys, in the Little Gallery. She would get £13 a month. It was the end of her stage career. Gwen lent her £10 to buy shoes, hat and stockings; the uncles sent her the repayment, pleased she had found a proper job at last. And though she was wretchedly disappointed in herself, she eventually concluded that all the most significant events in her life, including all the success and all the genuine love, came as a result of her years at Heal's.

5

Vendu

DODIE was not temperamentally suited to the shopgirl's humdrum life of clocking in from nine to six, nine to one on Saturdays, with three days' holiday bonus if one was not late for a whole year. ('You know what really gets me down?' says the ex-actress turned shopgirl in Dodie's play *Bonnet Over the Windmill*. 'Friends dropping in and asking me to come out for a cup of tea. That brings it home to you. It's sort of humiliating that you can't get out, even for ten minutes.') But what did appeal to her about Heal's was its style. Tottenham Court Road had several furniture shops (Shoolbreds, Maples) but none of the others had the prestige of Heal's, founded in 1810. Behind its handsome, colonnaded façade in Portland stone was an elegant, uncluttered, parquet-floored space lit by

119

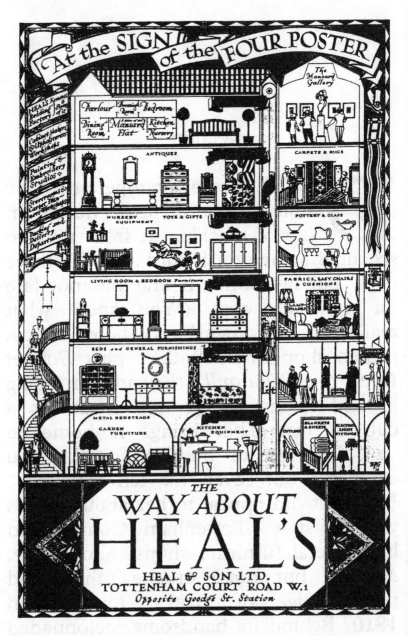

*1928 poster for Heal's
(R. P. Gossop)*

enormous floor-to-ceiling windows. The hall and gracefully sweeping circular staircase set the tone of the shop. Old-fashioned perfectionism gave it a classic quality — despite its gleaming modernity — displayed in its vellum-bound ledgers and the fine lettering on its show cards.

Bedmaking and feather mattresses were the foundation of the business; Heal's had placed their advertisements in all seven of Dickens's novels from *The Pickwick Papers* to *Our Mutual Friend*, and a Heal's bed was reputedly the best that money could buy. The shop had stood since 1840 on the same site, of a former farm which became a hostel for the shop's living-in staff, demolished not long before Dodie arrived.

She had first heard of Ambrose Heal — not yet Sir Ambrose — while at the Everyman, as he was one of the theatre's founders. AH, as Dodie referred to him always, had ruled Heal's since his father's death in 1913 and it was he who transformed Heal's from a furniture shop to a focus for pioneering design, ahead of its age and yet devoted to past masters. It was also Ambrose who, as a calligraphy and typography enthusiast, designed the fourposter trademark and masterminded the distinctive look of Heal's catalogues, posters and carrier bags.

Dodie found the shop an unexpected spiritual home. At first, she was merely number five assistant — which she deeply resented — to Harry Trethowan, who ran the china department and whose empire included the Little Gallery. She found Trethowan conceited and bossy and full of his own importance. Within six months Dodie and Trethowan had a showdown. Ambrose Heal had apparently told Trethowan that little Miss Smith might 'get up off her seat' and help Trethowan when the china gallery was busy. Outraged, Dodie marched into AH's office for the first time, amusing him vastly ('Surely I didn't say "seat"?' he said), and as a result he agreed to turn the Little Gallery into an autonomous department with Dodie in sole charge of buying and selling its lithographs, woodcuts and fine prints. So Dodie got what she wanted. 'Mr Heal beamed on me, and I beamed back.' And the next thing she wanted was Ambrose Heal himself.

Doris Parker, who arrived at Heal's as Miss Harris, junior office girl, shortly after Dodie and spent forty-two years there, says the staff were fascinated by Dodie. 'She was a quaint little character. A largeish head on a slim petite body, teetering along on very high heels, in clothes she had made herself, with bobbed hair that swung from side to side as she walked. We used to say she looked like a little horse. We were very tickled by her, but we found her aloof and private and hard to know.' Anthony Heal, Ambrose's son, remembered her as 'small but very determined, a very independent character. Quite pig-headed of course. She regarded herself as being a cut above the other girls. She had a sense of failure about having given up the stage; it was a comedown to work in a shop.'

Ambrose Heal was generally disliked and feared; even Anthony found him 'quite a fearsome figure'. His first wife had died young, leaving him with a son of six. His second wife, Edith Todhunter, lost her firstborn child, a daughter, in infancy. Then Cecil Ambrose, the son of the first marriage — born in the

123

same year as Dodie — was killed in the early months of the First World War when he was just eighteen. Anthony Heal remembered being taken by his parents, at seven, to Weymouth to say goodbye to half-brother Cecil as he left for France. 'That was the last we saw of him. He was shot by a sniper at Poperinghe in Belgium soon afterwards. I remember my father's grief. It was a tragic blow to him, as he had expected Cecil to take over the firm, in the fullness of time.' The family lived in Beaconsfield, at Baylin's Farm, bought by Ambrose in 1920. In this then still rural Buckinghamshire village, the sweet-natured and gentle Edith brought up the three Heal children Anthony, Pamela and Christopher, and worked in her garden every bit as hard as the two gardeners did. She seemed to know the answer to any question, being particularly well versed in the Greek myths: her father, John Todhunter, had been a Dublin writer, a Fabian and friend of Yeats. Meanwhile Ambrose went up to town every week to run Heal's — which meant he was free, on weekdays, to engage in amorous adventures, particularly with his long-term mistress, Prudence Maufe.

She was the wife of Edward (later Sir Edward) Maufe, the distinguished architect of Heal's new building and later of Guildford Cathedral. She had joined Heal's in 1919 as the firm's influential interior decorator. At the time Dodie went to Heal's, the classically beautiful Mrs Maufe would lunch with Mr Heal almost every day. Mrs Maufe was given to distinctive, tight-bodiced Edwardian clothes in exquisite materials, with leg o' mutton sleeves and skirts that swept the floor, and buckle shoes, wearing her hair parted in the centre and wound up round her head. Doris Harris remembers her as 'very, very grand'. Mrs Maufe ran the Mansard Gallery on the fourth floor, which established Heal's in the forefront of contemporary art. In 1919 Sacheverell Sitwell organised a show of French paintings in the gallery including works by Picasso, Utrillo, Matisse; drawings by Modigliani were sold for 2s 6d. (But not everyone was prescient enough to be impressed: the *Times* reviewer described having tottered from one 'ghastly' picture to another, until he found a sign reading

'No Escape By Way of Roof'.)

Dodie regarded Mrs Maufe as a rather humourless, bothering presence, but she was kind to Dodie, and also warned her that AH was extremely mean. Dodie had discovered that although she proved a better salesgirl than actress, AH was not prepared to pay her more money than he absolutely had to. When she first went to see him about her salary she wore her Guy Fawkes outfit: a long black coat with a white ruff, and a high-crowned black felt hat, made by Mr Faikosch. (The people who lived opposite her would watch her dressing in the mornings, and cheer as she left home.) AH interrogated her about her expenses, down to the smallest items; he was fascinated to hear about her custom-made clothes and the eighteenth-century room she was now renting. Dodie's interesting answer got her £4 a week plus commission, rising eventually to £350 a year.

She was then living with Phyllis Morris, who had walked out of her marriage, put on a brave hat with a brisk red feather and come back to London. Dodie and Phyllis set up together sharing a large bedsitter at 3 Great Ormond Street: a handsome, tall-windowed Georgian house which they decorated with yellow walls, matt black furniture, orange curtains and divans, cushions in green and magenta (from Heal's at cost price). They had a housekeeper to cook and clean and wash up, and to wake them in the morning. But Phyllis, who was still acting — she toured in the new Noël Coward play, *The Vortex* — was beginning to undermine Dodie with her writing success. After her two children's books, she had written a witty play, *Made in Heaven*, about two

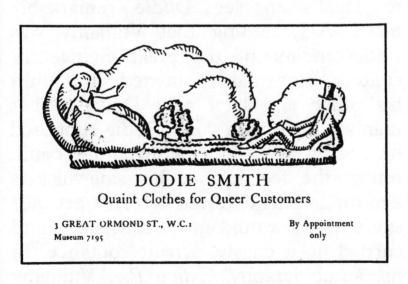

DODIE SMITH
Quaint Clothes for Queer Customers

3 GREAT ORMOND ST., W.C.1
Museum 7195

By Appointment
only

C. E. Vulliamy's design for Dodie's card (see p.126)

girls who share a bedsitter; it was later produced at the Everyman, directed by Raymond Massey and starring Adrianne Allen (soon to be Massey's wife), Gwen Ffrangcon-Davies, Gwen's friend Marda Vanne, and Claude Rains — enough to make Dodie rather jealous.

At weekends Phyllis and Dodie made some extra money by designing clothes. They had cards printed advertising 'Quaint Clothes For Queer Customers'. Dodie's card (see p.127) had a logo designed by C. E. Vulliamy, a young man who imported German woodcuts and came to Heal's to see Dodie remarkably often. AH, finding that Vulliamy was a descendant of the great eighteenth-century clockmaker, invited him into his office and later told Dodie: 'That man's in love with you.' Dodie supposed he mildly was, and wished she could return the feeling but his sidewhiskers and moustache deterred her. At weekends she and CE would go to museums, and carried on a chaste, artistic romance. In his autobiography *Calico Pie*, Vulliamy remembered Dodie: 'Her coloured shawls are vivid patches in the pattern of memory, and I have not forgotten a black dress with at least forty-five steel buttons.' And in a letter to Dodie, fifteen years after their liaison, he said Dodie's theatrical success had never surprised him, as she had 'always combined being sympathetic with complete unscrupulousness'.

Dodie's lack of scruple in personal relationships was now quite brazen. She ended the liaison with Vulliamy, who later became a considerable author himself (biographer of Mrs Thrale, George III and Boswell), because she had started an affair with a handsome soldier named Bill. This came about when Bill rang up one midnight, having picked her telephone number out of the directory at random. His pleasant clipped voice was so persuasive — he said he and his friend were 'two lonely young men' — that she and Phyllis had got out of bed, dressed and received Bill and his friend Bobby there and then. It could not have been a more disreputable start to an affair (no wonder Dodie used to say that she and her friends from the Three Arts had been 'just clinging onto their amateur status' in such matters) but the soldiers proved to be charming. They admired the amusing decor with the oranges painted on the cornice, and the distinctive clothes Dodie and Phyllis wore. Phyllis succumbed quickly to Bobby, but Dodie kept her handsome (married) captain Bill waiting for some months, a romance which 'made the winter more interesting, and ended without giving me one moment's unhappiness'.

In 1925, Dodie went to Guernsey with Phyllis and her sister Hedwige, but spent the rest of the summer alone. She had decided that in order to write she must have a room of her own, so she found a new bedsitting room at 192 Marylebone Road opposite the Town Hall, and rewrote her *Pirate Ships*, about the artist, his wife and mistress. Its unwitting hero, Norman MacDermott, decorated the small room in Italian palazzo style, painting a wall panel of a voluminous lifesize woman in blue and silver, recumbent on a grassy sward. In that room she hung a white and gold mirrored witch's ball, reflecting a hundred prismic images, which became her talisman. MacDermott also supplied her with a chest painted with dragons, and a small stone lion, which always remained in her study as mementoes of her youth.

When Dodie decided that it was time for AH to be 'collected', as she put it, she planned her seduction with a single-minded cunning that bore out C. E. Vulliamy's opinion of her. While organising a woodcut exhibition in 1926, she had a good excuse to see more of AH, and felt confident that he might be interested enough in her to become her lover. It took time. On St Valentine's Day, she sent him a verse:

The days of dear romance are gone,
Drowned in our noisy jazz and
    beano:
St Valentine is quite outshone
By Rudolph Valentino.

But now that Spring is here once
    more,
Small memories are waking
Of trim and formal days which saw
The House of Heal's in making.

O thou, on whom the gods did
    shower
Ambrosial gifts of healing power . . .
But personal remarks, I know,
Are not considered comme il faut.

What can I offer, I who own
So little wit or beauty,
But my allegiance to your house,
My service and my duty.

She ended with thanks 'for far, far more than salary' from 'The Little Gal of the Little Gallery'.

AH was suitably flattered, showing the Valentine (which he kept all his life) around the shop, amused by its unmistakably flirtatious, not to say lickspittle, tone. Dodie hoped to make some headway with him by Christmas, but ended up spending the holiday with Phyllis and her family at Birch Grove. The Morrises were a large, eccentric family — Mrs Morris, a rabid Spiritualist, used to play her trumpet in the attic — and Christmas at their long refectory table was jolly, but Dodie felt depressed. Phyllis, that year, had seen her play

The Rescue Party ('a good bouncing comedy' in James Agate's view) staged at the Comedy Theatre for fifty-five nights. Dodie was frankly envious. She would make her wishes on the tall cast bronze cat on the windowsill of the Heal's staircase, which she decided had magic powers. (When she eventually sold the cat for £40, it was retrieved from the astonished customer and re-labelled, by Ambrose Heal, 'Heal's Mascot. Not For Sale.')

In the new year of 1927 everything changed. One morning, Ambrose came into Dodie's stockroom. He picked up from the floor a small dark red ticket which had fallen off a French painting, marked in gilt lettering VENDU, and pinned it on Dodie's dress. He smiled; she gazed at him; nothing was said. But later in the day Dodie went into his office and said coquettishly, 'Apropos of that charming little "vendu" ticket, how long is one supposed to hold goods for customers who don't take delivery?' It was a clever and typically Dodieish remark, and it did the trick. He asked her why she wanted there to be anything between

133

them, and she replied, 'Because I love you.' They arranged to meet that night, at the pied-à-terre he kept in Fitzroy Square. She had told him this was not an evening, unfortunately, on which an affair could start — her time of the month — and besides, he was just leaving for one of his long Continental holidays. So they merely talked.

He pointed out all the disadvantages of a liaison: that he was twenty-three years older; that if she really cared for him she would end by being unhappy, because he did not want to lose his wife; and that he had never had an affair with anyone on his staff — except Mrs Maufe, who was always around. He wanted her to understand that, as he already had a wife and Mrs M, there really wasn't much left for anyone else. 'I said, half a loaf was better than no bread.' He said there wasn't even half a loaf. 'Well, crumbs, then, from a rich man's table,' said Dodie shamelessly, and he did not argue further. He also said something which she later used verbatim in her play *These People, These Books* (in which a publisher has an affair with his secretary):

'You see, when I have a really good assistant, I shouldn't care to lose her when . . . well, these things always end.' Dodie was determined. She assured him he would not lose her. Neither of them would have believed, she later wrote, that when it did end, it would be Dodie who ended it. She left Fitzroy Square feeling ecstatic.

While he was away, she organised an exhibition of old maps and model ships in the Mansard Gallery, and when one of the directors, Hamilton Temple Smith, interfered she wrote at once to AH — who was already writing her charming and indiscreet letters, which she reluctantly burnt — asking him to 'call the dog off'. This he tactfully did. On the day Ambrose reappeared in the shop, he and Dodie clasped hands, in front of several staff; how could a handshake convey so much? Dodie went to Fitzroy Square that night. The next morning he arrived in her office and conspiratorially handed her a large hairpin. This was a tactless move: Dodie's hair had been bobbed since 1919; so the pin must have been Mrs Maufe's — Dodie had seen her uncoil her hair in the ladies' room, and it just touched the ground.

As AH told Dodie, none of his mistresses had ever prevented him from being devoted to his wife. He was not an obvious Don Juan. He had freckled skin and fluffy red-gold hair, small eyes, a long pointed nose and a thin mouth. She supposed he had charm, but she never thought him really handsome. He was of medium height, small-footed and with an extremely light tread which she could always recognise as he approached. His voice was high, breathy and slightly affected — the kind of voice which suggested he was looking down his nose through half-closed eyes, as he often was.

For the next six years, they would spend evenings together at Fitzroy Square or in her little room in the Marylebone Road, where the saintly housekeeper Mrs Groom would cook them dinner, and remove the plates, after which 'it was always so quiet that we just took the chance of interruption'. It was thrillingly risky: but Ida Duncan, her handsome barrister landlady, had wisely said that a house full of women (she had two other tenants beside Dodie) could only get on if they 'kept themselves to themselves' and did not fraternise, and this rule was stuck to.

If she went to Ambrose's Fitzroy Square flat she left in the small hours; they never spent a whole night together. Dodie found his apartment gloomy and masculine, haunted by Mrs M who still dined there once a week, and AH invariably managed to convey his guilt and the warning that the affair could not last. She would walk home along the Marylebone Road, sometimes with tears streaming down her face. In her own room, by the light of a dozen candles, and firelight in winter, and decorated with yellow roses and madonna lilies in summer, the atmosphere was always happy.

As the years went by, Dodie felt slightly more secure, but never content — which made the interludes of happiness more intense: 'a satisfactory love affair is a wonderful enhancer of small daily pleasures'. One morning she rescued a small wounded bird in the Marylebone

Road, rang the bell of the house where Dickens had lived and asked the dimwit maid to take her into the garden. She then wrote 'Helping wounded bird' as a reason for lateness in the Heal's late book.

Though Ambrose did once tell her she was the most satisfactory mistress he had ever had, he never actually said he cared for her, and only when she gradually ended the affair did she realise that he must have done. And Dodie suspected that though his friendship with Mrs Maufe persisted until his death, their physical relationship probably faded during Dodie's regime — if the word 'regime' could be applied to her abject and furtive situation.

'The nearest I ever came to telling any friend about my new and surprising happiness was when, in response to questioning from Nadine March, I admitted that there was someone who was quite a bit older (actually nearly twenty-four years). She did not press for detail, but from then on frequently asked "How's your old gentleman?" He was far from old but did frequently stress his age in comparison with my youth.

When I pointed out that I was thirty he said wistfully, "What a delightful age to be".' (She gave this line to ageing Lord Crestover in her second novel, except that Merrie, the girl he addressed, was only fourteen and a half, though pretending to be twenty-one.)

She found AH could be bullied out of his meanness, and he began to pay for her holidays, with presents of cash or grants from the firm if she went abroad on business. He also gave her presents: antique jewellery, a watch, money for clothes, an emerald ring, a fine table, and at Christmas in 1929, the Underwood typewriter which was so vital to her ambitions. She gave him presents too, including a tiny painting on wood, of a madonna holding a candle and a madonna lily (she had it specially painted) inscribed with a verse: '*Madonna of the candlelight, whose heart will stay the same, 'Til this fair love-lily withers, 'Til the wind blows out this flame.*' When AH wrote to congratulate her on her marriage, twelve years later, he told her: 'I still have my madonna.'

Dodie felt she was popular at Heal's

in spite of the violent temper she found it necessary to cultivate to get her own way. Harry Trethowan alleged that she flung one of his assistants, a heavy girl, across the china department. Without her temper, she felt she might have been downtrodden by the elderly men who were chiefs of department. The staff called her outbursts 'Smith's brainstorms' and they always ended in her victory. But what she particularly enjoyed about those years was the intrigue of the affair. None of the staff suspected it, including Anthony Heal, who told me that although he was managing director of Heal's at the time, he had not noticed any clue, beyond the fact that Dodie always appeared to have unlimited access to his father's office. AH warned her she must tell nobody, so she did not even tell Phyllis, then or later in life. The one person who guessed was Alec Beesley, the young colleague who fell in love with her, and eventually became her husband.

Alec Beesley had arrived at Heal's to work in the counting house at 30 shillings a week. He was a striking figure: tall, slim, dark, with matinée idol good looks compounded by a small Ronald Colman moustache. He spoke to Dodie about his family as if they were completely in the past. His father, Lawrence Beesley, had survived the sinking of the *Titanic*, about which he had written a book. But although Alec had had a happy childhood in the rural outskirts of London, his mother had died young, and Alec was hated by his stepmother Muriel: nothing he did seemed to please her. Alec's only ally in the family, which lived in a large house at Northwood, Middlesex (where his father later established a private school in another large house named Disley Mount), was his beautiful half-sister, Laurien. Laurien says of her father that he was 'handsome, extremely clever, a Cambridge First and a winner of all the Classics prizes, cool as a cucumber but he was not eager to please people. And my mother seemed to try to make life awful for poor Alec.'

As soon as he left Dulwich College — which he had found 'totally without interest and totally without joy' — Alec had been sent off by his parents 'to sink or swim' in Canada and the USA, at sixteen.

He had been a logger and a bank clerk in British Columbia; he had worked on the Seattle power project in Washington State, and been a railroad ganger in Alaska. By the time he arrived at Heal's he was a gentle, self-contained young man with an original attitude to holidays. He would go to the car-free island of Sark, alone, to swim, explore and read, cooking his own food and enjoying the solitude. He had a natural artistic flair and regarded Heal's as his university, since it introduced him to interior decor, craftsmanship, typography, paintings and architecture; he was soon appointed secretary to the board, handling the firm's advertising with Ambrose Heal. Visiting Dodie in her office, he would tell her about his adventures in Canada, and she thought how attractive he would be to some young woman. Being seven years her junior, he seemed to her a mere boy. But he was interested in all things artistic, in Dodie's creative clothes, and in the theatre. In 1928 they became theatre-going companions. Dodie and a colleague named Ruth Dibb, blanket buyer at Heal's, were queuing to see

The Trial of Mary Dugan at the Queen's Theatre when Dodie remembered that Alec had wanted to see it too, so Ruth left the queue and rang him at home; the two women kept a camp stool for him and at the end of the evening he walked both ladies home, before going home to Northwood.

Dodie and Alec began to spend Saturday afternoons together, sometimes going to watch cricket at Lord's. Then Alec's stepmother forced him to leave the family home and he took a room in Covent Garden, still returning on Sundays to help with household chores, until the stepmother put an end to that too. Once, and once only, Alec took Dodie home to Northwood, and the stepmother was so unpleasant to Dodie that they never met again. On Sundays Dodie would write all day, in longhand, her interminable 'An Eye on Posterity', so Alec was forbidden to arrive before nine o'clock in the evening, when he would turn up with ham sandwiches, sixpence each from the Baker Street coffee stall. Sometimes, too, he would meet her in Regent's Park on weekday mornings so that they could walk to work together. Later he found a room in St John's Wood and would travel home with Dodie too. This was an unforeseen complication since she liked to get on the same bus as AH after work, but felt she could hardly explain this to Alec.

Ambrose Heal was mildly amused and also irritated by the young man loitering outside his office door whenever Dodie was in there, and sometimes peering in, whereupon AH would usher Dodie out in a hurry. When Alec worked overtime with Dodie at Christmas, he bought her a Heal's pure down eiderdown covered in gold (still in use sixty years later), and offered to redecorate her room. For the first time in her life, at thirty-three, she found she had at last an affectionate man friend who was unselfishly devoted, utterly reliable, helpful and kind: he would always lend her money at the end of the month, sometimes pawning his silver cigarette-case on her behalf. Dodie realised Alec was growing seriously fond of her, and thought she had better tell him she was already involved with someone else. His response was to explain his feelings for her in terms of time. He had never been in love before, he said, but if four o'clock was 'in love', then he was just at about half past three. She lent him her Rupert Brooke, so that he might read the poems of unrequited love, but he found them embarrassing; the one he liked best was 'Heaven', Brooke's famous poem about fish. Alec adored his pet goldfish and was heartbroken when they died ('his feelings about those fish,' said Dodie, 'were well up to three forty-five').

As his Dodie clock moved towards four o'clock, he suspected the affair with AH, long before he told her he knew of it. One of the presents AH gave Dodie was a valuable papier mâché chair which had arrived at Heal's in need of repair, and had been seen by many of the staff. When AH presented it as a gift to Dodie, she had to hide it from Alec, and also from Mrs Maufe who came to lunch one day at her flat. Dodie's maid enjoyed that piece of intrigue. She had previously been maid to a kept woman and told Dodie, 'Many's the time I've hidden gentlemen in my kitchen.' 'I've never managed to be kept, Alice,' said Dodie. 'Never mind, madam, there's always hope,' said Alice.

In 1929 Dodie made her second trip to the Leipzig Toy Fair to buy toys for Heal's, accompanied by 'Master Anthony' Heal, who spoke German, as interpreter. She and Phyllis, who had joined her there, went on to Innsbruck and to explore the Stubaital in the Austrian Tyrol. And it was here, at a small inn at Medratz — run by a jovial, harp-playing Tyrolean in lederhosen and embroidered braces named Anton Steiner — that she collected material for *Autumn Crocus*. Dodie walked on mountainsides, explored villages, felt a mystical sense of peace, and indulged in gloating reveries about Ambrose. They went over the Brenner Pass to Bolzano where she found a shop selling model French hats and returned wearing a black velvet veiled concoction with curious velvet ears, for which she designed a matching black bolero suit with white georgette veil and crystal beads, one of the 'special outfits' of her life.

When she returned, it appeared that

Mrs Maufe had found out about their affair. (Dodie had paid a farewell afternoon visit to AH at Fitzroy Square, and while she was there, someone tried the door. It must have been Mrs Maufe.) AH greeted the returning Dodie with the news that Mrs Maufe was furious, and that Dodie might have to leave Heal's. Did she want to go? No, she answered. 'Then I shouldn't,' he said, smiling. Dodie was miserable, and could not confide in her friend Alec. But then AH appeared in the Little Gallery, said Mrs M's rage had blown over, and invited himself to dinner the next day. Nonetheless a grain of resentment remained.

At Christmas 1929 Dodie stopped writing 'An Eye on Posterity' to practise on the new Underwood typewriter. She had outlined to Phyllis her idea of the plot of *Autumn Crocus*: supposing two women like themselves had gone to the inn at Medratz, and one of them had fallen in love with the innkeeper? But Phyllis, currently playing a maid at the Everyman — 'tripping on daintily with a sugar-basin and a little light badinage with another Lower Order' as she described it — was disinclined to use it as she had loftier notions of writing 'a play of ideas'. Norman MacDermott's wife told Dodie, '*You* should write that play.' AH had just had his tonsils out; Dodie visited him in the nursing home one Sunday (narrowly missing his family) and popped into the church next door, Marylebone Old Church, to pray for her lover, the last church service she ever attended in her life.

While AH was away convalescing on the Continent, Dodie was free to sit at home and, having drawn her gold damask curtains, she lit five candles, placed a vase of narcissi where she could see them, settled down on her divan in front of the fire with a large blue unlined exercise book and wrote her play, with greater ease and enjoyment than she had ever known. The first draft took six weeks. She seemed to recapture all the pleasure of the holiday in the Tyrolean mountains. She finished the heart-wringing love scene at the mountainside shrine, thirty minutes long, one Sunday evening just as Alec arrived with the ham sandwiches.

She decided on the pen name of

C. L. Anthony. She had always wafted prayers towards St Anthony, her girlhood favourite saint, and she had writing paper printed with an image of a pig with a crutch, St Anthony's emblem, since the Order of Hospitallers founded in his name allowed pigs to roam freely in the streets.[1] Alec had also had a crutched pig carved in ivory for her.

Phyllis, a true friend, took the play to her own agent, Dorothea Fassett at the London Play Company, and Phyllis's father enlisted a former German governess to supply the German in which much of the first scene was written. (It was a brilliantly eccentric stroke to have the first ten minutes spoken entirely in German. As Dodie said, she had often missed hearing the opening scenes of plays because of people arriving late in

---

[1] If Dodie named her handbags 'Anthony' after Anthony of Padua, the patron saint of lost property, and was now thinking of him, she was confusing two St Anthonys. The pig-loving St Anthony was the third-century St Anthony of Egypt.

the stalls.) The draft was professionally typed and bound, and Dodie sketched the sets herself. *Autumn Crocus* was not the first play she had sent to an agent (a letter from Spencer Curtis Brown in January 1930 regrets that they can 'find no trace' of her play *Pirate Ships*), but it was admired by the agents whose responses survive. 'I agree with you it shows a great deal of promise,' wrote Geoffrey Whitworth of the British Drama League to Ambrose Heal, who had sent it on Dodie's behalf. 'This is a difficult play. The tale is a sour one. But it is extremely well written and the characters are admirably drawn,' wrote the director Auriol Lee.

The first person to read it at the London Play Company was a young man named Laurence Fitch. He was a clergyman's son from Somerset, stage-struck ever since seeing Gladys Cooper in *The Letter* at the age of fourteen. Through a friend of his mother's, he had been given the job of general factotum at the London Play Company. He gave *Autumn Crocus* an enthusiastic report, and his boss Aubrey Blackburn sent it to the producer-director Basil Dean.

At the same time, Ambrose Heal had sent the play to his impresario friend Nigel Playfair. The report Playfair's reader sent to AH was approving: 'Steiner, a man of address and charm, keeps a small hotel in the Tyrol. He takes a sudden fancy to a pretty guest who is not nearly as young as she looks, and makes with her an appointment at a shrine on a nearby mountainside. Here he tells her he loves her, and very casually mentions his wife. This is a bombshell: not only to the pretty guest but to the audience, who think they have been watching a straightforward love affair.

'Eventually the woman renounces him and departs. That is the plot — which seems to me to require another turn of the screw. But the play is a matter of atmosphere, and depends for its principal interest on glamour of time and place, and surprise and neatness of dialogue. The work has many debatable points, but it is very much out of the common.'

Playfair decided he would put it on with Athene Seyler and Nicholas Hannen; but as soon as his rival impresario Basil

Dean heard about this, his 'managerial hackles rose' and, in order to outsmart Playfair, he offered Dodie a contract. Basil Dean, who had produced Margaret Kennedy's *The Constant Nymph*, had started out as an actor, first seen by Dodie from the sixpenny gallery of the Gaiety Theatre in Manchester where he was playing Jack Barthwick in *The Silver Box*. During the war, as Captain Dean, he had directed Dodie in *Niobe*, at Aldershot Camp Theatre, but he had then sacked her for taking an unscheduled lunch break at Ripon. Dodie had never forgotten (or quite forgiven) him for that. 'It would be pleasant to sell a play to a man I had once been sacked by.' Now he was offering £100 for her play.

6

'Shopgirl Writes Play'

DODIE always claimed that the first indication of her success was when she bought herself a Sunday lunch with two vegetables instead of one, at Flemings in Oxford Street, where you could get a wing of chicken with bread sauce and milky coffee for half a crown. (It was the day of the R101 airship disaster, so she felt guilty to be so ecstatic.) But suddenly having £90, after agent's commission, she bought a short ponyskin coat for herself for twelve guineas, and a dinner jacket for Alec, as he had been saving up for one and then had had his pocket picked. With the help of AH's beneficence, Dodie had already begun to behave in a fairly prosperous manner: she was having her clothes made by Nadine March's dressmaker Georgie Roberts, and she never again sewed a dress for herself. At the same time Uncle

Eddie, the youngest of her three uncles, died, leaving her £40 a year, which increased her guilt about not having gone home to Manchester even when she heard he was dying.

Once the contract was signed, Dodie met Basil Dean, the theatre world's most feared tyrant, for the second time in her life. He took her to lunch on oysters at the Ivy, where she told him candidly that his nickname in the business was 'Bloody Basil'. He called her 'Miss Smith'. 'I had the feeling I ought to keep our relationship strictly professional,' he told her. Basil describes Dodie in his book *The Theatre At War*, wearing 'a white fox fur and black button boots'. Button boots! Pure fantasy, Dodie said: she wore restrained black, relieved by a single white camellia.

What appealed to Basil in *Autumn Crocus* was the quality of the dialogue: 'Charm is often sought by young dramatists,' he said, 'but it was never more gracefully won than in this play.' The cast he chose was flatteringly top-notch. To play the heroine, 'the lady in spectacles', he picked Fay

Compton — who, as James Agate later pointed out in his *Sunday Times* review, was much too beautiful to be a little spinster schoolmistress from Eccles, 'a suburb of Lancashire, and home to the sad cake of that name'. Dodie wanted Gerald du Maurier for Herr Steiner, but du Maurier said he hadn't the legs for lederhosen. Basil scoured Europe for an Austrian who could speak comprehensible English and found the Czech actor Francis Lederer, who had bucketloads of the vitality and charm by which the whole play must stand or fall. Basil also signed up the pretty young Jessica Tandy and Jack Hawkins — who later married — to play 'the couple living in sin': an expression Dodie had to change, for the Lord Chamberlain's sake, to the absurd and ambiguous 'the couple living in freedom'. Martita Hunt was in the cast and so was the critic Agate's sister May, a former pupil of Sarah Bernhardt, in the comic role of the buxom, perspiring German tourist Frau Feldmann.

That Christmas AH gave Dodie a coral cupid and a rose diamond eternity ring. He had the jeweller deliver it to Heal's, where Alec unpacked it, as he dealt with all AH's mail. Since the ring later appeared on Dodie's finger, Alec's suspicions were confirmed, though he did not divulge this to Dodie. But one day that spring, Alec telephoned Dodie and recognised at once the 'Hello?' of AH — who then quickly hung up.

But the fact was, as soon as this dramatic change in Dodie's fortunes had occurred, and she had the entrancing distraction of having a play in production, she began to tire of AH. One fine evening, as she was getting off a bus to dine with Nadine March, the poem by Dante Gabriel Rossetti entitled 'A Little While' flashed into her mind. It begins

A little while a little love
    The hour yet bears for thee and
        me . . .

and ends

I'll tell thee, when the end is come,
    How we may best forget.

AH had gone off on another of his Continental jaunts, hurtfully telling Dodie he would not be back for her first night. But he gave her unlimited time off to attend rehearsals, where — beginning as she meant to go on — she made so many whispered criticisms that Basil stopped her sitting beside him in the stalls. In the end, however, she usually got her way; she had had so much practice, at Heal's, in battling with men, that she was never overawed by power. 'Despite her inexperience as a dramatist,' Basil later wrote in his autobiography, 'she had no intention of being present as a mere symbol of authorship. Quite the contrary. Watching her at rehearsal put me in mind of a particular robin in my garden who arrives every autumn, so tame that I have known him to alight upon a lately used spade, watching my every move with sharp eyes, and ready for swift action against any intrusion upon his territory or privilege.'

Two days before the opening, Dodie records in *Look Back With Astonishment*, AH sent a telegram, 'Coming back for your first night. Trust you can find me a *strapontin*.' ('What the hell was a *strapontin*?' wrote Dodie, adding that it turned out to be a fold-down seat.) This is a nice story, but the actual telegram, preserved in Dodie's archives, reads simply: 'COMING TO YOUR PERFORMANCE SATURDAY HEAL.' By this time the only available seat for the first night at the Lyric, Shaftesbury Avenue — in fact not on Saturday but on Easter Monday — was a place in her box with Alec. Mrs Roberts made Dodie a long white silk crepe dress with a short black velvet bolero; Alec gave her camellias for her shoulder. The opening night had been fixed for 6 April, the Easter bank holiday, specially to get in two days ahead of a musical also set in the Tyrol — *White Horse Inn*.

The first night was remembered by Dodie as a nightmare. The play seemed to drag. The audience up in the gallery was restless and rowdy, shouted to Fay Compton to speak up, and imposed its ill-humour on the whole house. Muriel Aked, whose scene Basil had called 'a hole in the play, my dear', achieved a comic success as 'the lady with the lost underclothes'. But there were loud sniggers and raucous jeers at the supposedly poignant ending when the heroine drove away from her married lover to the sound of a Tyrolean motor horn from a departing bus. Then there were boos and cat-calls from the gallery; so the stalls (containing a large claque of Heal's staff) began booing the gallery, whereupon Sir Edward Marsh, who was in the stalls, stood up and shook his fist at the mob. But a boo, as Dodie said, sounds like a boo wherever it comes from. In all her theatre-going she had never heard a more disastrous reception. She asked Basil forlornly, 'Is it just a bank holiday crowd?' 'They just didn't like it, dear,' said Basil, at once beginning to calculate how soon they might take it off.

Ambrose Heal had insisted on organising a first night supper at the Savoy for Dodie and Alec, Basil, Phyllis, Basil's American backer Kenneth Macgowan, and Mrs Maufe, who reportedly commented: 'He's never done as much for *me*.' It was a flat, even funereal, affair. Basil was gloomy, and Dodie sat silently in the midst of the forced chatter. Finally they piled all the flowers into the car — including the bouquets from AH and from Mrs M; and Alec's perfect crocuses from Scotland, thoughtfully set in a trug he had painted himself with crocuses — and drove home to Dodie's new top flat off the Marylebone Road (which she had taken at £100 a year). There Alec and Phyllis unwired and arranged the flowers and tried to cheer her up. She begged them to take away the orchids: 'They make me feel like death.' 'It can't fail,' Dodie said to Alec. 'Because if it does, I can't go on.'

Early the next morning Alec arrived with the papers. The notices were astonishing: all were enthusiastic. Alan Parsons, Viola Tree's husband and *Daily Mail* critic, called it 'the love story's triumphant return to the stage' and said later audiences would know how to appreciate the play. Charles Morgan in *The Times* gave it a lengthy assessment in which he likened it to Turgenev's *Torrents of Spring*. (Dodie hadn't read that novel, and didn't like it even when she did so, later.) AH, who read only

The Times, said 'I never had the slightest doubt,' and went back to the South of France.

That morning at Heal's Dodie was at her desk as usual at 9 a.m., surrounded by telegrams. Nineteen journalists turned up to interview C. L. Anthony, alias 'shopgirl Dodie Smith', the photographers slightly disappointed that there were no counters at which she could be photographed serving, the reporters equally dismayed to find that she was no lowly assistant but the head of a department with a staff of three. Nevertheless, SHOPGIRL WRITES PLAY proclaimed the *Evening News* billboard. The *Evening Standard* offered her £50 to write about herself: 'It's never too late for love, by girl playwright Dodie Smith' (the 'girl' being thirty-five years old). Heal's was festooned with *Autumn Crocus* posters. While Dodie was at the shop, blithely telling reporters she would not dream of leaving Heal's until she had made a great deal of money, 'Bloody Basil' was at the theatre making twenty minutes of cuts. When Dodie arrived, they had a blazing row. Basil said, 'I'm trying to save your play.' Dodie: 'Well take it off then.' Eventually he let her cut it herself.

She went to lunch at the Ivy that day with Phyllis, who wore her orchids. She could now lunch there as often as she liked, and lunch she did: Kenneth Macgowan, Basil's American backer, liked being seen around with 'the new girl playwright', and Alec, on whom she had become increasingly dependent, was always available. She soon moved into another top floor flat in Dorset Square, and AH himself designed her new cream and gold bedroom — a huge, north-facing room — with magnificent cupboards in the *dernier cri* Heal's 1930s style, and a custom-built ebonised desk. The whole flat was a study in monochrome: black, white and silver. The walls were dead white with no pictures. The front room overlooking the square had a black metal-topped dining table, a speckled black and white carpet, a black Blüthner piano, black glass flower vases, silver candlesticks, and curtains and cushions in black and silver. Anthony Heal remembers Dodie fussing over the lighting on her dressing-table which, she said, had to be thrown onto the mirror; he told her it was nonsense, she must have light thrown on her face, but she was adamant, so he designed a light-fitting that looked as if it threw light on the mirror, but actually diffused it.

While the decorating of the flat was supervised by Alec, Dodie went off on a cruise to the Canaries via Malaga and Gibraltar. Seldom had she loathed anything so much. She sat at the purser's table, bored stiff, and sailed back into Southampton to the strains of 'Happy Days Are Here Again'. She gave AH dinner in Dorset Square — now, suddenly, it was Dodie and not AH who decided when they should meet. Her new maid — who expected Dodie to have cocktails in the bath, and had literary pretensions, copying out chunks of Aldous Huxley's *Antic Hay* and claiming them as her own work — served AH over his left shoulder with a whole, burnt-black chicken. 'Am I supposed to eat the whole bird?' he asked. Dodie was as dependent as ever on maids and cooks, about whom she could, she said, have written a book.

With plenty of time to think about her life while on board ship, Dodie had determined on leaving Heal's. First, she suggested to AH that she might work part-time at Heal's and be paid by the hour, since the play was earning her £130 a week. (It was not only playing to capacity but they had had to install 35 additional seats. 'Woman's play makes fortune,' ran a contemporary headline, 'but she still works in shop.') He refused, quite angrily, and they quarrelled. But then AH took a large party to the play again, and afterwards relented and said she might reduce her work to four hours a day. Later this became two; then just a few hours a week. But even at Christmas 1931 she was still doing all the toy buying, and went back to run the department full time. It was not until well into 1932 that the accounts department begged her to leave properly, because her odd hours played havoc with their books.

She returned again and again to the Lyric to see her play, sitting in a side box, never staying for the love scenes, which she found 'too embarrassing'. But she loved seeing the House Full board in Shaftesbury Avenue. And on 4 June that year, 1931, Boo Laye held a *Mr Wu* reunion party, after which Dodie and Alec started a new hobby: first-nighting. From then on, they went together, always in evening dress, to every first night — 'one of the greatest pleasures of my life' — with supper afterwards at the Café Royal. Over breakfast in bed the next day Dodie would meticulously record, in a pretty little notebook, the play's cast, her comments, marks out of ten, and her predictions for the length of the run; also crisp notes on the stars. Over the next five years these notes amount to a comprehensive theatrical record of an era. 'Delysia is getting old'; 'John Mills brilliant as comic Cockney private'; 'Celia Johnson much improved — facial contortions seem to be going'; Sybil Thorndike in an unconvincing thriller — 'good grim acting by Sybil — "You're too good for this rotten play!" shouted the gallery to Sybil.' *George and Margaret*, Irene Handl's famous début walk-on in Gerald Savory's comedy, was 'just a slight story about a crazy Hampstead family, but funny from beginning to end; Alec laughed until he ached and nearly fell off his seat. This is the first time I have ever given +10 to a play.' Unlike *Bats in the Belfry*, 'a very very bad light comedy, about a mad family in a country vicarage, which made one squirm at its inanity'; *He Was Born Gay* had Gielgud and Emlyn Williams giving 'nervy and mannered performances' and ran for two weeks. She praised Robert Morley in *The Great Romancer*, Marius Goring in *Satyr*, though it was 'really too sexually shocking for the stage', Noël Coward's *Tonight at 8.30*, with Coward and Gertie Lawrence, and *Hands Across the Sea* 'a weaker edition of *Hay Fever*, funny but damn irritating'. There were also notes on promising young names like Margaret Lockwood, and on established ones: 'Ralph Richardson falling off badly'; 'Marie Tempest shewing her age at last, but still marvellous for 73.' But the general impression is of plays 'fatuous', 'dreadful' and 'God-awful'.

Dodie had become, almost overnight, richer than she had ever imagined possible; she bought a glamorous grey coat, which bore the label 'Gwen of Devon', for forty guineas. Her financial success was listed in the *Daily Telegraph* along with other big hits of recent years: Noël Coward's *Bitter Sweet*, R. C. Sherriff's *Journey's End* and Rudolf Besier's *The Barretts of Wimpole Street*. But she was already worried about repeating her success, and vaguely 'frightened of the future'. On 28 July she gave her first — and last — large party. AH arranged for her to buy quantities of champagne from Nigel Playfair, who had overstocked during the slump and felt he could not give showy parties as his drawing room was visible from the road. Playfair came to the party but AH refused; he looked wistful as he called in, on his way home to Beaconsfield, to collect his birthday present from Dodie. It was the new Gollancz edition of *Autumn Crocus* specially bound in vellum, with a separately bound set of watercolour sketches Dodie had done herself for the scenery. With a collector's acumen, AH decided she should not write in it, as that might damage its value. (After he died

Dodie asked his son Anthony to let her have it back, which he did.) Later, she wondered whether that was the evening when she realised she was no longer in love with AH. The excitement of her daily life was now such that she hardly needed the intrigue of the affair. The party, incidentally, was a great success, with guests — who included the actors Jessica Tandy and Jack Hawkins, Evelyn Hope and Arthur Hambling — staying most of the night; but the new table had so many champagne stains it had to go back to Heal's for treatment, and Dodie vowed never to give another big party.

That Christmas of 1931, she went home to the Manchester family. She found Harold, the last uncle, wizened and ill, and Nan exhausted from sheer irritation with her marriage, and with years of housekeeping for her brothers. The atmosphere was wretched. But the tables were turned, as Dodie — who had made £4000 from the play already, and had begun a portfolio of investments — was able to give Harold a gift of £100.

By then, the play's business was falling

off, since Fay Compton had left the cast for a pantomime commitment. Dodie told Uncle Harold she had yet to face her tax bill, and had spent extravagantly — on the decorating of her flat, and on her first-night dresses in silver lamé from Lilian Lawler in South Molton Street. Uncle Harold said: 'So it hasn't been a great success, then, after all,' with a somewhat Mancunian air of satisfaction. When he had first read *Autumn Crocus* he had told Dodie it was clever but 'not really a play, though, is it?' But then, he didn't think Shaw wrote real plays either: he preferred Henry Arthur Jones and Pinero. This was partly the habitual nostalgia of the aged for the works of their youth: Dodie, as she got older, and found her plays no longer the fashion, began to see Uncle Harold's point of view.

What, she asked Uncle Harold, are you planning to do this year? 'I plan to die,' he replied, and he did so, soon afterwards.

It was a relief to get back to London. Dodie was now the family benefactress, inviting Aunt Nan, Aunt Bertha and

Uncle Bertie, and Aunt Blanche, to her first nights, and even paying for their holidays. But the end of the play's ten-month run arrived: Basil took it out of the Lyric and into a suburban tour, before bringing it back for a last month at the Savoy. It had run for 371 performances. Though she was still at Heal's on one afternoon a week, Dodie could now follow a writer's regime of rising late, walking in Dorset Square, working from eleven till one. Dealing with begging letters, invitations to speak at luncheons (always refused, after one disastrous experience at the Critics' Circle), effusions from old friends ('You're the only one of us old Barnes girls who has distinguished herself' from a RADA contemporary; 'How proud your uncles must be of you' from a Manchester schoolfriend) and dozens of manuscripts from aspiring play-wrights, to which she gave the most careful consideration, all occupied swathes of time. She was trying, that spring, to turn *Autumn Crocus* into a novel, but became bogged down, unable to discard any dialogue, despairing of finding an authorial voice, and gave up.

In August she set off with Phyllis for a holiday in Corsica — hoping that bandits might inspire a plot. As Alec was seeing them off in a taxi Phyllis said, 'Poor Alec! I expect you wish you were coming,' and the minute they arrived in Corsica Dodie cabled Alec to fly to join them, which he did. Corsica proved wild and uncomfortable, and Phyllis persuaded them to retreat to the Austrian Tyrol, whereupon she pined for Corsica. At Innsbruck and at Medratz Phyllis's behaviour was 'uniformly bloody'. She eventually admitted that she could not bear seeing Alec's affection for Dodie. She wasn't jealous, she didn't want him herself, but she could not stand seeing Dodie receiving affection when she had none. Dodie found her egotism 'staggering' — Alec was heroically tolerant — and they all went home, Dodie to the urgent prospect of having to write a second play, to prove that she was no mere one-off fluke; although, as she reflected, 'Shopgirl writes two plays would be rather like Cinderella getting two princes.'

She told newspapers that she and Phyllis Morris were writing a musical about Corsican bandits called *Vendetta*, but instead she began a rural drama with the terrible title of *Grace Before Meat*. Then one day in her bath she had a much better idea: to write about the Depression. Unemployment in Great Britain was at 2.75 million. One furniture shop, Shoolbreds, had been driven out of business, and the staff of Heal's had been asked to take a ten per cent reduction in their salaries, reflecting the drop in profits. She would write a play called *Service* about a shop like Heal's, a family business facing recession, and its staff's efforts to save it, with AH the obvious model for the character of Gabriel Service. Writing at fever speed in Dorset Square on her Heal desk, she was almost driven mad. She started it a dozen times and tore up every draft. But eventually she gave it to Basil Dean. He was dubious: it had thirty characters, six different sets and no love interest. But Bronson Albery happened to need a new play for Wyndham's, and by late summer of 1932 it was being cast: a queue of hopeful actors formed outside Basil's Adelphi office. Jack Hawkins,

Ann Todd, Joyce Kennedy were signed up, and Phyllis took the part of the charwoman Mrs Munson. AH supplied most of the furniture for the sets from Heal's. He realised of course that *Service* was about Heal's, and told Dodie the play was 'sheer nonsense, my child, and you know it'. But the shop is plainly Heal's, starting with the description of Service's as an ancient foundation that once sold 'all sorts of Genoa, Dutch and English velvets, Padusoys of all colours, Lutestrings, Mantuas, Sarsenets and Persians; likewise, Cherry-derrys, Prunellas and Calimancoes . . . '

On the first night in October, Dodie sat between AH and Alec. Although elegance was hard to achieve, for a woman five foot high with her hair cut like a medieval pageboy, Dodie felt she achieved it in a superb new long white dress with enormous white fur stole and cameo necklace. The gallery applauded her arrival so loudly she felt she should stand up and wave — showmanship, said one paper the next day, which would have done credit to Edgar Wallace. The play took nineteen curtain calls. Basil had implored Dodie not to make a speech, but when the calls for 'Author!' became tumultuous she felt it was ungracious not to respond, and gave 'rather a good speech', she noted. From the start, *Service* went superbly. 'Woman Writes Best Play of the Season' ran one headline. Several critics likened the scope of the story to Dickens, and Gordon Selfridge himself told her it gave an accurate picture of shop life. *Service* is a deeply sentimental play. ('I must confess,' wrote St John Ervine, the Irish dramatist, 'that I have seldom felt so put out as I was when a rainbow appeared in the last act.') However, it also had the Priestley-like touch of common humanity, and as James Drawbell, editor of *Woman's Own*, said, 'Dodie Smith is much nearer to the hearts of the ordinary people than most of her fellow playwrights; and certainly nearer than any of the critics. She knows what people want, and she has the ability to give it to them with complete sincerity and conviction.' At the Savoy first night party, Basil told her: 'You're established now.'

Autumn Crocus was about to open at

the Morosco Theatre in New York the next month, November 1932, and Basil invited Dodie to accompany him there. Before she sailed to America on the *Aquitania*, Dodie felt she must confront AH, who had guessed that her feelings towards him had changed. She invited him to a farewell dinner, and pretended it was 'one of those days which could not end in the way his visits usually did'. Since she could not bring herself to run an affair with two men at once, she and Alec had not yet technically become lovers, but a few days later they did so. They had, God knows, said Dodie, been near it for years. And she feared the occasion was not a very happy experience for a 'devoted, idealistic and inexperienced young man.' The trouble was, she reflected, that she was still relatively sexually inexperienced despite her three clandestine affairs. She had hitherto depended on the technical expertise of married lovers. Also, her once lively sex drive had now so atrophied that she asked Alec not to send her love letters in New York, as even the words distressed her.

'Little Dodie loves big New York' said a headline in one of the New York papers as she and Basil installed themselves at the Hotel Gotham. She had told Basil she needed a suite on the ground floor because she might sleepwalk. Basil fixed one on the third floor 'so that if I sleepwalked I would not be killed but only maimed'. Despite being lionised and invited everywhere in New York, meeting Esmé Percy and Clemence Dane, Charles Laughton and George S. Kaufman, she was lonely and depressed. The first night of *Autumn Crocus* was a disaster. Francis Lederer, in his spiked mountaineering shoes, managed to fall off the mountainside not once but twice, the second time almost landing on the orchestra. Several people walked out before the end. The entire play was miscast, with the Dublin actress Patricia Collinge 'coy, sentimental and embarrassing' in the Fay Compton role. Lee Shubert, the producer, agreed. 'I have waited and waited for your beautiful play,' he said, 'and it is being spoilt by an actress who might be pushing a baby carriage. Shall I close it at the end of the week — or get a new leading lady?'

He engaged Dorothy Gish instead, but the whole thing still lacked charm, and flopped. The reviews were patronising, the audiences lukewarm.

However, at the Gotham Dodie met someone who was going to be important to her: John van Druten, the British-born playwright currently enjoying great success in New York. He invited her to a cocktail party where she met the poet John Drinkwater and his wife Daisy, in whom Dodie confided, without mentioning his name, about AH. Daisy Drinkwater declared that Dodie should end the affair completely or she might be put off sex for life. As soon as she got back, sailing on the *Europa*, where van Druten introduced her to the champagne cocktail, and Charles Laughton overcame her aversion to games by introducing her to deck quoits, she went to see AH and passed on Daisy Drinkwater's theory, attributing it to 'a New York psychiatrist'. She managed to convince AH she must lay off sex for a while — assuring him there was nothing between her and Alec — but AH persisted in coming to see her almost as often as before. He now seemed more willing to take her out and be seen with her. Once, she took him to a first night, but everyone asked 'Where's Alec?' and AH proved a much less amusing companion than Alec; so she never asked him to the theatre again, except to share her box with Alec on her own first nights.

She realised she was not now and never had been truly in love with AH, despite having assured him she would be faithful to him through eternity. And she also realised that whereas she could bear to hurt AH, she could not bear to go on hurting Alec, and keep him waiting and hoping. All this Dodie reasons out in her journal, and fairly accurately represents in her published autobiography (giving Ambrose Heal the pseudonym 'Oliver'). She was not in love with Alec, but he had become the most important person in her life; he was the best of companions and they simply enjoyed being together, liking the same things. When van Druten introduced her to the work of James Thurber, and she brought home from America *The Seal in the Bedroom*, Ambrose Heal was mystified and unable to see the jokes, whereas Alec was 'convulsed and enchanted'. Dodie rightly concluded that she should not waste time on anyone who did not respond to Thurber.

But Dodie also realised that sex itself did not really interest her now that she had fame and fortune. Having once longed for the security of three pounds a week, she now had a hundred times as much. 'I work when I like, go where I like, do what I like,' she told James Drawbell, who interviewed her for his book of profiles of distinguished women (*A Gallery of Women*, published in 1933) along with Greta Garbo, Elinor Glyn, Vicki Baum, Ethel Mannin and Dora Russell.

She and Alec had become lovers, but this was not as important to her as it had once been, and their sex life was 'not easy'. Yet this did not seem to matter. Alec spent all his spare time working as Dodie's secretary, assistant, and business manager — he had even prepared *Service* for serialisation in the *Daily Sketch* while she was in New York — and this appeared to be enough for him. As she recorded much later:

'I have often thought the fact that I was no longer violently interested in sex has partly accounted for our long and lasting happiness. I seem to have no feeling whatever for the men I cared for when I was highly sexed — the feeling of affection ended as soon as the sexual attraction did.' In later years, she had dreaded meeting AH, whereas she could not imagine ever ceasing to care for Alec. 'It is as if we slid from great friendship and ideal companionship, into a state of love beyond being "in love" — or at least, I did. I was in a state of dependent and devoted love, lasting and ever-increasing, but not "in love".' She admitted feeling guilty that Alec had been 'swindled' out of romantic love; and she missed the sensation herself, too, which she felt affected her work: 'There was no romantic love in any of my plays after *Autumn Crocus*. And in my novels I have only been interested in writing about romance for the very young — trying to re-capture my own youth.' This was certainly true: Dodie wrote repeatedly about the passions of avid teenage girls, and faithless middle-aged men: apart from *I Capture the Castle*, she found it almost impossible to write convincingly about romantic love.

'I think the main reason that I tired of AH, and became less interested in sex, was that I became successful. Women have for so long been conditioned to equate sex appeal with success. And although I considered myself highly sexed, I think much of my sex was, in D. H. Lawrence's phrase, "sex in the head" — quite a good place for it in my opinion. I partly longed for affairs as status symbols, an expression we did not use then but the idea operated all right. Certainly, to "collect" the managing director of Heal's struck me as a substantial status symbol, particularly as I had not been overburdened with masculine admiration — although for an undersized, not pretty girl I seem to have done fairly well. Success with *Autumn Crocus* satisfied my ego far more than a love affair could. As soon as I had that success, I no longer felt romantically excited by AH, even in 1931. The romance really meant more to me than the sex, and when the romance was no longer needed, the sex followed it.'

Dodie wrote those words in 1965 in her journal. She thought it unlikely that Alec would ever read it, even if he survived her. 'He might dip into it, but with me gone, it might sadden him.' So, she told herself, she was setting these things down for herself, to be stored with her other unpublished writings, in case someone might one day want to read her record of a life. But if Alec ever should read it, she added, she wanted him to know that her attraction to him was never part of the status symbol hunting. She loved him for his character, his intelligence, his looks — and though it was neither romantic nor carnal, it was a much more lasting and dependable love than anything she had ever known before. Oddly enough, Dodie never examined, even in a private journal, the reasons why Alec (so young and attractive) should love her (older, and plain) so devotedly that he could embark upon a physically low-key, emotionally unpassionate affair that would lead to a companionable marriage, and ask for nothing more than partnership in return from her. But this he apparently did: Alec seemed satisfied with being Dodie's best friend and life partner, or at least he never evinced a moment's discontent.

In 1933 another new play was awaited. She decided to write one that took place on the first day of spring — but it was so cold that spring she abandoned it. She began a comedy called *You Can't Go Wrong*, its heroine a spinster novelist who feels that her love stories are too innocuous because of her own lack of experience, and decides she must have an affair. That too was aborted. She started on a play called *Three For A Wedding* but it did not prosper.

There were distractions. She bought her first car, a Vauxhall, which Alec learned to drive. Dodie had one lesson, but met another car, grazed a stone wall, and gave up. Alec drove her around East Anglia, Devon and Cornwall, and up to Scotland; but she was curiously depressed, itching (literally, in Scotland, because of the horseflies) to get back to playwriting, and not much fun to be with. This did not bother Alec, who was already showing every sign of being possessed of 'invincible happiness'. Whenever others moaned about their lives, Alec would say: 'Well anyway, *I'm* happy.'

While they were in Scotland, Dodie had the idea for her third play, *Touch Wood*, set in a John o'Groats hotel ('once a hunting-lodge, a pleasant old place, still retaining some of its original atmosphere') where a childless couple return fifteen years after their honeymoon. But she had first to break off and return to the Tyrol for the filming of *Autumn Crocus*, which was to star Ivor Novello with Fay Compton, under the direction of Basil Dean.[1] Berta Ruck, the novelist, whose son was with the film unit, accompanied her. They found the Medratz hotel empty, out of season; they had to knock up Herr Steiner and his family at midnight, but the entire unit were given supper and

---

[1] Basil Dean's assistant director on the film was Carol Reed, the illegitimate son of Sir Herbert Beerbohm Tree; young Carol was too gentle, Basil predicted, ever to have a successful film career, which shows how wrong he could be.

beds, and stayed 7 weeks, held up by incessant rain. (Basil Dean was convinced that Dodie must have been in love with Herr Steiner, but he was in reality nothing like Francis Lederer or Ivor Novello: he was pleasant but stout and elderly, and devoted to Frau Steiner.) Alas, there was not an autumn crocus to be seen, so Basil had ten thousand paper ones made and stuck rather obviously in the grass, though Dodie told him there had never been more than a small clump. The villagers were given lucrative roles as extras, and when their local church procession took place it stayed in the last reel of the film, where all the villagers are seen staring hard at the camera as they pass.

London had a hot summer, and Dodie began to feel old (at thirty-seven) and curiously bored. After years of being woken at 7 a.m. ('I couldn't feel worse than if I was going to the guillotine . . . it's getting up and fighting your way on buses that gets me down,' says Billie the shopgirl in *Bonnet Over the Windmill*) she had not yet adapted to the disciplined freelance life. Alec, still working at Heal's, would dash home to his flat at six, pick up Dodie and they would drive out to the Essex countryside and swim. They had fallen in love with the countryside near Basil's home, Little Easton Manor, where Dodie befriended Basil's various girlfriends, including the actress Margaretta Scott. Dodie warned Basil that Margaretta was a Catholic and if he married her (Miss Scott tells me he never asked her) he would have to have all the children God sent. Dodie said Victoria Hopper was a better bet, and Basil did indeed marry her. At Basil's Dodie also met J. B. Priestley — who had just had his first play success with *Dangerous Corner* — and re-met the Drinkwaters. She and Alec spent Christmas Day that year in Highgate at the Drinkwaters' enormous house, complete with butlers. Daisy confided to Dodie that her poet husband liked a grander life than they could afford.

Touch Wood was soon ready. Basil delayed the opening and Dodie flew into one of her rages ('You mustn't say things like that to Mr Dean, he's terribly upset,' she was told, but she thought he would survive). The upshot of this row was that Alec decided to leave Heal's and become Dodie's full-time manager. She would pay him the same salary as he got at Heal's, and relieve him of the tyranny of nine-till-six.

In fact, Heal's was now enjoying a post-Depression resurgence in the vanguard of design; Mrs Maufe's 'White and Off-White' exhibition that year echoed the white-and-cream craze started by Syrie Maugham and Oliver Messel. At the same time Mrs Maufe was devising ways of making good Bauhausian design accessible to young couples, Habitat-style, with a complete '£195 house' and a '£350 house' — the theatre critic J. C. Trewin and his wife bought a set when they married in 1932 — including everything from the bed to the bath-mat. Heal's were spending about £450 a year on advertising, which had been Alec's department. Dodie was rightly anxious about wrenching him from this commercial career — and also about having thus sealed their joint future. Luckily Alec was blessed with a rare temperament which did not find it difficult (as many men would) to accept a bread-winning wife.

They had found a home to share. Or rather, Alec had found a thatched cottage called The Barretts at Finchingfield, a much-photographed village in north-west Essex whose Norman church, duckpond, hump-backed bridge and windmill have adorned the covers of dozens of magazines and Olde England calendars. 'Five roads led to a green and a pond, surrounded by cottages,' as Dodie described it, 'and there was an almost indescribable rightness about the composition of the place, just as one finds in great works of art.' Anyone arriving there today for the first time feels that time really has stood still — until in summer coach-parties clog the village green. The Barretts was originally a pair of cottages, a mile down the road from the green, between 300 and 400 years old; the builders unearthed a Charles II coin when digging the well. In 1934, it was a ruin: damp and decaying, with broken doors hanging off their hinges. The price was £425, with three acres, and no mains water or electricity; it needed thrice £425 to be spent on it.

On her first visit, Dodie did not quite see its idyllic potential. She sat glowering as Phyllis and Alec ate their picnic lunch in the dank barn. They could see its charming possibilities: the barn was to be a guest suite and music room, its hay-loft would be a gallery bedroom. Dodie was sceptical: she merely found the aroma of hens and tramps sickening. But she bought it, to please Alec; and The Barretts was to be their home base for ever after.

The new play, *Touch Wood*, was as different in tone as could be from *Service*: light, quick, and funny. It still reads amusingly (though nobody performs it today) from the opening lines:

ELIZABETH: Has the post come, McKenzie?

MCKENZIE: Well, miss, it has and it hasna'.

ELIZABETH: What on earth does that mean?

MCKENZIE: It came, but there wasna' any.

Unusually, for a formula hotel play, the hotel owner is never seen. The guests included not just one of Dodie's precocious children, but a family of three bright orphans, the eldest of whom, Mab, is twenty-two and ready to fling herself in Dodie fashion at a married man. Basil insisted on his girlfriend Victoria Hopper playing Mab, and Dodie had written the part with her in mind — but she was under contract to Sydney Carroll, who was at first reluctant to free her 'to play a bitch on heat'. Gerald du Maurier wanted to play the male lead (and Lady du Maurier, meeting Dodie at a party, said, 'The part *is* Gerald') but he was deemed by the manager of the Haymarket to be too old: 'I can't have a man of sixty making love to a young girl in my theatre.' In fact, du Maurier died just as rehearsals began.

There were histrionics off-stage. Dodie witnessed a scene in Victoria Hopper's dressing room with Basil down on his knees before a rigid-faced Victoria, who had broken off their engagement with a poise and courtesy Dodie found astounding in one so young. It was an 'awful and ludicrous' evening. Dodie pleaded; Basil pleaded; Victoria put on face-powder and coolly went back on stage. Dodie and Alec took Basil home to Victoria Square where he wept copiously and was put to bed by Alec. It was extraordinary, said Dodie, that someone with such a brutal personality — notorious for making actresses cry — should weep so incongruously. 'Even my second wife,' sobbed Basil, 'would get upset if she saw me in this state.'

The company, waiting to rehearse, found these shenanigans tiresome. Flora Robson, playing her usual role as the eternal spinster — she later wrote to Dodie, 'Couldn't you write me a part one day about a successful wife?' — was quite unsympathetic. Basil returned in dark glasses, the essence of gloom. Dodie took over giving the cast their movements. She and Alec spent the weekend at Basil's, walking in the garden at midnight, drenched by rain and tears. Eventually Dodie persuaded Victoria to promise to marry Basil, and two weeks later they went to the registry office at Great Dunmow where Victoria became the third Mrs Dean. Dorothy Hyson replaced her as Mab.

Two weeks before opening night in May 1934, Dodie's thirty-eighth birthday took place, and she received a most disconcerting present, which would change her life. It arrived in a hatbox, presented to her by Alec and Phyllis in her Dorset Square bedroom while she was breakfasting in her accustomed splendour. What woman, she instantly thought, wants a hat she has not chosen for herself? But the hat box wriggled and lurched, and out onto the bed poured a Dalmatian puppy.

True, she liked dogs. All her clothes were black and white; she lived in a black and white flat, and she had often said in jest that all she needed now was a Dalmatian. But she didn't want one *yet*. And she wanted to choose her own; a small puppy, not this clumsy, half-grown creature. Alec and Phyllis, after all their subterfuge and planning, were dismayed to watch Dodie get up, peevishly, to face life with the boisterous Pongo. She took him to the Haymarket Theatre for a rehearsal and he lifted his leg everywhere. Marie Ney, the leading lady, dropped him and he already appeared to be slightly lame. Basil said, 'You're going to make a fool of yourself over that dog,' and he was right.

At night, alone with Pongo in her flat, Dodie discovered a regime that was the nearest thing to motherhood she ever knew: she was woken every few hours by his howls. He stopped only when she put her fingers through the bars of his kennel to be chewed. ('Perhaps the most important thing for happy Dalmatian ownership,' declares the leaflet 'Beyond the Spots' issued by the British Dalmatian Club, 'is to understand that Dalmatians NEED PEOPLE.') And he was not house-trained, nor did he comprehend the idea. Ellen, the maid, a hefty farmer's daughter, would drag him round Dorset Square for hours, without results; then she would carry him up 72 stairs, and he would perform at once in the hall. Maddened by all this, Dodie sent Pongo back to the kennels, to have some peace until after her play opened.

Once more she offended the Lord Chamberlain, this time by referring to Mab in the script as 'a raving nymphomaniac'. She had first met the Lord Chamberlain's veto when she was not allowed to use 'the young couple living in sin' in *Autumn Crocus* (while Dodie's keen interest in sex had now cooled, that of her characters had not), and she had apparently offended the citizens of Letchworth with the mischievous line, 'My parents live in Letchworth, but their souls are purest Penge.' Now, a pleasant young man from the censor's office arrived and eventually conceded that Dodie could allow a character to say, of Mab, 'she's just a nymphomaniac'. It was the first time the word had ever been passed. 'So,' as Dodie remarked, 'it's all right to be a nymphomaniac, as long as you do not rave.' As for the child Nonny, who, as Dodie pointed out, adopted a high moral tone towards her erring elder sister, the Lord Chamberlain insisted that she should not be at all 'in on' scenes concerning sex. Dodie asked if it would help if, for the scene in which Nonny revealed that her sister had gone off with a married man, she wore a fairly long evening dress. The censor thought it might. So Basil put little Pamela Standish in a long white muslin dress with a blue sash, straight out of Kate Greenaway, which had the effect of making her look even more babyish.

This was to be Dodie's first play under her own name instead of the pseudonym C. L. Anthony. 'I never wanted to be called Dodie Smith: such a silly name, I thought. As a girl I would invent grand stage names for myself — "Beryl Lascelles" or "Margaretta Challis",' Dodie later recalled. 'But Basil Dean said to me: "If you use your own name, I will put it up in lights".' So Dodie Smith became herself. The effect, Basil found, was to encourage her to interfere even more in the directing and the sets. Basil, who like most directors candidly preferred authors to be dead, ignored her interventions. So Dodie smuggled another director, Murray Macdonald, into rehearsals to work privately with Marie Ney. In Dodie's opinion, Murray saved the play.

And surely, she told her journal, she knew better than any director how the sets should look. She insisted on the right lighting for the sunset scene; not a gaudy blood-red, Basil dear, it had to be the pale yellow light, with a tinge of green, that she had seen on her Scottish trip. It reflected Coleridge's lines

All this long eve, so balmy and
    serene,
Have I been gazing at the western
    sky
And its peculiar shade of yellow
    green.

Basil replied airily that he *never* read authors' stage directions and Dodie 'rampaged'. In his memoirs Basil describes Alec handing him, through an open car window, a sheaf of his notes of changes Dodie wanted, 'as formidable as a Petition of Rights'. Dodie never forgave Basil his obduracy. She pretended to, praising him fulsomely in her first-night speech, dragging him on stage with her from the wings. 'Thank you for mentioning me,' Basil remarked coldly afterwards. Then she and Alec dined *à deux* at the Café Royal.

An hour after she got into bed, Alec woke her to say the morning paper reviews were all good — the best she had ever had: *The Times*, *Telegraph* and *News Chronicle* considered it her best play yet. Noël Coward wrote to Basil that he had come away 'fairly bubbling with pleasure at having once again seen English writing, acting and production at their best', and to Dodie: 'I really did enjoy it so very much and came away feeling a good deal more cosy about the English theatre than I have felt for a long time.'

The next morning, she was photographed with the newly returned Pongo at her flat. Pongo became adept at looking appealing for the camera, sitting on a seat in the stalls, until one day he got folded up inside one. These pictures, with photogenic dog in lap, became her ideal self-image. 'Portrait of a happy woman', she captioned them. Apart from the hairstyle, a rigidly marcelled new perm, they represented Dodie's idea of

Dodie in heaven. Even Pongo, with his Dalmatian 'smile', seemed to know he would be loved for life. This was one day which, long afterwards, she wished she could live again.

Part Two

1935 – 1953

Part Two

1985 – 1075

7

The Casting of the Die

DURING these weeks of her third consecutive triumph, Dodie and Alec were furnishing The Barretts. They had engaged an architect but soon paid him to go away. At her basement antique shop in Baker Street a Miss Coates found them cottage-sized pieces of pine and walnut furniture, and stripped them to match the cottage's lime-bleached beams. Dodie considered her chosen mixture of furnishing styles simply perfect — nothing Olde Worlde or Jacobean, no dark oak or fake latches — and always resented anyone who failed to exclaim in admiration upon entering The Barretts for the first time. Heal's had supplied bright poppy red curtains and pale sofa covers, but very little of the furniture: which is why, Dodie supposed, AH and his son Anthony found so little to praise when they drove down to see her new home.

One day when she and Alec arrived to supervise the builders — who were adding a gabled kitchen wing and installing an Aga boiler — they found John Gielgud and his friend John Perry 'snooping around'. Gielgud and Perry had just bought Foulslough, a mill across the fields, where Dodie and Alec had done a bit of snooping too. In June of 1934, Dodie, Alec and Pongo, Ellen the hefty maid, and Phyllis Morris, all went down to stay at The Barretts for the first time.

Life there was not perfect. The sun brought a plague of flies, and Dodie would not even allow sticky flypaper, let alone any swatting. There was an invasion of bugs in Alec's bedroom, and he was badly bitten. The well failed to supply enough water even when they paid £60 to have it dug deeper. There were no good walks nearby — no meadows, just arable farmland where footpaths petered out, and Pongo, now a heavy dog, was not fond of walking and had to be carried home. Phyllis, as usual, was 'a mite difficult'. (The bugs, incidentally, left with the weeping maid Ellen, who was shortly dismissed.)

Alec busied himself with creating a garden, planting chestnuts and birches, acacia and lilac, fuchsia and clematis, while Dodie took herself off for long solitary walks along the still traffic-free roads to the High Crossroads from which she could look down on the cottage, the barn, the orchard and the pond, and marvel that she owned it all. But she soon realised she could not write with Alec and Phyllis about, and with all the interruptions of visitors and calls from local people. Basil Dean had assured her that if she set up home with Alec, the locals would be too scandalised to call; but call they did. Dodie returned none of the visits, except (out of curiosity, because she wanted to see inside their house) to the local grandees, Sir John and Lady Ruggles-Brise at Spains Hall, who were sorry, when she arrived alone, that she had not brought 'that nice Mr Beesley'. One can imagine the reaction of this rural community to the new owners of The Barretts: an eccentric lady playwright, her handsome young male companion, and their spotted dog.

(Sir John Ruggles-Brise, now in his late eighties, remembers Dodie's ménage in just those terms: 'She was a formidable cookie who "wore the trousers" . . . her husband did all the shopping, always with a large white dog with black spots all over.') A. J. A. Symons, author of *The Quest For Corvo*, lived in the village and showed signs of being a 'determined friend'. They explored the countryside with him but he insisted on reading his work aloud to Dodie which lulled her to sleep. From London came every friend they had; and from Manchester came the relations: Aunt Bertha, Uncle Bertie, cousins Esmé and Ronnie and Ronnie's fiancée Frances, all enraptured by the white thatched cottage.

Dodie began to long for the peace of Dorset Square where she could be alone all day. What with the gardener, the builder (captain of the local fire brigade) and garrulous tradesmen being barked at by Pongo, she made no progress with her writing. At last, one day that summer, Dodie was left alone in the cottage (apart from the housekeeper, who swindled them for a year before being discovered drinking gin in bed and ordering huge steaks from the butcher). She sat in the sun on the lawn, playing her hand-wound gramophone with Pongo beside her. She was now devoted to Pongo, and whenever he saw Dodie his welcome was hysterical. The corn was golden. She played 'Saturn', the Bringer of Old Age, from Holst's suite *The Planets*. 'I was conscious that I no longer felt really young and that — as for the married couple in *Touch Wood* — "the magic dies". I wasn't exactly unhappy; I had too much to be happy about. But I believe some tinge of melancholy was born then which has been with me ever since.'

By September, audiences for *Touch Wood* were dwindling. People were said to be shocked by its immorality. Aunt Blanche told Dodie, 'My dear, that girl ought not to have done that.' When the Haymarket Theatre owner Horace Watson died, the new management decided to take off *Touch Wood*, replacing it with a play that never did as well as *Touch Wood*'s worst week. Dodie was aggrieved, but was already at work on a new play — in a spacious, uncluttered new flat she had taken, in a mansion block called Rossmore Court, overlooking Regent's Park, with Alec in a separate one-room flatlet next door. With two new establishments to pay for and furnish as well as the cottage, she needed the money: she was still shopping extravagantly every day.

While she wrote, Pongo would be walked in Regent's Park by her maid. Maids were a problem. A gloomy Swede stayed a year. Another disappeared, and was found by police saying she could not face life with Dodie's white carpets. One was heard on the telephone ordering things from Selfridges, saying: 'The price is of no consequence whatever.' Another was Madeline Smith, who claimed to be related to the late Lord Birkenhead, Dodie's girlhood hero; she had a son in jail and 'undoubtedly stole a good deal of jewellery from me:' a gold wrist watch, an emerald eternity ring and a platinum ring all disappeared. Finally she found Eileen Potter, a former actress, intelligent, well-read and agreeable — a treasure who stayed for years; and also Jean Batters, an interesting young woman who made an excellent secretary, dogsbody and general factotum. She was the daughter of a coalmine-owner, and had played tennis and badminton for North Wales, but gave these up in her passion for theatre-going. She was an aspiring playwright (and Christian Scientist), happy to travel with Dodie and Alec to out-of-town openings of Dodie's plays.

Dodie's new play was finished at the gallop, and *Call It A Day* remains the frothiest of that run of early successes. Nothing she wrote, Dodie said, amused her as much. *Call It A Day* was the play she had started the previous year, in which all the action takes place, in accordance with Aristotelian convention, on one day, the first day of spring. It follows the members of a single family, the Hiltons, who are all in various states of temptation, proving the truth of the adage 'The first spring day is in the devil's pay'. Since Dodie had actually invented this saying herself, she was astonished to hear it quoted on the BBC years later as a famous old saw.

Disgruntled with Basil and their rows

over *Touch Wood*, she took *Call It A Day* to Hugh ('Binkie') Beaumont, managing director of H. M. Tennent, the legendary figure whose controlling power almost monopolised the British theatre from the 1930s until the 1960s. He loved the play and said he would be happy for Dodie to co-direct it — with Basil. First she had to extricate herself through a loophole in her contract with 'Bloody Basil'. She got so embroiled in the legal web that her solicitor Harold Rubinstein, a playwright himself, told her she could have shone in the law as she had in the theatre. Of course Dodie won the battle.

The play, set near Regent's Park in St John's Wood, has a curiously springlike, evergreen quality, which after an easily parodied, cosy start contains plenty of lines that caused prolonged laughter, such as Marie Löhr's 'Oh to be naked with a cheque-book!' on the pleasures of shopping in Harrods sales. And 'You can't shock a person whose favourite king is Charles the Second' was thought very witty. The younger daughter, Ann, is one of Dodie's precocious schoolgirls who quotes ecstatically from Rossetti and from Alice Meynell's desperately romantic sonnet 'Renouncement', a favourite of Dodie's youth. In fact Dodie privately coached Alexis France in the part of Ann. 'The only photograph in any of my plays is Ann in *Call It A Day*,' Dodie once told a reporter, 'who is myself in my girlhood.' Ann is clever, literary, arch. But it is her sister Catherine who flings herself at a famous artist while being painted by him at his studio (shades of Dodie and MacDermott) right under the nose of his complaisant wife.

The cast of sixteen was almost perfect, with Phyllis taking over the important cameo of Mrs Milsom, the gloomy charwoman who takes food home saying, 'It's not fit for human consumption — but it'll do for my husband.' Dodie had lifted that line from real life, from her Dorset Square daily.

But Dodie and Basil Dean once more found they could not work together without a battle. There were shouting scenes over the lighting, with Basil menacingly brandishing his umbrella:

'I will not be taught my business by you.' (Fay Compton dashed into Owen Nares's dressing room: 'Owen, come quick — there's going to be a fight.') The final breakup with Basil blighted the pleasure of her fourth success. Another Basil, Basil Dearden, later to become a film director, was stage manager: Dodie and Alec afterwards used the phrase 'doing a Basil Dearden' to mean displaying unreasonable caprice.

Call It A Day was a tremendous hit. It got ecstatic notices and ran for 500 performances at the Globe. When it arrived in New York, directed by Tyrone Guthrie and starring Gladys Cooper, Robert Benchley wrote in the *New Yorker*: 'Well, I'll tell you how I feel about *Call It A Day*. The night after the opening being Critics' Night Off, I went back to the Morosco and saw it again. The New York producers, however, became nervous about one scene, which had sailed past the British Lord Chamberlain unmolested. In this scene the Hiltons' neighbour, a charming young interior decorator named Alistair, tries gently to lead astray the Hiltons' son Martin, inviting him to see a new film at the Curzon ('the Curzon's a bit expensive, isn't it?') followed by a motoring weekend in the Cotswolds, and even offering him a partnership in his decorating business. 'I say, it's jolly queer when you come to think of it,' says Martin, 'that we do get on. We've hardly a thing in common.' Alistair was beautifully played by Bryan Coleman, with Owen Nares's real-life son Geoffrey playing the clean-limbed, cricket-playing Martin, who is actually keen on Joan, the girl next door. But Coleman — tall, blond, athletic — later told Dodie that the homosexual tag had seriously damaged his career for years. (When Warner Brothers made the film, having bought the rights for $50,000, they removed the homosexual scene altogether, and according to James Agate's review in the *Sunday Times* 'entirely destroyed the pattern of an admirable little play'.) Agate, incidentally, referring to another scene, in which the husband confesses to his wife that he has had a flirtation with an actress friend of hers, made a thoughtful comment on the play: 'Dodie

Smith always has one scene in her plays in which she appears to be writing very much better than she knows.'

The play achieved the longest run ever for a woman dramatist: fifteen months. The playwright Ian Hay wrote to invite her to join the all-male Dramatists' Club, to which 'certain distinguished lady dramatists' could be elected. Dodie was now forty and earning around £500 a week in royalties alone. But she had to pay Alec, the housekeeper Mrs Potter, her secretary Jean Batters, a full-time gardener at The Barretts, and a chauffeur. She and Alec would take friends to the Ivy, the Café Royal and the Caprice. She had begun to be a magnanimous and thoughtful present-giver, bestowing hampers, framed portraits, Christmas trees. She spent lavishly — on books by the score, after years of lending libraries; on jewellery (encouraged by Alec); and on dozens of designer dresses, including one from Molyneux, and one in red corded silk with a beaded jacket, which cost £70 and which she wore so often that Batters heard someone say, 'It's so nice and homey of Dodie Smith always to wear the same dress.' Her Blüthner piano in unpolished walnut was put in the new music room in the barn. In the secluded environment of the galleried guest bedroom above, she found the perfect space in which to write, stepping down the spiral staircase at interludes to play her piano.

'I had a beautiful flat and a beautiful cottage, and the legend of my success was ever increasing. I should have been very happy,' she says in *Look Back With Astonishment*. But after twenty years of Christian Science and never seeing a doctor, she began to get mysterious illnesses: hay fever, colds and sneezes, aches in the back, pains in the stomach. She had tonsillitis and trouble with her gums: 'Once I began to make money, small illnesses seemed to think I could afford them.' Pongo too became ill, and seemed likely to die, until Dodie engaged a Christian Science practitioner named Waddington who came along in a bowler hat and merely gazed on him. Pongo at once took a turn for the better and within weeks he was his old self.

Dodie's own cure was supposed to be

effected by a six-week Continental tour. She and Alec supplied themselves with a driver, whom they disliked intensely, and took their friend the director Murray Macdonald, who got on their nerves. They went to Brussels, Holland, down the Rhine to Vienna, Dubrovnik, Budapest — where Murray mercifully left them to return home — and then once more back to Medratz, to the *Autumn Crocus* inn. But by and large Dodie found it all 'hellish' and she never ventured onto the Continent of Europe again for the rest of her life. Pongo, they found on their return, had grown Falstaffian under Phyllis's care.

Alec had now ordered a Rolls-Royce, a custom-built pale grey Sedanca-de-Ville they had seen at the Motor Show, chosen because it had an electrically operated glass partition so that they could ride along in front with the top open while Pongo kept warm inside. The bodywork was by Freestone and Webb and it cost £2000. John Gielgud for one thought it absurd to drive such a car in rural Essex, but it was a splendid vehicle in which to arrive at first nights and Alec lavished every care on it: when eventually sold in 1960, it was still so immaculate he was able to advertise that it might have been kept in the dining room. They had a blessed summer, driving around the countryside exploring castles and great houses. With Gielgud one day Dodie and Alec went to look at an old house; Gielgud recalls wading through oceans of mud to find a kitchen full of unwashed crockery and old newspapers, and a sinister old bachelor who went off shooting as they arrived. Sometimes Gielgud brought his house party over from Foulslough; Dodie also found Tagley, a nearby cottage costing £200, for Gwen Ffrangcon-Davies, who had set up house with her friend Marda Vanne. Nadine March too bought a cottage at Sawbridgeworth. So the thespian fraternity had a summer as blue and golden as the pre-First World War summers of Dodie's childhood.

★ ★ ★

Binkie Beaumont had already lined up Diana Wynyard to play the faithless actor's wife in the unnamed (and unwritten) Corsican comedy, but Dodie never got further than Act II, and resolved never again to discuss a play before it was finished. Having turned out four consecutive hit plays, she was now regarded as infallible. A journalist who suggested to her that she seemed surprisingly modest received the reply: 'But I'm very conceited inside,' which was quoted in the *Observer*'s Sayings of the Week. A Fleet Street news agency commissioned her to write a series of six articles entitled 'These Six Tremendous Years' — 'You must have a wonderful insight into life and humanity generally, always to hit the right note which means success.' She discussed, with the composer Vivian Ellis — who later wrote *Bless The Bride* — a musical called *Wedding Day*. Ellis told her, 'You would be my ideal collaborator,' and came down to the cottage where, he recalled to me shortly after his ninetieth birthday, he took an instant dislike to Alec ('an early specimen of the species Toy Boy') and found the garden somewhat too Golders Green for his taste. But in

June 1937 Ellis was about to volunteer for the RNVR, and anyway Dodie was polishing off a fifth play, which involved many stormy tearings-up and rewrites and readings-aloud with Binkie, Batters, Phyllis and Alec. It was called *Bonnet Over the Windmill*, and would feature a windmill on stage in the last act. She enlisted Sir Ambrose Heal's help in establishing where the expression 'bonnet over the windmill' came from: he replied ('My dear Dodie Smith . . . ') that he had put a London University professor onto the query, who reported that the phrase '*jeter son bonnet par-dessus les moulins*', meaning to act recklessly and defiantly, to fly in the face of convention, was originally a lazy way of finishing off a story to children. Sir Ambrose was impressed with her outline of the play and for the first time he became a backer, investing £200. Dodie and Alec put £500 into this one too.

The play incorporated many Dodie fixtures. It was set on the roof (like the Three Arts Club roof) of a students' boarding house near Regent's Park, 'the nicest park in London', where the young tenants gather for picnics. The middle-aged landlady, Billie, makes her appearance in lacy underwear and is clearly Dodie, being 'a tiny woman' five feet tall, a former failed actress who now works in a shop and finds that 'selling dresses is easier than getting yourself parts you can't play from managers who don't want to give them to you'.

Dodie was to co-direct with Murray Macdonald, who discovered how hard it is to direct with the author breathing down one's neck and fussing over minute details of costume ('she must wear her best day dress; probably a red silk: it must convey originality without looking too expensive or too definitely arty; but must be striking in colour and style . . .') and with Alec hovering protectively. They decided to go for new talent for the juvenile leads. Anne Firth, who played Janet, supposedly a young RADA student with the unmistakable spark of genius — a difficult part to get right — was over-emotional, petulant and 'mysteriously unpleasing'. Among the young, only William Douglas-Home, whom Dodie had first seen at a RADA end of term prize-giving, was any good. He took the part of the amusing and debonair Brian, and made it twice as funny. But James Mason, who originally read so badly that Dodie suspected he could not read at all, did not 'come over' in the part of the dashing playwright Kit Carson.

Incidentally, it is worth noting here that Dodie's characterisation of Kit Carson, a playwright who has failed to get any of his plays produced for four years, is strangely prescient. Kit Carson is told, by the wise actor-manager's wife, that it may be that he cannot write successful plays any more because 'your life's all wrong. You're focusing on it [your work] too much. You're out of contact with life . . . It's emotional contact that's lacking.' She tells him the obvious solution is to fall in love. Kit says he has had enough of being in love to last him a lifetime, whereupon she challenges him: 'Have you? Do you really think that at thirty-two you've had enough emotion out of life to enable you to sit back in that windmill of yours and write masterpieces for the rest of your days?'

This is precisely the kind of diagnosis

that Dodie might have applied to herself and her playwriting life a few years later.

Typically, the plot once again involves the seduction of an older married man — Sir Rupert Morellian, a theatrical knight (played by Cecil Parker), by the young actress Janet. Sir Rupert advises Janet to have a few affairs. 'Would they be good for my art?' Janet asks. Sir Rupert: 'I've a feeling that if I said "yes" you'd fling yourself into the arms of the nearest man.' Janet replies: 'No wonder you're nervous. You're the nearest man.' A situation that was by now a Dodie staple.

Dodie's *Bonnet Over the Windmill* first night flowers and cards are carefully preserved and annotated ('Orchid Spray from Ivor Novello, Heather Horseshoe from Marie Löhr, Gladioli from Marie Tempest, Bouquet of Lilies from Ambrose Heal', etc.) and the telegrams from W. Macqueen-Pope, Noël Coward, Robert Morley et al. — 'May the windmill revolve endlessly'; 'Success Darling Bonnie Dodie' — testify to a general faith in her popularity. But the pre-London opening at the Grand Theatre, Leeds, seemed to Dodie 'unbearably long'. She got her usual cheers and made a speech, but left the theatre knowing the play would have to be drastically cut. Reviewers found it deft, full of life, full of real characters; but Charles Morgan, after a hot evening at the London first night in September 1937, took the trouble to write a long, considered review for *The Times*, in which he said that Turgenev would have dealt with the subject more profoundly. 'It fails, and it is something better than a paradox to say that the failure is worth more than all Miss Smith's past successes . . . She is in mid-stream; her serious work as an artist is on the farther bank.' Dodie realised he had understood her theme better than anyone, and though gratified to be reviewed so intelligently, she felt 'I had failed him'.

A. E. Wilson, the *Evening News* critic, pointed out that few writers could match Dodie's run of five successes in a row: 'Shaw, Maugham, Lonsdale, Coward and others have all had their failures from time to time, but Dodie Smith has never had a setback. She may now consider herself the most successful woman playwright in the history of the theatre.' In the second week, *Bonnet* began repaying its production costs, and Dodie and Alec went off to New York for a short holiday — Alec longed to see New York — leaving Pongo with Batters and an envelope addressed to Batters 'should Alec and I both fall off the *Queen Mary* or be bumped off by gangsters — Poor Pongo' bequeathing £100 for Pongo's maintenance.

Alec, like Dodie before him, found New York 'disappointing'. They drove to Boston and disliked that too, cut short their trip and arrived home in December — to find *Bonnet* coming off, after only three months. Dodie felt wretched about losing investors' money for the first time. But she was honest enough to see that the play might have been at fault. 'It began as a gay play of young people on a rooftop. Much of the second act was sophisticated and faulty shrieking comedy. And in the last act I was trying to deal with a psychological problem — the heroine's mixed motives in determinedly losing her virginity, trying to be honest about her own sexual needs — which made sense to no one but me. No one cared a damn what happened to Anne Firth. Binkie said it might have been different with Vivien Leigh.' In ruthless retrospective self-criticism Dodie decided she had written this play just to please herself. She had therefore played her audience false, and shocked the older ones, although she had letters from young people who identified with the heroine. She had learned, she told one correspondent, that 'nothing on the stage is really quite like life'. She would think out her next theme more carefully, keeping her audience strictly in mind.

Moreover, Alec (who kept the accounts) told her the next play absolutely had to make money, and dissuaded her from moving, as she wished, to a yet costlier flat. By April 1938 Dodie herself had received only £18 17s in royalties from *Bonnet*; Alec sent Sir Ambrose Heal a cheque for £6 11s 2d, hoping bleakly that there might be some more takings from repertory companies 'but these are not likely to amount to much.' Sir Ambrose wrote a frosty 'Dear Beesley' response, and a warmer one later acknowledging £90 'which I am thankful to have'. So he lost about half of his £200 investment.

Dodie was now plotting, with a cool deliberation, *Dear Octopus*, her most famous play, and the only one still performed nearly sixty years later. She had received a letter from the playwright Gordon Daviot (alias the historian and thriller writer Josephine Tey), whom she had invited to stay at The Barretts for Christmas. 'Will you kindly go into winter-quarters and write a play with no one in it under thirty,' wrote Miss Tey. 'This completely personal edict is because young love wearies my desiccated soul and because Dodie Smith has observation, talent and humour which is wasted on young love.' Dodie decided that most people liked family plays, in which youth and age mingled. What could be a better centrepiece than a family reunion for a Golden Wedding celebration at 'the Randolphs' country house in North Essex? Until rehearsals began it was still called *Golden Wedding*. It was 'bliss to write, and easy to finish'. While writing it, she and Alec went to see Gielgud (and Gwen) in *The Three Sisters*, and Gielgud told them, backstage, that he had 'such difficulty in finding plays for himself, apart from the classics . . . ' Dodie decided she must have Gielgud for her new play.

So she wrote the son Nicholas's 'Grand Toast' speech with Gielgud in mind, beginning, 'We are a very ordinary family. We own no crests, no heirlooms and our few ancestors are very badly painted . . . ' She wrote this speech in free verse with short stressed lines, then ran the lines together, which worked rather well, and in the speech found the central theme of her play: the durability of the family. This would always strike a chord with an audience. Everyone has a family of some sort, whether they like it or not. 'Oh, the family, the family — I'm never quite sure if I love it or loathe it,' says Nicholas. The family is 'that dear octopus from whose tentacles we never quite escape, nor, in our inmost hearts, ever quite wish to'. Yet, as he also says, 'There's something rather heartbreaking about family gatherings.' Everyone in the audience would respond to such lines.

All four generations of Randolphs, gathered under one roof, sprang to life: the septuagenarian parents, the eccentric daughter, the bovine married daughter, and the guilty one who had not been home for seven years while having an illicit affair ('me again,' said Dodie); the bachelor son, the lively great-aunt Belle who says, 'My hair has been so many shades I forget its original colour,' and the amusing children, including the one who says the rudest thing he knows: 'District Nurse'. There was a quarrel scene, a nostalgic tea in the old nursery, and an unexpected romance.

Dodie wanted her play to show 'the other side of the medal to J. B. Priestley's *Time and The Conways*. Brilliant as it was in many ways I believe the picture of family life in that play hurt a lot of people.' She had specifically set out 'to give a picture of a family who were, on the whole, pleasant'. Yet though Dodie felt pretty pleased with it, Alec, Phyllis and Batters found it 'depressing'! Alec 'could not follow the relationships'. Phyllis saw Dora Randolph as her own mother, with whom she had never got on.

(Curiously, Dodie always relied on the views of this same tiny circle of people, though they were hardly dependable, since they had all loved *Bonnet* at once.)

Binkie, however, assembled a glamorous and prestigious cast. He managed to seduce John Gielgud — as Gielgud put it to me — with a large salary, even though the role of Nicholas was hardly of his accustomed stature (Hamlet, Shylock, Richard II) and would lock him into one theatre for nine months. Dame Marie Tempest, though almost too glamorous even at seventy-four, was engaged to play Dora Randolph in a white wig. Binkie said Dodie could direct it herself, or pick anyone she liked. This was real power and control. Later she discovered that Gielgud had offered to direct himself 'but Binkie refused him, as John drives companies mad by constant changes of movement and mood' — but Dodie would have let him, had she known. Instead, she selected the actor-director Glen Byam Shaw, and he was a perfect gentleman: he let Dodie decide the moves.

'*Dear Octopus* is a play of lamplight, candlelight, firelight, sunset deepening into twilight . . . ' she wrote. Luckily the lighting man George Devine, later the founder of the English Stage Company at the Royal Court Theatre, respected these important subtleties. Dodie and Alec went off touring English cathedral towns with Pongo, elatedly feeling the play could not possibly fail. 'Yet I was intensely melancholy,' Dodie writes, 'without reason.' (Thirty years later, Dodie was asked if *Dear Octopus* was meant to have an 'end of an epoch' quality and she confessed she had known even then that it did; and their tour of provincial cities too proved to be a farewell jaunt around England.) Still, although there were no rancorous rows, there were tears from Valerie Taylor as Cynthia the renegade daughter, and Marie Tempest behaved like an autocratic dowager who seemed to have no inkling of the rudiments of the plot. She could not memorise and was hopeless at doing business. Her techniques had always been taught her, as if to a child, by her late husband Willie. Without him she could not do the simplest things — so folding napkins into water-lilies while talking, as she was required to do, was quite beyond her. (No normal actor, sniffed Dodie, would have found it a problem.) And Dame Marie hated having a woman author who watched. She said there was one scene she would never be able to play if Dodie was there: Dodie offered to duck down on all fours while she played it. But John Gielgud assured Dodie that Marie, by acute concentration on herself, would always come out all right. And she did. 'But although in the end she was superb, Marie never knew what the play was about: she told one journalist that *she* was the Octopus.'

As the play toured the provinces, Dodie hardly realised that war in Europe looked ever more threatening, and 'staggering as it may seem' she barely noticed the menace of Hitler who had by now annexed Austria and was targeting Prague. Even after her 1936 tour of Europe, Adolf Hitler was little more than a name to her. She knew Alec had been a pacifist since his schooldays at Dulwich, so they had discussed what he would do if war came: they would leave the country. There were, in fact, several alternatives for conscientious objectors who wanted to avoid jail, Dodie found out much later, such as farming; but since they did not really expect the crisis to come, they never investigated this. 'I am told there will be no danger of war until November 7th,' wrote Josephine Tey briskly in a letter. 'Hitler may not have heard of the date, of course . . .'

John van Druten, the playwright she had met in New York, came to the first night of *Dear Octopus* in Newcastle and pronounced it her best play. Aunt Nan came to the Manchester run, and brought flowers, signing her card 'from the last leg of the old Octopus'. But the real first night at the Queen's Theatre on 14 September 1938, began gloomily. The crisis in Czechoslovakia was on everyone's mind. During the first half, the house was subdued, faces grave and laughs few. It seemed to have become dull. Then, in the first interval, a dramatic *deus ex machina*, Charles Morgan, arrived from *The Times* with the news, which spread like wildfire through the theatre, that Neville Chamberlain was flying to meet Hitler at Berchtesgaden. 'It was as if the whole audience heaved a sigh of relief. And from then on the play went superbly, and built to a magnificent reception.'

At the curtain, there was no question of Dodie making a speech this time. Marie Tempest was used to making first night speeches, and had been forbidden to, so Dodie was not going to infuriate her by speaking herself. It was decided that Dodie should walk on stage, stand between Tempest and Gielgud and simply bow, which she did, gratified to hear the applause rise and the calls for 'Author!' increase. She then held out her hand to Marie — but Marie refused it, and drew her chiffon skirt away with a flourish. So she held out her hand to Gielgud — who refused to take her hand also. Later Gielgud explained to Dodie that if he had accepted her hand he would have shown up Marie's rudeness, which everyone was talking about afterwards. (That is Dodie's version of the story.) So Dodie stood bowing alone, and waved to the gallery as usual. Later, she heard that Noël Coward had gone to Marie Tempest's dressing room and asked why she had behaved so rudely, to be told by Marie that she had had 'seven weeks of hell'.

There was a party at Binkie's Hyde Park flat afterwards. Marie Tempest waylaid Alec: 'Ask Dodie to come and see me.' Alec advised Dodie to do no such thing, but Dodie said if Neville Chamberlain could speak to Hitler, she could go to Dame Marie. Dame Marie did not mention the curtain call, merely asking if her performance had pleased the author. The author assured her it had. (It was in fact Dame Marie's final starring role in the West End; after that, her memory went completely.) And the play was a certain hit. James Agate in the *Sunday Times* said four of the characters had been worthy of Chekhov. The houses were full; the fan letters came pouring in — from Ivor Novello, Emlyn Williams, and Mollie Keane (the writer M. J. Farrell), who said how much she envied Dodie for having written *Dear Octopus*.

The shadow of approaching war, however, remained. There might still be conscription, and Dodie and Alec felt they should leave England, just in case. As it happened, the impresario John C. (Jack) Wilson, who was Coward's boyfriend, provided them with a legitimate reason by deciding to open *Dear Octopus* in New York, and saying he needed Dodie's help in casting. So they could leave 'without appearing to run away from war.' But Dodie knew that running away it was; and she hated it.

They secured visas and passages without difficulty, because of having to be in New York to cast the play. (Other people who were frankly trying to get away were refused visas.) Rhodes the chauffeur would drive them to Liverpool, and Bertha Martin, their country housekeeper, would look after Pongo. The underlying plan was that if war broke out while they were away, Pongo could be shipped out to join them. While Alec organised it all, Dodie knelt in her navy blue dress on the white-carpeted floor of her Rossmore Court bedroom, packing her vellum steamer trunk. She loathed going, she loathed packing, and she very nearly loathed Alec for deciding to go. Who really had the upper hand, in making this decision? Alec would never have insisted, if Dodie had asked him to stay. But she told him he must decide.

Traffic poured past the window of Rossmore Court, laden with people leaving London for the country. The ARP services were being mobilised, enlisting hordes of volunteers; in a hectic rush, cellars and basements were requisitioned as air raid shelters; and trenches were dug in parks. When a girl arrived at Dodie's flat to deliver gas masks, Dodie told her they would not need them as they were going away, but she implored Dodie to take them: 'So many people seem to blame me for bringing them.'

The Munich agreement was signed on 30 September, two weeks and a day after the opening of *Dear Octopus*. Chamberlain's 'peace for our time', announced to a cheering crowd in Downing Street, came late one afternoon. The relief, Dodie said, was unspeakable.

However, she hated the actual crossing as much as ever. She was still racked by 'vanity and a writer's curiosity', wanting to be there in London, to see whatever happened next: a reaction markedly different from her youthful apathy about the 1914–18 war. She brightened once they had arrived (via Toronto and Quebec) at the Pierre Hotel in New York to find herself in the thick of casting, which she soon realised meant simply accepting 'the least worst' cast. Once that was finished, they sailed home again on the *Île de France*, arriving just in time to hear that King George and Queen Elizabeth[1] would be at *Dear Octopus* that night, and managing to get to London in time to sit on the dress circle steps and gaze at the royal box. The following week Queen Mary came too.

During these last months in England, as if to persuade herself that she was going to stay at home after all, Dodie took steps to buy the house she had always dreamed of: a handsome Nash corner house on the Outer Circle of Regent's

---

[1] Fifty years later Queen Elizabeth, by then the Queen Mother, saw *Dear Octopus* in a 1988 revival at Windsor, and wrote to tell Dodie how much she had again enjoyed it.

Park, no. 1 St Andrew's Place: bay-windowed, cream stuccoed, charming. She kept for ever the Folkard & Hayward brochure which described the house as 'thoroughly modernised and decorated in a chaste manner'. They went back again and again to view it. The Crown lease was for twenty-five years at a reasonable rent. An art dealer promised to lend Dodie modern paintings for the walls. But they did not buy the house. It is still there today, as handsome as ever, its stucco and its black iron railings pristine; but it now stands opposite the Royal College of Physicians, a concrete 1964 building by Denys Lasdun hugely admired by architectural cognoscenti, which Dodie certainly would have detested. Regent's Park continued to feature in her plays and novels; she never lost her hankering for it and she felt her fortunes were somehow bound up with its Nash terraces, and trees, and gardens sloping down to the canal. Whenever she met anyone who lived in the area, she would tell them, 'If you see a girl with bobbed hair and a straight fringe, wearing a bright green dress and a circular black cloak, that will be myself when young, going to wish on the wishing mound.'

As the phoney peace continued, Dodie would lie awake in Rossmore Court imagining how undignified a last-minute dash from London might be. They no longer had the excuse of casting in New York to take them away. Men were flocking to join the Territorial Army. She came to a sudden decision, then, that they should go to America for a year 'just to see America'. She practised saying, with little conviction, that they wanted to travel while there was still a world to travel in. She even tried to sell herself this excuse. As a writer she was insular, she told herself: Phyllis said she ought to see more of the world (Phyllis herself had recently been down a coal-mine, she boasted) and Dodie pretended, publicly at least, to want to broaden her experience. Alec agreed: anyway he was convinced Chamberlain had done the right thing, that there would be no war, and he genuinely wanted to travel.

'My reasons for this,' Dodie wrote thirty-five years later in her journal, going over again the decisions and indecisions, and visions and revisions, of that time, 'I saw clearly then as I see them now. Alec had been a pacifist ever since his schooldays at Dulwich in World War I, when he refused even to bang a drum in the corps.' Dulwich had turned him into a conscientious objector, Alec said, with its hypocritical exhortations (a) to be kind to all living creatures and (b) to stick bayonets into young soldiers' stomachs. The roll of honour of pupils killed in the Great War particularly sickened him: 'boys from my dorm, dead in the mud in France'. Meanwhile Dodie's own pacifism was melting away, 'not from any patriotic motive — I still believed one should even be killed rather than kill in self-defence — but because I dreaded being sneered at by theatrical London, and because I longed to be in on the war, as a writer and a lover of excitement. It would be good copy.' But that would be a ratting on Alec and all he believed in. 'I had taken so much from him, I had let him give up his own job — not that he hadn't wanted to — and he was now faced with a decision which mattered enormously to him, and might mean the difference between life and death. I simply could not let myself decide for him.

'One evening he went, alone, to a peace meeting and came back and sat on my bedroom floor; I was in bed. I can see him now, leaning against one of my cupboards which had a white lamp with a pleated shade on top, from which the light shone down on him. He wondered if he should not stay and face the future with fellow conscientious objectors. It seemed to *me* obvious that he ought, but I could not tell him so. Then he said he would not be thinking only of himself: he wanted to get me out of the war. It dawned on me that we must go, if he wanted to. If we stayed I might very easily let him down. I did not realise what good company he would be in. I saw ourselves as being completely ostracised' ('The rats are leaving the sinking ship!' Marie Tempest had reportedly said, and Madge Compton told them the whole theatre world was gossiping about their departure) 'and I knew I should mind that. I doubt if anyone can have as much success as I had had without getting an ego which minds public opinion. Alec has never cared what people think of him. I always have.'

But Alec also said that if they were going to travel together, they should get married. Before that, Dodie could not recall his mentioning this possibility: he had seemed quite happy as things were, and did not give a damn what people thought. (Dodie's remaining Manchester family still speculated as to whether she and Alec, with their neighbouring flats, were actually 'living together'. The fact is, they were living as closely together as they always would, not sharing a bed but bound together as a couple. Whether or not they still made love is impossible to say: Dodie never again mentions the subject.)

At Christmas in 1938 they gave a small party at the cottage — including John Gielgud and his Foulslough houseparty, with Binkie and John Perry; Gwen and Marda from Tagley Cottage; Phyllis and Nadine March and Joyce Kennedy. Picturesquely and memorably, it snowed. Dodie pencilled the view onto a canvas, and thought to herself, 'I shall not be here to paint this.'

The complications of this departure were overwhelming. They could give up their rented flats, but could not keep The Barretts as their residence, or rent it out, without becoming liable for both British and US income tax. As the letters about their visas testify, Dodie's financial standing at this time was that her earnings, never less than £2000 a year since 1931, had risen to £12,000. On New Year's Eve, by the firelight of the old range in the cottage kitchen, with Pongo asleep in his basket, they decided not to sell The Barretts but to offer it to Binkie to live in rent-free, as long as he paid the domestic staff. (And, Dodie sourly noted, over the years he came to resent what the cottage cost him, even though she could have been earning a decent rent from it.)

Dodie kept up the bright pretence of having 'a suddenly reawakened desire to see the world' — 'I, the woman who was homesick after a week on the Continent, and who never returned to England without the most intense and grateful thankfulness.' Those who suspected that Dodie and Alec were making their escape, at least pretended to accept the 'travel' excuse, and the explanation that they had to be away six months at least or it would not be worthwhile putting Pongo through quarantine on their return.

In a wild rush, Dodie again packed all her clothes, in a fantastic number of leather trunks and boxes, and gave up her beloved new Heal's furniture to the landlord (the aviator Claude Grahame White) along with the lease of the two flats. But Jean Batters's letters, after Dodie's departure, reflect how much was left undone. 'A demand for Sur-tax has arrived this morning for the rather unpleasant sum of £1402 10s 6d . . . ' 'You have a dividend of £18 2s 6d from Woolworths.' ' I have found your stage makeup box with some rather sweet souvenirs in it including a letter from the Everyman engaging you as a walk-on at a salary of 3s 6d a night!' (Batters could not have realised the sentimental significance of this keepsake.) Batters dealt with a stack of leftover bills, invitations — including one from Marie Stopes — and dozens of begging letters: from the lady in the chocolate shop 'fallen on adversity', from the Dumb Friends' League and other animal charities now accustomed to Dodie's cheques, and even one from her stepfather Gerald.

She wrote farewell letters, one of them to C. E. Vulliamy, her old friend from Heal's days who now wrote biographies. He confessed he had never been to her plays, or to any theatre since they had gone together to *St Joan* in 1924. 'I dislike intensely all masses of people — crowds, mobs, audiences or congregations — & I love more and more the sea and the hills and large uninhabited open spaces; and books. Most people are just appalling, aren't they?'

About Dodie's imminent departure, her old friend was extremely perceptive. 'You must be a crazy little fellow to go running about all over the American continent without an adequate reason. I believe you are afraid of warfare in Europe. Or have you always had a desire to travel? It must be delightful to have lots of money — and those who pretend they can do without it are humbugs. Yours infinitely . . . C. E. Vulliamy.'

A few days before leaving, Dodie went to say goodbye to Ambrose Heal. She had never called him Ambrose; in fact she had never, to his face, called him anything. She remembered the many times she had visited him in this same office, particularly the time she had stood by his desk in 1927 and told him she loved him. Now she had to tell him that she and Alec would be married in America. Absurd though it seems, one reason why she had not considered marriage before was that she thought it would distress AH. She explained that she and Alec could hardly travel all over America unless they married. He said, 'I should have thought you could.' Apparently, she noted, AH still believed that there was nothing between her and Alec, except a working partnership. It was a sad and embarrassing interview, but Dodie told herself she was so damned miserable anyway it hardly mattered. Perhaps Sir Ambrose was genuinely distressed at this leave-taking. Very shortly afterwards he made Mrs Maufe a director of Heal's.

There was a last conciliatory supper with Marie Tempest. She told Dodie about her late third husband, Willie Graham Browne. Apparently he had never, in all their years together, before or after marriage, entered her bedroom without knocking — which Dodie thought 'a jolly good idea'. She and Alec drove home on a foggy night, the fog horribly apt for Dodie's confused feelings. She looked longingly at no. 1 St Andrew's Place, a house that was to become the home of Mr and Mrs Dearly in *The Hundred and One Dalmatians*, which was as far as she would go in exorcising the desire to live there.

The farewell to The Barretts was made in the gathering dusk of a January afternoon. The memories of both farewells remained painful. Part of her mind always rebelled at the decision which filled the rest of her life with wistful what-ifs and if-onlys. 'Perhaps I am like Lilian, in my new novel [*The Town in Bloom*],' she wrote in 1965, 'trying to repossess her whole life and somehow change it; yet if I could be back in 1939, no doubt I should still force myself to do the same thing — even though I have never been quite sure it *was* the right thing.' Phyllis Morris and Jean Batters came to see them off at Southampton. They had been told of Dodie's marriage plans, and 'neither approved', Dodie says without explanation. (Phyllis, having encouraged Dodie to widen her experience, did not really want her to go off around the world.) Mrs Potter, the housekeeper accompanying them, became emotional and had to be given brandy — and she *wanted* to go, remarked Dodie. They watched as Pongo sprang lightly ahead of them up the gangplank in his Dalmatian way, pulling at the leash. 'It was the casting of the die. We followed him. And exile began.'

8

'Will We Ever Get Out of Limbo?'

'I HAVE burnt my boats; I have brought my dog Pongo out of England.' So began the 1939 diary in which Dodie began to 'sell herself happiness', writing with her gold Yard-o-led pencil, on the thick pages of a ledger bound in coral leather that Alec had given her, and which today has aged to a deep bronze. Originally she had intended to type up the entries and send them home to friends as a travel bulletin: 'hence the self-consciousness of the early entries, and the ghastly bright insincerity of the tone.' But she soon found she was writing entirely for herself. This journal ran on for 4,330 pages, taking her through the fifteen years of exile. When she eventually embarked on her autobiography in 1965, she reckoned that together with the journal she kept after the return to England, she had written two million words, including a 189–page resumé of the years up to 1939: 'And I have left out dozens of memories . . . and what the point of the whole thing is I simply don't know.'

Unfortunately, she had just read Arnold Bennett's journals and had decided that 'intimate and secret experiences are intensely boring to others; it is *facts* that make the journals of Arnold Bennett such fascinating reading. So let us have facts and no bits of embarrassing self-analysis, except to mention that I am highly self-conscious when writing anything that isn't a play.' As a result the first six months is chiefly a travelogue of bright pretence, with no real recognition of her own misery.

She began, for no discernible reason except an awareness that she was beginning a new phase, with a factual summary of her life so far: 'A happy childhood with enormous family of grownups — grandparents, mother, uncles, aunts; seven unsuccessful years as one of the world's most sacked actresses; eight years as a reasonably successful businesswoman; and eight years as a very successful playwright — six plays in eight years and five of them successes. The last one is running triumphantly in London and, rather less triumphantly, in New York. What a fortunate woman I sound! And yet, I think I never felt nearer flatness or boredom than this winter. I saw, if I continued fortunate, a long string of years spent between Tudor cottage and new flat, the Ivy and first nights. And if I proceeded to write flops, the same life, gradually dwindling, never quite sure of the moment for retrenchment — till one awakens, minus one's savings, without sufficient means to keep one in a bedsitting room. Not that I didn't like bedsitting rooms — they are the nicest rooms in the world.'

Does this mental stocktaking ring true? Not really, although the line about waking in a bedsitter minus one's savings is one she gave to Kit Carson, the fading playwright in *Bonnet Over the Windmill*, so the threat of possible failure and penury had been on her mind for some years. She alleges that she felt she was becoming complacent and middle-aged, and again pretends to believe she ought to see more of the world. There is much mendacious self-justification here for what she at once knew in her heart was a bad move.

She explains (for the mythical new reader) that she is accompanied by Alec 'my manager and greatest friend' and by Mrs Potter, who, sociable and gregarious, was soon involved with a pleasant-looking male fellow passenger. It was Dodie's fifth Atlantic crossing, 'so rough that the *Queen Mary* appeared to stand on its head'. She read Beverley Nichols's novel *Revue*, which John Gielgud had given her the night before she sailed: 'full of cleverness and vitality — but extraordinarily unworthwhile'. Alec did jigsaw puzzles in the next door cabin.

These 95 pages form a remarkably longwinded and self-righteous diary of an unhappy woman. 'I am even a little nervous of writing this journal in case it revives a certain egoism which nearly all young writers possess and which I have trampled on ruthlessly, ever since I became a professional playwright.' (Refusing to confide in her private journal about her inner feelings, she could shield herself from unpalatable truths.) She thinks she is a 'tolerably good' playwright now and intends to become a better one — not by improving dialogue, humour or character, which she knew very well were all fine — but 'a great play needs a great theme, and they don't come my way'.

The journal is full of detail about odd American ways with food like serving chicken with marrons glacés and orange. 'But Alec and I are going to fine each other sixpence every time we criticise American customs ... Agate's diary contains too much about food and Arnold Bennett's too much about illness, and this entry' (she had been seasick) 'offends on both scores.'

But at least Pongo enjoyed the voyage. In the dog-house on the top deck he howled heartbreakingly at first, but the kennel man assured them he would get to like it, which he did, barking at any woman wearing a pixie scarf. (He was always acutely conscious of headgear. At the Caprice, the man behind the cold meat buffet had to take off his chef's hat when Pongo came in.) He began to look slightly wild and to gaze with bright eyes on a lady spaniel. Dodie took to climbing inside the kennel with him, and got a dog's eye view of the deck, all legs.

So they arrived in New York with their Rolls-Royce, and found that they had to pay duty on Pongo ('they seem to think him a rare dog of enormous value'). Also that poor Mrs Potter had been put, Cinderella-like, in the service wing of the Pierre Hotel along with 'cabaret people'. But Mrs Potter was a brick. In the interminable rain, she would put on her mac and find lunch for 50 cents at the Automat. Dodie was harder to please. She claimed to be trying to like this city, a haven of freedom for all races, but she could not. She liked skyscrapers and shop-windows, but found the slums, festooned with fire-escapes, hideous and frightening, with none of what she saw as the redeeming picturesqueness of London's. She bought cutlery and crockery in Macy's and could not find a satisfactory teapot. 'At Heal's, every teapot was tested carefully. That is a *rotten* teapot. And I wonder what they would think of beds here? They are wildly comfortable, but Sir Ambrose would disapprove of them strongly because they are not really firm — one bounces off them when one rolls over.

'And there are a few other little matters. The sewage system, the telephone . . . And the restaurant menus are too sumptuously detailed and lyrical: surely "fresh killed baby lamb" and "boiled alive baby lobster" is self-defeating salesmanship? At one New York restaurant they brought the live lobster to the table, as if to give one a chance of making a pet of it first.'

They went at once to see *Dear Octopus*, and were furiously disappointed. ('One must see Lucille Watson as Dora to see exactly how good Marie Tempest is.') On a second visit Dodie found it frankly 'agonising'. 'Scarcely one line of humour is put over as it should be. Lucille Watson is uncharming and ungraceful; acts like a piece of wood, throws away the sentiments and can't time a laugh. Lillian Gish is more comic. The part of Cynthia seems to dwindle without Valerie's strength of personality. Jack Hawkins as Nicholas misses no points — but he is not John Gielgud.' Others were dreary, shadowy, awful, shocking, 'killing laugh after laugh'.

Jack Hawkins and Jessica Tandy, who had met in *Autumn Crocus* and married but were soon to break up, came to luncheon. So did Gladys Cooper. They dined with other playwrights: Gerald Savory, fresh from his success with *George and Margaret*, and various Americans whom Dodie envied for their energy: 'they can dash about the country, toss off films, produce each other's plays and write their own.' Arthur Kober, author of the play *Having Wonderful Time*, asked them, why doesn't Britain fight? Dodie replied, would Kober be prepared to stick a bayonet in a young German? 'He seemed a little shaken. So few people seem to ask themselves that.' She found much anti-British feeling, and the assumption that the British were effete, complacent, decadent, lazy — 'and our plays reflect it. We are fiddling while America burns, with patriotism and an intense desire to go to war.' Some American critics had disapproved of *Octopus* because it ignored the political crisis. Yet Dodie's original play had mentioned the possibility of war, but those lines had been removed 'because they brought the troubled world into a happy evening. I am as convinced as ever that the theatre's job is to entertain, not to instruct.'

She and Alec went to the theatre every night: *Outward Bound*, with Vincent Price, 'made me instantly long to write an equally original play; but I would more likely write a pale imitation of it'. They saw *Miss Swan Expects*, set in a publisher's office; she had wanted to set a play in a publishing office for years (and eventually she did). They approved of George Abbott's *The Boys From Syracuse* with score and lyrics by Rodgers and Hart; they liked Noël Coward's *Set To Music* with Bea Lillie; but *The American Way* by George Kaufman and Moss Hart was the worst play Dodie had ever seen, yet taking $40,000 a week.

And as soon as the sun came out, she stepped out to Bonwit Teller, Lord & Taylor, Bergdorf Goodman, Saks, 'full of gay fresh springlike dresses, Valentine windows with blue hats, pink

255

birds, jewellery and flowers': 'femininity at its most enchanting; heartshaped boxes with cellophane and sprinkles of sugar hearts among parti-coloured clothes. How pleased St Valentine would be.' 'A note on New York hats. There are hats with wimples, hats with fishnets, hats like plates, witches' hats, tartan hats, bonnets, flowers, feathers, net, tulle, hats where a reel of cotton is bigger than the crown. The favourite shape is like a little bird's nest tied on with a veil.'

Dodie began to bore even herself with such touristic, suburban observations. Batters was sending review cuttings about the latest West End plays like *Design For Living*, and adding her own pungent comments: in *The Importance of Being Earnest*, she said, Gwen Ffrangcon-Davies, had been 'ludicrous': 'She played Gwendolen, and was therefore Edith's daughter. As they are about the same age and look it, the whole thing is absurd. The imagination can go so far and then it refuses.' Dodie was achingly homesick for those first nights. In New York half the people did not wear evening dress to first nights, she noted scathingly, and anyway

Dodie and Alec knew nobody in the crowd. Playgoers' reactions were babyish: they would gasp like anxious children when two sympathetic murderers (in *The Gentle People*) almost gave themselves away to the police. New York audiences were docile, biddable, sheep-like, infantile theatre snobs who would only go to what they were told to like.

She was sure her play would soon fade into oblivion, taking Jack Wilson's money and £200 of hers. It had cost her nearly $500 to come over and help with casting; she had forgone all royalties since Boston, when she had $200 in advance. The pre-Broadway reviews had called it 'a family comedy about decent folk ... a play that encourages one to like one's fellow men, from England's most sugarbowl playwright', but Walter Winchell spotted that it was 'old lavender, a little too old, and the lavender a little too faded', too British in scene and tempo to stir America. And Lee Ephraim of Warner Bros told her *Octopus* was 'too middle-aged in sympathy for the films'. But Glen Byam Shaw, who directed the American production, wrote consolingly: 'It is a true picture of English life as I myself have lived it and if it is not "understood" in this country then it does not reduce the merit of what you have done by one iota.

'Anyway, my dear Dodie, you must go on and write. You have a very beautiful talent: there aren't many people who can bring happiness onto the stage nowadays and that is a very wonderful thing to do. Don't let America do anything to you. Simplicity is worth all the tricks and slickness ever invented . . . I firmly believe that you will write a great play and I think you are right to get away from ordinary London life, if you feel tired of it. Great energy is needed to write creatively and no one can gather energy by sitting still.'

Yet all she wrote was an introduction to a volume of her plays which Heinemann was bringing out. She would spend whole days at her desk in the hotel just writing letters home. Alec typed up the business ones, meticulously and laboriously. If only she could think up a play unaffected by topical events. She wrote a protracted dialectic on this subject, about how

Chinese theatre re-tells 1000-year-old stories, while Broadway seemed to insist on drama reflecting the heat of current social problems, imagining that this could change old habits of thought. 'If war came to America's own doorstep I think even the earnest New York audiences would turn and send the managements who rub their noses in it to *Hellzapoppin*.' She herself might be 'only a lightweight playwright'; but 'a great number of people have found escape, if not liberation, from watching my plays, and laughter is a pleasant noise for an author to hear.'

Charles Morgan reported in *The New York Times* that there had been a slump in the London theatre. Even *Dear Octopus* had slumped, but revived, and was now taking £2000 a week again. Dodie, however, was cast into gloom; one night she depressed Alec for two solid hours. She forecast years of exile, a world war in progress, losing her audience-sense by being away from England, and possibly also losing all her capital. On three out of four counts her forecast was absolutely correct.

In this rather low-key mood, she and

Alec went shopping in Fifth Avenue one day at the end of February and bought a wedding ring. As they wandered home, Dodie — aged nearly forty-three — thought of her past romances and unhappinesses and her conviction that she would never marry, and was greatly relieved that the buying of a ring had not, after all, been fraught with 'excitements, doubts and slight hysteria'. That evening they went to Lillian Hellman's *The Little Foxes*, and found it 'offensively melodramatic and the characters overdrawn'. Alec wrote to advise Binkie that he shouldn't risk his money on it.

The following week, on Tuesday morning, they got a train to Philadelphia and were quickly and unobtrusively married in a judge's private office. A lawyer named Maurice Speiser arranged everything. While they waited for the licence in an ante-room Dodie read a notice that no book was to be taken from the bookshelf without permission. On the walls was mounted a collection of guns which had each been used in a murder. After the ceremony they went back to Mr Speiser's and had some champagne, then caught the three o'clock train and were back in New York in time for tea.

They had chosen not to marry in New York to avoid a Wassermann blood test and 'to avoid publicity', but they need hardly have bothered: they merited a few inches in the New York papers. 'We have told no one in New York except Pongo, which is like telling the bees.' They went to the theatre that night. 'When I was a girl I used to say that if I ever married I should like to do it so unobtrusively that I scarcely noticed it happen, and I have certainly managed that. At first, Alec and I found it rather a good secret joke, but that will wear off and I hope it leaves us exactly as it found us. It should, for it is after our very happy years together a distinction but not a difference.' She was gratified when newspapers telephoned from London about her marriage ('I can't help feeling a little flattered') but dismayed when she received the clippings: 'She gave romance to thousands, now she finds it herself,' read one absurd headline; and they had dug out a first night photo in which 'Alec looks like a drug fiend helping himself to a shot of cocaine; I look every inch a shopgirl' (with corrugated hairstyle and two huge kiss-curls on her forehead).

Sir Ambrose wrote to say he had heard the news a week ago, but had been busy opening a Danish shop 'with the Crown Prince of Denmark: a perfect iceberg and about the same size.' He said he had confidence in the sound sense of both of them, and was sure they had done the right thing. He liked the fact that Dodie said of her wedding, 'We scarcely noticed it ourselves.' 'Tell Beazley,' he added — he always referred to Alec in this superior, mis-spelled way — 'I always felt he was cast for a big part and have no doubt that he is set for a long run to good houses.' But he also added meaningfully, 'I have my Madonna of the Candle on my desk here to remind me . . . '

Then she heard that her play was to come off after 53 performances at the Morosco. The cast had offered to carry on playing for $50 a week: 'But when plays fail they fail, and I think it unprofessional to alibi on whether Lent or even natural catastrophes caused the failure. What it boils down to is the fact that the critics didn't like the play and the public here are sheep. Those sheep who strayed through the hedge by accident enjoyed themselves, but didn't baa loudly enough to their friends.'

They went to the docks for the arrival of the *Paris* and met Margaret Rawlings, who was to appear in Charles Morgan's *The Flashing Stream*. If only Dodie could jump on board, she thought, and return to England, and see the daffodils. She tried to rough out a play set in a castle in the English countryside, but seemed to have no time or peace. She would be interrupted by the waiter, the chambermaid, Mrs Potter, the telephone, Pongo wanting a game — but she knew these were mere excuses. 'I fondly imagine I shall find peace on our trip south, or in the south of France, or back in England: but I know that one does not find peace, one makes it . . .' As Jean Batters said in a letter, America was Dodie's hair shirt: 'There is no need for you to wear it.' Which she already knew.

Then they set off in the Rolls-Royce with Pongo for California via the Deep South to see the real America. They travelled to places with magical names: Monticello, Virginia; Charleston, South Carolina; Baton Rouge, Louisiana . . . A painter might be inspired, but what could a playwright do with the cypress gardens of Charleston or the magnolia gardens of Georgia which John Galsworthy thought the most beautiful in the world? She thought of General Sherman marching along, burning his country's priceless heirlooms, and was repeatedly enraged by neon signs. 'It is utterly humiliating to realise that the taste of the world is getting worse. What would the men who planned this beautiful town say if they could see what modern commercialism had done to it?' In the land of rocking-chairs on verandahs, Pongo barked at 'darkies' who were terrified of him in turn. In one hotel there were large flying beetles outside: Dodie asked the porter if they ever came inside and he replied: 'Well, Ah guess they do sometimes, but we hurry them out.'

She was anxious and homesick, guilty to be holidaying in the sun while England was under mortal threat, evacuating its children, billeting soldiers, issuing ration books. She felt she made Alec's life a misery ('he bears it like an angel'). How could she plan new plays when she had no idea what sort of plays the British audience would now want? 'I have no axes to grind, I just want to offer people refreshment and recreation and yet it does seem somehow wrong to be dreaming of delicate charming plots with the world in such a state . . .'

On through Alabama and Louisiana and Texas they went, like a travelling circus. Wherever they stopped, a crowd collected to ask about the Rolls and the dog, and once they were chased along the highway and plied with questions. Did Pongo bite? How much did he weigh? The car was enormously admired: 'Gee, look! Oh boy what a car! See, a Rolls-Royce!'

Somewhere in Texas, she reflected, there must be her cousins, children of her Uncle Tyrrel Moore; she remembered his Southern accent and large hat. In New Mexico they searched in vain to find somewhere beautiful to walk Pongo: 'for a moment of beauty we get hours of ugliness'. The aridity of California immediately dismayed her: was there no soft grass, no shady trees, no mountain meadows or streams? And no escape anywhere from cars tearing past, and gas stations? It was 'wretched walking country for dog and man, except in National Parks which have designated picnic places.'

Binkie wrote that all he wanted from Dodie was a cable: 'Play finished ready for autumn production'. He was in a panic about re-casting *Octopus* in London, having to replace John Gielgud. But as soon as she arrived in Hollywood, Dodie was snapped up by movie studios, despite the fact that films had barely figured in her life until now: she was a theatre-goer, not a cinema-goer. MGM wanted her to work on the screenplay of Noël Coward's *Tonight at 8.30*. Warner Bros took her to lunch at the Brown Derby; Universal wanted her; so did Fox and United Artists. She had sworn she would never work in Hollywood. But, she reasoned, wasn't the European situation so menacing that she could justifiably keep herself occupied and get a handsome salary too? On the other hand, a contract with a film studio might be a sword of Damocles; would one's imagination feel clipped and thwarted? Supposing all creativity dried up? Surely dialogue hashed and re-hashed would become stale and dull?

She took advice from Charles Brackett, a 'Mayflower American' ex-novelist and former *New Yorker* drama critic who, after much success writing with Billy Wilder, had become a producer. He told her Hollywood was 'a beachcombing life', but assured her she could get $3000 a week without difficulty on her reputation. (In fact it was always up to 'the boys in the front office' who after haggling would offer $1000 to talk, $2000 to jot down ideas . . . and so on.) She met Hitchcock who had arrived to do *Rebecca*, and went to see Sam Goldwyn's *Wuthering Heights*: dreary beyond words, she thought, lacking any Brontë atmosphere. 'The Lintons' manor looked like a luxury hotel, with white paint and net curtains, and the party dresses dripped satin and lace and obvious modern lamé . . . Merle Oberon's fur trimmed hood made her look like Nanook of the North. Flora Robson was wasted and miscast. If this is a masterpiece I have little further interest in films, either as writer or audience.'

Hollywood was an insidious place: 'One might stay here for years, scarcely realising what one was doing,' she wrote in April 1939, 'while one's energy and creative power slipped away.' She remembered the lines about Limbo in *Dear Octopus*: 'People there aren't happy and they aren't unhappy — they aren't anything.' 'Increasingly I believe most of the English in Hollywood are asking the question Scrap asks — "Will we ever get out of Limbo?"'

John Gielgud wrote to ask if he could use her Bluthner while she was away, and it made her think she might be walking up the garden path of the cottage, seeing the firelight through the leaded window . . . Homesickness gripped her. The play she wanted to write at this moment was one set in a vicarage during a church festival, like the one at Thaxted in 1915, when Gustav Holst was there, and the girls in their white dresses sang on the lawn in the late summer twilight. Reading Elizabeth Bowen's *The Death of the Heart* made her regret the house in Regent's Park which had seemed so exactly right. 'And yet,' she admonished herself, 'I feel sure no house will bring you any happiness that you don't bring with you.' One consolation was that she and Alec were such good companions. They would talk into the night, agreeing with each other about her work and about life in general: 'I have never known any two people who could agree on so many topics so volubly and at quite enormous length.'

They drove on to Carmel, stopping to picnic at Point Lobos and seeing the seals leaping out of the water and clambering onto rocks with noisy barks. Carmel was then 'a pretty, unsophisticated but unspoilt artists' colony, with an old mullion-windowed church 200 years old'. She noted there was no booze, and no dogs allowed in the dining rooms; fifty years later when Clint Eastwood became mayor, there was no eating ice-cream on the sidewalks either.

In Britain there was now conscription — to the delight of Americans she met, who seemed to long to see Britain up against it. Were they jealous of us? asked Dodie. Did they yearn to be able to come over after a while and pull us out of our troubles? Somerset Maugham believed the mass intelligence of a theatre audience to be several degrees lower than the individual intelligence of its members. In the same way the mass mind of America seemed to Dodie to be more vicariously belligerent than any individual American.

Well, at least she could now say she did not wish to live in a country that endorsed conscription of its young men. She came to the last page of her leather-bound journal in April 1939. 'It would be nice to write, "and they lived happily ever after",' she wrote, 'but I shall be grateful if we even live happily for a few weeks, I am so tired of moving on.'

And so they stayed for seven weeks just outside Carmel, at a little place called

Robles del Rio, in a bungalow with views of green hills. Here they began their habit of 'serious reading' starting with Tolstoy in the OUP pocket edition from the Carmel bookstore. She was asked to work on *Rebecca* with Hitchcock; but she did not particularly like the novel, as she explained to Hitchcock in a letter, and there was no scope for humour. Meanwhile, Pongo had bitten a five-year-old child at a swimming pool. A court case was narrowly averted; Dodie and Alec gave the child a handsome present, but their peace had been shattered, and they journeyed on to San Francisco, arriving in an intense heat which had Pongo in a state of collapse. Back they drove, 3000 miles, to Vermont. For the first time since arriving in America, Dodie felt that Manchester, Vermont, was a place where she could feel at home. Mrs Potter, who had fallen in love (with a married man), joined them. They all settled into a charming old white weatherboard house with its own stream, and patterned wallpapers and tufted rugs, like an English house; they sat by the radio and listened to the news, which on 3 September announced that England was now at war.

From then on, they lived from day to day. Should they go, or stay, with Alec more and more entrenched in his conscientious objection, and Pongo threatened with quarantine? The decisive factor was the offer of a screenplay set during the First World War, about a Canadian soldier who meets an American prostitute on Waterloo Bridge in the blackout and falls in love with her. Dodie's salary for one month's work, $2000, would keep them for months. Again they set off in the Rolls with Pongo, and drove 3000 miles back to California. Mrs Potter went ahead by train and greeted them at the Beverly Hills Hotel.

Dodie soon discovered that in Hollywood the storyline of any film underwent such changes in the endless discussions that it no longer resembled the original in any detail. And whatever she wrote would be rewritten anyway. However, she agreed to work on it — at home, she stipulated, in the house Alec had rented from Marion Balderston (wife of the author of *Berkeley*

Square, the play based on Henry James's *The Sense of the Past*) in Cove Way, Beverly Hills, surrounded by eucalyptus and mimosa and with a view of Mary Pickford's Pickfair estate. Eventually, she was released from her contract: 'Sidney Franklin wanted a subservient writer, and I should never be that.'

But they decided to stay in the Balderston house, with its windows overlooking the Pacific, over which the sun obligingly staged an admirable show every evening, with a view of amusing seals and curious deer. In fact it was like a stage set: with two entrances to the garden, a door to the bedrooms, a door to the hall and a double door to the dinette. There was a large open fireplace, and 'the whole room,' said Dodie in a letter to Binkie, mimicking her own stage notes, 'may be said to have a "pleasant, lived-in feeling".' There was still an insistently breezy tone to all her letters to friends.

She was reading E. M. Forster's *Aspects of the Novel*, Percy Lubbock's *The Craft of Fiction* and Henry James's *The Art of the Novel*. Plainly she was planning to write a novel herself. Over dinner one night (at a Hungarian restaurant where they ate marrow-bones 'which tasted of nothing whatever gone slightly bad'), she asked A. J. Cronin for his advice on writing a bestseller. He replied: 'First, intensity. And in your case, stop reading Henry James.' She never took this advice. At the same time she was writing an autobiographical series, 'My Seven Tremendous Years', for a London news agency. This put her in the mood to write about her family and childhood: after all, her family were far funnier, she said, than any character in her plays. The words flew from the typewriter; and by the time she had covered her life to the age of twenty she had written 150,000 words. 'The whole book,' she said, 'would need to be longer than *War and Peace*.' It was packed away and remained unlooked-at for thirty years — when it became *Look Back With Love*, volume one of her autobiography.

She was perpetually homesick and anxious; certain that they were now tainted by the stigma of cowardice.

A. J. Cronin, now back in Connecticut, wrote approving of Alec's bravery in having the courage of his convictions. But most British people, now mustering their Blitz spirit, would condemn Alec, Dodie was sure; and she could not refrain from reminding him that but for him, she would be able, like many other women of her age in England, to share the war experience and yet have no part in fighting it. Surely she was entitled to whatever benefits there were in being a woman who was 'getting fairly old'? Must she suffer for someone else's principles? The normal husband of a woman her age (forty-three) would be pushing fifty (instead of a mere thirty-six) and beyond military service, and could maintain his principles without being menaced. However, she could not let Alec down and she was sure his feelings were genuine; so she went on, 'grumbling tearfully'.

She and Alec moved back to Carmel, to a house on the Seventeen Mile Drive, and found a housekeeper named Miss Hickson who spoke exquisite English and adored Pongo. It was a kind of idyll, despite the terrible news from England. The Savorys gave them a portable electric gramophone that changed its own records; galvanised by this, Dodie began her collection of records starting with Brahms' First Symphony, Prokofiev's Classical Symphony and César Franck's Symphonic Variations; soon she added madrigals, Purcell, Scarlatti, Bach; Handel, Schubert, Debussy, Ravel, Vaughan Williams; Mexican music, and West Indian calypso, which ever after reminded her of Carmel.

Dodie had by now become a chronic and loquacious letter-writer. Partly it was a way of jollying friends and acquaintances into remembering her, and not condemning her; partly it was an excuse not to write a play. Alec turned the spare room into a workshop where he spent most of the time packing parcels for English friends: clothes, food, lipstick, soap, 'to give them a bit of a lift' — including sugared almonds for Ambrose Heal, who wrote his thanks to 'My Dear Sugar Plum Fairy'. Over the next few years Dodie's address book was annotated with people's preferences:

'W. Macqueen-Pope is a diabetic. No more chocolates.' 'Special likes butter, bacon, sugar, milk.' 'Tea, coffee, eggs; a hot-water bottle for Nadine, and nylons size 9.' To Esmé Wynne-Tyson: 'Are nuts much good to you? Warn us off if you'd rather not have them.' Allowing for Dodie's naturally generous nature, it is nonetheless a form of manipulation, to send unrequited presents. And it certainly helped to salve her conscience for not being at home all through the war. (Esmé Wynne-Tyson's letters almost invariably start, 'You perfect darlings! your beautifully packed parcel arrived this morning . . . as for that creamed honey, honestly darlings I've never tasted anything so delicious.' 'Oh! darling, what an exquisite little winter nightie! I've never felt anything softer or lovelier, like Angora wool without the tickle.')

That spring of 1940, there was a carpet of wildflowers between their house and the Pacific. Dodie bought miniature vases to hold the twenty-two different species. It made her long more than ever for Essex. She began to work on a novel about a house built onto the ruins of a Suffolk castle named Wingfield, which she had seen on sale for £3000. She invented an eccentric family who lived there, now familiar to countless readers of *I Capture the Castle*. She completed five chapters in a whirl. 'I knew those people. I lived in that castle.'

Then she was struck by writer's paralysis. For one thing, she was stumped by trying to draw American characters, and the novel had three; for another, Rudolf Hess had just descended by parachute into Scotland. Dodie thought this meant the war would soon be over, and they would soon be going home. Just at that moment, John van Druten, ebullient with the success of his play *The Damask Cheek* in New York, arrived in Hollywood to work at MGM. He was a pacifist like Alec, and a Christian Scientist like Dodie. Gradually 'like stiff-legged dogs beginning to wag their tails at each other' she and her rival playwright began to be friends.

Van Druten was an interesting character: vain, plump, garrulous, homosexual, generous in some ways, greedy ('I once said of myself that *one* chocolate, *one* canapé, *one* cocktail were no good to me; I have to know that there are as many as I can want, even if I don't want them'), and avid for compliments and affection, which he lapped up from Dodie. He had begun as a playwright at the age of twenty-five with *Young Woodley*, set in an English public school, a huge success, at which point he gave up teaching law at University College Wales, to devote himself to the theatre. He had had several lean years, but consistently produced amusing plays: *There's Always Juliet*, *The Distaff Side*, *Old Acquaintance*. When he left England in the same year as Dodie, he had stood outside Charing Cross Station, imagining London being bombed, thinking: 'If I ever get out of this, I will go to America and never ever come back.' Now he had become an American citizen, and grew dates and corn on his ranch in the Californian desert. 'I love my home; my house is full of books that are important to me; the garden is bright with flowers, and there are tall trees; all of these seem like an achievement for me to have won for myself, so remote are they from anything that my first thirty years of life had prepared me for. Had a novelist written me, I would say that he had done a very bad job of preparation for the switch in background, venue and even character — in what I hope is no more than the middle of the book.'

Van Druten and Dodie shared a link in the distant past. In the 1920s van Druten had begged Norman MacDermott to let him watch rehearsals at the Everyman, to observe how actors reacted to the director and to each other, so that he could learn how to write a play. MacDermott was reluctant, but van Druten was so earnest and persuasive he let him sit at the back of the stalls. Then van Druten went off and wrote *Young Woodley*. And another factor propelled van Druten towards Dodie: in his youthful years his plays had always been directed by Auriol Lee, on whom he had depended utterly for advice. But Auriol had been killed in a car crash in 1936. In Dodie he found the longed-for substitute.

During 1940, Pongo suddenly became mortally ill. He had never been strong after the kidney trouble of his youth, but at seven he was still puppyish enough to chew slippers. Now he had begun breathing heavily and coughing. They took him to a vet at San José, and stayed in a hotel while he was treated, but the flick of his tail got weaker when he greeted them, and on the third day he could not even drink. His death caused Dodie more grief than anything since her mother's. She wrote page after page about him, agonising over the possibility that since it was Pongo's quarantine that kept them in America, she might have subconsciously wished him dead. Alec too missed Pongo terribly. Dodie had a superstition that no dog could enter heaven until it knows that its owners are protected by another dog. So she would have to get another, quickly: or even better, two dogs. Luckily there were several Dalmatian breeders a mere 400 miles away in Beverly Hills. Chauffeured there in van Druten's limousine (the Rolls was being serviced), they found a beautiful six-month-old black-and-white bitch which they named Folly, and a two-month-old liver-spotted male formally named Freckles of Finchingfield, but always known as Buzz. Two puppies were, they discovered, four times as much trouble as one dog. 'I'd like to take them down to the shore,' she wrote to van Druten, 'but I'm afraid they might damage the sea.'

They wrecked everything in sight and obliged Dodie and Alec to move to a larger more isolated house inland, where one room could be a dogs' playroom with all furniture removed except a built-in window seat, which the dogs chewed to pieces.

Dodie was still writing endlessly — but only letters and journals. By March 1941, she calculated to Nadine, she had written 700,000 words of letters since arriving in America, 'which is rather a frightening thought for a professional writer whose plays are normally 20,000 words, and who isn't exactly earning anything'. She spent some time writing a carefully argued defence of *Lady Chatterley's Lover* for Sidney Campion's book on Lawrence. She described how she had discovered Lawrence's poems in her early teens, and had admired him ever since. She had read *Lady Chatterley* at express speed (the book was in her possession for only two days) but thought the sex scenes 'all justified, beautiful, and of poetic loveliness'.[1]

When she finally got down to a play — *Lovers and Friends* — set in Regent's Park in World War I, the Japanese

---

[1] 'It is a modern convention,' she wrote, 'that certain words, known to all men and to most women, are unmentionable . . . So writers have to rack their brains for ways of so stirring the imagination that the reader will supply the missing words himself . . . This seems to me far more indecent than Lawrence's way of taking the "objectionable" words in his stride and giving them no undue significance.' What, she asked, could be more indecent than a row of asterisks? She had been distressed, in youth, to be told that certain things like the lower strata of her underclothes, flannel petticoats etc., might not be mentioned 'before gentlemen'. 'I fancy the time will come when Lawrence's "objectionables" will become as mentionable, though not as obsolete, as flannel petticoats.'

bombing of Pearl Harbor intervened and America, too, was at war. In the ensuing social upheaval Dodie wrote at speed a screenplay about a Californian family facing the outbreak of war and unwittingly harbouring a spy ('Fifth Column at the Fosters') for which Metro offered $20,000, but after six weeks they cancelled the deal. Worse, Alec was now eligible for the American draft, and America, they discovered, was much tougher than Britain: unless he had the full backing of a church like the Quakers, he could be jailed. They lived — in another, smaller house, without Miss Hickson to help — in a state of suspense. How could Dodie exist with Alec in jail? Who would cook for her (Alec did what little home cooking they did) or help her with the lively young dogs? While he was away for a night seeing the Draft Board, she wandered the lonely rooms in misery, playing her white grand piano, spending hours writing to van Druten. Even the British Vice-Consul had assured them that if they went back, Alec would have to join the armed forces: fire-fighting duty would not suffice. There was nothing for them to do but to stay, and for Dodie to get on and earn some money in films.

They gathered up their Carmel treasures (cashmere rugs, books, records), took a last Seventeen Mile Drive to gaze at Seal Rock, and consoled themselves by finding another beautiful new home with Monets and Picassos on the walls and an exquisite Le Douanier Rousseau ('my favourite painter') at $260 a month on North Palm Drive, Beverly Hills. Alec, it turned out, could stave off the threats of the Draft Board by working as a counsellor to other conscientious objectors. And although jobs in the films were becoming scarcer, Mary Martin's husband, Richard Halliday, managed to get Dodie an offer from Paramount to work with Charlie Brackett on adapting *The Uninvited* by Dorothy Macardle, a sub-*Rebecca* ghost story set in a lonely house on a Devon cliff-top.

Though Dodie found in Brackett a true ally — 'Has anyone ever told you that you write like an angel?' were his words on reading her first draft of the script — and though she was paid a soothing

$1250 a week, her experience was no happier. Another writer was brought in to make 'a few technical changes'. Charlie told Dodie she was writing down to her movie audience because she despised them; and that she was over-sentimental. The Hollywood habit of hammering things out incessantly was a pleasant enough way of working once one stopped feeling guilty about it, but the constant unpicking and patching meant the original plot was quite lost. ('Now do remember you're better than Dorothy Macardle,' said Charlie one day. 'Who?' said Dodie: after four months she had forgotten even the author's name.) But Charlie was amiable to work with, a true friend and ally. He suggested that Alec, who looked so like Hollywood's idea of the English officer, should take a screen test (Alec was sure he could not act, and declined) and even offered Dodie a small part in *The Uninvited*, playing the lunatic: a good story with which she could amuse friends. But most importantly he understood her exiled misery in the way that only another writer could: 'for he realises that it is not only suppressed love of country which worries me, but suppressed desire for copy'.

A copy of *Horizon* would arrive, with a Mass Observation description of life in wartime: 'What a field for the writer there is in England now,' said Dodie wistfully. Charlie said he had a vision of her with her nose pressed up against the war, longing to get in on it; he had the same feeling himself. To rub salt in her wounds, Binkie, flushed with putting on Noël Coward's *Blithe Spirit*, was writing lyrically from Finchingfield about how 'everyone is quite amazing in their spirits, courage and smiling faces, and however low you may be feeling, it does cheer one up to see people being so good' and about cooking wholesome blackout dinners for John Gielgud who shared his London flat: 'it is surprising how pleased one is to have company and never to be alone for a moment.' Ambrose Heal wrote about having to make Utility furniture, and about the lack of transport, the dearth of books, the foreigners and Jews 'swarming over Beaconsfield', the arrival of evacuees at Baylin's Farm ('and not very nice clean children at that — the great complaint is of the chronic bed-wetter'). He was doing a roaring trade in blackout material at Heal's, but reported that it was not much use to have the money to buy ten Players, when you couldn't get cigarettes. (Dodie sent a giant pack at once.)

It caused Dodie untold pangs of regret not to be there. Charlie reassured her. 'He thinks that if a writer has missed the Blitz, he has missed everything; no writer could write at the moment without fearing it would all be out of date soon. He very strongly believes that there is no course for me except to stand by Alec.' Her dreams of England tormented her. While half-awake each morning, still in England in her dream, she would feel aglow with happiness and would tell herself, 'This is real, this is true,' and let the longing for England flow over her like music. Then she would really wake, and feel an aching regret that spread from her solar plexus all over her body. Every day she realised again what she had lost and left behind, how damaged was her reputation, how she had robbed herself of pleasures which might never return until she was too old to enjoy them. The diaries of these weeks show with what clarity Dodie perceived her self-inflicted exiled misery.

The great consolation was that van Druten came over often with his friend Carter Lodge, and they indulged in theatrical gossip and tore everybody to pieces. This shocked Alec, but Dodie found she enjoyed his company and the fact that he always brought books to lend and discuss. A correspondence began which persisted for seventeen years and ran to more than a million words. On the surface, it was two playwrights discussing their craft, with such an eye on posterity that each kept carbons of every letter. (So there are now two complete collections, one in the Berg Collection at the New York Public Library, and Dodie's 400 miles away in Boston University.) Van Druten hoped they would be published in their entirety, but Dodie always wondered if they were quite as good as John smugly thought them. Dodie often received his carbons, since he would let his typewriter ribbons get so faint only the carbons could be read. What is certain is that this letter-writing to van Druten sapped much of Dodie's creative energy during her years of exile, and represented a safe, cerebral and literary form of affair. He thought nothing of writing two long letters in a single day, of the type that inspired an instant answer. Sometimes Dodie suspected (reasonably) that he liked her letters better than he liked her. 'Or does he like writing to me far better than he likes me or my letters? And do I feel the same?'

The correspondence had begun when Dodie was feeling 'most horribly nervous' while writing the third act of *Lovers and Friends*, 'and I really think it may do me good to "visit" a little with you (how oddly this country uses that word visit, but it's one of their peculiarities that seems rather folksy and nice to me)', and from then on she regarded van Druten as a repository for her more girlish and Cassandra-like sentiments. 'Dearest John' (on New Year's Eve 1942) 'Do Eves get you as they do me? Almost any old eve will do: New Year's, Christmas, Easter, Midsummer.

The actual day of anything has never meant much to me. Even as a child, there was always a sort of flat depression about Christmas Day for me.' She acquired some new writing paper simply headed DODIE SMITH in red, remarking 'Classy little bastard, aren't I?' In these letters she became coquettish, playful and conspiratorial. She would hymn jigsaw puzzles, fireflies, Jews ('but I do rather draw the line at them being Jewish') and American insects and animals 'but I can't seem to work myself up to people'. They would exchange gossip, bitch about other people's writings, swap books and reminiscences, moan about actors who couldn't act and directors who couldn't direct and whether they cared what audiences liked. Of the two, van Druten was more apt to crow about his work in progress: he once wrote to Dodie, 'Sometimes I am frightened by my own technique. It's so good.' Dodie said Thurber might draw this: 'Portrait of the Dramatist Frightened By His Technique'.

Then one day at the end of November 1942, van Druten brought Christopher

Isherwood with him, and Dodie found him at once one of the most congenial people she had ever met. 'My first impression of him was that he radiated goodness . . . a sunniness of temperament which enabled him to like and be liked by almost everyone.' He seemed to like Dodie just as much, because he came again the following Sunday and every Sunday thereafter for many years. 'Well, I thought you'd like each other,' remarked van Druten tartly, 'but not quite so much.'

9

Christopher and His Kind

ISHERWOOD'S first impression of Dodie, says his biographer Peter Parker, was that she was slightly 'crazy' with her animal obsessions, but he immediately took to her. Being short himself, he liked small people simply for being like him; he took to Stravinsky for the same reason, though he had no interest in his music. He found Dodie a good listener and talker, and having rapidly established his place at her Sunday lunch table, came back on Christmas Day, renouncing his vegetarianism for the day to share the turkey and bringing his friend Tony Bower, a sergeant in the US army.

Dodie was struck by 'a very charming simple quality' about Isherwood — 'almost humble'. When imparting information he would preface it with 'As you, of course, know . . .' but then Dodie had not mingled enough with the English upper classes to realise this is a commonplace mannerism *de haut en bas*. She longed to see him more — preferably without van Druten who invariably dominated the conversation. But Isherwood was shortly going to live in the Swami Prabhavananda's house, the Vedanta Temple in Hollywood. She was deeply suspicious of 'all this Eastern religious stuff'. 'Also I am never quite at ease with very *good* people — Alec is about as good as I can stand,' she wrote in her journal.

She felt motherly and protective about Isherwood's genius. At thirty-eight he was just eight years younger than Dodie, but famously boyish in looks, and having found him, she could not bear to lose him to 'the Swamitage', especially since she considered him to be 'on the fringe of greatness'. '*Mr Norris* was such an enchanting, wildly funny book; there should have been singing in the streets when Christopher first burst upon an apparently unastonished world.' Moreover she found him hilarious, with his 'killingly funny imitations of Nöel

Coward in *In Which We Serve* and his silly jokes and puns, picked up at a Quaker workshop (where he had gone as a conscientious objector) like 'Praise the Lord and pass the malnutrition'. But Isherwood would sit cross-legged in his white socks and extol the pleasures of the Swami's house, which he was due to disappear into in four weeks' time and which sounded to Dodie 'horribler and horribler'. That a brilliant writer should wash dishes in a small household, bursting with people from eighty-year-olds to children of school age! Isherwood was to live in a room off the dining room, where the nephew of the Swami also slept in an alcove. The inmates would have to do all the housework and be perpetually together. Would religion steal a fine writer away, as it had Tolstoy, she wondered. How would he write *Prater Violet*? The Swami had said, 'The cobra has bitten you, Mr Isherwood, you will die soon.' Dodie supposed he meant die to the world. She imagined seeing Isherwood's small slight figure receding into the Swami's temple on Ivar Avenue on Sunday evenings, between rows of cypresses, leaving behind 'the teeming awfulness of Hollywood Boulevard'. 'But Christopher looks sunnily saintly and says they are all "so nice". He has a curious habit of smiling at me across a room. At first I thought it was just a friendly glance and returned it, but I find it goes on and on and one feels so discourteous when one has to turn away from it to pour the tea or talk to others. But really if I don't turn away I don't see how it would ever end. Presumably we should just beam and beam on each other till we just floated upwards in mutual goodwill. As it is, I forget all about it and turn back half an hour later to find Christopher still beaming.'

Just being with him made her and Alec both feel physically more alive, even after hours of talking which would have been exhausting with anyone else. Why did he insist on going into 'the monkery'? 'Apparently he longs for the discipline. He cannot just follow his religion alone. He doesn't appear to like the Hindoo side of it but is willing to swallow that because he likes other things about it. I simply cannot understand the craving for *discipline*. If I wanted to be good in his way, I would do it by myself. He seems to want to force himself beyond his own inclinations. He has given up smoking and longs for it; he will give up drink when he enters the order. He will entertain friends there and even visit them; but not go to parties or restaurants. I fancy the truth is that he has led a muddled and rather dissipated life and feels he might slip back. It's hard to imagine such a thing for he is so genuinely good, but now that I have read *Goodbye to Berlin* I can understand a little better. He has lived with such extraordinary people and one fancies his friends might lure him to a lower life if he does not shut himself off from it. But I cannot like the whole business. It seems fairly hysterical for a man of his age.

With the coming of Isherwood, Dodie and Alec's life was 'a whirl of sociability' compared with the isolated idyll of Carmel. Christopher soon brought with him his new friend Aldous Huxley, then living in the Mojave Desert. Dodie was greatly flattered but she did not find Huxley easy to talk to, and left the discussion of pacifism to Alec. Huxley was 'very very depressing about the future of Europe'. Dodie felt conversationally at sea; she concluded, 'I am never at my best with people I look up to too much.' (Years later, when van Druten had invited Huxley to dinner — and Huxley had brought Hubble the astronomer — Dodie wrote to van Druten: 'I am sure I should like Huxley if I really knew him. My fear is that I never really could. And I slightly feel that he despises me — whereas I know damned well that I am not despisable.') Huxley, Isherwood told Dodie, was greatly interested in the Swami too and might even enter the order if he were not a married man. Dodie was contemptuous. 'They are such brilliant and erudite people, but I don't feel they are normal in the way Alec and I are normal . . . and that sort of abnormality worries me.'

Another friend of Isherwood's, named Denham Fouts, arrived, a fellow conscientious objector and the wealthy bisexual son of the owner of Safeway, who lived in a small Santa Monica apartment with a very large Picasso. (He is featured in Truman Capote's novel *Answered Prayers*.) Dodie found him offhand and casual. 'And again,' wrote Dodie in her journal, 'the queerness.'

'I am getting to a difficult point in this journal. I write it for myself alone . . . but I cannot write wildly libellous things. To have certain things recorded in pen and ink makes me feel faintly uncomfortable. Yet a journal bores so much if one makes reservations of that sort.' So Dodie decided to record that 'many of the people we are associating with are completely *different* from us. I am always using mental reservations when talking to them and can never be quite honest and admit that I know they are different. If I could — and they admitted it — our relationship would at least be honest. As it is, it is the game of double-ostrich — both sides pretending something each must know the other knows. Or perhaps they think we resemble blind bats rather than ostriches. And we certainly "act bat" very well.' Dodie saw that the above was a 'piece of circumlocution'. As she said, anyone who met Isherwood, van Druten and his friend Carter Lodge, or Denham Fouts, would 'guess it in one'. Isherwood was flaunting a cache of envelopes with 'Kiss the Boys Goodbye' and a large red mouth on them, to be skittishly used for his farewell notes to men friends.

The week after Christmas, Isherwood brought Tony Bower again, this time with van Druten and Denny Fouts. When they had all gone and the house was empty, Dodie and Alec said in the same breath 'Oh I do like you,' and collapsed on each other's shoulders with relief. Isherwood obviously regarded Dodie as some kind of trophy to be shown off to his gay friends. On another Sunday he brought Tony Bower's mother, Mrs Duff Gordon, who disconcerted Dodie; younger than Dodie herself, she was also much prettier and smarter: 'Somehow I always imagine the mothers of grown men to be old ladies in black silk and fichus.' Isherwood advised Dodie to give up perming her hair — she loathed going to the hairdresser anyway — and just to put it under the tap. She grew out her perm from then on, and when her hair fell to her waist she wore it in a plaited bun for the rest of her life.

More importantly, Dodie quickly became one of the very few people with whom Isherwood discussed his writing. As Dodie made plain to Isherwood, she and Alec valued him more highly than any other element of their American life. They saved things up to talk to him about. He became their family, but without the drawbacks of relations. Isherwood too had no interest in families and preferred his friends to be childless. He thought Alec dashing and glamorous: a type of British individualist who sided automatically with the underdog. Isherwood's need for Dodie and Alec was, for a time, as great as theirs for him: when Dodie was away, he later said, there was nobody to ask him, 'Well, Chris, how was the week?', no one to whom to reply, 'Oh — *assez mouvementée.*' What use was it, to have a hair's breadth escape from the cops (as happened one night when he was stopped outside a party and made a foolish remark about marijuana) if he had nobody to *tell* about it?

Dodie was fascinated to hear that Isherwood's ancestral home in Cheshire was Marple Hall, a great Elizabethan house with Queen Anne additions, very near her own roots in Lancashire. Isherwood had inherited the house but had given it to his younger brother. How painful to hear of a great house unloved by its owner, with the soot of industry heavy on its leaves and grass. It reminded Dodie of her unfinished novel, *I Capture the Castle*, which she doubted she would ever go back to. 'It is in the romantic vein I could scarcely recapture, and the original impetus is now gone.'

Isherwood had supplied a useful new word for her vocabulary. She had urged him to turn some of the *Goodbye to Berlin* stories into a play, and he had replied, 'But where would the wow be now?' The 'wow' was the sensation that inspired creativity: the rush of conviction that a particular plot was possible. Van Druten gave her another expression she adopted: 'Oh, that's your holy grail mood,' he would say, meaning her determination to abandon her old style of play, to pursue the holy grail of the truly Great Play. Van Druten said a writer should 'do his best and not fuss'. Dodie said a writer need not fuss too vocally and bore his friends, but fuss he should. She felt an almost physical urge to embark on a new kind of work, without any thought of audiences. It amazed her to think that she was now forty-seven ('unbelievably for little Dodie Smith of Kingston House') and experiencing the kind of artistic growing pains that should have come in her thirties. She wanted, deep in her solar plexus, to write a better type of play. 'It's a sort of physical urge — rather like when Buzzle wants to roll on the grass. For better or worse, I am now one of the holy grailers.'

Van Druten also revived her interest in the notion that one could ill-wish other people. She had heard this first from C. E. Vulliamy in 1924: 'He was one hell of an ill-wisher and claimed to have caused numerous deaths. He said the will to wish ill went out of him almost unconsciously, and he would watch the results as an almost horrified spectator.' Dodie had found herself being very civil to CEV after that. Van Druten's view was that when people crossed him, they *just had to go*: it might even be through death, but they just had to stop existing for him. Much later, Dodie too became quite adept at that: she almost ill-wished van Druten himself, and Alec, for his part, completely edited him out.

Meanwhile, daily life in California remained sybaritic. They could walk the dogs through a sun-filled winter, in a garden cascading with semi-tropical flowers — though rather than walk, Buzz always expected to be carried uphill despite being in radiant health — and Dodie earned $20,000 without too much pain from the film studios. Darryl F. Zanuck once sent a telegram asking her to 'polish *Lady Windermere's Fan*'. It was ludicrous, but Hollywood's boys in the front office would pay her $2000 just for giving Charlie Brackett an hour's advice 'which he would have been welcome to on any of our Monday dinners for free'. At one point she found herself 'improving the dialogue' on an appalling script for Charlie. Charlie had already added laboured, unfunny lines like 'I'm afraid we're an unsmoking household. Grandfather had a cigar blown down his throat when he was on the bridge and lost his taste for tobacco.' It made her weep: how could Charlie, so amusing and even erudite, write such stuff? When she asked to have her name taken off the credits, Charlie just laughed and said he would instead add another credit: 'Bad taste by Charlie Brackett'.

Van Druten once pointed out that if she and Alec had not gone to a party at the Balderstons' in 1938 they would never have met him, and through him, Isherwood — it was 'an argument for going to parties'. Alec replied, with a disarming lack of tact, 'But the truth is, we should have got on perfectly well on our own.' Dodie affected to agree with Alec, but she privately knew how much she lived for these new literary friendships. They were vital to her, almost to the exclusion of everyone else. 'John and Christopher and Charlie were my chief wartime acquisitions,' she wrote. First, it was pleasant to be so popular among these three men, two of them gay and therefore wifeless, and the third, Charlie, with a wife who was conveniently 'ill' (actually an alcoholic) and soon even more conveniently dead.

Second, they gave Dodie professional support; they admired her, and provided her reading with an extra dimension: 'All my writing life I have longed to talk to other writers.' She exchanged views with Christopher and John on everything they read and wrote, not always agreeing. Van Druten could not read Henry James, while she was increasingly dazzled by him. Christopher lent her Arthur Waley's translations from the Chinese, but she found them irritating; she could not read such playful, highbrow, mock-simple fairy tales. They exchanged new novels — by Isherwood's distant cousin Graham Greene (which Dodie hated) and by Evelyn Waugh (she referred to his books as 'the Horrors of Waugh') and Henry Green's *Concluding* ('which ought to be called *Neverending*'). They joked about *The Heat of the Day*, *The Death of the Heart*, *The Heart of the Matter*; or was it *The Heat of the Heart* or *The Death of the Day*?

Van Druten was proving a friend of the most determined kind. Unlike Isherwood, he would not only turn up several times a week, but would talk on the telephone for an hour every day. 'We constantly criticise him — but I never find him boring. He and I talk continually about our respective plays just as Phyl and I talked continually about our respective love affairs. I think in both cases I listen the most. I doubt if John would continue to telephone unless the balance was slightly that way.'

He would sometimes write Dodie four letters in a single day, which would arrive by Special Delivery in a van. Alec understandably found this tiresome. Van Druten was argumentative, critical, but resentful of criticism; Dodie only had to question a detail in his new play for him to become petulant and practically to kick the furniture. At least when she criticised him, she wrapped the negative up in blandishments. She had lent him *Prunella*, by Harley Granville Barker and Laurence Housman. 'I wonder if he knows how the line "Here's a nice garden — let's pull it to pieces" is typical of *him*.' When he came to dinner, he was 'astonishingly talkative, almost uninterruptably so. Alec frequently walked out in exasperation.'

Once she noted mildly: 'John was never a bore and much of what he said was interesting, but he did say it at great length and the evening developed into a lecture rather than a conversation.' Yet Dodie remained amused and tolerant.

She was delighted that van Druten invited himself over for 31 December 1942. Alec disliked sentimental New Year's Eves, and last year had retired to bed leaving Dodie to sing a solo 'Auld Lang Syne' holding Buzzle's crossed paws. This year it was all hard talking, with no time for sentiment. Van Druten showed Dodie his journals, much less personal than her own, full of extracts from his reading. For several days after that, Dodie copied extracts from her own current reading of the Goncourt Journals, on the subject of literary birth pangs, and 'the travail, the torment, the torture of the literary life . . . It is as if you had a sheet of blank paper in your head . . . the dismal weariness, the infinite despair, the shame, with which you feel your powerlessness . . . you tell yourself that you are incapable of doing anything, that you will never be able to do anything, that you are void.' Obviously this mirrored Dodie's own despair. She had finished her new play, *Lovers and Friends*, but had little confidence in it.

In her 1943 journal is an account of a single telephone conversation with van Druten, which covered thirty pages. Even though he had spent the previous evening talking to her, van Druten kept her on the telephone for more than an hour. As the call dragged on, Alec, waiting to go shopping, kept dropping frantic notes in front of her, but to Dodie every word of van Druten's was 'of absorbing interest'.

What was it about? They began by discussing whether characters in novels had to be larger than life, with every trait exaggerated: van Druten cited Virginia Woolf and Elizabeth Bowen, who would take an ordinary character and make her full of exquisite perceptions and altogether of such a rarity that nobody would believe her to be real. (Dodie found this question, of artistic licence versus humdrum reality, of perpetual interest, and had copied out a letter of Oscar Wilde's in which, defending himself against the charge that his characters were unrealistic, he declared: 'Quite so. If they existed they would not be worth writing about. The function of the artist is to invent, not to chronicle . . . Life by its realism is always spoiling the subject matter of art. The supreme pleasure of literature is to realise the non-existent.' Dodie contrasted this view with that of Chekhov, who believed theatre should 'show life and men as they are, and not as they would look if you put them on stilts'. It was the difference between a Franz Hals painting and a Rembrandt.)

Dodie believed that ordinary people were all in their own way odd, even a little mad. If van Druten drew Dodie in a play, with all her apparent eccentricities, 'it would show how dangerous photography is because those things would give no impression of the real me at all — which shows how fake our portraits are . . . ' (Dodie and van Druten used the expression 'photography' for realism or naturalism, and even applied 'photographic' to dialogue.) They went through all their mutual friends — Isherwood, Brackett, Peggy Webster:

they would all be 'full of exquisite strangeness' in a novel: 'John, by the way, is convinced that Christopher is so obsessed by sex that all his reactions are conditioned by it . . . which might be magnificent for his work. So many of us get bored by sex and it makes for flatness in work.'

Halfway through the conversation Dodie broke off to go shopping with Alec, while van Druten went to write up their conversation in his journal, which he then read aloud to Dodie in another telephone call. And on they went — through Ibsen, Tolstoy, Shaw, Henry James — and back to Elizabeth Bowen:

JOHN: She writes about people's exquisite hands fluttering over the delicate china . . .
ME: She damn well does no such thing. You've only read one Elizabeth Bowen.
JOHN: Oh, what a hell of a lot of reading one's got to do ever to be able to finish an argument.

Her conclusion after their marathon discussion was: 'John slightly resents my desire to improve because he is jealous . . . a perfectly healthy feeling for the writer. But one must be well-mannered about success. I have regarded every moment since we left England as failure for me. I hope that if I ever again experience success, I will know how to hold my drink.'

Dodie was convinced that the correspondence with van Druten was 'good for us both'. She especially loved discussing techniques of stagecraft with him; she was horrified when he reported that two characters in his latest play passed one another a cup of coffee by mistake, and got such a laugh it became a set piece of business. She had been furious when two characters collided on stage in *Dear Octopus* and Glen Byam Shaw had 'kept it in'. All this theatrical chatter was therapeutic to her: even when she wrote about being 'dead tired' or 'hating life', her letters to van Druten were bursting with vitality and creative energy.

The danger — which Dodie did not understand till some years later — was that she was dissipating her creativity in these letters, and that van Druten was in fact a leech. It is an aggressive form of parasitism to bombard someone with letters. But Dodie was his willing victim. They were the closest and deadliest of rivals, enjoying one another's failures with *Schadenfreude*, while commiserating and jollying each other along with suggestions. Dodie gave as good as she got — but being honest, she was the loser, especially as she could not resist showing van Druten her works in progress.

'It's wonderful to have John to argue with — I enjoy it more than I can say. But John does not extend my mind as Christopher does. John finished today by asking what plays I was going to write with my "fine new sensibilities". I said the only idea I had was what I call Project Two — the play where several people are unconscious of their extreme jealousy. Either John will tell me this is a bad idea — or write something like it himself.' A premonition of what he was to do with *Lovers and Friends*.

This play, which Dodie had just completed, was destined for Broadway.

A thrilling cable had arrived from Jack Wilson: 'Katharine Cornell mad about play and very anxious to do it.' Dodie was amused by the open American nosiness of the telegraph office girl, who read the cable and rang excitedly: 'Hey, Katharine Cornell wants to do your play!' But oddly, Dodie let Wilson go ahead with the production without getting involved in it herself at all. 'I want this play to be a success, to justify itself, to make money for the future. But more than anything I want to write *better*.'

This was not an idle posture. An article had come out in *Horizon* by Arnold Goldsmith about the 'cosy' school of playwriting, the well-crafted middlebrow comedy (later very vocally despised by Tynan, Levin and other critics of the 1960s). Goldsmith's article said that van Druten had been head of the cosy school, but had been superseded by Dodie, whose plays had 'the fidelity of the touched-up photograph'. She felt that from the article, the reader might suppose that both van Druten and Dodie were now dead. 'And I believe that, as a writer of the Cosy Play, I am.'

Reading E. M. Delafield's *The Diary of a Provincial Lady*, she found the domestic problems left her quite depleted, and she was determined never again to write a play in which anyone said 'Cook sez' or one that made the audience nudge one another saying 'Isn't that like your Auntie Annie?' She burned to write a play that would have significance and relevance to the British in wartime. With no first-hand experience, she had intended to draw upon the graphic letters written by Jean Batters about her fire-watching. But these letters had come to a sudden and peculiar end in 1941.

Batters had been a most extraordinary secretary: an intelligent young woman whose acid comments, acute observation and pungent, critical style of letter-writing easily matched Dodie's. (Later she became Secretary to Dame Edith Evans and wrote a book about life as Edith's slavish dogsbody, which had driven her to drink and a nervous breakdown. When I met her on the publication of that book, in 1977, a genteel spinster of seventy-one living in Eastbourne, Batters told me that while working for Dame Edith had been hellish, working for Dodie had always been 'tremendous fun'.)

When Dodie and Alec first went to America, Batters had seemed to be very much on their side. But later, as the war took over her life, Batters became increasingly absorbed in her fire-fighting at the 'U' fire station in Devonshire Close, Marylebone, which she described in microscopically detailed letters: the hours on watch, the German planes like 'bloody bluebottles' overhead, the table tennis, the dancing to 'Hutch' on the gramophone, the endless drinking of tea and Bovril, the listening to the wireless, the peaceful nights after the air raids. It was the kind of information for which Dodie was avid. Then Batters suddenly fell silent, and resigned as Dodie's secretary. Apparently she had fallen in love with a fellow fire-watcher. At the same time she took offence when Dodie sent her a Christmas cheque in 1940. In January 1941 she wrote to say she had passed on the £5 to Esmé Wynne-Tyson — the former actress now turned playwright and novelist, who was a pacifist and a Christian Scientist of a most unswerving and evangelical kind, and who had taken over Dodie's secretarial duties — because she was 'damned hard up'. 'I shouldn't be consistent in accepting it,' wrote Batters, 'and it would be very strongly against my conscience. I think you know how strongly I feel about this war and about people who take no part in it, and therefore, feeling as I do, it would be impossible to accept your money.'

Worse, she turned on Dodie for the three years she had spent working for her. 'I know you resented my not being grateful for suites at those lousy station hotels because I always have stayed in suites, whereas for a normal secretary it would have been marvellous. But it felt all wrong. Sometimes in those little rooms I used to see all my youth going, and I'd given up all the things I used to love like dancing, tennis and people my own age and having a car, and I would walk along the sea wall with Phyl like a snail and think, why am I crawling along like this when I might be playing tennis?'

Dodie was astonished by this turned-worm letter. (Batters had a tendency to write letters 'in the heat of the moment'.) She wrote back a stinging one herself, starting off in her usual, fulsomely charming tones, 'Please don't imagine I resent your giving Esmé the money; I am glad about it. I'm sure you'll understand that my conscience likes to feel clear too.

'For I *have* a conscience, you know; my principles are just as rigid as yours and have necessitated great sacrifices. I suppose, strictly speaking, I disapprove of you as much as you disapprove of me. You still don't tell me why you stopped doing my work without warning; I suppose your phrase "You know how I feel about this war" is meant to account for everything. But in view of the affectionate letters you sent me, it was quite impossible for me to guess this. Then you stopped writing . . . and you even put me off the scent by your cable, "Too busy and too unbelievably happy to write" (that little classic came shortly after the fall of France, I think.) So still I was deceived.' No other friends, Dodie added, had expressed any disapproval of her leaving England: they had remained as affectionate as ever. 'That, I suppose, is the essence of friendship: to remain faithful to one's friends even when one disapproves of them.' Dodie went on in this wounded, waspish vein: 'You happen to be very young for your age,' she told Jean, and even rebuked her for 'the rather unwitty hats' she used to wear.

Dodie put Batters's curious onslaught down to a kind of wartime psychosis. Batters had met 'the common people' at her fire station, and wished to discard previous associations with people with money, culture and fine feelings. 'I quite liked Jean,' she told her journal, 'but suffered no emotional pang over her sudden change in character, her impertinent and patronising behaviour. What saddens me is the knowledge that England is now full of Jeans and I can never make contact with them again. Imagine writing for a public of Jeans!' She could not imagine there ever again being theatres packed with well-dressed people willing to pay 12s 6d to see a play. 'Perhaps it will be a good thing — but I hate the world to lose its charming graces, even in a good cause like the equalising of wealth. I sometimes feel that in Russia, for instance, all the graces are gone and people aren't any happier than they were under the tsars. Anyway, brotherly love has found it necessary to execute far more people than the worst tsars.'

Lovers and Friends was now in production, but Dodie did not go to New York for rehearsals or even the opening night. She suspected she would not get her own way on Broadway as she had in London. In any case, she had a new distraction at home in California: a litter of Dalmatian puppies. Just after delivering her playscript for typing, she and Alec had decided that Folly and Buzz should mate. Armed with textbooks, they watched Buzz clamber at first onto Folly's head. Despite this canine ineptitude Folly became pregnant and the pups were due in July 1943.

Dodie and Alec had read up the facts about whelping, but were nevertheless quite unprepared for the reality: each pup emerging in its transparent little sac, and the bed flooded in what looked like green ink in various shades from lime to bottle. Only later did Dodie learn that the placenta is normally green; at the time she and Alec thought Folly must have swallowed some green carpet dye. It was altogether an alarming and unforgettable experience. Dr Jones the vet had expected seven pups; with mounting consternation they counted nine, ten, eleven, twelve . . . The thirteenth puppy was born apparently lifeless, pale yellow in colour, but was revived by Alec's tenderly rubbing it dry and working its tiny legs, until it gave a few little gasps and twitches, and was alive: the process is described in the book of *The Hundred and One Dalmatians* (and later shown in the Disney film) and was graphically related by Dodie in interviews. The final tally, at the end of a long and exhausting night, was fifteen pups. Buzz slept peacefully throughout his mate's parturition. At sunrise, Dodie the midwife was still wearing the black lace dress she had put on for dinner.

They happened to be without a housekeeper, having just fired the Danish incumbent for her temper and her rudeness over the lack of butter. That day, Dodie had been working at Paramount, and had had Isherwood, van Druten and Charlie to dinner. With the birth of the puppies, domestic chaos ensued. Folly had managed to tear the guest house mattress to pieces, wrecked a chair and ripped a bedspread. She herself could not possibly produce enough milk to feed all fifteen pups: Dodie and Alec had to find tiny feeding bottles and were advised to look for a foster mother. Alec drove out to a dog pound and, somewhat miraculously, came across a Dalmatian mother who had been picked up, minus her pups. She was under-nourished, rickety and un-house-trained but she did have milk. At first, she appeared to be about to bite the puppies' heads off, and both mothers kept sitting on the babies. They found someone to take six of the pups and the foster mother, but within twenty-four hours the woman was on the telephone saying they must come and take the foster mother back again as she would not stop barking.

In the end they managed to get the saintly Miss Hickson to return, and gave up their lives entirely to puppy-feeding (and Dodie's obsessive re-counting of them) until the pups could feed themselves in the garden, shaded by a scarlet poinsettia bush and gradually growing their black spots. Charlie, Isherwood and van Druten came over to admire the brood before homes were found for fourteen of them, and for the foster mother.

Dodie revelled in the fact that she and Alec now had a reputation as eccentric hermits who never went out, entertained only their three men friends, and were besotted by their dogs. (One day Alec came back quite distracted from a shopping expedition: he had lost all three dogs — Buzz, Folly and Dandy, the one pup they had kept. He had driven all round Beverly Hills searching for them. He had been to the police. And all the while, the dogs were contentedly sleeping on the lawn: he had forgotten to take them with him.) That summer Dodie basked in days of journal and letter writing, reading Henry James and E. M. Forster and listening to Beethoven's late quartets, pleasures shared with Isherwood, while the puppies and their mother continued to wreak destruction on the house, which belonged to Loretta Young. Their next move was to a far grander house ($600 a month) at 1141 Tower Road, re-named by Isherwood 'Ivory Tower Road', with wooded hillsides, views over Los Angeles and the Pacific, sloping garden with sycamore tree, swimming pool, and an enormous underground bolt-hole in case of earthquakes. It belonged to Mrs d'Arrast, the former Eleanor Boardman, star of silent pictures. Disagreeable, said Dodie, was a mild word for her.

Lovers and Friends proceeded to its November 1943 opening on Broadway after much anguish for Dodie, hearing everything at second hand. Raymond Massey's new wife Dorothy, who had told her husband it was 'a woman's play that would make a lot of money', had sent seventeen foolscap pages of notes on how the play should be altered to suit Ray better. Massey did not care for the play: 'It seemed the longest play I ever acted in,' he said in his autobiography, *A Hundred Different Lives*. 'It was written in British tea-talk, rather twittery.' He found his leading role 'a deadly bore'.

But being just out of the army and forgotten on Broadway, he badly needed this job opposite the star Cornell. Dodie was nervy and cross to hear about the cuts and revisions, but Jack Wilson said there would be 'lots of lovely money for you, darling'.

On the first night, Dodie and Alec sat in their palatial sitting room with Buzz, Folly and Dandy, waiting to hear about the reviews. Dodie filled in time by writing pages of journal, imagining the theatre: 'The curtain will have been up nearly an hour now. The second act will be starting. Katharine Cornell in a blue crepe dress, Carol Goodner in a printed silk . . . ' This unleashed her nostalgia about the London first nights, the flowers, the curtain calls, the parties. Did she actually care more for the excitement of the first night, the applause and congratulations, than for the play itself, coming to life? Not being there, she felt as guilty as a mother who had handed over a child as soon as it was born . . .

Then van Druten's telegram was telephoned to them, with news of the first notices. It ended 'Deepest love and angry sympathy' and advised her to go and have a soothing dinner in the bath. During the minute that Alec took to write the message down, Dodie's spirits sank to 'a terrible new low'. So that was that. Luckily Alec had brought some new jigsaw puzzles and they managed to start one: 'They are very good as a drug.'

Van Druten's commiserating telegram was especially poignant. When she had shown van Druten the first draft of her script in 1942, he gave constructive advice: 'I still find your first act curtain wrong. It *dribbles* down. And I think Act II Scene iii is an anti-climax. The "bloody inconvenient" line is an obvious *act* curtain line.' When it was finished, he sang its praises, and told her she had lost none of her skill. In brief, the plot concerns a soldier named Rodney, meeting his girlfriend's best friend Stella; they fall in love in an instant, in the play's prologue, set in Regent's Park in 1918. In 1930, they are seen happily married, until Rodney falls in love somewhat unconvincingly with a priggish young woman, and Stella seeks solace elsewhere. In an epilogue they are back together. The play has many witty lines but lacks charm. After giving Dodie his advice on its construction, van Druten went off to his ranch in the desert below Palm Springs and wrote his own play, on a strikingly similar premise: with an actress heroine, whose best friend has stood up a soldier on weekend leave, so that in the course of the play the soldier switches affections from one girl to another, just as in Dodie's prologue. His play was called *The Voice of the Turtle*.

True, van Druten had sent her a postcard asking if he might 'borrow an idea' from her play. Since this episode merely constituted the preamble to Dodie's play, and van Druten had given her much-needed encouragement, she generously told him to 'go ahead'. He dashed off his play, she noted sourly, 'in about three weeks'. The irony was that, as a result, her play and his opened at the same time in New York. *The Voice of the Turtle* turned out to be the most successful play van Druten ever wrote, and ran for 1000 performances. Dodie's play enjoyed a modest run, but the *New Yorker* said it was 'written with that peculiar bird-like lilt that makes British clichés so much more irritating than our own.'

The sad truth is that van Druten's play was better than Dodie's: tauter, funnier, and with more amiable characters. *Lovers and Friends* is Dodie's weakest and least credible performed play. Still, despite the notices, receipts were $23,122 in the first week, and there were capacity houses for its brief run. Gerald Savory reported to Dodie candidly that it was a charmless production ('pauses to make your hair stand on end'), that Miss Cornell was incompetent, abetted by Mr Massey who was 'nothing more than a gifted amateur'. 'Never for a moment is Cornell a believable person. She slouches about the stage, is difficult to hear, does 101 little tricks that can only be described as cute. You have always had the most wonderful gift of charm and spontaneity and a complete lack of contrivance. In *Lovers and Friends* I could not feel that.' Dodie thanked him for the first honest and constructive criticism she had had.

A. J. Cronin, too, wrote to report that there were eight curtains the night he went, and that 'You ought to be a proud, proud wumman, ye wee, and clever wee, thing!' The critics 'don't know what vintage wines are, only hard liquor in snootfuls or snorts or whatever they call them. They cannot bear a drawing-room comedy with no machine-guns or gangsters on view.' This made Dodie wonder what she and Cronin would write about in future. Reviews of the film of *Dear Octopus* (which Esther McCracken had faithfully adapted, with a cast including Margaret Lockwood, Michael Wilding, Celia Johnson, Roland Culver, and Athene Seyler) referred to 'the stinking rich'. She wrote to Cronin: 'Do we all have to write about workers of the world uniting now?'

Van Druten returned to them all smiles, after his dazzling notices for *Turtle*. Dodie wondered if she might have been more cheered if he had flopped, 'for misery does love company, and playwrights become more envious than they know'. There were no more mentions of plagiarism for the moment, however, and van Druten reminded her that the lines from *Dear Octopus* —

BELLE: Nicholas — and not married or anything?
NICHOLAS: I don't know what you mean by 'or anything'

were 'a direct steal' from his earlier play *There's Always Juliet*; he had improved upon the same joke in *Turtle*:

SALLY: Were you engaged, or anything?
JACK: We were engaged, and *everything*.

'I do not propose to sue you,' he told Dodie.

Van Druten had brought them the record of *Oklahoma!*, the hit of the season, and constantly sang 'I've got a wonderful feeling everything's goin' my way'. To Dodie's credit she did not find this irritating. Van Druten was earning around $7000 a week, and the film rights of *Turtle* had been sold for half a million dollars. Isherwood joined them all for the Christmas turkey and brought

The Screwtape Letters, three Merediths, the new Raymond Chandler and a Frank Sinatra record as a 'horror present'. Having Chris there, said Dodie, made everything seem an adventure. Dodie, surrounded by all this male warmth, was still nagged by frustration and despair and homesickness. She wrote a poem:

Nothing in this lovely land
Seems to make me understand.
Mountain ocean flower tree,
Only as through glass I see.
Nothing enters into me.

Isherwood kindly said this was beautiful; van Druten more truthfully said it didn't make sense. But then, she reflected, the *Four Quartets* didn't make sense to him either. After Christmas, Dodie began manic note-writing, another substitute for creativity. At speed she wrote fifty pages entitled 'In Search . . . ', the search being for a 'new' kind of play, which would convey its meaning on a deeper level than realism. It later struck her as 'a fairly crazy piece of writing by someone I no longer know'. Though she left Alec to look after all business matters (such as the sale to Warner Bros of *Autumn Crocus* film rights for $20,000) and had no domestic work to do, she never seemed to have time to get any new work done. 'What curse is on me about time? Alec's desk is always piled high with work: his trouble is, he is so painstaking, a thorough worker but a fairly slow one. If he hurries too much he gets irritable.' It was typical of Alec that when Paramount wanted to hire the Rolls-Royce for a film, for a sum amounting to a month's rent, Alec polished it until it was dazzling — too dazzling for the cameras, so it had to be dulled down on the set. He blamed others for inefficiency; but, Dodie pointed out, the world could scarcely get along if everyone took as much trouble as he did over everything. 'I think my lack of time is caught from Alec for I don't remember its being so bad in my early days before Alec became my manager — with a view to leaving me more time to work in!' Paradoxically, Alec's very presence in the house seemed to make writing more difficult for her. She could almost feel the peace in the air when he went out. And he seemed to feel the same way about her.

'I suppose the constant exchange of ideas between us depletes us. We can even read better if we are quite alone. Yet I don't like it if he is out of the house for more than a few hours. I fear I may have lost my ability to enjoy solitude.' She had discussed with Isherwood the idea of choosing not to marry. They observed Miss Hickson with her spinsterly ways: 'her own little luncheon tray, her own dog, her own garden'. Dodie recognised elements in her own character that might enjoy such autonomy. She had told Charlie that if she had ever had a child she would prefer it to be illegitimate, 'because then it would be all mine'. 'I think I can only manage marriage because Alec and I like a certain amount of privacy, though he is a much better sharer than I am. On the whole I'd rather give than share.'

As she listened to the reports of the Allied invasion of Europe — never in the presence of Alec, whose response was very different from hers — she found it all quite thrilling. It nagged at her that her letters home might arrive simultaneously with German bombs. To make light of the war, while in England, would be brave; to make light of it from California looked merely callous. She ached to share D-Day so that she could write a Britain-at-war play. How would she know how England felt after the war, if she could not be there? 'One must know if England swings to the right or left, for one thing. And oh, one needs to be there, to feel it in one's bones, not just to read about it.' She could envisage the flood of happy relief she would feel at being back in England but she really did fear that opprobrium would be heaped upon them when they returned. She could not forget that she had selflessly left England for Alec's beliefs, to come to this 'meaningless' place. She was reminded of a line from Henry James's *The Immortal Hour*: 'There is no backward way for such as I . . . No, there is none. What I have lost, I have lost . . . and one will not trace that bit of pattern in the carpet for many years.' Dodie became extremely fond of this carpet metaphor, and used it often. But she told herself briskly to stop this 'soul-shrimping', and get *on*.

She heard from May Whitty that Noël Coward had said Dodie might have written a really great play had she stayed in England, 'which harrowed me rather'. Van Druten agreed it was 'very trying' of Noël to say such a thing. 'I still think I could have written something pretty good, just about people's everyday courage. When I read cheap English papers like the *Daily Mirror* and see pictures of little working girls, girls in the services etc., I find myself quite dazed with envy, sometimes.' To compound this feeling Ambrose Heal, in his letter dated 4.4.44 ('now isn't that neat?'), sent an *Observer* review of Esther McCracken's *No Medals*, in which the reviewer suggested that it was just what Dodie might have written, if she had been around: 'Miss Smith would have splashed cosily about in the domestic troubles of the wartime housewife; Miss McCracken has picked up her mantle.' 'She's very welcome,' responded Dodie to AH. 'I have no desire to write that sort of domestic stuff again, I am trying very hard to grow up as a writer before I grow old as a woman.'

'Worse than homesickness is the knowledge that I have really missed the war in England now, and that even if some miracle took me home tomorrow, it would be too late.' Batters's three-year silence had left Dodie ravenous for the telling detail of everyday life. Ambrose Heal sent a facetious article from *Punch* about food parcels, which seemed to Dodie utterly unfunny. 'So possibly I shall never again be able to make the British people laugh.'

In 1944, three years after her last letter, Batters suddenly wrote again, all contrition. Dodie sent a cable at once ('there is no need to talk of forgiveness') and at last felt she could start work on her Britain-at-war play, drawing on Batters's experiences. It was called *The Sofa and the Window*, 'just a nice little thing with one set, a few characters and lots of comedy' set in a decaying Elizabethan manor house in Suffolk, where the grand-daughter, Sarah Hampden-Hidden, brings home her touchy working-class cockney lover, Albert, whom she has met in the fire service, to meet the family. For Sarah and Albert she drew heavily on Batters's punctilious accounts — 22 pages of single-spaced typing — of life in the watch room where she had observed a deb named 'Cav Ben', Barbara Cavendish-Bentinck, being courted by a humble footman from Marlborough House.

The set had a semi-circular bay window overlooking a country estate, and a sprawling old sofa; the sofa and the window were to symbolise the two kinds of people there would be after the war: 'on the sofa, those still burying their faces in the past; at the window, those ready to face out to a new kind of future'. The play's theme was creeping Socialism, and the prospect of inevitable changes in society after the war: 'Communism, Socialism, we're definitely in for something of that sort, aren't we?' 'But it'll be gradual. A sort of inching in of a drab grey tide.'

As an analysis of war's effect on society it has nothing like the power of Priestley's *Time and the Conways*. The picture of wartime Britain evoked by Dodie at second hand, rings false: 'It's in the towns that it's so ugly. Oh, Elliot, the women's faces, the cheap makeup. The rudeness in the shops and the shoddy goods. The drabness, the peeling houses, the cracked china and nowhere feeling really clean. I could write a poem — "these I have hated".' 'Were you in London during the Blitz?' 'No.' 'God, that sky was wonderful . . . ' and so on.

She sent it to Binkie marking the laughs with an X in the margin: one of the Xs comes at the point where someone says, 'Is the motor of the pump out of order again?' and receives the reply, 'I fear it's definitely retired for the duration.' But its fatal flaw is a total lack of conviction in the character and dialogue of the proletarian Albert: if Dodie had ever been familiar with the rhythm of cockney speech, she had plainly forgotten it.

She sent her play to Sir Ambrose, who received it while lying on a sofa in the window of a hotel in Lyme Regis, having crocked his knee while hopping on a bus.

She gave it to van Druten who found it dull, depressing, and unoriginal. But at least it meant resuming contact with Binkie, who had not written to her since 1940, when their friendship had suddenly and mysteriously dried up.

In the first year of the war he had written to her euphorically about the joys of life at The Barretts, its garden a riot of lupins and delphiniums, marigolds and goldenrod and sweet peas. Finchingfield was the only place in England, he said, that still looked exactly as it did before the war. His mother, who lived at The Barretts while he went only at weekends, had become quite a land girl, growing enough walnuts, apples, blackberries and plums (500lb) to feed half Essex, and having the cottage distempered and scrubbed and prettied up. Binkie himself had dug out all the plants to allow mains water to be laid, and then planted six dozen rose trees. Soldiers would call for baths and meals (his mother, he said, was all too sociable and some locals were 'oh dear! rather boresome'), the inglenook fireplace was the perfect air-raid shelter, and they had four cats. Their small theatrical colony, with Johnny Gielgud, and Gwen, and Diana Wynyard, was flourishing.

But suddenly there had been a misunderstanding over payment of the rates. Dodie had intended to pay them, but it was left to Binkie. One marvels that he should object to paying rates, when he was enjoying this rural retreat rent-free, but for whatever reason his letters stopped, and the silence lasted until 1944. Suddenly, Binkie wrote to tell Dodie that Terence Rattigan was offering to buy The Barretts for £3000. Dodie replied cordially that, after consulting several people, they could not consider selling for under £5000. It is notable that Dodie barely mentions The Barretts in the wartime journals; her nostalgia was only for London. Binkie now brought her up to date with gossip: Peggy Ashcroft had had a baby, the Lunts were enjoying capacity audiences at the Aldwych, Bea Lillie was magnificent in *Staff Dance* with Robert Morley. Dodie was thrilled to have his letter, and immediately sent him *Sofa*, certain that it was the play he had been waiting for from her.

Eventually he replied, telling Dodie her play would be 'wrong for the mood of the moment' — it was April 1945 — since the war seemed about to end. Dodie was desolate, or as she said to Binkie 'a little wistful' that he hadn't put it on while the country was swinging to the left: 'It might have been the one play to reflect the trend of the times. Now it will always look as if I was wise after the event.' The quarrel with Binkie was never truly repaired; two decades later, the director Frith Banbury told Binkie how hurt Dodie still was, 'and Binkie, who was an elephant who never forgot, shook his head and said, "It's no good".'

Isherwood was still a dependable Sunday visitor. He inscribed a copy of his *Prater Violet* to Alec and Dodie and the dogs, 'those great philosophers who have achieved the Truly Organised Life after extraordinary austerities in following the little-known path of Dalmatian Yoga, from their friend and worst disciple, Christopher: this little token of affection and gratitude for the sobering east wind of their criticism and the eternal summer of their kindness.' Dodie was confident enough of his friendship to make him, with van Druten, her joint literary executor. Christopher had now left the ashram — he was 'fed up, sick and tired of hearing them yacking about God' — and was working for Warner Bros on Wilkie Collins's *The Woman in White*. He shared none of Dodie's longing to get back to Britain: he associated England with too many hated people, starting with his old headmaster Geoffrey Fisher who was now Archbishop of Canterbury. He despised Stanley Baldwin and he hated the exile of the Duke of Windsor: 'all childish reasons,' said Dodie, 'for a man of Christopher's intelligence.'

So Isherwood and Dodie would spend Sunday afternoon on the patio 'gazing down on the view which seemed to float in a golden haze making us feel that neither it, nor we, were quite real. Alec shared in our conversation but not, I fancy, in the sense of unreality in which Chris and I encouraged each other. We both of us liked to feel we were on "the edge of otherness".' She never tired of seeing Isherwood, though she gradually decided he was less 'sunnily good' than he had been when still in the Temple, and she disapproved of some of his failings — which derived largely from sweetness of character, and a habit of loving too easily — more than Alec did, who tended to shrug and say 'Chris is Chris.' Isherwood told her every writer was in danger of becoming a megalomaniac, and of feeling superior to other people: 'As a writer, as a creator, don't you feel rather arrogant, don't you say to yourself, I can write, none of these people around me can?' Dodie denied feeling any such thing; she spent more time feeling furious with herself because she could not express things better, or find greater things to express; she always wanted to do better next time . . . 'Ah,' said Christopher disbelievingly, 'a high state of spiritual advancement.' But it was true. Perhaps, she reflected, she *should* feel more arrogance and confidence. 'Humility doesn't go with art, which is in some ways a form of vanity itself. And I'm not really too bloody humble.' This at least was frank. The tone of her thousands of words of self-analysis in the journals is far from humble.

They were moving house again. They considered Rudolph Valentino's, John Barrymore's, and one that had belonged to 'fun-loving Mamie Boomhanger' (who had been murdered, and left a house filled with trophies). They settled on Anatole Litvak's house, at 19139 Roosevelt Highway, Las Tunas, on the way to Malibu. It had a bedsitting room with a vast desk, the only one Dodie ever found big enough, and a playroom for the dogs at beach level, and quarters for Ruth and Eric, the Scandinavian help. It was modern, simple and expensive, with an Utrillo and a Dufy on the walls, and chestnut leather furniture. Dodie was happier in this house than at any time since coming to America but she continued to listen to accounts of the Allied invasion of Germany and thought, as she wandered through the dawn light, of women getting up in England to go to factories. How would she have stood up to all that? She only knew that if she had her time again she would have chosen to be there, where her roots and all her nourishment were. Nothing would give back those seven years when she should have belonged to England. She could not write in America because her heart did not want to. Van Druten did not have this problem, she decided, because 'he has the same superficial intensity that is inherent in the American character. His emotion and theirs are intense on the surface, as children's often are.' (He had said to Chris, 'What a pity Dodie can't get to like Americans,' and Chris had replied, 'Has she ever met one?') The journal soothed her conscience, for life was gloriously comfortable, with walks along the shore (not bathing, as the Pacific rollers knocked her over), reading Proust, Henry James, Ivy Compton-Burnett, playing Verdi's Requiem very loud, walking shoeless at midnight; living in slacks by day and a kaftan, or what the Americans called a 'hostess gown', for evening. Charlie was right: Hollywood was a beachcombing life. Alec had found that he could fish from the sun-porch when the tide was in. Much of her journal was taken up with 'the ever-fascinating behaviour of three deliriously happy dogs'. And most satisfyingly of all, she had gone back to her novel, *I Capture the Castle*.

10

Capturing the Castle

'**I** WRITE this sitting in the kitchen sink . . . ' The first words of *I Capture the Castle* rank with 'Last night I dreamt I went to Manderley again' among the most striking and quoted first lines in modern British fiction. 'What a marvellously Dodiesque opening,' wrote Ambrose Heal, when she sent him the finished book.

As early as 1943, Dodie had shown the first chapters to her Hollywood agents, and MGM invited her to discuss it as a film. But they wanted her to dictate the rest of the plot to a secretary — 'slightly difficult, as I had forgotten the rest' — and she shelved it the following year to write *The Sofa and the Window*. To fill in time while awaiting the call from Binkie about *Sofa* — which never came — she sat down, on 27 February 1945, to write the novel which is unquestionably her masterpiece, the only one with all the qualities of imagination, originality, exuberance and convincing character-creation that had been lacking in her work since she arrived in America. It summoned up a spirit of England and Englishness that can only have erupted from the recesses of her memory, six years into her exile. At first, she doubted whether she still had the 'wow' for the story. She was nearly forty-nine. Might she have grown up too much as a writer to assume the naivety of her seventeen-year-old journal-keeping heroine? She re-read the chapters written in 1943 — and found the wow *was* there. So, at Anatole Litvak's huge desk in front of tall windows open to the Pacific Ocean and the endless blue sky, she set to work.

(She kept a book called *Eastern England* to hand, to remind her of the Essex countryside. As Miss MacQueen in *Sofa* had said, remembering a period spent in Canada: 'The sudden sight of even a map of England would bring tears to my eyes. A picture of an English lane on a calendar would upset me for the day. I don't think anyone who hasn't lived in exile could know what I went through.')

Told simply, the tale of *I Capture the Castle* is romantic: two young sisters live in penury in a house built into the ruins of a castle with their exotic stepmother Topaz and their difficult, eccentric father Mortmain, who once had a *succès fou* (and *d'estime*) with an experimental novel, but now has a bad case of writer's block. ('We have been poor for five years now.') Into their lives arrive two half-American brothers who own the castle, and the boys' American mother. Predictably perhaps, the girls will fall in love with the brothers. But there is nothing predictable about the course of events, nor the endearing, characterful and lively style of Cassandra's observations. The *dramatis personae* are original and oddly convincing, in particular Topaz, an artist's model who wafts about, naked under her mac, communing with nature.

Dodie's notebook — several hundred pages on the writing of *I Capture the Castle*, reflecting her attention to every detail — shows that Cassandra was originally called Sophia. But one factor remained constant: Cassandra was, in most respects, pure Dodie. Nowhere is Cassandra more Dodie-ish than when she writes: 'I have never felt happier in my life. Perhaps it is because I have satisfied my creative urge . . . or it may be the thought of eggs for tea.'

She took the romantic picture of a childhood in a castle from the vivid autobiography of Margot Asquith, who had once walked arm in arm with Dodie around the toy department of Heal's saying indiscreet things about Lloyd George. The Tennant girls — Margot and her sister Laura — were self-willed, passionate, bold and fierce, possessed of beauty, temperament and impulse. They grew up 'children of the heather' at remote and turreted Glen, their baronial home in the Highlands. 'I remember nothing unhappy of my glorious youth except the violence of our family quarrels,' Margot wrote. She and Laura had walked on the turrets by moonlight, shared a night nursery/sitting room, kept their clothes hanging in a tower, read ghost stories and argued all night by candlelight: 'We were wild children, left to ourselves.' On several occasions the same men proposed to both of them — significant in view of what happens to Cassandra and Rose. The Tennant girls were considered 'fast' as they received people in their bedroom, but a family friend, Godfrey Webb, told them that 'people who were easily shocked were like women who sell stale pastry in cathedral towns, and he advised us to take no notice whatever.' In Cassandra and Rose, Dodie created an impoverished middle-class version of the Tennant sisters.

She approached her plot as if it were historical research. The action took place in 1934. Mortmain, the girls' author father, was now forty-eight, having published *Jacob Wrestling* — an equally important but slighter work than *Ulysses* (1922) — in the early 1920s, and having been lionised in America for it. His ego had been swollen by the lionising; but Joyce had gone further along his own lines, cutting the next rung of the ladder from under his feet. After a spell of imprisonment (for attacking his wife)

Mortmain had felt ridiculed, and had withdrawn more and more from life — hence living in this isolated castle, to avoid neighbours. But his creative powers were moribund, as he felt his progress was blocked by the work of writers like Joyce. With the arrival of the American family, the Cottons, Topaz would sense a cooling from Mortmain in his fascination with Mrs Cotton, 'the highly intelligent but exhausting and too talkative type of American'. She would captivate Mortmain, 'who is starved of flattery, so that one can really feel he might leave Topaz'. But should Dodie mention *Ulysses* at all? Would naming a real modern work in a piece of fiction be like sticking a snapshot in the middle of a watercolour?

In her notebook she kept a detailed record of all such doubts. The London Fox-Cottons — the Americans' cousins — she could see very clearly: they would be 'arty, Chelsea, Bloomsbury, phoneys in a way'. But how to keep minor characters like the girls' younger brother Thomas, the schoolmistress Miss Marcy, the dog and the cat, 'in play'? Stephen, the orphaned farmhand who moons over Cassandra, was a problem character who fought his way into more importance than she had first intended. And how could Simon and Cassandra's names be found in the register of the inn, without implying a physical love affair between them — and how acceptable would that be in a story told by such a young heroine? 'But then Cassandra is fully grown and at seventeen knows all the facts of life — and doesn't, as she says, think much of them.' Just like Dodie herself. Although she claimed to be embarrassed to identify herself so completely with a seventeen-year-old girl, she knew that therein lay the book's real claim to be 'in some tiny way, a work of art'.

What makes Cassandra so beguiling is that although precious and whimsical at times (garlanding herself with wild-flowers on Midsummer Day) she is also sharp: of Stephen's good looks, she notes that he is 'fair and noble looking, but his expression is just a trifle daft'. Her exquisite sister, 'a pinkish person who looks particularly fetching by firelight' whose candle reposes on a chest of drawers painted to imitate marble 'but looking more like bacon,' is a constant target for Cassandra's waspish barbs. Rose's ensnaring behaviour towards the richer brother makes Cassandra write: 'There were moments when my deep and loving pity for her merged into a deep desire to kick her fairly hard.'

The fulfilment of hopes, and arrival of longed-for money in the family, Cassandra discovers, 'brings no kind of feeling'. 'I wonder if there isn't a catch about having plenty of money. Does it eventually take the pleasure out of things . . . It does seem to me that the climate of richness must always be a little dulling to the senses.' It certainly changes Rose enough to turn Cassandra spiteful: 'Oh go and sit in your bathroom and count your peach-coloured towels.' Cassandra is no Pollyanna: when the school-mistress Miss Marcy suggests she might read to old folks in the evenings, she stares at her with astonishment, having decided that 'I don't believe the villagers like good works being done to them'. The vicar perceptively defines Cassandra as 'the insidious type, Jane Eyre with a touch of Becky Sharp. A thoroughly dangerous girl'.

At times as she wrote Dodie became depressed and hopelessly stuck; her handwriting would then deteriorate into illegibility. The death of Hitler was announced on 2 May 1945, the eve of Dodie's forty-ninth birthday. In the ensuing week, when the European war reached its end — the very thing she had longed for — she found herself with a terrifying case of writer's nerves. 'My inner ear — that faculty for hearing every word spoken in my head before I write it — suddenly went out of gear; or it became impossible to pull it out of gear because it never stopped, morning or night. It worked while I was writing, reading and even sleeping. Always I heard words battering at me, trying to form their own satisfactory sentences. I became obsessed by rhythm. I have always fussed about the balance of my writing but in a very amateur way. Only recently has it dawned on me that every word of a novel ought to be as carefully balanced as every speech in a play. Since then, life has been quite nightmarish. I found I was trying to impose on sentences the rhythm of poetry. I heard every word said with exaggerated accents. Moreover I couldn't get any relaxation in reading because my ear listened to the rhythm of everything I read and I couldn't take in the sense. And nights have been almost more exhausting than the days for I dreamed in words as well as happenings.'

So when Charlie Brackett rang at the end of May to ask her to do two weeks' work at Paramount on improving the dialogue in *To Each His Own*, she seized the chance of a refreshing rest from the novel, and a cheering $4000, which would pay eight months' rent. Six days a week of working nine till seven on the film, with an hour's driving each way, had the effect of removing her novel — in which she had reached Chapter XI — completely from her mind. It was 'the Paramount parachute; following the Hess parachute'.

After that, there was a new problem. The Swedish couple who kept house for them announced they were leaving in six weeks' time: Ruth, already worn out by too many guests, threw a tantrum about catering for someone so rich as van Druten who had been invited for lunch. Ruth and Eric, who had previously worked for Katharine Hepburn and had many tales to tell, had hitherto been 'bliss'. Only to van Druten did Dodie ever confide the recurring drama of the domestic help problem: 'One so often gets to *hate* them; and it's a dreadful thing to share a house with someone one hates.'

She stared blankly at the page in front of her. No further ideas came. It was a struggle to get back to the scene where Cassandra lets Stephen kiss her, and to the misery of Stephen's unrequited love, and Cassandra's for Simon. In any case, were the half-American brothers believable? And was Cassandra too facetious? Should Cassandra fall in love with Stephen after all? Could Dodie get away with leaving the ending unfinished, unsettled? She had been told that doubtful endings were unpopular. Should Simon actually propose to Cassandra? Didn't the entire story, even though the characters seemed vividly alive to her, have 'a curious unreality'?

Despite such nagging doubts, whenever she opened her manuscript at random she found it better than expected, so she toiled on. 'Well, well, I must get on with it. This handwriting looks as if I am disintegrating, mentally and physically.'

On Tuesday 8 September 1945 she wrote the last words of the last chapter, 'none too happily' as the ending was not at all as she had expected it to be. Just the day before, maddeningly, she had read a review by Edmund Wilson of a novel by André Malraux called *La Lutte avec l'ange* — which was the same title, after all, as *Jacob Wrestling*! God knew she did not consider herself in the same line of country as Malraux, but Mortmain *was* meant to be in that league ... On the whole she thought she had written a charming and amusing book, but had she been mistaken to mix a girlish love story with the story of an author of Joycean calibre? Would people think she had based Mortmain on Sanger in Margaret Kennedy's *The Constant Nymph*? 'One oughtn't to try to draw genius, even the conventional unconventional kind,' she scolded herself. 'And I fear I haven't brought off my American characters at all.'

The great consolation was that even at the end, she still liked Rose ('my usual, "difficult" girl: beautiful, rather violent') and Topaz, and Stephen; and Neil wasn't bad. 'It's Simon who is so shadowy.' The whole work seemed to represent the last fling of an exuberant adolescent spirit she had not realised was still within her. 'Damn it, there are times when it reminds me of *Our Hearts Were Young and Gay* — a book I loathed. Of course that did sell over a million copies.' And best of all, she still loved Cassandra, and the book stands or falls by Cassandra, who is sharp and decidedly funny. When Rose declares she will earn some money — 'If necessary I shall go on the streets' — it is Cassandra who tells her she couldn't go on the streets in the depths of Suffolk. Cassandra's 'Noble deeds and hot baths are the best cure for depression' is almost as familiar as Sydney Smith's advice on the same lines. But my own favourite exchange is the one between Cassandra and Simon, when Cassandra is beginning to realise that she and Simon have a literary rapport that Rose cannot possibly share with her fiancé:

CASSANDRA: Let's see, what could Chesterton's dog Quoodle smell? Water and stone and dew and thunder . . .
SIMON: And Sunday morning — he was so right about that having a smell of its own. Oh it is so amicable being with someone who knows this . . .

There, surely, is Dodie herself: surrounded by close friends who read the same things, and enjoyed literary cross-references. It cemented their friendship, for instance, when she discovered that both she and van Druten had once read, and never forgotten, a wonderfully awful Ella Wheeler Wilcox poem, 'The Duet', about 'Maud, my wife and the tenor McKey'. Van Druten knew it by heart.

On 15 September she gloomily started her revisions. She decided the whole book lacked form, and it would take her four days just to revise six pages. A whole year later, she was still spending nine weeks revising the 34-page chapter set on Mid-summer Eve. And everything conspired against her getting on with it: Charlie, who was in high spirits, having just won, with Billy Wilder, an Oscar for *The Lost Weekend* starring Ray Milland, was pressing her to help with a film called *Alice Sit-By-The-Fire*, which she did, for several well-paid months.

She also stopped work completely to move house, as the owners wanted the house back. Isherwood and his friend Billy Caskey, who had been living in the chauffeur's room at the side of the house for the summer, had gone off to Morocco. But revising *I Capture the Castle* dominated the whole of 1946, her fiftieth year. She moved the date of the action from 1934 to 1935, and made notes from the Paramount archives of all the events of that year. It was the Jubilee year of King George V and Queen Mary, so she would have to mention the London street decorations. She got stuck again and again at the page mentioning James Joyce. The concentration of effort caused blood to rush to her head; she would type each page over and over until she felt quite dizzy. Meanwhile her psychological scrutiny of each character and his motives continued. Her analysis of Mortmain and his writer's block, for instance, is like a psychiatric or even neurological case study. Once again Dodie was proving the truth of Sheridan's 'easy writing's vile hard reading', or rather its converse, easy reading always involves extremely hard writing. A novel, she decided, was at least four times as much work as a play.

Somehow she had time that summer to write to Aldous Huxley giving him detailed advice on a hypothetical play. But she could not make a chatty correspondent of Huxley as she had of van Druten — who continued to bombard her with his letters almost daily.

What was the appeal of this correspondence, when she was so preoccupied with her first novel? Clearly it was bolstering, to have a fellow playwright with whom to mock other playwrights, for one thing. They used a shorthand expression for works they found boring: it was 'veldt', since Dodie once said she hated plays about the African veldt. When they discussed Orwell, van Druten wrote,

'Yes dear, novels about the lower classes are — and always have been — *veldt* to me too.' Dodie said her veldt was as large as the Veldt. 'It includes sea stories, low life subjects, folk plays; anything dealing with rugged Maine fishermen, Hillbillies, Welsh preachers, Irish peasants — any damn peasants at all.

'I confess, with less shame than I ought, that I really only run happily towards books and plays about fairly sophisticated characters, or I get a slight feeling of depression in the solar plexus.'

She was flattered that van Druten enlisted her help with a title for a new play. If only Americans knew the word 'don', he said, he could use *Coldly Sneers the Don* . . . He was left with *The Ivory Classroom*. 'Oh, Mr van Druten, I 'ate it, I'm sorry but I troofully do,' replied Dodie (borrowing the voice of Miss Blossom from *I Capture the Castle*.) 'What about *The Stone and the Stream*? Have it put up in lights and see if it's any good.' They exchanged views on censorship, immorality in plays, the secret of Coward's comedic sense, whether Maugham would date, why Pip befriended

Magwitch in *Great Expectations*; Jane Austen, Emily Eden, translators of Tolstoy (Maude vs Constance Garnett), Olivier's Hamlet, Rumer Godden, Graham Greene, Rupert Brooke, the music of Debussy and Mahler; and whether J. M. Barrie was homosexual.

Through van Druten Dodie could share a much more sociable and gregarious life, and live vicariously in the world of Broadway. He went to all the New York plays and musicals, and to Gian-Carlo Menotti's new opera; he met Charles Addams the *New Yorker* cartoonist and his slinky black-haired wife, a ringer for Morticia. He had noticed a new writer named Truman Capote: 'I am not prepared to prophesy how *important* a writer he is going to be, but I am staggered by his talent.' He constantly made Dodie laugh: when looking for a new name for a character, he had come across the name of the Governor of Puerto Rico 'who sounds like an American playwright's oath: "Jesus T. Pinero". Isn't that unbelievably delightful?' Dodie never minded van Druten using letters to her as a kind of jotting-pad. Their minds were alike in wanting to preserve their every observation, make links, and share perceptions; and they both had the writer's acute childhood memory, sharing Edwardian references to forgotten sights — cab-runners, crossing-sweepers, lamplighters, knife-grinders, hatboxes, modesty-slips — without boring each other. It was pleasant, too, for van Druten to burble inconsequentially to Dodie about his cats, Clancy (which resembled Eliot's tabby Jennyanydots) and Pyewacket. To Dodie he could show off about how his work was going (*'Bell, Book and Candle* has one good scene anyway — the best I've ever written') or about how clever he had been: 'I made a remark the other day which had a sort of Emersonian simplicity about it, and which haunts me as a theme for meditation. One of those obvious simple truths. A man I know was complaining of someone else's lack of integrity and said, "I do at least ask of people — To thine own self be true." And I — to excuse the accused man, who is an unhappy and insecure weakling — replied, "Yes, but you have to be awfully sure of what your own self is before you can be true to it." I still think that rather good.'

Dodie's tolerance towards van Druten at this stage was almost infinite. They included Isherwood in the tripartite correspondence, watching each other's reviews, ready to pounce, and she loved being the pivot of these gay men's exchanges. Van Druten was 'astonished' by the good reviews for Isherwood's *Prater Violet*: 'Did *you* see all that in it? Did Chris *mean* all that?' In turn, when *The Mermaids Singing* swiftly came off, Isherwood told Dodie he thought 'a flop would be good for John's soul'.

'Forster is on his way to California,' wrote Isherwood. 'Auden is getting quite fat, and has switched to a girlfriend! He is rather shy and cagey about her.'

'Apparently jealousy between Starkey and Carter is beginning to rear its delightful head,' Isherwood also reported, of van Druten's two lovers. 'Johnny was very demure about this. But I don't know why I'm being so catty! I've no call to be, for actually my own life could hardly be nicer. I have Caskey, the apartment, lots of new clothes, and am working, and dinner (which Bill is just fixing) smells delicious . . . Also, I am in a state of rude health, due to my new hobby, a gymnasium run by a cross-eyed Swiss called Joe Pilates . . . ' ('Darling Chris,' wrote Dodie, '*must* you have your chest expanded three and a half inches?')

But there were now other interruptions in her life as, with the end of the war, English friends began to travel to America. Murray Macdonald, who had directed *Touch Wood*, was the first friend to fly in to Los Angeles, and they went to meet him: it was Dodie's first visit to an airport. She felt it was 'a vision of the future', but she never flew in an aircraft herself. Dismayingly, Murray told her she would not like Britain any more; the theatre had lost its glamour, and she would be an exile from the past. As she wrote to Ambrose Heal, the British already seemed to 'miss' the war now it was over; it had given an excitement and zest to life which was now gone. Dodie wept when Murray left, newly conscious of the pitiless Californian sunshine, and the hideous Los Angeles streets — and the fact that she had no real excuse to be there any more.

In January 1947 Phyllis Morris arrived to stay for three months. She had invited herself, hoping to get work in films, and offering to housekeep for Dodie; the war, she said, had taught her to become 'heavily domesticated — but I am sure that in your lovely house there is no drudgery'. Isherwood, van Druten and Charlie watched with amusement to see how Dodie would manage another woman in her life (but they all rallied round Phyllis, whom they liked, with flowers and opera outings and offers of apartments). Dodie dreaded her arrival: they had never managed to live peaceably together as girls, so how could they now, in this small house? And indeed Phyllis, having arrived in a preposterous black bonnet with a bright pink feather, proved 'a most restless, unhappy guest', who talked herself into a state of indignation, with Dodie and with life in general.

She accused Dodie of vegetating 'out here at the end of the world with no friends' all because of those stupid, vicious, ruinous dogs — 'I've told all our friends that I'm going to put a bomb under you' — and what did she mean by writing a *novel*? Alec was frequently driven out of the room in exasperation. Dodie could no longer work without the quiet evenings to which she was accustomed, when Phyllis invariably wanted to talk. Eventually Phyllis, whom they had introduced to Charlie and various Hollywood agents, was given a part in a Hitchcock movie playing a housekeeper, and moved into van Druten's Chateau Marmont apartment. 'Just listen to the glorious silence,' said Alec. 'We are always happiest,' wrote Dodie, 'to be on our own.'

Meanwhile there were sixty Christmas parcels to send off, and a time-wasting offer from George Cukor at MGM: $35,000 for a finished script — money they suddenly needed badly, but it would have consumed five months. She was experiencing the rushes of blood to the head again. She turned down the film, and revived her Christian Science reading. Charlie came back with another offer, this time one she could not refuse: $16,000 for a film treatment of Henry

James's *Portrait of a Lady*, intended as a vehicle for Olivia de Havilland. On 12 May 1947, she started re-reading the 900–page novel, a favourite of hers but quite different when read as a duty: 'It was a hellish job. I never liked one less, or worked harder.' What with her devotion to Henry James, her sleeplessness, and her new habit of rewriting every paragraph six times — she kept every draft — she thought she would go crazy. She finished it in seven horrendous weeks. The one consolation was that Christopher, now staying with his mother in Cheshire, sent her two of Henry James's letters he had found, addressed to one of Christopher's relations: Dodie was greatly touched.

William Douglas-Home wrote to her from the Hirsel, the Homes' family seat. She had written to him sympathetically when he was imprisoned for insubordinaion, having refused, as a tank commander, to carry out an order that he considered an act of murder during the battle for Le Havre. He was now out of prison and wondering whether to continue on the stage or go into politics. 'What do you advise? As a profession I

Dodie's father,
Ernest Walter Smith.

Her mother, Ella, in 1911,
after her second marriage.

A Furber family wedding at Kingston House,
Manchester, 1903. *Left to right* Grandima, Uncle Harold,
Dodie as bridesmaid, Aunt Bertha, Uncle Bertie Slater,
Aunt Madge and her husband, Uncle Eddie, Dodie's
mother, Uncle Arthur.

Dodie's favourite photograph of herself, at twenty-five.

'Bud' (Leonard Paul) Duval Dodie's Canadian admirer.

Three Arts Club Fancy Dress Ball, with Dodie *centre front* showing her legs.

Above left Portrait of Dodie Smith as successful young playwright, 1932.

Inset above Ambrose Heal, Dodie's employer at Heal & Son, whom she was determined to 'collect'.

Left Fay Compton and Francis Lederer in the first production of *Autumn Crocus* at the Lyric Theatre, 1931.
(Mander & Mitchenson Theatre Collection)

Felix Irwin, Angela Baddeley and John Gielgud *right* in the first productioin of *Dear Octopus*, 1938.

Phyllis Morris with Dodie, Alec Beesley and Pongo at The Barretts, Finchingfield, Essex, 1934.

(Mander & Mitchenson Theatre Collection)

Left Alec with Dandy at Malibu Beach, California, during the war.
(Jon Wynne-Tyson)

Above John van Druten, Dodie's friend and rival.
(Mander & Mitchenson Theatre Collection)

Folly with some of her fifteen puppies.

Christopher Isherwood *right* with Dodie and Alec in California on Christmas Day, 1945.

Two of Dodie's sketches for *I Capture the Castle* with Miss Blossom, the dressmaker's dummy, in the bedroom, *right*.

Above left Janet and Anne Grahame-Johnstone who illustrated the first edition of *The Hundred and One Dalmatians*.
(Anne Grahame-Johnstone)

Inset above One of the Grahame-Johnstone twins' drawings of Pongo and Perdita.
(Anne Grahame-Johnstone)

Left Dalmatian pups from the Disney film version, *101 Dalmatians*. *(© Disney)*

The Barretts in full bloom, with Alec, Dodie, a Dalmatian and some of their many pigeons.

Dodie at ninety with Charley the last Dalmatian, photographed by Jane Bown in 1986. *(Jane Bown)*

hate acting, but for six months or so, I rather like it — and do you think it would necessarily militate against one's future as a Premier? After all, Mr Disraeli was a cheap-jack novelist — or do you think like Mr Sheridan I should stick to the reputable profession of playwright?' Dodie replied: 'Are you never going to act any more, dear William? Will you play a part if I write it?' and gave him advice about playwriting: 'Characters who are forced to tell the wrong story are like dogs who are taken the wrong walk. They stage a sit-down strike.' She advised him to write notes on each character and plot development, 'as Henry James did'.

She told Ambrose Heal she was living in a state of suspended animation, not knowing what England was feeling any more. She could not write for an American audience: 'I can only write about things that are in my bones, and America just ain't.' (W. A. Darlington, the *Telegraph* critic, said 1947 – 8 was a low point in an undistinguished theatrical decade: 'There are few subjects the contemporary dramatist can tackle without either pretending the war did not happen, which would be absurd, or by bringing the war in, which is not likely to be popular.')

On Monday 4 August 1947 she handed the finished *I Capture the Castle* to Alec, with trepidation. He rarely liked novels, and they both felt 'typescripts of novels are curiously repelling — particularly bad ones, full of spelling mistakes' (though Dodie was an almost perfect speller). After one day Alec told her he was enjoying it; a day later he finished it, 'wildly enthusiastic'. He had the same sensation as when reading his favourite novels, Elizabeth Taylor's *Palladian* (which had been published the previous year, also with a heroine named Cassandra), and Nancy Mitford's *The Pursuit of Love*. Alec was a hopeless liar; Dodie would have known if he was not sincere, so she could now relax. Except, of course, that Alec produced fifty foolscap pages of suggestions. He questioned the book's topography. He said Dodie had not succeeded in making the reader feel the weight of the castle's *stones*. He felt the dog, a bull terrier, had no physical presence. He greatly disliked

Miss Blossom, the imaginary barmaid type with whom the sisters conduct cockney conversations ('I find her a little hot-making myself,' said Dodie, 'but I think her value outweighs this and anyway, I can't remove her') and he said there were too many sunrises, and too much *mist*.

Did Alec's painstaking and pernickety involvement irritate her? Apparently not. But it was hard sometimes to keep her own ear true, and to maintain the trick of catching Cassandra's idiosyncrasies, and her literary background, while satisfying Alec's desire for clarity. They spent a fortnight going through the book page by page, in three sessions per day, adding commas, changing words like 'jolly' and reading every word of dialogue aloud. Phyllis read it too: she liked it, but she was 'outraged' about Mortmain's book: she had the same reaction as the general public to *Ulysses*. Dodie would somehow have to appease the less highbrow readers, and 'sell' them the idea of Mortmain's enigmatic appeal.

On went the revisions. At the same time she had to write her condolences to

Sir Ambrose Heal whose wife had died. Feeling it almost an impertinence, 'as I knew her so little,' she paid tribute to Lady Heal's unassuming manner. 'She somehow managed to convey, when visiting Heal's, that it was unusually kind of the assistants to serve her and that she really ought not to take up their valuable time. I remember her introducing your children to me and giving the impression that they were almost being presented to royalty. I doubt if there have ever been bosses' wives with that particularly graceful brand of good manners. It seemed to go with her low and very beautiful speaking voice.' Dodie added that she still thought of Sir Ambrose every day of her life, 'morning and evening, and often in between'. Sir Ambrose replied nobly about his wife's 'simple considerate ways, the fine gallant spirit behind that quiet modest demeanour.'

By 5 November Dodie had spent ten gruelling weeks on revision, and felt dazed and ill, near to breakdown, from the exhaustion and rushes of blood to the head. These would arrive, out of sheer dread, every time she was ready to start work, and every time she was in difficulties, dozens of times a day. She would lie in bed in the morning, her heart racing at the very thought of work. And she would wake in the night fearing death — not for its own sake, but because her book wasn't finished. 'Never, never have I suffered so over any piece of work. Sometimes I would spend two hours without getting one short paragraph of revision right. And always I was dogged by the fear that my creative powers were fading for good, that I should never be able to write anything else in the future.' But she wrote to van Druten's actor friend Starkey (Walter Starcke, who had written sweetly to her after coming to stay, and had, like all her friends' boyfriends, been charmed by her) that she hoped soon to toss off a few plays in record time: 'Theatre is so much shorter and — to me — easier than novels.'

No play had ever consumed as much time and thought. Dodie even began to see in her novel an allegorical quality — the English characters trying to get money and material aid from the Americans, Mortmain being revived in spirits by contact with the Americans. This slightly worried her because, since the war, hatred between the two countries seemed to be growing. Did Rose seem rapacious for financial rescue from the American family, like England's own greed for America's support? Also, Alec wanted her to 'pin the story to reality' by mentioning other famous works of innovation in the text: Picasso's, or Beethoven's last quartets. Finally she agreed to mention Henry James 'as a talisman'. Joyce and Proust, she said, were the real begetters of this novel: 'strange forefathers for a book whose content may strike some people as suitable for Peg's Paper!' Already the typists, Mr and Mrs Massey, had told her it was 'superb material for a film' and in their enthusiasm had actually mistyped 'Greensleeves' as 'Screen Sleeves'.

And yet, a week after the book had been sent to the Masseys, all her misery faded. Was it like the pain of childbirth receding from memory? She was still tired, and still suffering the rushes of blood (which may have been menopausal; she was now fifty-one); but she began to think of new plots for plays, and increasingly of the possibility of returning to England. Binkie wrote to say that The Barretts was looking enchanting: he had had all the woodwork painted, and yet promised she would find it exactly as she left it.

Both Isherwood and van Druten had gone back to Britain and reported enthusiastically that they suffered no hostility for their wartime exile. Van Druten assured her there was 'none of the "deserter" business, not even from the *Horizon* gang'. Isherwood reported that England was 'straight out of a Hollywood film. Winding lanes and hedges. A two lane highway is called a dual carriageway, and there are things called roundabouts.' He was staying with his energetic seventy-eight-year-old mother at icy Wybersiegh Hall, near Stockport in Cheshire, snow all around outside 'and the gas fire shrunk to a dim arctic glow on the horizon'. His old nanny was now an ancient crone sitting by the kitchen range being waited on; his younger brother seemed old, withdrawn, pathetic and odd. Isherwood tried to fascinate them all with tales of American life, retiring to his room when exhausted to wallow in old photographs, books, manuscripts.

He found England socially and politically much to his liking: the Labour government was 'really doing and planning *marvels*'. He might even stay and write theatre criticism: 'Mr van Druten's great play triumphed over every obstacle, even Miss Sullavan's performance . . . ' 'Dodie darling,' he added valedictorily, 'I can never thank you and Alec enough for all your kindness to me during these years, and the haven you provided for all my crises, problems and escapades.' Nonsense, Dodie wrote back on what would normally be 'Chrisday', i.e. Sunday, it was he who had made all the difference to *their* lives. Van Druten too missed her. 'Dodie dear,' he wrote from England in June 1947, 'I feel these letters are taking the place of my morning calls. But they are strangely lonely and one-sided, a bit like masturbation. (The simile breaks down, I realise, since *you* share them with me).'

Van Druten, like Isherwood, wrote enthusiastically: of 'castles, churches deeply embosomed in trees, much greener than I remembered'; potted shrimps, underdone cold roast beef, salad served on crescent shaped plates, Heinz salad cream, stewed fruit served in silver bowls; politeness in the bank; 'war-damaged houses that look like Miss Havisham's, blackened and scarred with twisted girders and roofs open to the sky'. Dodie devoured all this with a mixture of anguish and amusement. 'So the Atlantic wasn't Lethe! Someone has come back to tell us about life after death!'

In March of that year Dodie received a letter from England that shocked and grieved her. Aunt Blanche Guthrie — really her grandmother's cousin, but her dearest 'Aunt' — had died at eighty-four, and in harrowing circumstances. She had been sitting by the fire writing a letter to Dodie, when she fell forwards, her head against the grate. All her beautiful silver hair had been burnt off, and she died that night. Dodie could not rid her mind of the image of Aunt Blanche's last agony in the fire, and her calling out to the

God she worshipped. She remembered her childhood visits to Aunt Blanche in London, and their going on the great suffragette procession together. It was Aunt Blanche who would bring Dodie a ten shilling note every Christmas at Heal's, and she had been so excited and proud at Dodie's first nights, when she would wear Dodie's mother's scarf, so she seemed to represent her. Of all her family, Blanche had written the most amusingly, with shrewd comments and an appetite for life. She had relations on three continents and often visited them: only the outbreak of the Second World War had prevented her, at seventy-eight, from going halfway round the world to see an eclipse of the sun. Even her last letter, in a firm large legible hand, was full of vitality, mentioning that she had taken a large party to see the film of *Dear Octopus*. That her last thoughts should have been of Dodie, and that she should fall so suddenly from a happy, busy life to excruciating pain and death, seemed too horrific and unfair.

Their first step towards getting back to England was to leave California, in a new green DeSoto station wagon, for Netherby Farmhouse in Pennsylvania — 3,000 miles nearer home. And at least they would be able to do some theatre-going again: it was eight years since they had seen a play.

On Twelfth Night 1948, Stanley Salmen, of Little, Brown the Boston publishers, telephoned. He had received the manuscript of *Castle* the previous Friday, read it over the weekend and was enthusiastic — but he wanted her to cut it from its present 145,000 words. Ruffled, Dodie asked for the manuscript back, with the result that, despite bitter weather, Salmen turned up in person on their doorstep, agreeing to publish it in full. One thing he would not agree to, however, was anonymous publication, which Dodie had fancifully requested. (The original typescript read 'I Capture the Castle by Cassandra Mortmain'.) They told her it would be impossible to rouse interest in such a book; the personality of an author was a vital commodity nowadays. So she capitulated; and spent six months designing charming endpapers, still used today, little sketches of the high-raftered castle kitchen, of the girls' candlelit bedroom with four-poster; and of Belmotte mound.

She tried to warn herself that it might, after all, be received as the merest of light novels. She would find that hard to bear, after so much work. Alec had read the manuscript a dozen times, and the proofs four times. He even made a clay model of the castle so that Dodie could draw from it, cleaned her sketches, and sharpened every pencil a dozen times a day. More importantly, 'His critical sense is amazing. No inexact word gets past him, no trick of over-writing, no cumbrous sentence. He doesn't over-persuade me to make changes. He just points out the faults and leaves it to me. In nine cases out of ten I come round to his way of thinking. And he has been wonderfully good and patient: his faith in the book has buoyed me up again and again. I wanted to dedicate it to him but he wouldn't let me — he thinks dedications are embarrassing, a little cheap; and I rather agree with him. But I here and now do dedicate the book to him.'

When the Literary Guild ordered 550,000 copies, Dodie was dismayed: they were lower-brow than the Book of the Month Club, and known to do 'bosom books' (what would now be called bodice-rippers, with well-endowed women on the cover). But they would pay her a $42,000 advance. Dodie always had a Micawberish theory that if one behaved extravagantly, 'supply' of funds would turn up, and this was a classic example of 'supply' landing when it was needed, just when they had made the expensive move to Pennsylvania where there was no lucrative film work for Dodie.

The cuts demanded by the Literary Guild were curious. They did not care for the line 'We doubt if the vicar's wife exists who father could stand.' They did however make one wise suggestion, that Cassandra should act a little more kindly to Stephen. Alec agreed on this point. So Dodie added just two lines, satisfying everyone, about Cassandra intending to be kinder to him (though she firmly retained the phrase 'in a determinedly sisterly way'). And she was relieved to be allowed to keep the ending ambivalent:

she wanted readers to finish the book hoping that Cassandra would marry Simon. Astonishingly, the Guild said they would have preferred Cassandra to marry the humble Stephen. 'I see,' she wrote in her journal, 'how dangerous to the integrity of the author these book clubs are.'

She was happier than she had been for years. 'This really is happiness: notice it, will you?' she told her journal. Having her first novel accepted was surely as good as having her first play performed, and the advance of $5,000 from Little, Brown, and $42,000 from the book club, would keep them going for several years. But she already doubted that she could ever write anything as fresh or amusing again.

11

'His Majesty's is Still There'

IN the week of the publication of *I Capture the Castle* in October 1948, she took up her novel notebook again, just to record John van Druten's opinion of it. He had read the novel in seven hours, accompanied by hot buttered toast. 'But he made it abundantly clear that he considered the book little better than trash. (He also considered *Jane Eyre* trash; I am well content with such company, above my station though it is.) He even managed to make his enjoyment of it sound insulting — as if he felt a little ashamed of it.

'When I asked point blank if he found the book funny, he said he could see where the laughs came, but wasn't much amused. No, he didn't find Cassandra interesting — not as well done as my Ann in *Call It A Day*. The only character he liked was Topaz. The others he considered flat and conventional. Again and again he came back to his gleeful leitmotif: that he was *surprised* that I, with my "extended interests" — he meant my recently acquired fondness for James, Proust and T. S. Eliot, none of whom he liked, so he resented me liking them — should waste three years on something so *unimportant.*'

One can understand Dodie's fury, that her friend and confidant should so cruelly stress the book's lightness and ignore its virtues. It contrasted notably with her own kid-glove treatment of van Druten whenever he showed her his plays 'on which he has usually spent all of three weeks'. Alec and Phyllis managed to laugh at van Druten's remarks, saying 'What did you expect?' but Dodie was racked with anxiety that her novel might be, after all, too trivial.

She need not have worried: nearly half a century later new readers are still discovering the novel, and old readers rediscovering it, with a sense of enchantment. On 20 October 1948, *I Capture the Castle* was published, with the 40,000 first print run already subscribed by booksellers. Dodie was charmed to handle the finished copies, with her own illustrations. But compared to the first night of a play, the lack of focused excitement filled her with flat dismay. The crude adverts ('This is the novel that starts in the kitchen sink' . . .), the brevity of the reviews . . . the fact that she was suddenly invited, as an author, to review other novelists' work ('dog should not eat dog, and especially, new dogs should not eat long-established dogs') made her 'ill with rage and disappointment'.

But two reactions to the novel were particularly gratifying. She had sent it to Ambrose Heal, apologising that it might not be at all his cup of tea. He replied that he had revelled in it, and went into the kind of detailed appreciation authors adore. He couldn't swallow the farcical bear hunt scene. But he liked the music, the religion, and the Vicar with his madeira, so pleasant and wise. 'Where have you learnt about all this? I enjoyed it all — very much *you*, all of it. Like I enjoy good sherry and crumbly biscuits, crumbs and all.' The character he had really adored was Topaz. 'She reminds me a lot of someone I used to know. I wonder if you know who that was?' Dodie herself, of course.

(Dodie, in turn, took care to write rapturously of Ambrose Heal's own books: she had examined the finely engraved illustrations in *The Signboards of Old London Shops* with a magnifying glass; then re-read it to the accompaniment of Handel's Concerti Grossi, 'which seemed appropriate'.)

The other thrilling reaction was Isherwood's. His last letter had confessed he was 'drinking too much and committing indiscretions' and exhausting his guardian angels, while he was writing a screenplay of Dostoevsky's *The Gambler*, living in a squalid hotel in Santa Monica. Then he had gone to South America with Caskey, so he was away when the book came out. When he returned, Dodie sent him the novel, telling him lightly that her book was 'a little piece for *Peg's Paper*, written with a care that would not have disgraced Flaubert'. He was not to feel that he had to be kind: 'I am sure that nothing you say will hurt me.' When his response came, it proved to be infinitely the most cheering: 'To say "I couldn't put it down" is hardly original, but true . . . Your tremendous strength is detail. It is like really good carving; the more you look at it, the more you see . . . ' He loved the religious bits, he was charmed and moved by the locking up of Father in the tower: he felt that at times he had only just escaped being locked up by Dodie himself. '*Jacob Wrestling* and the work in progress are two of the really convincing books in all literature.' He liked Neil better than Simon and rather hoped Cassandra would get Stephen '(but perhaps he would have been a bore — a bit like Stewart Granger'.) He loved Dodie's drawings; 'I think it is a book that will be very much lived in by many people; because you can live inside it, like Dickens.'

Dodie read this letter a dozen times; it was 'manna in an arid desert', she told him. 'For as you have obviously guessed, no critics seem likely to find anything in the book beyond a rather extra-funny, lightweight, sentimental story . . . You can imagine how your letter has helped me.' And to her relief van Druten wrote again, still surprised that it had turned out to be 'that kind of book', 'coming from you, with all your newer and extended interests, and after spending so long on it', but having spent a whole evening discussing it with a very drunk Isherwood — 'glassy-eyed, fix-stared, with very deliberate diction, but perfectly coherent and extremely intelligent, just talking too loud and a little too ponderously . . . '

'Oh Dodie, dear,' he wrote, 'do you really need praise? I could go on giving it to you for ever . . . But you really will have to get out and about a bit more . . . There are so many people just waiting to see you to burst into paeans, I know.' He needed to see her and so did Starkey ('He is almost jealously anxious to share everything I do . . . but also he does like you both so much, regarding it as a huge privilege to know you.') Eight pages of this flannel, including much hypochondria about pains in his legs, caused Dodie to reply by return, eight more pages ('typing at fever speed'). 'Well, the correspondence is certainly back on top of its form!' She told him firmly why the book mattered to her so much, and why van Druten should keep his criticisms to himself. 'Perhaps you think I'm making mountains out of a very childish molehill. But it ain't no molehill to me. I *love* my book, and I think it is a very *original* book — and so does everyone else but yourself who has read it. Grrrh!' As for his aches and pains, they were just nerves and cramps, said Dodie briskly: and if he was feeling a bit broke, well, 'it's the karma backwash of your great success.' But please would he be a pal and not tell anyone about her book? 'Oh Johnnie, Johnnie, you are a terrible TELLER!'

Incorrigibly, van Druten replied, twenty minutes after receiving her letter, with another eight pages, about his sexual obsessions ('Just occasionally I get visions of myself in my sexual moments that rather humiliate me with the visual picture of what I must look like'), about Huxley ('has a sick mind and — like Hamlet — has had bad dreams. I wonder if he is perhaps fundamentally homosexual, and unconsciously resents normal intercourse?'), and about whether Rupert Brooke was offensive when he wrote (in his sonnet 'Lust'): 'Your mouth so lying was ' most heaven in view/ And your remembered smell most agony.' This letter was followed by yet another the following day, still concerned that he might have said anything to harm the reputation of Dodie's novel. 'Oh dear, it's an awful situation . . . Oh Dodie, I feel the termites are at our friendship . . . Love and distress, John.'

That Dodie's need for his approval outweighed her inevitable irritation is clear: van Druten and Starcke arrived on Christmas Eve, just after his E. F. Benson play, *Make Way for Lucia*, had opened to poor notices. Shortly afterwards, hankering for sunshine, Dodie and Alec drove across to California once more, to take again the Balderston house in Cove Way, Beverly Hills, lately vacated (with its upholstery wrecked by cats) by James Mason. They agreed to refurbish it — 'spending money has always had a therapeutic effect on me', said Dodie — because *Castle* was now published by William Heinemann in Britain in

April 1949, to enthusiastic reviews: George Malcolm Thomson referred to Dodie's 'pert command of the artful-artless' and George W. Bishop in the *Telegraph* found the book 'rich in clean sentiment as an English spring is full of blossom'. It sold 57,000 in two months, and sat at the top of the *Sunday Times* bestseller list.

Just after Christmas, Isherwood wrote to tell Dodie that Denny Fouts was dead, of drugs or drink in Rome: 'Now I wish with all my heart that we could be back in Entrada Drive, even with the little boys and the scandals and all the fights included.' Dodie replied that she had 'mentally drawn the line' under Denny after learning of his 'peculiar tastes' (for little boys) but now she felt one never ought to draw any line, with people one liked, and she had liked Denny, who was 'like a sweet, loving, wicked child'. (What she really objected to about Denny Fouts was his neglect of his dog Trotsky.)

Dodie, infinitely happier than she had been in the same house ten years before, still longed to go home. A playwright friend named Warren Chetham-Strode,

who had just written *By Bread Alone*,
wrote from Chelsea in April 1949
pertinently guessing that she was staying
away from England only because she
was afraid of the reception she and
Alec would get. But, he said, nobody
had pilloried or shunned Huxley when
he came back. 'In time of war we
accept the genuine pacifist. And when
war is over we forget, with the most
amazing rapidity, what people did or
thought. Most of the present Cabinet
were conscientious objectors in the First
World War.' Anyway, he adds, theatre
people are such success snobs, they will
be at Dodie's feet for having caused a
truly great stir with her first novel.

Her little white cottage was waiting,
Warren wrote, and so was the good Essex
earth, and the dogs would soon get over
their quarantine, and she surely must
have enough money. 'Are you crying
yet? I rather hope you are. You see,
I felt that probably no one had written
to you like this — so I thought I
would dare to. Your work is needed
here. *You* are needed here.' Warren
had even investigated kennels for her,

visiting one near Great Dunmow in the pouring rain and reporting that the dogs looked perfectly happy. He also gave her a thoughtful résumé of how the welfare state had changed England. 'The spirit of getting something for nothing engendered by our interpretation of Socialism is creating a mean type of mind, a mind far more selfish in the mass than it ever was in pre-war days. And restrictions of all kinds — some quite unnecessary — have put mild dishonesty into the forefront of our daily lives ... The daily scrounge, the petty double-crossing are, I regret, having their moral effect on the children. And worst perhaps of all, is the replacement of a love of adventure and its necessary courage, by a demand for security beyond all margin of common sense.' (Ironically this analysis sounds almost identical to that applied by many commentators to the effects of the Thatcher years on society forty years later.)

Dodie suffered real anguish over having missed the war and its aftermath. She felt that only by winning British hearts with a new play could she assuage the unhappiness and guilt of her American exile. By August 1949, she was reading religious books — Evelyn Underhill, C. S. Lewis, Dorothy L. Sayers — and keeping a notebook of her spiritual progress, as she had with *Castle*. The setting for her new play, *Esmeralda and the Cloth*, was Thaxted, where Dodie had spent that weekend at the Noels' vicarage in 1915. The main character, a newly-ordained country vicar, had been evolving in her head ever since. In the play he meets a London dressmaker, Esmeralda. He thinks that making seventy-guinea frocks in the austere, rationed post-war world, is immoral. She thinks his religion is mumbo-jumbo. He is fixed on celibacy, but they fall in love. Dodie was happy with this play: 'There was a good deal of comedy, and a happy atmosphere; I was hopeful.'

She had good reason to be, because *Esmeralda* is charming. The opening scene features another of Dodie's sharp pubescent girls: 'Funny to see you without your dog-collar,' she says to the vicar. 'You've seen me without it countless times,' says he. She: 'Yes, but not since you were a dog.' Esmeralda is an original character, whose genius as a couturier is somehow believable, and whose enthusiastic embrace of Suffolk village life is the reverse of Dodie's. (She agrees to talk to the Women's Institute, and makes an instant dress for the fattest woman there, who has a 48-inch waist.) The subplot features a village girl who gets pregnant, a theme treated with Dodie-ish permissiveness. It is mentioned that 64 per cent of babies are now conceived out of wedlock, and there is a comment from the girl that would have had Tory cabinet ministers of the 1990s spinning: 'Nowadays, you can't count it against a man so much when he won't marry a girl. He knows the Government'll take care of her.' The evangelical theme, too, is prescient of the 1990s: 'The Church of England is right back on a missionary basis,' the vicar tells Esmeralda, 'and I'm a very new broom.' As with *Castle* it is striking that Dodie could so accurately reflect English country life, after eleven years of exile. Murray Macdonald, when he came out to California again, read *Esmeralda* and said he wanted to do it with Binkie. Binkie cabled 'yes'. He still had a mighty grip on the fortunes of the West End theatre and his patronage was essential.

Meanwhile she was doing a little lucrative Hollywood work on *The Mating Game*, spending lavish amounts of 'therapeutic' money, and dining on her terrace alongside bougainvillaea, jacaranda and hibiscus. She caught bees from the pool and revived them in a bee-cage. She also rescued sundry cats, dogs, and an opossum with an injured leg. One night a collie dog with a fish-hook embedded in its mouth scratched at their door: Alec gently released the fish-hook. They told van Druten about it, who said: 'You are the most extraordinary couple. I have rarely known you to show affection for human beings, but I'm quite sure that if three goats and two bees knocked on your door in the small hours, you'd get up and let them in.' Alec said, 'Well of course.' Dodie said: 'What happened to the third goat's bee?'

They watched the filming of *Sunset Boulevard*, invited by Charlie to see Gloria Swanson shoot William Holden.

At Christmas came Charlie (and grandson Tigger), Isherwood and Caskey, as well as Phyllis, who was now doing so well in movies she was driving herself around in a Chevrolet coupé. They met Michael Wilding and Marlene Dietrich (who ignored Dodie) and Irene Selznick, who was working with van Druten on his *Bell, Book and Candle*, in which Rex Harrison and Lilli Palmer were to star. Van Druten went off to New York for the opening, while Dodie struggled with *Esmeralda*'s third act. She also began work on *Letter From Paris*, a play based on Henry James's short story, *The Reverberator*, about a patrician family's horror of the muck-raking press, and finished it in two months.

All that year Isherwood had been exhaustively discussing his new novel *The World in the Evening* with Alec and Dodie, but he became quite ill with the struggle over it. The main character was a homosexual doctor: 'I always liked your idea of treating homosexuality that way,' wrote Dodie, 'bringing it in as only one facet of the story, instead of blowing trumpets and saying, "Make way for the great daring novel".' But he wrote (28 March 1949): 'Dearest Dodie, Sudden despair! It is all so awful and false and bogus. This wretched rat of a Stephen and all these boring people, and the lack of movement, and the slowness, and the sort of grim-lipped Americanoid wry humor. What am I to do? I feel there is something integrally wrong. Stephen is neither objective nor subjective enough. I long for a *plot*. I wish to God I didn't have so much happening before the book opens. I wish — I wish —

'This is the real dark night of the soul, and I can only appeal to your insight. Don't just wince at this rubbish, try to see *why* it's so bad, and tell me. When you and Alec have read it, I'll come up, if I may, and talk. It is no use our discussing this any longer on the basis of what I would *like* to have done; you have to know the worst . . .' In another letter: 'You may yet save my sanity, health, wealth and art by your prudent and calming presence. Otherwise I fear it may be going to be one of my mad summers.'

Both Alec and Dodie were concerned

that Isherwood should make some money. One day, popping his head out of the swimming pool, Alec said to van Druten: 'If only Christopher would make a play out of Sally Bowles's story in *Goodbye to Berlin*.' He could not have foreseen in what manner this idea would eventually become a play, and — as *Cabaret* — a musical and a film that would make plenty of money for their friend. Van Druten, typically, seized the idea himself, went off to the Chateau Marmont and finished the play *I Am A Camera*, based on Sally Bowles's story, in ten days. He arranged a contract, giving 75 per cent of earnings to himself and 25 per cent to Isherwood, from which he refused to budge, writing bitter letters which proved to Dodie that van Druten had always been jealous of Christopher's literary reputation and was all the more rapacious about money to compensate for his own lack of repute.

At the end of 1949, something happened that really delighted her. The postman arrived on his motor-scooter delivering the London *Sunday Times* which, then as now, ran a Christmas feature called

Books of the Year in which celebrities named their favourite reading. There, at the end of the alphabetical list, was the composer Ralph Vaughan Williams and his nomination: *I Capture the Castle*. So this man who (for her) personified England, and England's music, and all that she was exiled from and nostalgic for, admired her first attempt at a novel — a novel which had kept her emotions and imagination all fixed firmly on England! She seized her Yard-o-led pencil and drafted a long, painstaking reply. First, she set the scene: California, the sunny garden, the mimosa, the bougainvillaea etc. She considered him the greatest of living composers, 'as great as many of the greatest dead'. There could be no greater honour, she told him, than his mention of her work.

His music filled her with 'the same feeling that I have about London, the English countryside, the past of England, Purcell and Shakespeare. It is a little like what Cassandra feels when listening to Summer Is Icumen In.' In fact, she had been going to let Cassandra listen to Vaughan Willams's setting of

Rossetti's 'Spring Moon': Rossetti was the favourite poet of her girlhood, and 'Spring Moon' was the first Vaughan Williams composition she had ever heard. Now she loved many of his works; she had been playing his Mass in G Minor only the night before. She carried all the themes of his Symphony in F Minor in her head. 'I wonder if I am making you understand a little how happy I am that my book has given you pleasure?'

Her letter was neither insincere nor exaggerated: she did not generally write in quite this extravagant vein. Dr Vaughan Williams, probably somewhat *bouleversé* by her response, wrote that he was pleased to have 'made friends through a chance remark in a newspaper'. He was glad Cassandra had not listened to 'Spring Moon', because he regarded it as 'one of the sins of my youth'. His own favourite at the time was a song called 'The New Ghost' with words by Fredegond Shove; but few knew it as it was not yet 'gramophoned'. He had never seen Dodie's plays, he confessed, but perhaps one of them might make him an opera? He was always looking out for subjects.

Dodie needed no further encouragement to send him *Autumn Crocus*, her only play of faintly operatic potential. Her friend Isherwood, she name-dropped, had suggested it. The comedy in *Autumn Crocus* had 'dated rather badly', 'but some of the writing in the balcony scene and in the love scene on the mountainside has a certain poetic quality which I never achieved in later and far more expert plays'. And she had, incidentally, thought of a good theme for an opera: a well-intentioned statesman of vision and integrity destroyed by power, proving Lord Acton's dictum 'All power corrupts; absolute power corrupts absolutely'. The idea was too large for a small woman, she said, but it had come to her while listening to Verdi's Requiem Mass. It would have to be written by a major poet — Auden perhaps?

Vaughan Williams duly wrote again; he and his wife had been reading Dodie's play aloud 'with great interest'. Alas for *Autumn Crocus*, among the composer's pet aversions were '1. Austrian mountains; 2. Tyrolean Folk Song and 3. Schumann's Music. So there we are!' On May Day Dodie wrote again, hastening to assure him that she too, despite *Autumn Crocus*, shared his aversion to Tyrolean folk song — she had never heard any when she wrote the play — and to Schumann. But a friendship had been struck, and two years later she invited Vaughan Williams to her next first night. 'Not much use my going nowadays,' he said, 'as I am so deaf; even with every electric gadget in the world' (he had by then an ear trumpet he called his coffee-pot) but he invited her to his birthday concert at the Festival Hall in October that year.

Another penfriendship cheered her: she sent a copy of *I Capture the Castle* to Miss Emily Allen, her old English mistress from Whalley Range High School in Manchester, one of her most important influences, always remembered in the classroom in her pretty mauve dress with 'The Meeting of Dante and Beatrice' in sepia just above her head. She told Miss Allen to note the passage where Cassandra hears through the open windows of the schoolhouse the children singing rounds, just as she once did during Miss Allen's lesson on Langland and Chaucer, 'and I seemed to capture everything together — medieval England, myself at ten, the summers of the past'. Miss Marcy, she added, was not Miss Allen, 'although she is small and nice. It is just the spirit of your teaching which, I like to think, drifts into the book occasionally.' Miss Allen replied that her memories of Dodie's class were equally happy 'but you mustn't forget, Dodie, that youngsters are apt to put haloes on teachers they like. What would happen if we met again? Would the halo drop drunkenly over my left eye, and then fall?'

In 1951 Dodie made her first momentous trip home for twelve years, to arrange the production of *Letter From Paris* and its casting. In all the years of exile she had not been separated from Alec for more than one night. Leaving him behind was like losing part of her brain. They now had 'a companionship so closely interlocked that, separated, we are simply not complete'. Alec brushed her clothes and suede shoes, packed and labelled everything in her luggage, insisted on packing cashmere rugs for warmth, and supplied her with a cheque book which she hadn't had to think about for years.

Before she sailed for London she stopped in New York to see *The King and I* which van Druten had directed, then embarked on the *Queen Mary* with a huge trunk, an old Asprey wardrobe suitcase, two suitcases for clothes, two for stationery, an attaché case, a typewriter, and two boxes of food for presents. Being in London again, staying at Murray Macdonald's house in Chelsea, drew her out of what van Druten called her 'hermititis'. Even when stuck in a train at Clapham Junction in fog, being home made her feel ecstatic. She met old friends — Max Adrian, Basil Dean — went to restaurants, theatres, and the Oliviers' party at Claridge's where she saw Noël Coward, Emlyn Williams, Sybil Thorndike, Peggy Ashcroft, Diana Wynyard, Edith Evans; she met Mary Martin at a party at Gielgud's. She went to the first night of *And So To Bed*, with charming Vivian Ellis music, and forecast that Keith Michell would be a star; and to another grand party at Binkie's on election night. In the Haymarket one day John Gielgud found her standing on the pavement. He loomed near and whispered, 'It's all right, Dodie. His Majesty's is still there.' She had marathon discussions with silken-voiced Binkie until late in the night at his newly acquired pair of houses on Lord North Street (later to become the home of Teresa Gorman MP). He was keen to do *Letter From Paris* — but not *Esmeralda*, as he disliked anything to do with religion. One weekend she and Binkie went to The Barretts together. Dodie was unable to disguise her dismay on seeing the overgrown garden, the paddock a wilderness, the brick path needing repair, the barn needing re-thatching, the cottage itself crammed with Binkie's ornate furniture, out of scale and period.

She went to visit Alec's half-sister Laurien in Buckinghamshire. Another day was spent in Manchester with her cousin Ronnie Reynolds-Jones, now a prosperous insurance broker, his wife Frances and two beautifully-mannered young sons — her closest relations now that all the uncles and aunts had died. She also met Peter Hamilton, vicar of St Mary's in Sale, Manchester, with whom she had had a long correspondence over *Esmeralda*; she saw Diana Wynyard, who graciously turned down the part of Esmeralda, saying she considered herself too old.

She went to see Ambrose Heal at Baylin's Farm, Beaconsfield, which he now shared with his son Anthony and Anthony's wife Theo, who had also worked in Heal's china department. Sir Ambrose, nearing eighty and a widower, annoyed Dodie by referring to Theo's dog as 'the creature'. She felt he was no longer himself now he was removed from Heal's, just as Heal's was no longer itself without him. Yet at this time his letters to her — once formal and distant — became increasingly affectionate and even skittish. 'My dear,' he wrote, 'How perfectly sweet of you. Some day if we live long enough we shall I trust establish a bond of intimacy when you will feel that you can address me without the absurdly ceremonious prefix [Sir].

How can we achieve this much desired consummation? A way must be found for plumbing further depths, but I thought you had already touched bottom? You are still holding back some secret delights? You rouse my curiosity — if that is the polite word for it. I have heard it called something else. What could it have been? Can you remind me? Yours rather stiffly, AH.' For an octogenarian writing to his fifty-five-year-old ex-mistress the style is remarkable for its facetious innuendo.

To her journal Dodie confided her appreciation for Alec's letter-writing. 'It must be seldom that such good love letters have been written by a near middle-aged man to his fully middle-aged wife. He could make the most trivial details of his daily life absorbing; conversations with Chris and Charlie; the garden, even California weather and above all, the three dogs.' He would take them to drive-in movies where they barked at any dog on screen. She was slightly perturbed by one letter from Alec which told how Isherwood brought young male friends to visit him 'no doubt to cheer Alec up. They were apt to get playful and swim about with flowers in their hair — Alec sent colour snapshots — and on one extra playful occasion they threw all our garden furniture into the pool.'

What had actually happened, Don Bachardy explained to me, was that Isherwood was trying to explain to Alec what 'camp' meant. 'And Alec simply couldn't get it. He suddenly got up and threw all the furniture into the pool and said "Is that camp?" and Chris said "No, that's farce".' Incidentally, added Dodie, Isherwood had once said he believed all men had some seeds of homosexuality in them. 'Except Alec,' Isherwood said. 'I somehow can't imagine it ever appealing to him.' Bachardy emphatically concurs.

There was an unforeseen hiccup over *Letter From Paris*. A woman called Mrs Winchester claimed she had already written a play based on Henry James's *The Reverberator*, and by chance her agents too were the London Play Company. But Mrs Winchester 'and her awful play *Scandal Sheet*' were sent packing by Laurence Fitch and there were no further accusations. Laurence had now taken over as Dodie's agent, though she had first to battle over her contract with Dorothea Fassett, her original agent at the London Play Company. 'How I loathe quarrelling with people and feeling that there is someone in the world who is angry with me! But Dorothea went just too far. And she was beastly and insulting to Alec. So exit Dorothea.' Laurence instead became 'a bright star' in Dodie's life.

She sailed back on the *Mauretania*, with a head full of projects, anxieties, and a longing to get back to Alec. English beds and pillows were too hard, and despite warm fires their houses were chilly: 'I think the English like to *see* warmth, but are careful to let it out of the house.' Still, she felt a wave of nostalgic love for England, and wrote lyrically about dogs, St Paul's Cathedral, taxis, buses and mists in parks, and took issue with Phyllis's criticisms: 'She is wrong. People on buses do NOT smell . . . And their faces have noses, not just nose-intentioned blobs, and good bones, and they are, to me, twice as interesting as many quite good-looking American faces.'

In New York on the way home she met a furious ('but still his own dear self') Isherwood. It seemed at this stage that van Druten was planning to give Isherwood no royalties whatever on the printed play of *I Am A Camera* (dedicated 'To Dodie who started the whole thing'). Dodie soothed him, and it was later arranged, after her intervention, that Isherwood would get a two-and-a-half per cent royalty during the play's run. Within a matter of weeks, with capacity takings and Julie Harris superb as Sally Bowles, Isherwood had made $20,000, and, in time, the subsequent musical *Cabaret* gave him a substantial income. Van Druten himself, Dodie guessed, easily made a quarter of a million dollars that year.

Yet she found van Druten grey with worry, nervous and irritable over *I Am A Camera*. Dodie sat up till 2 a.m. in his hotel room, helping him rewrite a scene: van Druten refused to let her order a midnight cup of tea (saying there was no time) and then kept her working another two hours, and was aggrieved when she got up to leave; meanwhile his friend Starkey ordered, and ate, a three-course supper. She ran into Rex Harrison and Lilli Palmer on the escalator at Penn Station, an encounter which made Dodie's day because Rex praised *The Sofa and the Window*, Lilli praised *I Capture the Castle*, and they both asked to read *Esmeralda*.

So she returned happily to Alec, to listen to him reading *The Golden Bowl* aloud. An agent named Jules Goldstone erupted into her life and persuaded RKO to offer $15,000 for a film option on *I Capture the Castle*. ('He is a small middle-aged Jew, not at all well known, and yet he had Howard Hughes himself telephoning me, which Charlie said was unheard-of.') Once more, 'supply' had descended — although RKO never made the film. But where *did* all our money go? asked Dodie. In rents, she supposed. Soon they were back again in New England, at a house in Wilton, Connecticut, and Dodie had a frantic burst of activity: she produced a stage version of *I Capture the Castle* in only two months, and started yet another new play, set in a monastery, which would be 'more original and modern than anything I've ever done'. She had not been so productive for years. She thought it was the stimulation of having dipped back into the London theatrical scene; Alec told her it was because she had stopped letter-writing — in particular, to John van Druten — that lashings of extra energy had been released.

And now in her journal Dodie confronted her grievance against van Druten, even more damaging to their relationship than her taking Isherwood's side over the *I Am A Camera* royalties, or his scathing reaction to *I Capture the Castle*. She had long suspected that van Druten stole ideas from her, although he had been candid when he snatched the theme of his *Turtle* from her *Lovers and Friends*. On their last journey eastward from California to New England, Dodie and Alec stopped at van Druten's ranch at Indio near Palm Springs. Dodie helped him with his new play, and showed him *Esmeralda*. Then when he came to New York to receive an award, he was too busy to visit them, but told Dodie that the play she had advised him on had 'died', and that he was working on another play, of which he would tell them nothing except the title, *I've Got Sixpence*.

Dodie said to Alec: 'John is going to plagiarise *Esmeralda and the Cloth*, and write a religious play. That is why he won't come and see us.' Alec said he had been expecting this, and so had Chris. A week later, van Druten wrote to say he was dashing ahead with what was indeed a religious play, claiming that it was a bit like Eliot's *Four Quartets*. Dodie and Alec drove to Hartford, Connecticut, to see a pre-New York performance and found it 'tough, sordid and disgusting. People around me were groaning audibly with boredom. The story bears no resemblance to my play, but the idea, use of prayer etc., completely derives from *Esmeralda*. John would never have written it but for my play. What is more, the actual idea is one that I mentioned to him.'

Alec was angrier than Dodie had ever seen him. Dodie was furious too; if he had asked her first, she *would* have minded, but would have told him to go ahead. Instead, van Druten was clearly avoiding her. When he eventually came, she told him she thought his play would damage *Esmeralda*'s chances in New York, at which van Druten turned instantly black with annoyance and said that was absurd. Dodie managed to be 'perfectly pleasant' for the rest of his visit, but their old closeness had gone. Dodie realised now how greedy and grasping he was, and began to resent and even to despise him. Alec implored her to end the friendship.

'I hope I shall never do anything at all vengeful, but as a giver-out of useful thoughts I have shut up shop with Johnny. I shall not let him read any play of mine in script form again. He has suddenly ceased to exist for me.' But like Hilda in *Dear Octopus*, she seemed unable to sustain hatred. And gradually their letters, after a period of perfunctory 'Dear Dodie' ones, with no 'Love' at the end, regained their old flavour, full of shared exchanges of views about Salinger, Betjeman, Gide . . .

Isherwood, 'as lovable as ever', returned

once more from England, reporting in letters that young men there were now so highbrow they talked of writers he had never heard of. 'Poor Chris! I don't think he realises this is a sign of middle age in himself. He blames the young; when similar things happen to me I blame the years.' She could not resist telling Isherwood about John's latest plagiarism. Alec did not care if he never saw John again, she said, but 'me, I can't go on feeling angry for long. And if one lets people read one's plays one mustn't grumble if they give people ideas. Still, it has made me feel I must be a bit more cautious where Johnny is concerned. Don't of course let him know I mentioned this to you. He knows how I feel, but I don't intend to show any more resentment. I felt it was wrong to feel so angry, so I meditated a little. And stopped feeling anything at all about him.'

In a telephoned interview with a British newspaper Dodie said she was soon coming back to England to oversee her new play, *Letter From Paris*. She would be on hand for casting and rehearsals 'as I always used to be. I'd like my first play after so many years to be my very best.' And so she sailed back on the *Queen Elizabeth* in June 1952, was met by Phyllis at Southampton, and took a suite in the Ritz with an ornately tiled Alma Tadema-style bathroom. Binkie arrived at the Ritz with two dozen eggs laid by his Finchingfield hens. But the 'maimed feeling' of being separated from Alec was back. His first letter recalled Dodie's 'harrowed' face as they parted on the dock in New York. Her letters to her 'Dearest' and 'Best Beloved' again showed a sweet concern for him, toiling away on her behalf. 'Oh my poor! as Laurence would say,' she wrote. 'Oh, my poor, poor! To think of you typing two whole acts of my play during all that heat! AND writing me long letters! AND looking after yourself while Esther was away!'

Another letter to Alec that September reflects his fussing concern about her clothes, and her almost formal, grand-motherly response. 'Of course, it is a damn nuisance not to have my fur coats as regards smartness ... But please remember that my Saks beige cashmere is a more luxurious coat than most well-to-do women come by in England. People rave over it. And few people dress well now. The lady dresses very well and very simply.' (This was Vivien Leigh, who was being wooed to play Cassandra.) 'But I certainly can't compete with her in smartness and it's no use trying. I will buy something new if I need to. If you join me, I will arrange for you to bring the Kolinsky cape and possibly the Saks suit. I don't want the lamb. I don't want the rough seal and I don't want the ermine. So stop worrying yourself my darling . . . I do appreciate all your neat, well thought out letters.'

She wrote in her journal: 'I reckon it must now be twenty past ten at night in Wilton. Soon Alec will take the dogs out for their last run, with the fireflies dashing about like stars on the loose. Then all three dogs will go to Esther's room for three Friskies each . . . Alec will get himself a drink, then he and Buzz and Dandy will go up to bed.' There would be Schubert's Octet on the gramophone, and the feeding of the tropical fish in the deepening twilight. 'Oh I do hope

I can bring back good news this time. But whatever happens I think we already know we possess the things that matter most.' This entry, when she read it later, seemed to have been written by a gentler, more emotional woman than she remembered herself ever having been.

12

The Woodspurge

LETTER from Paris looked promising. Binkie had assembled a strong cast including Maxine Audley, and a set designer, Oliver Messel, whom Dodie found at first enchanting, later 'utterly pig-headed'. Peter Glenville (son of Shaun Glenville, the pantomime dame, and Dorothy Ward, the idolised principal boy) was to direct, and he too seemed agreeable; 'dresses carelessly', noted Dodie, 'and is apt to have food stains on his clothes.' One of Binkie's favourite new gamines, Brenda Bruce, was to play Francie Dosson, who is supposed to be so ravishingly pretty that a portrait painter might swoon at the sight of her. Dodie had her doubts about this casting, but over dinner she found Miss Bruce 'quite taking'.

Binkie was just about to open a new Noël Coward production, *Quadrille*, with

Alfred Lunt and his wife Lynn Fontanne. Dodie considered herself low in funds despite her choice of the Ritz (Alec had said they must cut down on their lavish Christmas present-giving), and she was astonished to find Binkie buying, as a first night present for Noël, a magnum of brandy; and for the Lunts two Sèvres vases at £50: 'All such presents come off one's income tax, but I was beginning to be bloody doubtful if I should have any income.' (Binkie gave Dodie a modest Pierre Balmain shawl, £8, for her own first night.) On the opening night of *Quadrille*, Dodie, Binkie and his friend John Perry sat frozen-faced while Noël's glittering eyes bored into them. Only by recalling that Noël had kindly blown her a kiss during *Dear Octopus* did Dodie manage to keep her face in a fixed rictus, 'probably looking like the famous Smiling Man whose mouth was gashed into a hideous grin'. John Perry wore a mask, she reported, of agonised boredom.

On her own in London, Dodie again embarked on a round of films, parties and dinners. She rubbed shoulders with

Graham Greene in a squashed taxi; he made the mistake of asking her how he could kill some cats who howled at night. Oliver Messel had a party at his house in Pelham Place, South Kensington, complete with flamenco dancers. 'There are few noises I like less', said Dodie, 'than Spanish stompings and shouts of *¡Olé!*' She saw the film of *The Importance of Being Earnest*, and *South Pacific* with Mary Martin, and reported everything back to Alec in long letters. She went to the first night of *The Innocents*, another Henry James adaptation directed by Peter Glenville, and afterwards he took her to supper with Valerie Hobson: 'ten times prettier off the stage, or off the films, and almost ideal for Esmeralda, if she can act herself in real life.' Miss Hobson was wearing a simple Dior dress that had cost £250, and told Dodie that the couturier Victor Stiebel might do the dresses for Esmeralda 'very cheaply, as an advertisement'.

Dodie's most lyrical letter to Alec that summer brought vividly to life a London she thought had vanished but which was, in 1952, exactly as it had been for a century, except that the girls no longer wore hats. On a June evening, she wandered in luminous summer twilight, 'the sky a woeful soft blue as if lights were behind some blue woollen material', around Leicester Square, waxing reverent about streets with Georgian houses, pubs and little food shops; she had forgotten that people actually still lived in the heart of London. Hundreds of people sat on the steps around Eros: everyone looked happy and she often heard laughter. In St James's Street, the gentlemen's clubs were lit up so one could see 'the glittering crystal chandeliers, the old prints, fine staircases and galleries with ironwork around them'. Near Buckingham Palace, where the palace clock chimed, the light was fading and everything looked 'most amazingly romantic'. The sentries were on duty; there was a smell of hay and horses. Berkeley Square still had its charm, its great sycamores with gnarled trunks, and a few of its old great houses. A kind lady in Curzon Street stopped Dodie and removed a caterpillar from her neck, whereupon they both went in search of geranium leaves for it to eat.

As the production got under way, Glenville revealed to her that Binkie's friend John Perry had felt 'bitter resentment' at Dodie's recent return visit to The Barretts. Apparently it was to do with all the money Binkie had spent. Dodie was speechless: even a modest rent for a country cottage for fourteen years would have cost thousands. Ah, said Glenville: it was being under an obligation to Dodie that made them more resentful. And during the pre-London tour, Dodie and Binkie bickered like an old married couple. In a gloomy Birmingham hotel room which was 'like being inside a brown paper parcel' Dodie called him the Head of the Holy Beaumont Empire, which he rather liked.

Daphne Rye, Binkie's casting director, worked overtime. The young Frenchman cast in the lead was dismissed. Oliver Messel's Danish boyfriend Vagn Reiss Hansen (the rudest man Dodie had ever met, but also one of the funniest) had remarked: 'My dear, he is not only a queer; he is a *very queer* queer.' Then Daphne produced a delightful young man from the Sheffield Repertory Company, Peter Barkworth. Thin and sandy-haired, he read superbly, and was only twenty-three, although Binkie loudly remarked in the boy's earshot that he would 'never see thirty-seven again'. But before he came in at the last minute, the original cast had a fortnight in Manchester, to which Dodie invited her cousins. She met the Reynolds-Jones family at the Midland Hotel, including cousin Ronnie's son Christopher, then fourteen and intensely curious to meet his 'fairy godmother' who had gone off to America in the year he was born, and who had always sent wonderful parcels of chocolates and butter and biscuits. She sat with Christopher in an alcove and asked him to read the local papers' reviews of her play. She said he read beautifully, and asked him particularly what he thought of Brenda Bruce. They dined in the Midland, and he recalls that though Dodie spoke of her mania for animals she consumed two poussins the size of sparrows.

Then she sped back to London for the continuing rehearsals. Her play, she

427

woefully told Glenville's boyfriend Bill Smith, seemed to her 'like something the head girl of a finishing school wrote for the girls to do on Speech Day'. Both scenery and costumes were distracting, excessive: 'overpowering dresses, ludicrous wigs, quacking panatrope'. During the tour, *Autumn Crocus* was revived as a Sunday-night television play, with Phyllis now in the Muriel Aked part. Dodie watched it on a tiny TV set at her hotel. It made her feel oddly sad, anxious for the future, and full of misgivings about returning to London with an adaptation of James instead of something original. At the eleventh hour, Binkie was still begging her to forget about Henry James altogether and turn the play 'into one of your lovely comedies with lots of lovely jokes'.

Meanwhile, Peter Brook was approached to direct the stage version of *I Capture the Castle*, but when he eventually responded, he was not free for the next nine months. 'Damn it,' wrote Alec in one of his furies, 'according to Binkie he had the script over a month ago! They really are BASTARDS.' Vivien Leigh was still first choice for Cassandra, despite the fact that she was, at thirty-nine, a trifle old to play seventeen. But she could look young, she seemed enthusiastic ('Oh please please do let me dress as a bear!') and she had at that time more box office drawing power than Olivier himself. Miss Leigh, said Binkie, had given her word, which was as good as a signed contract; he gave a high-spirited lunch at the Ritz. 'THE LADY HAS SAID YES,' Dodie was able to cable Alec. But a week later the lady panicked: she realised she could never look young enough, and irrevocably backed out. 'She has a will of iron,' Binkie said. He made Miss Leigh tell Dodie herself. She came to the Ritz, gazed beseechingly at Dodie and said: 'I can't do it.' They talked for two hours, while Dodie fixed her eyes on the gilt basket of dying flowers on the table in front of them. 'You do forgive me, don't you?' Vivien said as she got into the lift. 'Oh no,' said Dodie sweetly, 'I shall go on liking you and admiring you, but I shall never forgive you. Because you would have been perfect as Cassandra.' She wouldn't, of course, as Dodie knew.

She might just have achieved a *tour de force* under Larry's tutelage, but he was tied up filming *The Beggar's Opera*. She was an unhappy woman, Dodie decided. And, she consoled herself, perhaps the beautiful star would have been 'a bit of a cope' needing red carpet treatment etc.

Peter Barkworth was switched from understudying to take on the leading role of Gaston Probert in *Letter From Paris*. He seemed to Dodie sweetly provincial and *ingénu*: when taken to the Ivy, he said it was his first visit there. 'One's first visit to the Ivy!' cried Glenville. Dodie also took him to see Coward's *Relative Values*, and Barkworth came back to the Ritz and sat for hours discussing Eliot, Auden and life in general, 'with that rather lost, wild look that used to come into his eyes (I never got to the bottom of that)'.

Then he came down with flu, and was taken in by Oliver Messel and Vagn to be nursed at Pelham Place. This caused ribald remarks throughout the company. 'Barkworth at Pelham Place, eh? *Very* interesting,' said Binkie. Vagn had administered brandy and lavished expensive, rationed food on Barkworth. He had been so solicitous, Barkworth told Dodie: 'You know Vagn's not a man to take no for an answer.' Dodie could not resist saying, 'You alarm me,' at which Barkworth roared with laughter. By degrees, he revealed to Dodie that he was rather shocked by her tolerant attitude to homosexuality. 'Actually,' Dodie added, 'I am sure that both Vagn and Oliver were activated by nothing but kindness.'

Barkworth became identified in Dodie's mind with the young man in the play she was planning, *The Treasures*. 'He is a most unusual boy,' she wrote to Alec. He was well read, he wrote, he composed, he could hum whole phrases from Vaughan Williams symphonies and discuss all manner of poetry: when Dodie said she found little beauty of language in Auden, he proved her wrong by quoting the very poems Isherwood used to recite to her. And yet he still seemed like a boy. He had never eaten an oyster: 'You have to swallow them whole, don't you?' he said nervously. Dodie found him 'a wonderfully useful link with modern youth. What surprises me is that I can find anyone so very young so very unboring. It is so necessary for a writer to keep in sympathy with the young, so I cross-examine him like mad' — even though she did not delude herself that he was at all typical. 'One pleasant change about him,' Dodie added to Alec, 'is that he is quite certainly not homosexual, and I don't think he will stray in that direction. Much as he appreciated the kindness shown to him when he was ill, he was quite a bit embarrassed because Oliver Messel would call him "dear".'

Barkworth was equally fascinated by Dodie. In his memoir *First Houses* (1983) he described the time he spent with the small, white-faced woman with straight dark hair drawn back tightly over her ears. 'Her features were a little too sensual to say she looked like a nun, but there was a withdrawn air about her, as though she was in part thinking about what she was saying, but in part remembering some far-off occurrence which would not leave her.' She was the most peaceful companion he had ever known: she spoke softly and rapidly and kept very still. What he admired about her was that while being compassionate she was also surprisingly tough. 'She stood up for what she wanted and said what she believed in, and wouldn't give an inch when other people made her cross or dispirited.' This made Barkworth reflect on how easily he vacillated or was thrown when people were unpleasant, how he capitulated in his desire to please. 'You should stick to your guns, Peter, when you know you are right,' Dodie told him. 'I admire people who have the courage of their convictions, and don't abandon them just to keep the peace.'

She was in her element again. She would pass the Lyric Theatre and think: 'This is my world, and I am absolutely happy in it.' But Peter Glenville was soon bridling at Dodie's interference. He wrote her a long letter, accusing her of not understanding the etiquette of rehearsals. 'You have a strong instinct to crowd the director at his work. At rehearsals you gradually increased your active participation to the point of addressing the cast from the stalls and on the stage. You followed me about on the stage and off it, so that I had to invent little ruses to escape so that I could think clearly. This is obviously distracting. You sat with me on the stage when I gave notes and expatiated on them. Sometimes you actually stood looking at actors rehearsing on the stage at a distance of three or four feet. This is impossible for all concerned . . . The director, like the conductor, can only perform his job properly when he is the sole interpreter to cast and staff. Changes have to be the sole prerogative of the director. It is unsuitable for the director to have to raise his voice to be heard over the author's.

'Actually, Dodie dear, you are intruding on my active work more than would be normal even for a co-director. I am distracted at having to keep another person's ego fulfilled and latterly have come to dread rehearsals. For some time this double act has been considered a joke in the present cast — a joke which makes us both look a trifle silly.'

Dodie drafted at once a soothing note: 'I shall always look back with joy on our time together.' But she had taken all he said to heart. She caught a cold, the leading lady a cough. On the first night

Miss Bruce tried to cough along with the audience laughter, and by the last scene — according to Dodie — was shedding real tears. 10 October 1952 was an odd, lonely first night for Dodie; her first ever without Alec, or Ambrose. She went with Laurence Fitch, who brought her a tiny silver box in the shape of an envelope with a Paris postmark, in which Dodie later kept her saccharin tablets.

The play failed. The sets were too heavy, fussy and ornate, they created the wrong mood: over-bright and without a hint of Paris about them. They took so long to change, the curtain was down for 52 minutes. 'We took too many curtain calls,' Peter Barkworth later wrote, 'and each time we bowed to the applauding stalls, the boos from the gallery got louder.' Harold Hobson commented that prolonged bowing 'always subjects players to a cruel ordeal'. The cast were thoroughly dispirited as they traipsed back to their dressing rooms and to the first night dinner at the Caprice. Next morning the notices were poor. Barkworth got some kind mentions for being 'agreeable' but it was plain that in his West End début he had not set the world on fire: it was twenty years before he had another leading role in London. Dodie told Barkworth he had been a triumph of acting over wrong casting. As for Brenda Bruce, only when Dodie looked glumly at the press photographs did she realise that Miss Bruce's face was 'somewhat plain and lined' as the heartless Kenneth Tynan, among others, pointed out. Unlucky Miss Bruce, for whom this was supposed to be a great chance, had to endure seeing her face over half a page in the *Evening Standard* next day with the question 'Do you call this a plain face?' 'That part really needed Vivien Leigh and nobody else,' Brenda Bruce says today. 'It was an unhappy episode altogether.' She cheered herself up by playing Peter Pan next. About the play itself, loyal W. A. Darlington said Dodie's skill was unimpaired, and wrote sympathetically about it in the *New York Times*. In a private letter to Dodie, when she wrote to thank him, he said another leading lady would have made all the difference. The *Daily Mail* headline was 'Ordeal to be there'. 'What

Miss Dodie Smith tries to say appears to be that Americans are brash and infantile and only the most sympathetic understanding will allow them even to set foot on the threshold of our ancient civilisation. How she says it is an ordeal for the audience.'

The first night bouquets — there were not enough vases in the Ritz for them all — included spider dahlias to 'dear, *dear* Dodie' from Vivien Leigh, whom Dodie had decided to feel sorry for: 'It can't be much fun to be a Trilby of thirty-nine,' she wrote to Isherwood, 'with a handsome and much sought after Svengali husband.' Looking down towards Berkeley Square from her Ritz room, Dodie thought of Rossetti's lines

From perfect grief there need not be
Wisdom or even memory:
One thing then learnt remains to me, —
The woodspurge has a cup of three.

There was a little darned patch on the Ritz's net curtains which she decided

437

was her woodspurge, as she stared at it so long, deep in thought. She imagined the reader of her journal asking, 'But did it ever occur to her that the play was to blame?' Yes, she said, the play had weaknesses. It was, in Brenda Bruce's view, a wooden piece of work.

But Dodie's old English mistress from Manchester, Miss Emmie Allen, loyally thought Dodie had improved on Henry James. 'In his novels, the characters are seen through a veil, darkly; your play brought them to life, they were more defined. There were some delightful and exciting scenes — the family reunion, the attack on Francie, the last scene. And the whole play moved along so surely without any wanderings down the garden path . . . I still don't understand the critics . . . Does no writer, dramatist or composer take a theme not his own and use it for his creative power? What about Shakespeare?'

To her credit, Dodie managed to put on a metaphorical cork jacket and bob on to the next project. The new choice to play Cassandra was young Dorothy Tutin, full of personality. She had already evolved a complete conception of Cassandra's character. Dodie took to her at once, especially when she endearingly said, 'My hairline's hideous — look!' sweeping back her hair to show it. Again Dodie sat up with Binkie till four in the morning planning the *Castle* tour, while *Letter From Paris* drifted on for just three weeks, to a handful of people and thin applause. The only recompense for Peter Barkworth and for Dodie was their friendship. Dodie was concerned that his first West End play should be a flop, and insisted on giving him twenty pounds when he said he was finding it hard to manage on the twelve pounds a week he was earning.

One night after the play Dodie took Barkworth back to supper in her Ritz sitting room: the first time he had ever eaten so grandly in private, the waiters wheeling in a table, arranging chairs and flicking napkins: hot soup followed by a cold collation, at which point the waiters left, to Barkworth's relief. This must be frightfully expensive, he remarked to Dodie. 'Yes it is quite. I suppose I'm absurdly extravagant, but I love it,' she said. When he asked, she told him it cost seven pounds a night, just for the suite, without food. Barkworth was astonished. She told him how she had once lived over a bakery, to save on heating, and that she had gone to Heal's for thirteen pounds a month. 'I think money should be fun,' she advised him. 'Even when I was very poor, when there was no unemployment pay, I used to enjoy working out what I could afford. I tried never to stint on clothes. I would always wear what I thought was appropriate for meeting people . . . You should never throw anything away. Actors should have large wardrobes: if it's a modern play it's much better to wear your own things; hired things rarely look lived in.' Barkworth told her that in Sheffield he had saved a pound a week. 'That's the way to do it,' said Dodie, 'and it's fun. It gives even missing a meal a purpose.'

But she became wistful when Barkworth said he had expected her to be a sort of Esther McCracken. She told him she had written McCracken's type of play, before McCracken. 'And she drifted into silence again,' he said in *First Houses*, 'thinking of her past successes, comparing them with the play we were both so heavily involved in. "Ah well," she said.'

She packed her trunk to go home, and Laurence arrived to help her with the bags. Dodie was painfully conscious that her failure with this play was a financial blow to him. Alone with quiet thoughts on the SS *America*, she found that not even the prospect of seeing Alec again could take the weight off the disappointment she was bringing home. It had been the worst half year since the threat of the draft board ten years before. She sat down to catch up with her journal and wrote 80,000 words, the length of a full sized novel; she wished to God she had written a novel instead. No wonder she had a callus on her middle finger. She had written fifty letters too, including a marathon epistle to Isherwood, who had reached page 100 of *The World in the Evening* and had begged for a postcard as a life-sign. He was seeing the Huxleys, and Gielgud, but 'without you there is nobody I can discuss things with, and no place where I really relax.'

She was wretched about all that work wasted. She had written to Barkworth, asking him to say frankly what the cast had felt about the director. His reply, which came by return, was like the opening of a floodgate. The cast had been in despair: fussed and worried, and yet given nothing helpful, just fidgety movements. Basil Dean wrote to her that the play just 'did not hold our interest in these revolutionary times. British audiences are less easily moved now, because of all their wartime experiences, than in the days when you and I were having our big successes together.' 'Its failure was sad and puzzling,' Dodie wrote three years later to a BBC producer, Mary Hope Allen, who was putting it on radio. 'Or perhaps not so very puzzling. Most people thought it was under-cast and over-decorated. No doubt there were faults in the writing too.'

When she arrived in New York to be met by Alec — who was now, she realised as if for the first time, quite silver-haired — she talked incessantly about her four months in England. Plainly, they had to leave America and come home for good.

America was killing her work; and they had to get back while they could still afford the move. Earning money was now a matter of urgency. She became engrossed in *The Treasures*, and after finishing the first draft forced herself to revise her strange play set in an Austrian monastery, *That Which Hath Been*. She could not bring herself to write much about those last months in America. She confessed that she had never been as frank as she meant to be in the journal, and now felt it was better to leave a gap altogether than adopt that old insincere brightness of tone. Her memory remained so tenacious that whenever she read over the past she always knew when there were undercurrents of misery beneath breezy entries. Yet Alec, who had read bits of her journal while she was away, said he found it 'so sad he could not bear to go on.' Dodie was distressed that he had read any of it, although there was nothing secret from him. She had asked him to read her draft autobiography: but he accidentally read the journal instead, happening upon the Malibu period when she was writing

I Capture the Castle, feeling ill and obsessed with the fear that she might die before finishing it.

√ In Wilton, Connecticut, they had their dreariest American Christmas ever. No friends came. The underlying anxiety about the future may have been the reason Alec became ill. He spent days watching sport and old English films on television (they had finally bought their first TV set, ostensibly for the maid). Binkie came to New York and arrived to spend a day with them, but Dodie suspected he would shelve *I Capture the Castle* for want of a leading lady, now that Tutin was tied up in Graham Greene's *The Living Room*. An ice storm left them without light or heat for five days; their priority was keeping Alec's tropical fish alive with hot water bottles, but they had plenty of wood for fires, and they cooked by gas. The monastery play progressed abominably. Alec disliked it comprehensively: 'he disliked the story, the writing, everything'. He could not understand the metaphysical element of the hauntings; and for the first time he could give no advice or help. Dodie had the horrible conviction that the failure of *Letter* had destroyed her husband's hitherto unshakeable faith in her powers. And in his illness — some kind of chill on the spine — he proved unnursable, wanting only to be alone. Dodie had never felt so utterly alone herself. 'Alec was just not there, as far as I was concerned. Perhaps it was psychosomatic: perhaps due to depression, anxiety about the future and general stagnation of life; or a subconscious procrastination of the decision to return to England.'

Dodie's respite came in poetry. She learnt vast tracts, and it was like a benign drug. 'It left me with many fragments shored against my ruin.' She learnt by heart every word of the *Four Quartets* and at last fully understood it. Also Gerard Manley Hopkins's late sonnets, Dylan Thomas's 'Fern Hill', 'In The White Giant's Thigh', 'Deaths and Entrances', 'Altarwise by Owl-Light', and 'Poem in October'. The learning of such poems during walks at sunset — 'murmuring, as if saying my rosary' — was her greatest solace this difficult year. But she had never been more unhappy since

1942. To be with someone and yet to feel so utterly alone caused 'a loneliness of spirit which takes some defeating'. She longed to talk to Isherwood — who was having his own troubles with Caskey, now a tragic figure menaced by drink — and wrote him vast letters, wishing they could sit and talk. In return Isherwood told her how he missed her 'amoral moral support and kind severity. You cannot possibly know how you have helped me.'

In December 1952 Isherwood had asked them to give a brief impression of Tyrolean life. He sent a long complex questionnaire — 'What sort of a small house would one rent? Village amusements? Canoeing? Behaviour and costume of the inhabitants?' to which Alec replied in businesslike detail and with commendable vividness, despite the distance of the memory: 'Forest — ye-e-es but not wild, primeval forest; larches, with the young green tips much lighter than last year's growth; and they smell heavenly in the hot sun . . . Wood: in 1928 you would haul it by ox-cart from the local saw-mill (turpentine smell) just down the road. Swimming: yes, in the lake, but bloody cold from the snow-water. Village amusements: Beer. The cinema. Fiddle and concertina, with heavy-footed dancing. *Schuhplattler* on special occasions. Church processions with costumes and draped saints on saints' days. Gossip. Illegitimate babies ... You must not forget the flowers which spring up as soon as the snow melts in June — millions of them, primulas mostly; one cannot walk in the fields or the hillsides without crushing them: mauve, red, purple, violet, white, yellow. And the clearness of the air, when fine. And the wetness of the drizzly rain, when wet. And the streams of melted snow-water rushing down to the lake. But why don't you read *The Constant Nymph* and *Autumn Crocus* and crib from them?' Isherwood didn't need to: he wrote back that he had been able to use Alec's material 'almost verbatim'.

It is striking, reading the Isherwood/Beesley correspondence, that Alec's letters are far more succinct than Dodie's and his critical instincts are no less sharply honed than hers: 'Dodie says, and I join her in saying, that there is no book we would like less than your suggested one on Etruscan art — unless it be one on Lincoln or the Jews in Israel! Than which!' 'Two disappointments: Denton Welch's *Journals*, well-written of course, but too florid for my taste — too much almond icing. And Anthony Powell, likened by some to Christopher Isherwood and taken very seriously by the English critics — *such* dull books, *such* a flat, boring style; and where the bloody hell's the humour? . . . Oh, and I loathed your god's latest one, *The Old Guy and The Sea* [sic] pure American marshmallow. I fail to understand how you and the critics (fie on you, Cyril Connolly!) can take that maudlin old driveller seriously. Alone in the critical wilderness, I despise you, Hemingway!'

Finally, although Alec remained vaguely unwell, they agreed to seize the moment and go. Quarantine was still a deterrent. Folly and Buzz were now aged eleven and Dandy was nine: would they have to wait until their dogs died? At that moment Charlie rang, offering another screenplay. Dodie forced herself to agree at least to read the book if he sent it. But that night she cried for hours, the first time for years. Did she *have* to accept, Christian Scientifically, whatever came? She sat in her Christian Science chair (her childhood armchair) and suddenly decided: 'I can't and I won't.' 'And my fantastic memory recalled the day when, as a small child, I suddenly knew that I did not want to face the glass of orange juice pressed on me daily. I just pushed the glass over, and wondered why I had never thought of it before. Well, I pushed Charlie's glass of orange juice away from me.

She told him no, even before the book arrived — and when it came it turned out to be a tear-jerker called *Lillie's Story*, the type of novel she disliked most, about mother love, 'one of my least favourite subjects'. She flew back to work on *The Treasures*. She sent Isherwood the monastery play, *That Which Hath Been*, asking for suggestions for a better title. 'It is too heavy, too portentous for such a play. It's a very fantastic, peculiar play. One needs an airy, starry title.' Isherwood had already given her advice about details of Benedictine monastery life, and his critique was thoughtful. He approved of Dodie's venturing into a metaphysical, philosophical play, of the kind he would like to write himself. But she felt he was pulling his velvet-gloved punches: his own narratives were so journalistic, he must surely be antipathetic to imaginative writing. Yet his only criticism was that there was a lack of a solid Nazi background in it. Dodie, feeling that her play was not important enough to be taken so seriously ('It's hellishly important to me of course, but I can't feel it's important *sub specie aeternatis*'), disagreed: 'I feel that solid serious Nazi background would be about as suitable to this play as a dissertation on the habits of wolves would be in *Red Riding Hood*. The Nazis are just off-stage villains, who fly planes and shoot off guns. They are the menace.' Although Dodie regarded herself as a completely apolitical writer, she felt strongly that the Nazis were by now 'just the last villains but one, having been made *démodé* by the Russians' and she frequently referred to the atrocities of Stalinism. And she aligned herself with Ivy Compton-Burnett's revulsion for making fictive use of any modern happenings. 'Reality has the same effect on me.'

In the middle of August, as they were packing to leave, Isherwood sent the manuscript of *The World in the Evening*, dedicated to Dodie and Alec in recognition of the many hours they had spent, over four years, having passages read aloud and discussing the story. He said the novel had changed considerably and now rather resembled Huxley's description of *Time Must Have A Stop*: 'A curiously *trivial* story, told in *considerable* detail, with a certain amount of *squalor*.' It turned out to be the only work of Isherwood's they had ever disliked. None of the characters lived; they seemed to have no physique. And the 'overpowering' amount of sex was not so much shocking as embarrassing. 'The narrator has one affair after another, both normal and homosexual. The homosexual love scenes are as bad as such scenes usually are, and the normal sex scenes don't, to me, ring true. There is little humour. In some parts the book is actually boring — unbelievable for an

Isherwood book.'

Isherwood had urged them to be *utterly frank*. They set to, and each wrote — five pages from Dodie, two from Alec — praising the descriptive writing, 'the vitality'. 'And we wrapped up our criticisms by saying we were probably fuddy-duddies as regards sex scenes (quite untrue, really).' Dodie suggested some alterations and hoped she had kept Chris happy. He told them that Speed Lamkin, of all people — 'a nice bright child,' said Dodie, 'but with an ounce of talent only, and not a reliable critic' — had also said there was too much sex in the book. So had Isherwood's American publishers. His English publishers remained silent: 'They may be dead of shock.' If she could speak in person, Dodie said, she would have been franker to her old friend.

'But I fear that no amount of tinkering will really save the book. And I fear it is the company Chris keeps,' wrote Dodie. 'He is destroying his sense of values and even his taste. He needs the company of his peers — as almost every writer does.

I believe America has almost ruined his talent.' (Isherwood had just recounted to them how he had got involved with a boy who, relying on 'the kindness of strangers', had become a tiresome leech, usually committing some act of violence and then coming to tell him about it.) And Dodie had written sternly about Caskey, who would never grow up, she said, if Isherwood was always there to provide him with travel treats. 'Incidentally, didn't he behave rather more sensibly when you were broke?' But Isherwood had already met Don Bachardy, who had typed the new novel for him. 'He is very sweet and intelligent and fun to be with and he types quite professionally and likes to cook. The snag? He's only nineteen!' Bachardy was devouring culture at voracious speed. 'Don is sitting at the other end of the room reading *War and Peace*, because he has a test on World Literature in college tomorrow . . . I know you would both like him very much — he has the immediate and almost universal appeal of someone like Julie Harris — and this year we have spent together is one of the nicest things that has ever happened to me.'

When the finished copies of the novel finally arrived, Dodie told Isherwood, 'I have found myself cuddling the book as one would cuddle a baby. Not that I ever would cuddle a baby, but it *is* done . . . We are puffed with pride that the book is dedicated to us for all to see.' It did mean a great deal to her to be thus honoured on Isherwood's flyleaf, even if she disliked the novel — which indeed proved to be his least popular. Isherwood's friendship was 'one of the few things that have made these fifteen years of exile worth while'. Later — though he knew, reading between the lines of her letter, how little she had liked the novel — Isherwood sent her the play based on the book, which he and Bachardy worked on together. 'We were very uncertain of ourselves,' Bachardy says. 'And we made up our minds we would send it to two friends, Dodie and Cecil Beaton. We would let them decide our fate. If they liked it, we would go on with it; if they didn't like it, we wouldn't. And neither of them liked it, so we just put it in the closet and there it remained.'

Since her American interlude really was finally coming to an end Dodie reflected at length — again — on what it had meant. She had left England with her sixth play showing to capacity audiences. She was returning fifteen years later to a very dubious future as a playwright — who would do the three plays she now had ready? 'Fifteen years ago they could have been sold "sight unseen." But beneath all her anxieties, she was convinced that merely to be in England again would guarantee happiness.

'On the debit side,' she wrote later, of her time in America, 'is the complete loss of my career as a playwright and I have realised more and more what it meant to me. I had come to think that it was largely the blow to pride that I minded; but what I more deeply regret is the loss of a beloved profession. I once said, in the thirties, that I only felt fully alive when I had a production in hand. After *Letter*, I never felt quite the same. The legend cracked. Fear of failure had crept in.'

Part Three

1953 – 1990

13

Very Snug Smugs

DODIE and Alec sailed for England at last on the *Queen Elizabeth* on 30 September 1953, with the dogs in the kennels and the Rolls hoisted aboard, and came home to the house lent to them by Murray Macdonald at 12 Cheltenham Terrace, Chelsea, where their luggage reached the bedroom ceiling.

Every day their priority was to visit the quarantined dogs, whose quarters were predictably unsatisfactory, the kennels cruelly unheated and the meat rations meagre. Dodie paid for new kennels to be built, heated by oil stoves and with grass runs; but by Christmas — when *Dear Octopus* was televised, though ignored by Dodie — Dandy was lank, listless and covered in sores. They had to employ a night nurse for him, a splendid woman named Jackson who cooked him chicken and slept on his pillow. When Dodie asked if she wasn't afraid of catching ringworm, Jackson said her husband had asked the same thing. 'I told him, "I shall probably come home bald as a billiard ball." That settled *him* all right.'

They plunged back into nightly theatre-going, Dodie still expecting Alec to be snubbed by people for his 'conchy' past. They saw Dorothy Tutin in *The Living Room* and the Oliviers in Rattigan's *The Sleeping Prince* where Vivien Leigh was gratifyingly 'little better than adequate'. Peter Glenville came to lunch, and Alec found him 'too pretty' — 'an odd criticism from Alec, who is so very tolerant of people's sexual predilections.' That same day, 22 October, the John Gielgud scandal broke. He had been arrested in Chelsea for 'importuning male persons for immoral purposes'. The papers were full of the subsequent hearing where Gielgud (described as 'a clerk' of Cowley Street, Westminster) was fined £10 and ludicrously advised by the magistrate: 'See your doctor the moment you leave here.' Dodie wrote at once to Gielgud — 'This damnable business will be forgotten in a few weeks, whereas the fact that you are the greatest figure in the present English theatre will remain unchanged . . . We think the world of you and always shall' — and for good measure she also wrote to his mother, Kate Terry Gielgud: 'Dear Mrs Gielgud, I find myself longing to send you our sympathy about John's misfortune . . . His magnificent achievements will never fade . . . No one in the theatre is more loved and admired.' Gielgud's mother replied gratefully: 'John has nothing to his discredit save one toast too many at a Chelsea party.' If Dodie came to John's next first night, asked Mrs Gielgud, would she come and shake her hand? Dodie sent all the newspaper clippings to Isherwood, including an article by E. M. Forster from the *Observer*, and Isherwood too wrote to Gielgud, who had been knighted earlier that year, expressing solidarity. 'But oh dear,' Isherwood wrote to Dodie, 'I do wish we had a better issue to join battle on than Gielgud's stupid indiscretion!'

The new Dodie Smith play, *I Capture the Castle*, now looked cheeringly propitious. Cassandra was to be played by Virginia McKenna: the prettiest girl Dodie had ever seen, but surely too ingénue, with more beauty than talent? Five minutes into her audition, all doubt was dispelled. Ginny was quite faultless. Her agent had sent her to audition for the prettier sister, Rose, but she was determined to play Cassandra. 'I just didn't want to be Rose. I felt so akin to Cassandra. I *felt* like her, and not a bit like Rose. I *fought* to play Cassandra,' she remembers. The equally beautiful Yvonne Furneaux became Rose. The respected character actor George Relph was to tackle Mortmain, and three of the handsomest filmstars of the 1950s were to play the young men: Richard Greene (soon to be Robin Hood) as Stephen, Roger Moore (later to be James Bond) as Simon; and the tall, dashing Bill Travers, who three years later married Miss McKenna, as Neil. Little brother Thomas was played by Ted Ray's bright fourteen-year-old son Andrew; and Ivy Stebbins by the splendid Vivian Pickles. Even the smallish part of the vicar went to a star, Cyril Luckham. It all looked immensely promising.

Virginia McKenna recalls that Dodie insisted she must have her long hair cut. 'So I did. And she said, "Not short enough." So I had it cut again. "Still not short enough." So I had it cut *really* short. And she said, "It's too short." She had very exact ideas of what each character looked like and you had to fit in to her vision, quite rightly so. She was forthright, but it didn't make you dislike her. She didn't couch things, so you knew where you stood.' So for Miss McKenna's wedding to Denholm Elliott, which took place at Holy Trinity Brompton two days before the opening night of the play, she had cropped hair; she was still 'the picture bride of the season' in Edwardian lace. Neither she nor her bridegroom missed a performance of their respective plays (he was in *The Confidential Clerk*) and there was no time for a honeymoon.

During rehearsals, Ginny had found Bill Travers enormously engaging and they had 'great giggles' together: 'In the scene where I appeared shivering in a bathing costume, soaking wet, neither

of us could ever keep a straight face.'
Neither her young star's wedding nor the
backstage fun were recorded in Dodie's
diary, which became — once again — a
saga of problems.

Murray Macdonald proved to be a
disappointing director, being ill and
irritable. George Relph got pneumonia,
and Dodie considered him incapable of
the broad bravura acting needed for
Mortmain. Roger Moore was whisked
off to Hollywood in mid-run. The play
seemed immensely over-long. People made
copious suggestions for cuts, changes,
rewrites. Alec was patience personified,
helping with music cues, soothing the
cast with interminable Thermoses of
coffee. (Joan White, who played Miss
Marcy, referred to Alec forty years later
as 'the linoleum salesman — wasn't he a
linoleum salesman once, at Heal's?') His
solicitousness for Dodie's wellbeing was
tireless and, to the cast, a bit tiresome:
he was forever finding her a comfortable
chair, and anticipating her every need.
Dodie was by now sitting, (in her mink
coat down to her ankles, on the stage near
the actors while Murray Macdonald sat in

the stalls. Two weeks into the tour, he announced that he could not work with the author there. Dodie riposted that she had not done anything untoward. It amazed and distressed her that one of her great friends 'found my presence completely inhibiting', especially as the cast had complained to her privately that Murray just could not direct. Tyrone Guthrie, who had directed *Call It A Day* in America, was called in from Ireland to rescue the production and pull the show together in twelve hours flat. 'Now keep quiet, Dodie,' he said sternly as he began. He had read neither the novel nor the play, and said it wasn't his cup of tea, but he was full of ideas ('I know what's wrong and I don't want any argument, is that clear, Dodie?') and made the cast roar, inventing bits of business and changing Topaz (Georgina Cookson) from an aspiring highbrow to a blowsy barmaid type, a comic *tour de force*.

In the midst of rehearsals Alec and Dodie visited the Vaughan Williamses in Hanover Terrace, Regent's Park, a house after Dodie's heart, 'admirably furnished in a surprisingly modern style'. What did she expect, busts of Beethoven? asked Vaughan Williams, who was eighty and too deaf to hear Dodie's reedy voice. (In fact, Ursula Vaughan Williams says, they had Empire dining chairs, a Queen Anne secretaire and 'a lot of eighteenth century stuff' so Dodie's observation was faulty.) There was a black kitten named Crispin that played on the piano keys. Ursula, 'obviously a wonderful wife for him', showed Dodie the box room behind the pedimented façade of Hanover Terrace. Dodie said she would like to set a play in such a room — apparently shambolic but orderly enough for the composer to find whatever music he wanted.

After the ten-week provincial tour they opened on 4 March at the Aldwych, a theatre with glum memories, for Dodie, of the doomed *Letter From Paris*, but with an amusing stage door-keeper's dog which flew into a fury if you whispered 'Rats'. An invited audience sat stony-faced in the dress rehearsal: why did people who had not paid for their seat find it so hard to laugh? But the first night was animated and rang with laughter and applause: not from politeness but from real enthusiasm. Yet when the notices came out they were middling. Dodie naturally saw them as 'terrible' and many of them 'insulting'.

The complaints were that the play was unreal, the characters non-existent, that the novel (which several critics had liked) was lazily adapted with too many scenes. Dodie felt — as so many playwrights have since — she was the butt of some invincible dislike and spite. The *Daily Express* dug up the old 'shopgirl writes play' tag, mentioned her Rolls-Royce, and ran a caricature of her with 1931 hairstyle and much aged face. Certainly, the critics, all male, seemed to enjoy brandishing snide expressions about women's magazine writing, whimsical sickliness, and 'giddy capriciousness' (Kenneth Tynan). Harold Hobson said the play would go down well with Aunt Edna, the imaginary playgoer invented by Rattigan 'who lives in Guildford, or maybe Harrogate, has about £1500 a year and reads all the nicest novels'. 'One of those fey families, poor but genteel, whose members are thick on charm and thin on credibility,' sneered

Milton Shulman. Ivor Brown mocked the Cinderella theme: Godsend Castle was of course Stonybroke Hall, Mortmain was Baron Stonybroke, the American brothers were Prince Charming and Dandini. *The Times*'s critic, by contrast, saw elements of *Dr Faustus* and *A Midsummer Night's Dream*. Only the *Church Times* discerned the acuity of the scene between Cassandra and the vicar: 'It is not often that an actor is given such sensible things to say about prayer.'

The one bright note was the universal praise lavished on Virginia McKenna, who was enchanting, ingenuous, charming, witty, graceful, exquisite, guileless, sensitive, high-spirited, assured, intelligent; she plucked the heartstrings; she conveyed the joys and despairs, the engaging precocity, and the coltish grace of youth; she radiated a spiritual beauty; she played with tact and intensity and a daffodil freshness (Tynan) and never put a finger wrong (W. A. Darlington). She pleased everyone, even those hardest to please. It was undoubtedly a triumph for Ginny. 'No critic seemed to realise,' wrote Dodie, slightly peeved, 'that you cannot achieve that kind of success in a badly written or unreal character.' Sundays, weeklies and magazines damned with faint praise. 'The whole piece ticked away with a dizzy mechanical speed, yet seemed to last half the night,' said Philip Hope-Wallace in *Time and Tide*. It was 'full of good theatrical material but woven very loose and thin'. Dodie was in despair. How could she carry on in the theatre at all? 'I don't know what to do,' she told Alec.

What had gone wrong? One glaring fault was Dodie's experiment with the cinematic 'blackout' technique between scenes. Even Binkie's Italian housekeeper, Elvira, sent a message: 'Tell Miss Smith, too much blackness.' Foolishly, she had not inserted in the London programme her explanatory preface, 'fearing London critics might think it patronising'. Yet within a few years, blackouts and jumps in time were commonplace on the stage. It is certainly true that there probably were too many 'vagrant' characters from the book who were not entirely germane, and made the piece too sprawling and episodic, full of minor elements that, without the ballast of the novel, lacked dramatic importance.

But people did like it. Marius Goring, an actor Dodie had revered ever since *The Red Shoes*, wrote to say how outraged he had been by the critics — 'who instead of rejoicing at something new (what else in Heaven's name is art for but to find new ways of seeing things?) reject anything that is not completely clear to them; these same people would write "Miss Dodie Smith repeats herself" were you to follow their advice ... ' He and his wife had left the Aldwych 'with a feeling of gratitude one too rarely has, for having been shown something one has not known before about the world in which we live, in this case, the world of a young girl's heart and mind. The ending alone forms one of the most enchanting love scenes I know.' Dodie gratefully wrote back, telling him that actually Goring had been her original casting for Mortmain, who was after all supposed to be in his forties, red-haired, dynamic with something of a suppressed volcano quality — all attributes Goring had displayed so effectively in *The Red Shoes*. Marius Goring, she added, 'might have made all the difference to the play's fortunes . . . '

The Vaughan Williamses went too, and Ralph declared he was violently in love with both Cassandra and Rose. 'The critics,' he wrote to Dodie, 'are blasteder fools even than I imagined.' Ursula Vaughan Williams's letter was perceptive. Having just re-read the book, she had missed in the play 'that acute sense of place and season which is so lovely . . . and the nice Jane Austenish quality in the sisters' relationship'. But she hoped the public would wake up to what pleasure and laughter was here. However, they were not to have the chance, since it ran only six weeks in London.

Dodie was in no mood to be pleased about John van Druten's success with *I Am A Camera*, but they went to the London first night anyway, and found Tutin 'too pure' for Sally Bowles. But she had 'a star quality which Ginny lacked — perhaps because Ginny was not ambitious. She was always saying she would really like to give up the stage and raise a family.' And Ginny meant it too; after she parted from Denholm Elliott (six months later) she and Bill Travers met again and they embarked on a happy marriage that produced four children and lasted thirty-seven years, ending only with Bill's sudden death in 1994.

The audiences at Dodie's play were enjoying themselves; Dodie had never heard more laughter; yet she accepted *I Capture the Castle*'s short-lived run with unusual equanimity, because of the overwhelming consolation of not having to go back to America. She gazed at her name in lights above the Aldwych on the final day and wondered if she would ever see it there again. 'But I don't seem to mind terribly,' she wrote to Isherwood.

This was because The Barretts was ready. Binkie's infuriating prettifications — he had recently introduced wallpaper and a suburban french window into the barn, plus a croquet lawn in the paddock — had been removed at his expense, and Dogs' Freedom Day was imminent. The Rolls stood outside The Barretts looking as good as when new. Dodie wished she showed the passage of seventeen years as little. The poplars they had planted twenty years ago, wondering whether they would ever see them fully grown, were now towering.

After collecting the dogs from their quarantine kennels — bestowing presents on Jackson the kennelmaid, to the disapproval of the vet, who said Jackson drank — Alec swore they would make it up to the dogs for those six months, and never leave them for more than a few hours again. They arranged to keep on Binkie's excellent housekeeper at the cottage. Constance Ridgewell, a woman of quiet dignity, had been born in the next village, and had gone into service as a girl with Colonel Henry at Hill House, Finchingfield, where she stayed until her marriage in 1933 to her childhood sweetheart Percy Ridgewell. They lived in the tied cottage near The Barretts where Mrs Ridgewell still lives today.

Life at The Barretts immediately felt right, despite the roar of the planes from the nearby American base. Dodie's bedroom, overlooking the placid pond, reminded her of Frances Cornford's lines:

My room's a square and candle-
lighted boat
In the surrounding depths of night
afloat . . .

She wrote to Isherwood in a state of ecstasy. 'Chris dear, do you remember good English bread? Bliss after that American nonsense.' And the wisteria and the apple blossom — she longed for him to see it. And, she went on rapturously, 'Scotch salmon, steak and kidney pie, lovely fires and baths in large, candle-lit bathroom, and dogs'. The barn awaited him, with its log fire and spiral staircase to galleried bedroom. There were three white ducks on their pond, known as the Marx Brothers. 'Our housekeeper is wonderful. And we have a rather peculiar gardener named Choat.' (She had asked him whether he spelt his name with an 'e', and he replied, 'No. We lost the e's years ago.')

'I have spent six months,' she wrote to Isherwood, 'looking at the world through a haze of love. You used to say my character would be all right if I could extend some of the affection I felt for insects to human beings. Well, all English human beings have more than insect status with me now.' The sunrises, seen through the chintz curtains, were like Samuel Palmer paintings, even though no more 'barbarous in beauty the stooks arise around' since farmers were straw-burning. And there was a blue moon on 8 October 1954 — the moon dyed turquoise by mist, caused by thin clouds of ice crystals five or six miles high.

In their old cupboards Dodie and Alec found locked-away linen, crockery, maps and baskets which revived memories of picnics by haystacks and water-meadows; there were even pre-war crumbs, and — most moving of all — white Dalmatian hairs from Pongo, who had never come back to his cottage. 'And out, at last, came my gold witch ball, which reflected my years in Marylebone Road, before *Autumn Crocus* was written. I always have a feeling that it holds within it all that it has seen, holds perhaps the end of my youth.'

They had missed Queen Elizabeth II's coronation, the historic event of 1953, but gradually Dodie began to get the feel of her England again — particularly from the Third Programme on the wireless. This represented, for her, England at its most unchanging, the accents, the tone of voice, the choice of music, the announcers comments: once when a performer was taken ill during a recital, the announcer said he had 'very gamely' come back to play again. The short talks in concert intervals were a lifeline to the returned exile. 'The experiences of a governess'; 'The life of a couturier's model'; 'How three young men took up housekeeping in a Chelsea houseboat': each talk revealed a way of life with which Dodie had lost touch, each almost a scenario for a play, opening up the lives of the kind of people who (she was sure) would have enjoyed her earlier plays. Controversy was raging, at least in the *Daily Telegraph*, because the BBC allowed Mrs Margaret Knight, a humanist, to lecture on 'morals without religion'. Dodie thought her talks extremely reasonable. How could one believe in a God who permitted evil, and animal suffering? Yet *Telegraph* readers were two to one against Mrs Knight. 'They are dishonest,' wrote Dodie. 'English churches are empty, yet the majority of English people think Christianity must be protected from any attack.'

That Christmas of 1953, spent at Gwen Ffrangcon-Davies's, Dodie felt suffused with thankfulness. 'Not even to give myself an extra fifteen years of life would I have faced again that long exile.' But what about Alec? In California, he would always look out each night at the lights and stars, and feel perfectly content. But his innate talent for happiness meant he could now distil pleasure from the less balmy Essex air, and pure satisfaction from his garden and from improvements to the cottage. He was effusively grateful to Dodie when she kept a steak and kidney pie (cooked by Mrs R) for him to eat when he got home from watching cricket at Lord's 'as if it had required great powers of imagination and organisation'.

But what would Dodie do with herself now? She sat down at her dear old

Bluthner piano and thought she might take up playing it again. Or perhaps she might do some oil painting, like Phyllis, who had just exhibited her 'rock fantasies' of New Mexico, of which the *Arts Review* said, 'Her style does not belong to any time or place, only to Phyllis Morris.' (Dodie thought them 'hideously garish'.) Instead Dodie opted for italic calligraphy. Hours each day were spent on improving her hand and she kept detailed notebooks of her progress for the next four years: 'I thought I had set my way of making ascenders with a kick to the right, so — *h, k, l, b* — but on this page I seem to be making the tops dead straight.' Letters were drafted in italic script, to be typed up later by Alec. In fact her handwriting, already neat and legible, became 'astonishingly' fine, and the Swan calligraphic pen became her favourite. Sir Ambrose, a collector of italic manuscripts, gave advice. Correspondence continued to obsess her: a letter to van Druten in September 1955 took two whole days.

To give herself a project she read systematically through the whole of Shakespeare. All her life the mark of the First Folio, even on a cheap Stratford souvenir, had meant 'more than any crucifix' to her. She thought Shakespeare's heroines — Juliet, Portia, Beatrice, Rosalind — were 'the best in the world' 'because they were none of 'em *coy*'. She decided she could spot exactly where the Great Mind was taken over by another writer, and said she admired the histories most 'because they tell a real story, not fantasy'.

Every evening at sundown she would have her bath by candlelight (though the bathroom did have a modern telephone installed in it), give the dogs their supper and settle down to domestic bliss: Dodie reading, and Alec typing up the letters she had handwritten during the day. 'You know,' said Alec, 'we're infatuated with our own lives — our own dogs, our own cottage, even our own food.' (When John van Druten wrote a play called *The Duchess and the Smugs*, she and Alec decided to refer to themselves as the Smugs 'because we are so bloody pleased with our cottage here. We are very snug Smugs with our giant fires and central heating.') One night when they were quietly reading together indoors, Alec said: 'Oh, the dogs and ourselves and books and peace — it's so *good!*'

They rediscovered the English countryside, driving back to Wingfield Castle in Suffolk, where the house was built into the ruins within the courtyard. Under the ownership of Baron Ash, it had become frighteningly grand; she preferred to remember the ramshackle Victorian interior explored at dusk in the 1930s. They retrieved a single Tudor brick from Rushbrook, a great Elizabethan house being demolished, and explored the deserted shrubbery of Gosfield Hall, another Tudor manor house — with lake, and mirror-lined ballroom in which one was reflected into infinity — Dodie recapturing the thrill of discovering the derelict houses in Whalley Range that had so fascinated and saddened her in childhood. (Later Gosfield was converted into thirty-five retirement apartments and Phyllis Morris took one, keen as always to be close to Dodie.) And sometimes she would wander through nearby farmlands — across the fields to the Toppesfield Road, and the woods beyond Foulslough, to find secret places, lanes filled with seeding thistles 'white as a meadow of the moon' and occasionally a disused cottage containing an old oil lamp, a couple of bedsteads, and a pair of elegant wooden shoe-trees.

One day in the woods she met the Ruggles-Brises' game-keeper, who was impertinent enough to mention that Dodie must be nearly sixty now.

'Sixty! It certainly is my next milestone, but to have it mentioned, loudly, in the open air, came as a distinct shock. And me in a bright orange linen coat over a white sunbathing dress which would scarcely pass the film world's test for cleavage! When I think of my grandmother, at much less than sixty, a silver-haired old lady with a wrinkled, parchment-pale skin, in black from throat to heels, and a bonnet! What few grey hairs I have grow tactfully underneath the brown.'

On another excursion she found herself at a chamber music concert at Thaxted Church, her first visit since 1915 when she stayed with her RADA friend Barbara Noel at the vicarage. Barbara had married her father's curate. She was still there: instantly recognisable by her 'unmanageable' hair. They kissed, to Dodie's surprise, and spoke of meeting again, both knowing they never would. Dodie went in search of other churches, little lonely places like the one at Tilbury-juxta-Clare; but she never once stepped inside Finchingfield Church. She met the young vicar, however, and told him she was a Christian Scientist, 'a very dull religion I'm afraid'. 'Yes it is,' the vicar said heartily, adding, 'There are some in the village if you want them.' Dodie did not; she had never met a Christian Scientist who didn't put her off Christian Science.

But she no longer minded talking to strangers. 'I am so bloody sociable you just wouldn't believe it,' she told Isherwood. 'People stop to admire the dogs and I positively like them . . . And the country hotels are so good — astonishing food, and they give the dogs presents.' (This may be the only record of praise for English country hotel fare of the 1950s.) 'Oh darling Chris, are you sure you are right to live in America? The lack of you is the worst drawback here.'

Dodie sought no substitute local friendships; she wanted no sherry parties or garden fêtes. However, the coterie of bachelor acolytes in America was partly replaced by their neighbour Henry Warren, a bachelor of about sixty, who lived at a cottage called Timbers. Henry was the author of several books on country matters, notably the autobiographical *A Boy in Kent*, *A Cotswold Year* and *England is a Village*. He gave the impression of being an upper-class Englishman of the intellectual type, said Dodie, but was in fact the son of poorish parents, a former schoolmaster who had become a broadcaster and poet and had been deputy editor of the *Radio Times*. He still wrote poetry, short stories and essays, and would flog the odd article to *Country Life* on how pleasant it was to live in a village where the Squire was still called the Squire. 'He particularly resents the comparatively large earnings of the lower classes, and all that is done for them in this "Welfare State",' noted Dodie. He seemed to have rich women in pursuit, offering him cars, houses, holidays. Dodie did a little prodding and got Henry to tell her about his private life, which was going through 'an unexciting patch'; he would lend Alec the Olympia Press editions of Henry Miller's books, which Alec piously refused to read. Henry confided that he had never actually been much interested in sex, but women always hoped to persuade him otherwise.

Alec and Dodie began taking Henry with them on their Thursday shopping excursions to Sudbury, the small and unpretentious Suffolk market town with half-timbered Tudor buildings, home town of Gainsborough, which Dodie now said she would not swap for the whole of California. The three of them made a habit of making a detour each week to some old Suffolk house, Domesday Book village or ruined manor on the way to market. 'All shopping is a chore,' as Henry wrote in an essay called 'Thursday is Market Day', 'and my friends and I argue that if we can extract virtue out of necessity, by shopping in a town we find congenial and by journeying to it through a countryside that is even more congenial, we are lucky.' Place names charmed them: Good Easter, High Easter, Abbess Roding, White Roding, Margaretting, Shellow Bowells, Pharisee Green. Suffolk abounded in discoveries: the remote and sparsely-populated Belchamps — St Paul, Otten and Walter; the Hennys, a huddle of hills and dales with narrow, sunken lanes, unchanged since feudal times; the sleepy towns of Lavenham, Clare and Long Melford. Isolated manor houses, white weatherboarded water-mills, secret gardens, derelict out-houses and cottages were their passion: once they found a perfectly trim and roadworthy pony-shay in an outhouse, once a collection of oil paintings in a ruined farmhouse; once a meadow overgrown with the Great Horsetail, one of the oldest forms of fossil plant life. Henry affected to find Dodie and Alec terrifyingly argumentative — he and Alec would argue on country matters: was that a woodpecker or a jay? etc. — but he too was dogmatic and uncompromising.

Dodie was shocked to find, over lunch one day, that Henry had seriously considered becoming a Roman Catholic priest just as a way of earning a living. She suggested that he should write a children's book instead, about the swan on Finchingfield pond. He began work at once with boyish enthusiasm. Dodie pondered: would she always be handing out ideas to friends, and getting nothing in return? As for her own ideas for new plays, she had given up confiding in Alec. 'He simply cannot visualise how an unwritten work will turn out and his anxiety to help simply makes him destructive. He has destroyed almost every new idea I have.'

Worse, Kenneth Tynan's article heaping scorn on Country House plays set in Loamshire came out in the *Observer*. 'If you seek a tombstone, look about you: survey the peculiar nullity of our drama's prevalent *genre*, the Loamshire play. Its setting is a country house . . . The inhabitants belong to a social class derived partly from romantic novels and partly from the playwright's vision of the leisured life he will lead after the play is a success . . . Loamshire is a glibly codified fairy-tale world, of no more use to the student of life than a doll's house would be to a student of town planning. Its vice is to have engulfed the theatre . . . Never believe that there is a shortage of playwrights; there are more than we have ever known; but they are all writing the same play.' He mocked the tea-parties in 'the living-room at Binsgate, Vyvyan Bulstrode's country house near Dymsdyke'. No wonder people of intellectual appetites were deserting the theatre for the cinema: 'We need plays about cabmen and demi-gods, plays about warriors, politicians and grocers . . . ' And he doubted whether our knowledge of our language had been perceptibly broadened by any national dramatist since Galsworthy. 'In writing plays the ear is paramount: when that withers, everything withers.'

Well, her ear had not withered, wrote Dodie angrily in her journal. Tynan, she decided, was 'an insulting and not very talented young idiot'. If one listened and rendered dialogue as spoken by the people, plays would be even drearier, full of clichés, the vocabulary minimal. The main fresh trends since Galsworthy's day were Americanisms. None of the popular playwrights of the 1900s had stayed the course for a lifetime. Maugham saw 'datedness' coming and stopped writing plays. 'Playwrights date almost as one is watching their first success. My dear friend Warren Chetham-Strode has a serial on the radio and the dialogue is full of "jolly" and "old man" and "hold the fort" and other clichés. I think I have cured myself of most of that.' Rattigan, she felt, was doomed to datedness. If she could see so clearly what dates a writer, could she save herself? A touch of unreality was needed; a trick . . . Humour dated desperately quickly. The idea of writing a funny play now seemed 'appalling'.

However, she later conceded, it *was* true that few modern plays addressed important subjects, and, she had to admit, plays such as hers were of no very serious value. So while she was 'almost permanently furious with Tynan', she did find herself becoming 'sympathetic to his longing for what he calls the theatre of passion and ideas. Would I myself not prefer to see a play of passion and ideas to an even quite clever comedy? Passion and ideas last; so little else in the theatre does.'

It is a crucial irony of Dodie's career that she returned to her home territory at precisely the moment when 'the well-made play' was being excised from the repertory. The new writers nurtured by George Devine at the Royal Court were in the ascendant, and in came Ionesco's Theatre of the Absurd and Artaud's Theatre of Cruelty; and the phrase 'well-made play' became for Tynan a term of contempt. Dodie felt intuitively that the real danger for her as a playwright lay with 'elderly critics who feel they ought to be "modern"'. Laurence Fitch had a theory that critics identified her plays with their own guilt about the carefree life of the thirties.

Dodie was still astonished about how little she minded the failure of *I Capture the Castle* as a play; but she was nagged by the question of how to make money if she could not re-establish herself as a playwright. The bill for doing up the barn was well over the builder's estimate. Repertory companies had begun to do *I Capture the Castle* but the royalties were negligible. 'All my life,' she fretted, 'I have never seen security ahead — in poor or rich days. I have always had to step out on the tightrope without being quite sure I could make the journey. But I always have made it. By being extravagant at certain points, and ensuring more supply: e.g. the $15,000 for the film rights of *Castle* came in just after we had undertaken the expense of moving from Beverly Hills to Connecticut, cutting myself off from film work. And I think of the pound notes that dropped from heaven into my handkerchief or my handbag, in really poor days.' But no management would take *Esmeralda and the Cloth*, or *That Which Hath Been*. All summer Dodie worked on *The Treasures*, set in a Westminster house like Binkie's in Lord North Street. It centred on a domestic quartet: a newly elected Tory MP named George (Dodie knew pitifully little about politics, but then so did George), his selfish wife Gwen, his clever young secretary Philip and Gwen's overworked dogsbody Cathy. Cathy has been having an affair with George; Gwen is idealistically in love with Philip. Once

489

again, her plot includes a young girl making a determined dead set at an older man. Cathy tells Philip: 'That's how I got George. I willed it . . . it was more than a wish, more like a spell. I said, "By the time these hyacinths come up, he'll start liking me".'

Lacking any professional deadline, she produced 45,000 words of journal, 5000 words a day, writing by the light of one candle close to the page. She covered 134 pages, largely about her relief at being back home. 'I don't believe I knew until these last months that one really does sigh with gratitude.' If she woke in the night, it was never as it used to be in America — when in the small hours she would be beset by the sense of wasted years, and 'one day nearer the tomb' as Henri-Frédéric Amiel told himself every night in his journal. Instead, in England, she woke up filled with relief and euphoria: 'We're here, we're home, it's true.' 'Never have I known such conscious, continuous happiness. I am almost afraid of it, afraid for it, afraid of fire, war, illness, death.'

But she still needed the stimulation

from van Druten's nine-page letters. He kept her in touch with what was happening on and off-Broadway as he dined with Enid Bagnold, and bitched about his producer Irene Selznick. He had written a 'slightly repellent' novel called *The Vicarious Years*, about an adolescent boy (trying to emulate Isherwood, Dodie thought), which Alec found unreadable. But her eyes filled with tears as she read his letter about his bad notices for his latest play, and its closure. And yet, did she not also feel a kind of relief? 'Do not all playwrights feel a slight pang of jealousy at the success of other playwrights, and a corresponding relief at news of failure? It is a dreadful thought, but I am horribly afraid it is true.'

The correspondence with Isherwood recaptured its old zest: he genuinely missed them both, and he too kept her in touch with the literary/Hollywood life. He had been to Key West to visit Tennessee Williams on the set of *The Rose Tattoo*, and described Anna Magnani vividly — 'brutally physical and flat-heeled and ungirdled and capable of farts and belches, but somehow also quite beautiful and flashing-eyed and nobly frantic, like a horse in a battle-painting by Delacroix, with huge snorting nostrils . . . ' but a month later it was 'God preserve me from Anna Magnani' who, poor soul, is proving nearly as much of a bore as Garbo.' Dodie had no star names to drop but she did tell of a Christmas present she received. 'How would you like a Devon Violets pottery barrel for Madeira (of which one drinks so much) complete with wooden tap and six dinky little thimble-sized beakers — the whole setup in a sort of pottery trough.' As for Anna Magnani, Dodie added, 'she looks *filthy* to me and I have an unfashionable aversion to dirty women. So has Alec. One gathers it is now pretty *vieux jeu* to wash.'

She sent Isherwood *The Treasures*, and he was blunt. After *I Capture the Castle*, he had decided that plays did not sufficiently stretch her talents, and that novels would better reflect what he saw as her extraordinarily sensitive and intelligent character. 'I feel it's below your standard,' Isherwood wrote. 'Not that the dialogue isn't often sharp and effective, in your best manner. Not that the plot isn't quite convincing . . . No, what it lacks is a surprise revelation, perhaps some quite vulgar surprise . . . ' Dodie's reaction to this criticism is missing; she kept no carbons of her calligraphy. But Isherwood was right, the play was not quite amusing or sharp enough, and unfortunately Binkie agreed with him, though for different reasons. Binkie did not wish for any added vulgar surprise. Binkie found it all 'too shocking' as it was. Dodie protested that there had been a change in the moral climate now — she wanted to say 'permissive' but that word hadn't come in yet.

But Binkie came to The Barretts and stayed seven hours, discussing how the play could be improved: make the wife nicer, the MP more interesting; attract star names, etc. But even as she rewrote, she had a sense of doom about it. An 'astounding' letter from Binkie duly arrived, congratulating Dodie on her 'magnificent' revisions but 'calmly bowing out of any interest in doing the play'. Dodie decided to fall out with Binkie on the spot, and the frost lasted for years. In a fever of rebellious indignation, and after a few days on angry journals, she started work on an entirely new type of project altogether: a children's story, which would be called *The Hundred and One Dalmatians*.

14

'A Little Book About Dogs'

ALITTLE history is required here. Dodie never particularly wanted to write about dogs. She didn't even like reading about dogs, as she told Esmé Wynne-Tyson's son Jon when he was starting the Centaur Press in 1954 and suggested that she might write something: 'I could no more write "a little book about dogs" than I could write an epic poem,' she told him sniffily. But now, two years later, she remembered an old idea. When Pongo was a puppy, her friend Joyce Kennedy, the character actress, had remarked that 'he would make a nice fur coat'. Dodie had thought at once of a children's play in which a wicked woman — to be played by Joyce — would steal Dalmatian puppies to start a fur farm. Pongo would be a canine Sherlock Holmes and conduct the pups' rescue from the lonely country house where they were imprisoned, with his friend Bob Airedale, his Dr Watson. But Dodie had never got round to writing it.

Then on 16 December 1954 she read for the first time a book by Enid Blyton, bought as a present for a little girl in a nearby cottage. Why should she not write for children too? That night she sat up in bed from midnight until 3 a.m. as her candle burned lower and the story of the Dalmatians unfolded in her mind. It would start with the birth of the fifteen puppies born to Folly and Buzz in California, and Alec's resuscitation of the runt of the litter, the Cadpig (a story often re-told by Alec, saying 'I felt like God'). The hero would be Pongo of course, though he would incorporate characteristics of both Buzz and Dandy. The villainess would be named Cruella de Vil, whose name became one of Dodie's lasting contributions to contemporary folklore.

She started writing *Dalmatians* on 1 March 1955, and completed a handwritten draft in seven weeks: 45,000 words. She typed it herself, breaking off for her fifty-ninth birthday on 3 May 'to write my journal and take notice of the spring'. Just as the dogs sprang to life on the page, her real dogs were in their terminal decline. Folly had just died at the age of fourteen, and her son Dandy appeared to succumb to a stroke, but recovered. Buzz too was ageing into canine senility, pathetically bewildered by the mysterious fading of his eyesight and hearing. 'Perhaps — nay surely — animals are lucky,' reflected Dodie, 'not to know who the enemy is.' The freshness of homecoming had now definitely worn off. 'It has been made very clear to me how little my past reputation for success now counts. Two failures have done irretrievable damage. No, not irretrievable. I shall try to write a play I shall think of as my retriever, but not until I finish *Dalmatians*.'

Their investment income was scarcely enough to live on. For a while they were cushioned by Margaret Truman playing in *Autumn Crocus* for a long summer stock tour in America. She was possibly not the world's greatest actress, wrote Dodie to van Druten and to Isherwood, but she was 'certainly the greatest actress who was the daughter of the president of the United States, and she played to record-breaking business'. Then Laurence Fitch sold a new film option on *I Capture the Castle* (the first option having lapsed) to J. Arthur Rank. When the contract was signed and £2,500 paid, Dodie celebrated by ordering seven bottles of Floris bath essence at 16s 6d each.

Dalmatians was bought by Heinemann for £100 advance, with generous royalties for the author if it sold more than 7,500 copies. Everyone liked it except van Druten who found it 'too doggy'. Don Bachardy wrote (in a letter describing how he and Chris slept under the stars on the sundeck of their new house) that they had read *Dalmatians* aloud to each other before going to sleep. Isherwood could not pretend that it was his kind of book, but he thought it a *tour de force*, and wished there was more of Cruella de Vil. He suspected Dodie disapproved of her: 'One never should, of one's villains.' Dodie said she hadn't expected Chris to be crazy about any book about anthropomorphised animals, but recommended him to read E. B. White's *Stuart Little* and *Charlotte's Web*.

That autumn was dominated by wrangles over *Dalmatians*. As we now know, it became a children's classic, and sold all over the world, but at the time, everything about it seemed 'so bloody complicated'. Alec and Phyllis each produced long lists of suggestions. Dodie fussed over the design, cover binding, endpapers and format; she sent Laurence Fitch an angry letter and a copy of what she considered a fine children's book — Eleanor Farjeon's *The Little Bookroom*, illustrated by Edward Ardizzone — demanding something similar. Ardizzone was first approached to illustrate it, but declined. Dodie was wistful: she so admired his moonlight and firelight drawings and his misty London scenes. Instead, Heinemann introduced her to Janet and Anne Grahame-Johnstone, twenty-seven-year-old twin daughters of the portrait painter Doris Zinkeisen. They had grown up with a passion for drawing and a reverence for animals, especially horses: they rode, sometimes sidesaddle, every morning in Rotten Row.

The twins drove from London (on a route supplied by the Automobile Association, as they regarded Finchingfield as the back of beyond) and were charmed by the cottage and by Dodie and Alec, who in turn found the blue-eyed, dark-haired, strikingly beautiful sisters — so alike and like-minded that nobody could discern who did which part of their joint work — quite captivating. Dodie was shocked to discover how little Heinemann were paying them (a flat fee of £100) and paid them £150 herself, buying the right, much to Heinemann's annoyance, to have as many illustrations as she liked. She showed them the Ardizzone book: could they illustrate the initial letters of each chapter like that? Alec drove them round the Suffolk villages, with Dandy barking his head off, to sketch the steeply pitched gables and densely thatched roofs, and the Tudor façade of Spains Hall. They also spent days in Regent's Park and on Primrose Hill, which they drew faithfully with its row of lamp-posts marching down the hill. Janet (who drew the dogs) sketched Dandy in endless poses, capturing to perfection the characteristic rocking-horse running gait of the Dalmatian, and Anne (who did the people) created a fabulously elegant Cruella. For Cruella's husband, she made a quick sketch of a furrier who appeared on the television show *What's My Line?* She found the Badduns and the Nannies easy but the Dearlys rather too bland to draw. The tailpiece of the book was to have puppies entwined round 'THE END': Janet was going to draw babies too (for the Dearlys) but Dodie said, 'Ugh! No — not *babies.*'

She drafted her own *Dalmatians* publicity, beginning 'Good news! Dodie Smith, whose *I Capture the Castle* sold over a million copies, has a new book and this time it's for children as well as grown-ups' (ironically, *Castle* too came to be regarded as a teenage girls' preserve, and was for years hidden from adult view on the children's shelves). She wrote a series of little articles for children: about the birth of the puppies, and the day Alec thought he had lost the three dogs; and how Pongo got shut up in the folding seat at the theatre. When two young people from Heinemann arrived, 'I found myself feeling like some grand old lady of literature . . . Every joke I made went a shade too well, and the instant I opened my lips no dog barked — except our own of course.' She had to upbraid Alec afterwards because of his remarks — 'Dodie always likes little Jews' and 'I think the sparrows must be Jews because they always get the best nests' — made without noticing, apparently, that a visitor named David Deutsch might himself be Jewish.

That year, Dodie found herself greatly exercised by Princess Margaret's decision not to marry Group-Captain Peter Townsend, 'a plot that only Shakespeare could do full justice to'. At the time of the Abdication in 1936 she had lunched with the historian and biographer Philip Guedalla and his wife, who had announced that they were going up to London to boo Stanley Baldwin. 'How strange it is that the behaviour of the Royal Family can still interest one so greatly! I find myself faintly disliking the Queen, strongly disliking the Duke of Edinburgh, in two minds about the Queen Mother, very sorry for Princess Margaret and far more sorry for Peter Townsend. As for the Archbishop, I remember he was Christopher Isherwood's disreputable headmaster at Repton. "Have you ever been troubled by impure thoughts, Isherwood?" To which Chris, with blue eyes wide, replied "Oh *no*, sir!" I'd quite enjoy throwing a tomato at him, but I would not heave a brick through Lambeth Palace. I would never damage any house for its owner's sins.'

Despite little flurries of appreciation for her old plays, like Christopher Hassall's plan to make a musical of *Autumn Crocus* (the fifth such attempt), she found it depressing to write, in fifty-five Christmas cards, the same news: that *The Treasures* had been shelved, that dear Folly had died, and that she had just written a children's book.

Finchingfield had just been electrified, and Henry Warren ruffled Dodie's feathers by writing a jolly article in *The Times* headed 'The 'lectric comes to Goose Green', in which he had referred to 'the village's only influential house, which combines a Rolls-Royce with oil lamps'. Dodie bridled at this and thought it snide. Long telephone calls ensued about whether Alec and Dodie were entitled to feel insulted. Such a waste of time! 'Moral: Never criticise any writer,' she wrote. 'What they need is praise, praise and more praise — Osbert Sitwell.' Still, they invited Henry to dine, on pheasant with port wine stuffing, with Isherwood when he arrived that January. Henry was enchanted by Chris's smile and quiet dignity (not after rather too many drinks, said Dodie) but Isherwood did not seem to like Henry much: 'Oh, I should think he's a very nice man,' he said, without conviction.

Isherwood brought with him Don Bachardy. He had written often about him and their 'uncle-nephew' relationship; 'We live together in a tiny apartment just below the Sunset Strip and he goes to college and studies German . . . we cook at home together and it is very snug.' He knew Dodie would be charmed, as 'Don charms everyone.'

Dodie was astonished by Don's youth — he was twenty-one, but looked to her fifteen — and by his looks: 'he has a strong resemblance to Dorothy Tutin, but with much more beauty.' He was one of the nicest boys she had ever met, English or American, she decided — and intelligent too, with a copperplate hand. Van Druten called him 'a badly written character', meaning one of those in a play who do not make enough impact to merit their presence on stage. But Isherwood explained that Don was paralysed with shyness when not at his ease — John Lehmann, Isherwood's publisher, would just pretend Don was not there — but he was fine with Dodie and Alec, who were welcoming and accepted that he might be interesting 'without demanding a performance of opinions and disclosures'. Isherwood had always appreciated the fact that Dodie and Alec took his lovers seriously, and appeared fond of them. Emlyn Williams had urged Bachardy to keep a journal and in it he described Dodie vividly: 'completely unlike her pictures, and yet unmistakably Dodie' . . . 'sweet and amusing, but also strange and secluded'. Physically, the most striking thing about

Dodie, as he recorded her at the age of sixty-one, was her dwarflike appearance. 'Her head, shoulders and breasts seem enormously over-sized for her shortness, and she looks even stranger when her very long hair is undone.'

Bachardy, the future artist at work, watched her keenly as she questioned people, never perfunctorily, and observed how her face changed while she listened to their replies. 'Her most vivid quality is her alertness. She is very quick and observant, and watches every minute. I could see her mind working, catching every gesture, weighing each word carefully and shrewdly. Her round dark eyes would suddenly look at me as I spoke, making mental notes. I was also aware of her tremendous honesty. She commented on people and topics instantly and decisively, out of habit rather than affectation. Falseness is completely lacking in her.' (Among her comments: that Starcke was 'a kind of sinister clown'; Binkie 'a two-faced, lying double-crosser'; Kenneth Tynan 'a swine'.) 'At times she may seem a little too emphatic, even insistent, but it's only her strong desire to please others, to make them comfortable and relaxed.'

He found her terribly sensitive about her work, unforgiving about criticism, and prone to make wisecracks with a perfectly serious face. The example Bachardy gave was that when Chris was describing the effects of mescalin, saying it sometimes produced feelings of horror and sometimes feelings of a oneness with nature, Alec asked what kind of horror. Dodie answered, 'I should think the feeling of oneness with nature would be quite horrible enough.' And she had loved Isherwood's story about a prim nurse who said: 'Personally, I never notice if a man's pants are on or off.' Alec, Bachardy decided, was a good, strong character 'and is not the least bit showy about it. He doesn't try to sell himself at all, but is only friendly and agreeable and unassuming. I admire him very much.'

As Dodie and Alec's first residents in the barn, Isherwood and Bachardy were model guests: polite, tidy, leaving the bath scrubbed. Don, reported Isherwood, was 'wildly enthusiastic' about both of them and about the thatched cottage and its 'children's storybook snugness'. Bachardy still has a home movie of that visit, with Isherwood clowning around doing his 'village idiot' act in and outside the barn on a freezing cold day. It was, he says, an icy walk across to the bathroom from the barn. Isherwood, incidentally, had been warned by both John Gielgud and Emlyn Williams that Dodie was now 'crazy', and he was relieved to find this was not the case.

While the boys were with them, a nine-page letter from van Druten arrived, full of religiose self-examination. He had produced a novel that did not sell, a play that did not make it out of Boston to New York. Dodie had spent days on consoling letters, but she also felt the envious playwright's relief. Dodie regretted allowing Isherwood to read the letter, thus exposing van Druten to his derision. John had sent love to Chris, knowing he would be there, saying, 'He will not be surprised at the news of my play, as he did not like it at all. In the same way I am not surprised at the bad reception of his movie *Diane* — but I hope we can both be sympathetic to the other about it.' Isherwood was much aggrieved. He was so proud of his *Diane de Poitiers* filmscript that he had brought it for Dodie and Alec to read; they too thought it was awful.

A week later, Buzz died in slow agony, since Dodie could never have a dog put down. He was fourteen and a half. Buzz was Dodie's dog of dogs, the dog of her lifetime. He had slept in a bed in her room, but would wake each dawn and clamber onto hers; she would pull a quilt over both of them and they would go back to sleep. Without him she felt demented with misery, with a physical longing to hold him in her arms. She filled page after page of her journal about him. 'He always managed to give the impression that he was only a *little* dog. He had such a sense of humour and a will of iron. When he wanted me to stop work he would not only climb on my knee but right up onto my desk. I shall never cease to miss him.'

Isherwood and Bachardy returned for a second weekend in February. They annoyed Dodie by coming on a later train than planned; Dodie suspected that they were 'lolling in bed' but in fact Isherwood was having a tooth capped. Isherwood spent the weekend making notes for *Down There on a Visit*, and would sit with an open bottle of ink on the arm of his chair: when Dodie pointed out that Dandy's tail might send the bottle flying, he capped the bottle laboriously after every dip of his pen. Eventually Dodie and Alec drove the boys to Cambridge to stay with E. M. Forster. Isherwood said to Dodie: 'Last chance to meet Morgan Forster!' but she didn't want to meet him; once, she might have wanted to, but it was now too late. Instead, she went clothes shopping for the first time since returning home; Bachardy had noticed that she wore the same dark blue wool dress every day. While visiting Forster, Bachardy was repelled by 'the school atmosphere and awful self-consciousness' of 1950s Cambridge, and the way Isherwood and Forster smugly accepted 'which colleges were considered desirable and distinguished and which, like St Cats, were not'. Then Isherwood and Bachardy went up to London — Bachardy, like the cat in the nursery rhyme, to see the Queen. He stood on the Mall for an hour, Bachardy told Dodie, 'until the Queen whizzed by at breakneck speed'.

While in London to harangue Heinemann, Dodie stood breathing in 'that sweet, stuffy, dusty air', filled with nostalgia for Heal's, and the Three Arts, and London summers. She would write (ten years later) a novel about it called *The Town in Bloom*. She watched the prostitutes in Shepherd Market, Mayfair. 'I don't know why people fuss about prostitutes. God knows, they live difficult lives and it's all rather grim for them.' During the beautiful summer of 1956 that followed, visitors streamed down to Finchingfield. She wrote extensive notes about her desire to write a non-realistic play, with 'heightened' language, influenced by religion and the rhythms of the iambic pentameter. She studied *The Poet's Handbook* by Clement Wood, which Isherwood had given her; she re-read Wordsworth and tried to re-train her inner ear to invent poetic lines of dialogue: beginning with 'Heaven lies about us in our infancy', she proceeds:

'Do you remember jewelled spiders' webs/ And stars entangled in the apple boughs/ And steel-bright raindrops springing from the lake./ What playthings had we then!'

Her strange, impenetrable monastery play, *That Which Hath Been*, had gone to Basil Dean who thought it finely written but full of 'whimsicalities'. Now she sent it to Gielgud, pointing out that with stars, it is like those spirits from the vasty deep, will they come when you do call to them? They might come if Gielgud called. Also, would he have a go at that terrible title? 'Apart from the fact that I don't like biblical titles, *That Which Hath Been* makes a sort of heavy, wine-coloured noise, almost maroon. Any suggestions for a deep blue title, preferably with a touch of silver, will be welcomed.' Gielgud replied that he was too busy directing Berlioz at the Opera House — but in any case he felt the play lacked humour, 'especially your particular and delightful brand of humour which was always the kernel of your success with an audience,' he soothed. But he added, more candidly, 'Unless you can interest really accomplished players in acting for you, I feel sure you would be better not to do this play at all. Forgive this destructive criticism, but I do feel it strongly. It was good of you to want my opinion and of course take no notice if you do not agree.' Of course Dodie did not agree, and wrote back in her best italic hand to say so.

The Hundred and One Dalmatians was published on 19 November 1956, perfect for Christmas at ten shillings and sixpence. The first notice appeared on 23 November in the *Times Literary Supplement*: 'A doggy fairy tale that will please a great many children, so light it is, so sentimental, so well illustrated, so easy to read, with not one slow word in its expert telling.' Noel Streatfeild made it her Book of the Month choice for the *Young Elizabethan* magazine. Another children's author, John Rowe Townsend, said, 'If dogs could read, they would be unable to put it down.' But the most glowing tribute came from Alan Melville on 23 December on BBC radio. He began by saying he estimated three per cent of listeners would hate it, so he would read the first paragraph aloud and then the three per cent could go away and throw up, while he went on talking to the remaining ninety-seven per cent. He finished by saying it would become a canine classic. (Even this charming and witty review made Dodie 'a mite resentful' about those three per cent throwing up.)

Foyle's Children's Book Club ordered 20,000 copies. Shoals of letters arrived from fellow dog-owners. Kathleen Farrell, author of a novel Dodie admired, *The Cost of Living*, wrote to ask, was the Splendid Vet by any chance Proby J. Cautley of St John's Wood? (Yes, replied Dodie. 'Our Splendid Vet is Proby Cautley. There couldn't be a splendider.') The novelist Olivia Manning wrote to ask if Dodie knew of an animal faith healer; her twelve-year-old Siamese cat had been pronounced incurable, and she had heard that a dog of Dodie's had been so cured. Dodie confirmed that in the 1930s Pongo had been mysteriously ill with a kidney complaint, and became skin and bone and too weak to stand and even Proby J. Cautley had been in despair; then a small man in a bowler hat had come along, and gazed at Pongo, who was soon boisterous, rather too fat, and lived another five years.

Dodie never wrote a perfunctory letter. 'There are times,' she wrote in January 1957, when a pile of letters lay in front of her, 'when I think letter writing will drive me to a genuine nervous breakdown.' But she never let a correspondent down; when Noel Streatfeild wrote asking how *Ballet Shoes* could be turned into a play, she prepared a thorough theatrical outline, 'but oh, my dear Noel, I'm afraid its very virtues fight against its being turned into a play.' Noel was thankful: she had suspected it was impossible, and now perhaps at last people might stop asking for *Ballet Shoes*, the play.

In February Stanley Salmen, from Little, Brown in Boston, rang with news that was 'both pleasant and worrying'. The Walt Disney studio had asked him to quote a price for the movie rights of *The Hundred and One Dalmatians*. In fact, Viking were to publish this book in the USA, but as an old friend, Salmen warned that Disney did not pay high prices, and she would be lucky to get $10,000. She wrote to Charlie Brackett for advice. He said, 'Ask for 25, hope to get 15 . . . ' It was Charlie, it turned out, who had given his own copy of the book to Disney: knowing Walt would never read the whole book, he told him just to look at the episode where the puppies roll themselves in soot to disguise themselves. This salesmanship had done the trick, and Charlie was rewarded with a gold season ticket to Disneyland, where he took his grandson Tigger every Saturday. Disney did eventually offer $25,000, and the contract came within months. The Disney men told Dodie she was lucky; the *Pinocchio* contract had taken three years.

The Disney factor was vastly important to Dodie's morale: it was 'the first really solid food my undernourished ego had come by for years.' So she had had beginner's luck with her first play, her first novel, and her first children's book. The money was welcome too. Not since the Literary Guild's $42,000 for *Castle* had they laid their hands on a substantial sum, and they were facing a huge tax bill from America which Alec had been keeping from Dodie, as he did all the bill paying. (Dodie made him cover up the tax form before she signed it; Alec said she couldn't stand the sight of her own blood.) Now they were back in the surtax bracket, which started then at £4000 a year.

During the success of *The Hundred and One Dalmatians*, Dandy, the last of their Dalmatian family, grossly overweight at 70 pounds, died on 7 September 1957 and was buried with the others under the mulberry tree. 'Such a relaxed little dog!' said Dodie in her journal. 'He used to look as if he had been poured into his chair.' The memory of Dandy set Dodie off on an orgy of remimscence about California, where Dandy would sleep in his own armchair in her study: 'My door would be open and so would Alec's. We would both be reading. Occasionally Alec and I would talk — across the little passage and landing which separated us.' With the nostalgia came the remembered sadness of exile. 'I learnt to accept it, to stop fighting it, to say to myself, "Well, there it is: there's nothing to be done. Just be patient — and hope." But it was always there — the feeling of being lost, slightly maimed, utterly displaced. And despite the numerous worries of the present, and the sorrow of losing Dandy, and Buzz and Folly, I realise that I now have a basic happiness here, which was missing even during our happiest times in America.'

Alec and Dodie decided not to replace the dogs, simply in order to be free to go to the theatre again. They had not seen a new play for three years, and people told her she could not hope to make a comeback unless she did. So they got rid of every dog bowl and leash, suffering pangs of regret each time they passed the dog bowl spot. With this new freedom, Dodie was soon summarising her thoughts on *The Entertainer*, *Roar Like a Dove*, *The Chalk Garden*, and *The Summer of the Seventeenth Doll*. And with the same sense of plunging into a new way of life, they drove into Braintree in the Rolls and bought a television set.

In her journal in 1955 she had written: 'I believe we are on the edge of a great change in the class bracket which audiences are going to wish to see. It was once the upper class; in my heyday it was the upper middle class. I think they will soon demand to see the lower middle and working classes, and television will bring this about.' If she was to be a working dramatist again, she had to find out what pleased the nation. Without television, she realised, she was like a playwright who could not make use of a telephone in a play because he had never used one. But lest it spoil the look of the cottage they put the television set in the back kitchen.

As a result Dodie completed a deliberately classless play called *Amateur Means Lover*, set in a rooming house in Camden Town. But it was still a hopelessly dated play, full of cosy small talk ('You'd better get to bed, Miss Edie. It doesn't do to hang about after a hot bath.' 'I did slightly boil myself') and prattle about Bovril versus cocoa as a nightcap. Among the amiable but fuddy-duddy boarding house inhabitants is a Dean's daughter named Cilla ('I love Eves, don't you? I like them better than Days'). But there is something ineffably depressing about this play; a 1950s ambience of dim light-bulbs, mean gas stoves, tinned soup, fishpaste sandwiches, dressing gowns, umbrellas and mackintoshes. It was sent to managements, but nobody took it — until five years later, when at Liverpool Rep (12 September 1961) it was well received by a packed house, and greeted by the *Times* critic as evidence that Dodie was 'accepting the challenge of the times' since it featured a kitchen sink.

Dodie now decided to lose weight. It was 'outrageous' to be only five feet high and nine stone: she would get back to what she had weighed at twenty-one, seven stone three pounds. This she did over six months 'without ever suffering a pang of hunger. Great was my pride and loud the resentment of some of my steadily thickening friends. Phyllis insisted that if a tree increased in girth as it grew older, a woman had a right to, too.' To show off her new figure her dressmaker, Georgie Roberts, designed a simple sheath dress; Dodie would send her beautiful materials, and back came dresses, a hundred of them over the next twelve years. Weight loss was, as Dodie said, 'one of the more valuable presents a no longer young woman can make to herself for use in the years to come'. But Dodie knew her satisfaction at slimming was partly compensation for her lack of theatrical success.

Van Druten reminded her that few playwrights did much good work after middle age, and said he and Dodie were 'back numbers'. (He was fifty-six, Dodie sixty-one; but she could not agree that one must let a new generation take over: the only young man whose work she admired was John Osborne.) Van Druten seemed increasingly to be bowing out, almost willing himself to die: in his last letter in the autumn of 1957 he seemed to Dodie to be 'at death's door through money worries. He is at the ranch now, taking things very quietly. I wonder if he will ever be quite well again. I don't think he will, unless he can find some metaphysical rather than medical cure.' He described a condition that sounds like myalgic encephalomyelitis (ME), an inability to raise enough energy even to brush his teeth or shave. On 20 December 1957, a cable arrived from Charlie to say that John was dead. Alec brought the news to Dodie while she was breakfasting in bed. And there were two letters from John on her desk, waiting to be answered! She had already rehearsed her replies, and was planning to write to him during Christmas lunch, to tell him about their recent visits to the London theatre . . . She was quite flummoxed that there was nobody, now, whom she could tell her thoughts to.

What with house-painters, and Phyllis's Christmas visit, it was a while before she was able to write down her thoughts about van Druten in her journal; and by then it was as if the skin had closed over a wound before it was ready to heal. 'Oh John,' she wrote, 'you must now be beyond all human petty envies. I often helped you willingly with your work: you never helped me . . . You were a jealous writer and I caught envy from you, though I had more reason to envy you than you had to envy me.'

Re-reading his obituaries much later she found the following in *The Times*:

'His plays . . . cannot be said to have made a lasting impression. They show him to have relied on superficial observation rather than on insight, and to have allowed the ready wit and pleasant lucidity of his style to be frequently swamped by a genteel sentimentalism, which seemed to be an inherent part of his view of things.' Dodie thought this cruel, ungracious; it would have hurt John, who strove for Chekhovian depth. But on reflection she decided it was just. And that it could also be said of her own plays, quite as justly. But then she never strove for Chekhovian depth ('except in *The Sofa and the Window*, and who knows what that wasted play contains'). 'We both, in our different ways, let surface detail dominate our plays.'

That Christmas Day, 1957, they went to Gwen's again, for a smoked salmon and champagne supper. Gwen, who never failed to entertain with style and generosity, was now playing Gielgud's mother in Greene's *The Potting Shed*. 'I know she doesn't like playing old women but she's glad to earn £100 a week.' Phyllis talked at length about her lessons at a London art college and about giving up the stage ('I seem to have made a name for myself as a depressed charlady, I'm never off the floor'). Exhausted by her, Dodie and Alec were in no mood to greet 'the boys', Isherwood and Bachardy, on New Year's Eve. Dodie had sent them a postcard to fill in regarding food; they said they could take anything except hamburger buns, sukiyaki and Chaplin's latest film. They particularly desired shepherd's pie, kedgeree, steak and kidney pudding, treacle tart, Jell-O, *crème brûlée* . . .

They arrived with primitive luggage including a bursting paper bag, Isherwood in his usual unsuitable clothes: 'a little thin towny suit and dreadful shoes. Why? He has made huge sums of money recently, nine solid months at 20th Century Fox, and has just bought a $25,000 house.' When she had rung him about van Druten's death on 20 December, Isherwood had seemed extremely upset. Now his distress seemed to have evaporated into bitter criticism of their friend — especially after Chris read

John's last two letters to Dodie, with their moans about money.

She decided that Isherwood, whom she still loved, was an increasingly weak character. He seemed to grow further away from himself at his best, and more distressingly vain. He was neglecting his novel to do another movie job. And he could be petty and mean about presents and entertaining, though he no longer had the excuse of poverty. 'I am now staggered at the things he expects friends to do for him and how little he does in return. I decided to voice no criticism to Alec, but then Alec astonished me by starting the criticism with a coldness I never expected him to apply to Chris. I must re-find some love and charity for Chris. I will *not* let myself turn against him.'

One day Dodie cornered Isherwood alone, and they talked of journal writing. She said her journal reflected how their friends repeated the pattern of their lives over and over again and made the same mistakes. Would anyone say the same of her? she asked. Well, Isherwood said, he had often noticed her extreme annoyance at the barking of the dogs when guests told stories. The three would rise up as one to bark down storytellers who spoke with too much emphasis: Aldous Huxley was the worst offender. Isherwood had therefore decided that Dodie only kept the dogs to punish herself. Dodie was flabbergasted. How could anyone as intelligent as Isherwood make such a facile judgement, so devoid of understanding? She brooded over it later. No friend in the world had ever meant to her, or to Alec, as much as Pongo, Folly, Buzz or Dandy meant. Any annoyance over the barking was directed at the friends, not the dogs, for dramatising stories when they knew it made the dogs excitable. Dodie had no sense of self-mockery where her dogs were concerned.

There was another annoyance: Isherwood encouraged Don to ask questions 'like an irritating child', so he would launch himself into subjects he knew nothing about. And Don took such an embarrassing amount of cream on his puddings that one had to look away, and when one looked back, he was still pouring. She could excuse greed in Don's case, because of his youth, but Chris was just as greedy (rolling his eyes and saying 'Oh heavens! so much food!' while accepting second helpings). Isherwood became quite ill, she reported, but still took three helpings of treacle tart.

Bachardy, for his part, was observing Dodie closely too. He related in his journal how he was left alone with Dodie on New Year's Eve (an account later copied by Isherwood into his own journal). 'Almost unaware of me and visibly hardly able to bear any longer the strain of the long day, she began pacing the floor, fidgeting, passing from the living room to Alec's study and back again, eking out a note or two of half-hearted conversation to keep me occupied while her mind was absorbed in something else. I watched her face; it was ugly with pain and tension and anxiety. The corners of her mouth drew down in grotesque expressions of tragedy, her thin nervous eyebrows met and parted in spasms, her whole face changed quickly and horribly in a succession of almost ridiculous stage-masks — happy, sad, fearful, resigned, hopeful, determined, grim — like waves of emotion splashing, flooding, disappearing and forming again over her face. At one point, after a short silence in which she was incapable of disguising her distraction and even, I think, completely forgetting I was in the room, so difficult was her struggle with herself, she sighed rather than spoke "*Johnny*." Not John, but Johnny, only just audible, as though she were speaking to him personally, intimately, alone.'

A few days later, Isherwood insisted on taking Dodie and Alec to see his friend Amiya, whom he had met *chez* the Swami. She had been 'an ordinary middle-class English girl' who had fetched up at the ashram. When the octogenarian Earl of Sandwich arrived there and fell ill, he was nursed by Amiya, who promptly divorced her husband in England and married George Sandwich. So now she was the Countess of Sandwich, 'a great bazaar opener', Isherwood said. Dodie was curious to see the Sandwiches' stately pile, Hinchingbrooke, so Alec and Dodie agreed to drive the boys there in the Rolls. It was a sunny day, but with a dusting of frost on the fields: Isherwood swathed himself in Alec's pre-war Teddy Bear coat, fur gloves, and two rugs 'as for a polar expedition'.

They were to lunch in Cambridge, Isherwood having offered to treat them and Alec having very firmly accepted. But Isherwood could recall no hotel or restaurant (despite having been at Cambridge for two years) so Alec spotted the old-fashioned University Arms Hotel, where he found himself ordering drinks and food as Isherwood was in his 'Oh heavens' mode. King's College chapel was closed; E. M. Forster was out; and they got lost looking for Isherwood's old college room at Corpus Christi; but eventually they arrived, just before dark, at Hinchingbrooke, where it turned out that the Sandwiches lived not in the great house, which had been given to the son and heir (Victor Montagu MP, who disclaimed his peerages), but in a mock Tudor cottage on the edge of the overgrown estate.

Isherwood had assured them that Amiya would be overjoyed to see his friends Dodie and Alec. He had also promised there would be a butler; very few butlers had come Dodie's way and she longed to see one. After a long interval, a man in a striped suit and a very loud tie opened the door. After a long wait, the Countess, 'a trifle overweight to be wearing scarlet', arrived and addressed Isherwood in loud, affected, gushing tones, regarding Dodie with a cold and withering stare. 'Are you staying to tea — or do you feel you ought to start back at once?' she asked them. Damn it, Dodie thought, they had been asked to tea, and stay she was determined to do. They were shown into a dim mustard-yellow room hung with modern paintings while the Countess talked at the top of her voice with many 'My Gods' and 'Jesus Christs' and references to 'this dump'.

Eventually the aged Earl appeared, his ancient tweed suit hanging loosely as if on a skeleton, and deaf as a post, so his wife carried on talking about him as if he were not there. She said, laughing loudly, that he had recently hurt his back trying to get two legs into one leg of his pyjamas. Alec handed round tea (black and cold) and managed a conversation with the old man who, Dodie realised at once, was both charming and intellectual, but incapable of hearing her high voice. When Dodie said it was time to go, everyone rose instantly and the Earl offered to show them his paintings, whereupon the Countess positively screamed: 'George — *they are going.* Stop him or he'll go on and on.' Dodie had never known a front door close behind her so quickly.

In the homegoing Rolls they became almost hysterical with relieved laughter, and the episode took on a Mad Hatter's tea party quality in retrospect: they had never encountered such rudeness. But to Dodie's astonishment Alec — usually much more generous and tolerant of Chris than Dodie — suddenly turned on Isherwood for his social ineptitude and gracelessness. Chris's *shoes*, noted Dodie, did something to Alec. Why, Alec railed, must he look so terrible and not know how to order a meal or tip a waiter, despite having travelled the world, made so much money, despite Repton and Cambridge and coming from a distinguished family and being the owner of two stately homes, even if one of them was now in ruins?

An interview in the *Evening Standard* indicated that Isherwood and Bachardy, after a stay in London 'seeing friends: Forster, Spender, John Lehmann and Dodie Smith', had departed for America. The interviewer described Isherwood's voice as 'the voice of the English public school boy now filtered down his nose': a precise description, Dodie thought, of Chris's voice whenever he was nervous or trying to make an impression. As for his Christmas present, it was a copy of his own *All The Conspirators* (which she already had) and a half-guinea box of biscuits such as she had given her neighbours the Pedders along with a book and a plant. Dodie was beginning to feel petty about signs of meanness in friends. Her old friend Madge Compton irritated her by denying herself library subscriptions, yet Dodie knew she had £12,000 from her late husband. 'As one who never inherited 12,000 pence' (she seemed to have forgotten the £40 a year from the Manchester uncle) 'I cannot feel too sorry for her, nor for Phyl, who has

£20,000 and is pushing herself into old age partly because of the pension she hopes to get.'

With Isherwood and Bachardy gone, Dodie had more time to fret about every writer's need for ego-food. Isherwood had told her that when he took his first screenplay to his producer Jerry Wald, Wald said nothing. So Chris said: 'Jerry, I must tell you I cannot *write* without praise'; on which cue Wald praised the work. But what meaning could there be in praise so elicited? She watched Henry Warren's ego being fed titbits in little ten-guinea cheques from *The Listener*. The Disney sale had given her own ego a blow-out meal; but she had sent Henry a handsome cheque so he could share in what he called 'the Disney lolly'. She had now quite lost the lyric happiness of the return from exile. Old possessions still had the power to waken emotions more poignantly than the beauty of spring. But candidly, her most cheering feeling these days was the thought of a good book over a good meal. Nights seemed a terrible waste.

She played old records, wallowing in

nostalgia 'for the vanished years and the vanished success'. 'I am always conscious of how *old* I must seem to young people now and yet even as I write I *feel* extremely young' (but then all her ageing friends said they felt young). After seeing *Dear Delinquent* by William Douglas-Home, she wondered if she might write a funny play again: 'laughter is such a nice noise.' She had finished writing a new play, but after twenty years, success seemed less probable than ever. 'There is something so peculiar about the whole business of writing plays. The difficulties and dangers are so great, the rewards of success are so great: I believe the ego of the playwright is more richly fed than that of non-dramatic writers. And success seldom lasts for a playwright as it does for a novelist.'

She began, twenty years too late, writing down the passages from books she wanted to treasure, wishing she had started in 1939, before she read Tolstoy, James, Proust, Compton-Burnett. Her first entry in the commonplace book labelled 'These Fragments Have I Shored Against My Ruin' was a poem from the

New Yorker, curiously remimscent of her own experience, by Robert Beverly Hale:

> I have outlived five dogs:
> Hector and Hercules, Genghis the
>   Golden.
> The fashionable Pamplemousse.
> And lately, Hans of Weimar,
> Hans of the amber eyes.
> You are my last, Denise;
> Life is but one dog more;
> Denise, my raisin-bread Dalmatian,
> Denise of the delicate crossed paws.

Dodie at once sent a copy of *The Hundred and One Dalmatians* to the poet and told him of raisin-bread Buzz and his delicately crossed paws. In a nostalgic mood she fretted over the cottage's 'clean, dogless rooms' and said to Alec: 'We have everything we want — except our puppies.'

In June that year, Dodie recorded her last visit to Ambrose Heal. She had been feeling guilty about not having seen him for four years; she continued to send him books at Christmas, at Easter and for his birthday, but his thanks had begun to be dictated to a secretary and signed 'Ambrose' in an increasingly shaky and spidery hand. He had not sent *her* a present for a quarter of a century. Suddenly there was silence. Dodie wrote to him; Anthony's wife Theodora replied that AH at eighty-five had become 'forgetful' and her books were lying unacknowledged, he having no idea where they came from. Yet she encouraged Dodie to come and visit.

Dodie dreaded it, with reason; it was a most embarrassing day. After a sleepless night they drove off on a bright June morning to Buckinghamshire where Theo welcomed them with her affectionate sheepdog pup. AH appeared, suddenly ancient and bowed, in a little-old-man's suit of liquorice-coloured cloth, with matching shoes. Alec had always thought him very ugly, but in his red-haired days he had personality and magnetism. Now even Dodie found him 'particularly ugly', with mottled face and hair too fine to look white. She had not bargained for a man without a shred of memory. Or perhaps he was just an irritable old man who found his visitors, their questions, and their patronising attitude, peculiarly tiresome.

To almost every question he replied: 'I don't remember.' To every statement he responded: 'What is the point of that?' and other rebuffing replies. He poured a shaky sherry and became irascible about the timing of lunch. Lunch, in Dodie's view, was inferior: cold chicken, new potatoes, salad, gooseberry tart, rice pudding and cream with good white wine. ('We should have given any visitor an infinitely better lunch — but no wine.')

Over coffee, Dodie tried to explain about the *Dalmatians* film but was floored by the question, 'What is a film?' When she tried to describe an animated film and the thousands of drawings needed to show just the raising of an arm, AH asked: 'But what is the point?'

She offered AH a copy of the book, explaining that it was really for children. AH replied, with an unexpected, formal lucidity: 'It may be a completely adult production, but I see no reason why I should get involved in it.' He seemed pleased with himself for saying this.

Then Dodie and AH were left alone. AH gazed after the departing Alec and said: 'Beesley's gone quite grey, hasn't he?' Suspecting that the ageing of others might be a comfort to the old fellow, Dodie pointed out that her own hair was quite grey underneath, and she supposed she would soon go grey all over. AH said, sharply: 'Why should it go grey?' 'Well, most hair does, eventually.' 'Nonsense. Why should it?'

Every conversational foray failed. Dodie told him she might soon have a play on again. 'But have you *sold* it?' he asked, with an air of shrewdness. Dodie asked if he found, as she did, the time passing swiftly as he grew older. 'No.' She asked if time dragged, then. He paused, thought, and said weightily: 'I have not noticed either of these things,' and stared at her very hard. Dodie realised he must think her chatter superficial and patronising, but could not find anything to say that pleased him.

In the afternoon there was an outburst by AH against Alec, for his description of a stove as 'Tyrolean' when it was actually Danish. Theo hastily suggested that they all leave AH and go to see the stove, apologising to Dodie that AH was being 'upsettingly difficult today' and 'making no effort'.

When they returned AH had his feet up in the study, reading *The Times*. 'Oh, must you go?' he said brightly, obviously greatly relieved. He became a smiling, relaxed, jokey AH now. Dodie told him how often they were reminded of him by the silver cigarette box he had given Alec (in return for help in dealing with letters of congratulation on receipt of his knighthood). 'Good gracious — what an extraordinary thing to give anyone. I must have been mad.' She also mentioned the Eric Gill woodblocks he gave her; but could not make him understand. She said he must come to her play (*These People, Those Books*) when it was produced. 'Oh, have you a play coming on? Have you sold it?' Here we go again, Dodie thought. Dodie told him for the second time that she had sold it to Murray Macdonald, who had been one of AH's co-investors in *Bonnet Over the Windmill*. Here, AH was right on target. 'Did he get his money back?'

he demanded. The mists of age, noted Dodie, had not clouded the memory of that £200 — which she had only allowed him to invest to please him; it had meant pushing out another backer whose money had already been accepted.

Alec and Theo went out. Dodie turned back and picked up a little brown deer she had bought in Austria in 1929 and given him as a birthday present. 'I gave you that,' she said. 'Did you? Why?' Dodie explained, and he seemed pleased. She went over and bent to kiss him. He looked surprised but eagerly raised his face. She found his skin warm and dry and curiously pleasant to feel, with none of the repulsiveness of his appearance. As she turned to wave him a last goodbye, he suddenly looked more like his old self, lying relaxed in the sunlight, smiling.

As they drove home she was oppressed with dullness, exhaustion, and guilt. Then she realised she was at her old game of imagining in other people the feelings she had herself. 'If he minded age as much as I would mind it, he would take more interest in life, religion, music, poetry — the real consolations for the old,' chided Dodie in her journal — seemingly incapable of imagining what it might feel like to be eighty-five. 'I am more and more convinced that one must lay up treasures for one's old age.

'But poor Theo — what a hell of a life she must have, looking after him. She is so pretty and likeable, and with a sub-normal eldest son too. Anthony is lucky to have such a wife.' They stopped in a nice old hotel near Rickmansworth for tea and sat luxuriating in the fact that they were themselves. Alec, said Dodie, had never forgiven AH his grudgingness. He was a master who never praised, as far as Alec was concerned, yet Alec would readily have remained devoted, had he not instead become devoted to Dodie. And he often saw Dodie made unhappy by AH. She wrote dutifully to Theo, thanking her warmly and saying AH looked well and contented and that Baylin's had never looked more lovely. But she knew she would never go again.

15

Disney Ex Machina

ODIE'S new play, *These People, Those Books*, was set in an old-fashioned publisher's. The head of the company, Ralph Medway, has a devoted private secretary, Margaret Grey, with whom he once had an affair, and who still secretly loves him. She is the mainstay of the firm, cherishing elderly authors but also taking on bright young writers including a talented Angry Young Man. The play has obvious echoes of the Dodie/Sir Ambrose relationship, and cross-references to her long association with Heinemann: there is a Dodie-ish bestselling author, Winifred Wing — played by Marie Löhr — who wants to write an experimental novel anonymously, just like Dodie and her later anonymous plays.

A happy company assembled for the long pre-London tour. John Stride — who had just played Jimmy Porter in *Look*

Back in Anger at Liverpool Rep — was obviously star material as the angry young man, a gardener's son. The other bright young things in the cast included Emlyn Williams's son Brook, Lucy Snow, and Georgina Ward who proved her skill one night by deftly kicking aside a chair that had collapsed beneath her on stage. The publisher's wife was played by the exquisite Diana Churchill ('the worry with the fringe on top' Emlyn Williams called her) who was loved by the company but whom Dodie found exasperating. Before rehearsals she would draw on a pair of spotless white gloves, which made it impossible to turn the pages of her script and easy to drop the small gold pencil with which she wrote out every movement in full, often having to rub out: 'Sorry, chaps, sorry, I know I'm a nuisance but I have to get things right.' Then she would go through the whole rigmarole again.

The young director proved quite inept. He would interrupt rehearsals to explain, Dodie thought quite unnecessarily, the psychological motivation of each character. A dinner was arranged at the Ivy to deflate him but he proved undeflatable. Even when shut up in The Barretts barn with Dodie, with a tray of objects in front of them on which to plan moves, he had no ideas, and his shirt was soaked in perspiration. Still, Dodie felt euphoric, fully alive once more, as she and Alec were flung into rehearsals, long lunchtime discussions, and provincial hotel rooms. They drove to Leeds for the opening — in the same theatre as *Bonnet Over The Windmill*, twenty-one years before — and caught the final dress rehearsal which went on till 2 a.m. The Oliviers, who were backers, came to the first night dinner and Dodie sat at Larry's right hand. Though he had once been to The Barretts with Gielgud, she did not feel she knew Larry well. But he singled out for special praise a line from the play — a sure way to an author's heart — which was Mrs Medway's 'How do you think it feels to have a civil, courteous husband who doesn't appear to know you're alive?'

Before the play proceeded to London, the producer Murray Macdonald agreed to take over the directing, but 'would only do it if Dodie kept out of the theatre' which outraged Alec, since Murray was responsible for landing Dodie with a hopeless director. They moved on to Manchester where Dodie made her first ever television appearance. She had dreaded it, but Isherwood had told her the best way to bear any unbearable fate, 'even being burned alive', was to accept it willingly. So she perched on a high stool, convinced herself there was nothing in the world she would rather do, and sailed through the interview, sorry when it was over.

She was also taken back to the scenes of her childhood by the *Manchester Evening Chronicle*. The Old Hall and Kingston House had been demolished, mere sites occupied by weeds and stones. But Thorncliffe still stood, black with dirt. There was a solicitor's office on the first floor, in her grandmother's bedroom, so the room once papered in rosebuds and satin stripes was now Dickensian with dusty files. Here Dodie had read Grandima's favourite book, Hervey's *Meditations Among the Tombs*, at eight. The cistern room in the attic where

Dodie wrote her first play, which lulled her mother to sleep, was still there. So was the window where Dodie sat writing 'As I Sit By My Window'. The garden was a mass of rubble, the laburnum and the weeping ash tree vanished. She was amazed to find how little emotion she felt: how could she be so resigned to the passing of time?

One beautiful autumn day, they saw a signpost to Marple, Isherwood's ancestral home in Cheshire. They found the house of red sandstone creating a sunset gloom about it. It was now little more than a ruin, with most of the roof gone, and the great staircase fallen into the hall. At the back, the land dipped in a dramatic ravine. Gazing at the stables and the crumbling façade, Dodie and Alec asked each other, how could he? How could he leave such a house to its fate? In fact, Isherwood had explained his hostile feelings about Marple Hall. His ancestor Bradshaw (his father was Frank Bradshaw-Isherwood, and Bradshaw was the name of his alter ego in *Goodbye to Berlin*), who presided over the court that condemned Charles I to death, had lived there, and Isherwood was convinced that Marple was haunted. As a child he had slept in a mullion-windowed nursery in the attic. One night, he arrived down in the servants' quarters, having traversed several staircases and hundreds of yards of stone-flagged passages, and yet with his feet still warm. He said his father had carried him — but his father was away from home at the time. And when his nanny went up to the nursery she found a heavy chest had been pulled across the door on the inside; there was no way for anyone inside to get out. Another of Marple's ghosts was a lady who had been divorced for her barrenness. Christopher's younger brother had seen her; she came into the nursery and told him he had no right to be there. It was a house 'full of evil', Isherwood said. Dodie wrote and said she hoped the ghosts of Marple would turn up at his Malibu dinner parties, as she had never seen a beautiful house in such an advanced state of neglect. 'We drove on, thinking of you very lovingly even though we shall never understand how you could leave Marple to its fate.' It must have been an impossible house, she realised; but she could not understand why Isherwood so little minded its ruin.

These People, Those Books contained more original ideas than many plays running in the West End in the late 1950s. Yet it never found a London theatre. This was a damaging blow — not even to achieve a West End airing! Murray Macdonald told her that impresarios found the play too gentle; and it just didn't say enough. So Dodie watched 'the death of a play that didn't deserve to die'. Phyllis and Madge Compton both told her they had found the affair between Medway and his secretary 'off-putting'. They said they preferred sex left out of plays altogether (which was rich, remarked Dodie in her journal, coming from 'two reformed old rakes — reformed only because they ceased to get opportunities for rakishness!'). They were like her Aunt Blanche who had urged Dodie to 'write a play about a nice girl who falls in love with a nice man and marries him'. Suffering one of her fiendish colds, not susceptible to Christian Science cures, she buried herself in her journal: was the 'traitor within' giving her a hint to keep out of the theatre?

She had sent Binkie another new play, with the unappealing title of *This Is Never I*, about the daughter of a distinguished art critic, jealous of her ex-artist's model stepmother (shades of Topaz), who sets up with an arrogant young farm labourer, a primitive painter. But she heard nothing. From a man who had lived in their house rent-free for fifteen years, what excuse could there be, other than his sudden death? Nor would he even accept their telephone calls. Only Laurence Fitch managed to get past Binkie's fierce secretary, and then only because she mis-heard and thought it was Peter Finch on the line. Finally Binkie was cornered into inviting Alec and Dodie to Lord North Street to discuss her play. He greeted her with a fond Judas kiss. They talked of the cottage, of his new country house, of his great success with *My Fair Lady* — anything but Dodie's play. Finally Alec brought up the subject, and Binkie said he was 90 per cent keen on it, but wanted some changes. Alec muttered, when Binkie left the room: 'He doesn't want to do it.' They left feeling despair about Binkie's slipperiness. And the play was never put on.

Dodie was mystified. She saw Pinter's *The Birthday Party* on television, and could not believe 'the repetitious dialogue, the dreariness, the obscurity! and the critics hypnotise me into thinking Pinter brilliant! Almost all the new playwrights have no story value at all. One couldn't care less what happens next. Older critics remark on it; younger ones appear unconscious of it. The theatre is in a chaotic state and even though it may slay me, I am fascinated to watch it in transition.' When interviewed, Dodie was careful to praise some playwrights — Osborne, John Whiting — but not Pinter or Keith Waterhouse and Willis Hall. The latest sensation was Shelagh Delaney's *A Taste of Honey*, which Dodie found 'pretty damned good' though 'that menace of a woman from Stratford East, Joan Littlewood, has dolled it up with all sorts of tricks'. She wrote to tell Isherwood that Delaney, pressed on television to give her view of *Look Back in Anger*, said, 'I thought it was bluddy awful.' 'She is an attractive girl with a terrific Lancashire accent. Fascinating to see what happens to her as a writer.' But critics today, she told Isherwood, only praised new trends: anything not new was doomed. She copied into her commonplace book a passage Henry James had written in 1895 when he was being turned down by magazines despite still 'burning with ideas and projects': 'I have felt for a long time past that I have fallen on evil days — every sign or symbol of one being in the least *wanted*, anywhere or by anyone, having so utterly failed. A new generation, that I know not, and mainly prize not, has taken universal possession.'

Meanwhile in Hollywood, the filming of *The Hundred and One Dalmatians* was completed. In July, Walt Disney and his wife, who happened to be in England, drove over to lunch. Disney at once established himself as the perfect guest because on seeing the cottage he stood transfixed, saying 'Wow!' Charlie had told Dodie that Walt's nickname was Mickey Rat, so she had expected 'a small, mean-looking Hollywood Jew; but he was tall, broad, mid-Western and good-looking'. A gentle, self-effacing man in her view, who answered questions courteously. Dodie told him about the fifteen puppies born to Folly, and their impact on her life, which inspired her book. He said *Dalmatians* had proved a natural: preview audiences loved it, and they had not loved *The Sleeping Beauty*. He assured her that he had really had to change and cut very little of her story — 'You should have seen what we did to *Peter Pan* and *Alice in Wonderland*.' They had excised the foster-mother Perdita, giving her name to Missis; but he had insisted on keeping the cows giving milk to the hungry puppies. Some of his people had feared this would cause offence: 'But I was once a farm boy myself,' he said. The only thing that spoiled this happy encounter was the absence of Dalmatians at The Barretts — Walt was sorry about that — and also the roar of planes overhead, which happened to be at their most intrusive. At each roar, Dodie said 'Yours', as they were from the nearby American air base.

That summer of 1959 was memorably hot, perfect for picnics. They took Henry Warren on more outings to churches, ruined houses and castles but he was disgruntled and quarrelsome, having had to forgo his £2 10s a week from the BBC in order to get his old age pension. And he would leave his gloves, glasses or cigarettes in the Rolls, and 'made a great fuss about trifles like having teeth out'. Dodie was beginning to find all her friends tiresome: 'scatty' Gwen and Marda gave them 'a particularly gristly piece of pork' at lunch and failed to ask Dodie a single question about herself. 'They parade their ego feeding so publicly,' she wrote. 'I suffer from ego starvation too, God knows, but I hope I feed mine in decent privacy; what's more, I believe my ego is less ravenous than it used to be'. Phyllis Morris, now living at Gosfield Hall, was getting deaf and boring. In fact none of their friends was ageing gracefully enough. Charlie, who was suing Fox for a year's salary over the filming of *Cleopatra*, and anxious about his grandson Tigger's hair-raising escapades, exasperated Dodie with his hardness of hearing: his telephone calls were punctuated with 'I beg your pardon?' People could be very annoying. A wasp, however, that stung Dodie and gave her acute pain for six hours (it was in her shoe) was 'the poor, poor creature'.

Even Isherwood and Bachardy were irritating. Isherwood looked 'distinctly older: dimmer and greyer'; Don was gentle and pleasant but Dodie now found him 'alas, not very interesting'. They all had lunch at the Ivy, where Isherwood introduced Dodie to Olivier as 'Mrs Beesley' as if she were someone Larry might not know. Isherwood, wearing 'his usual awful cheap-looking shoes', was carrying one of the knobbly parcels with which he always seemed to be burdened. His 'act of poverty' began to annoy her; and he was again a deplorable host, perusing the menu with 'Oh, heavens!' like an embarrassed schoolboy, so Alec did the ordering.

One thing that may have irritated Isherwood in turn was Dodie's refusal to believe he was not using the name Gavin Lambert as an alias. Isherwood had praised Lambert's novel *The Slide Area*, bestowing on it the cover-line 'I wish I had written this book.' Dodie thought the novel quite obviously Isherwood's work: it was 'maturely compassionate' and 'on page 48 there is a conversation which exactly paraphrases a conversation of yours with your dear headmaster, now our beloved archbishop. And who but you could have invented the Instant People joke?' Isherwood's repeated denials failed to convince her. He protested that Gavin Lambert was the editor of a very good British film magazine called *Sight and Sound*; but eventually admitted that he and Lambert, who lived near him, were friends and were 'collaborating' on television plays.

After lunch they all went at Isherwood's suggestion to the Serpentine, where they sat, chilly and windblown, on broken chairs on the dried grass, watching the non-existent swimmers. Then Dodie and Alec delivered Bachardy and Isherwood to the Spenders' for a party (driving via Regent's Park which was full of secret servicemen for the visit of Dwight D. Eisenhower to the American ambassador's residence, Winfield House). When they said goodbye, Isherwood and Dodie exchanged looks that were meant to be loving, but were actually despairing. 'Something has gone,' Dodie noted. 'Quite frankly, I did not find Chris interesting — and I suspect he felt just the same about me.' She did not believe she *was* less interesting, but the contact was broken. Nor was she reverent about the work of either Isherwood or Bachardy. She found Bachardy's portrait of herself too truthful to be pleasing. In Isherwood's new manuscript, which was inside the knobbly parcel, she found the story 'Mr Lancaster', the young Isherwood therein 'deeply unsympathetic — cute, conceited, slightly nasty'. (It formed part of *Down There On A Visit*, eventually published in 1962.) Christopher responded: 'I quite agree with your criticisms of my handling of my younger self . . . Yes, I fear Mr Lancaster is dull. I have no satisfactory excuse for this.' Dodie began to think Isherwood could not have written anything as good as *The Slide Area*.

In her journal for January 1960, while again waiting to hear from Binkie about her new play *The Zing Thing* — a little farce set in Mayfair with a dotty actress heroine and a plot based on Gestalt therapy, and Dodie's Positive Thinking — Dodie recorded 'one sadness; even more sad because it saddened me so little'. Theo Heal had written to say that Ambrose Heal had died peacefully in his sleep on 15 November. The obituaries were long and complimentary. Dodie's first reaction was not sorrow but worry: would Theo and Anthony expect them to go to the funeral? Alec would hate it, and since Theo and Anthony must guess Dodie's relationship with AH (they didn't) she felt her presence would not be 'quite suitable'. In the end she just sent an especially exquisite bouquet.

'I was so shocked at my lack of emotion,' she wrote, 'that I spent some time remembering the past and trying to revive something of what it meant to me. I can always feel emotional about vanished youth. But what I felt was a sadness for myself, not any real tenderness for AH.' She mulled over the memory of

Christmases in the Marylebone Road and her little tree trimmed with gold, which AH always came to see. The gold witch's ball still hung downstairs: what pictures it had once reflected, and kept safely hidden. 'And I remember Alec touching it and wishing on it — and my saying "Don't wish for what can't happen". He said: "It might." And I think somehow he knew it would.'

In this nostalgic mood she embarked on the writing of *The Town in Bloom*, the most autobiographical of her novels, candidly based on Three Arts Club life. She dug out an old photograph in which she and her gang were in fancy dress for a ball: 'You all look like tarts,' Henry said. Out of William Gerhardie's *Pretty Creatures* fell a Heal's chit for Little Gallery sales of flower prints, and 'it was as if the me of those days was with me in some way more vivid than memory.' There was a picture of herself at twenty-three, just before the Everyman days, wearing her hair in a fringe and a yellow jumper she had knitted herself, that was her favourite: a vivid, eager face that she felt represented 'the inner and eternal me'. 'And I feel sad for it, sorry that the girl it represents had such a lot of misery ahead of her. Was it quite as bad as I think it was? Yes, I really did have hell for years — no money, a disastrous love affair, and such a long wait for real success . . . ' This photograph arrived from her cousin Esmé, in a box containing her father's relics and a picture of her parents with Dodie as a baby: 'How soon their happiness was to end,' she mused. And here was her mother at forty, already ill, but with 'an eagerness about her face, a curious youthfulness and a touch of desperation in the eyes.

'She had such bad luck. She was brave, optimistic, gay; and a very loving, generous, deeply sympathetic woman. What quality drew such disasters towards her? I don't know — unless her extreme tenderheartedness caused an unconscious desire to punish herself, to share the sorrows of others.' Dodie believed she had inherited her mother's masochistic tendency, but she had the toughness to cancel it out. She decided that *The Town in Bloom* would be the wrong novel to follow *I Capture the Castle*, a favourite with schoolgirls (the only book, one woman told her, that had ever taken her daughter's mind off horses), since one of her heroines would be a kept woman, and another would 'anticipate her wedding'. She put the photographs firmly away.

A BBC television revival of *Dear Octopus* in March 1960 distracted her but the aftermath was depressing. Despite an audience of eight million the notices were hostile, led by the *Daily Mail*'s, headlined 'The Octopus is Dead At Last'. The kindest review was in the *Observer*: Maurice Richardson, who always liked her work, had watched it with friends and reported that they 'seemed to think Dodie Smith was single-handedly responsible for the Spanish Civil War and the Munich pact'. 'I am now obviously doubly villainous,' Dodie realised glumly. 'I represent both the Establishment and the hated 1930s.'

Laurence Fitch told her one manager had said her plays were 'too pleasant'. She decided to resuscitate *The Treasures* with its unspeakably unpleasant heroine. She also exhumed *This Is Never I*, insisting that Laurence offer it anonymously. But nobody liked it, name or no name, 'so they can't dislike it just because it's mine. They just don't like it.' Only one new impresario, Michael Codron, seemed keen, but said he could not do it unless given the name of the author. When told it was Dodie, he was no longer interested. Dodie said sadly to Laurence that her name was obviously a drawback, and he admitted it was true. She tried another experimental play, *Between You and Me*, linking a theatre festival production of *Measure For Measure* with the permissiveness of modern life. 'But it seems to make managements furious.' That too languished in Laurence's drawer, where all seven scripts remain today: *The Sofa and the Window*, *Esmeralda and the Cloth*, *Between You and Me*, *That Which Hath Been*, *The Treasures*, *This Was Never I* and *The Zing Thing*. Her ideas notebook reveals how many plays she was planning: *A Room With Two Fires*; *Octet*; *Take Over Biddy*; and one called *Ann & Anne*, in which a rich girl named Ann longs to join the masses, and

561

a secretary named Anne longs to move up in society.

But in the face of constant professional rebuffs her imagination stagnated. It simply would not function. She had no idea what happened to the characters. And since the Disney advance had dried up Alec said they would need, for the first time in their lives, an overdraft of £350. What rankled, again, was the realisation that all her friends had some inherited money; Phyllis had £30 a week unearned income, 'every blooming friend' had capital, and even Henry had been given his house and various legacies. Only Dodie had had to earn almost every penny. Yet she and Alec seemed to shoulder all the hospitality bills, were expected to transport Henry and Phyllis on shopping trips, and were still handing out presents which they could no longer afford.

She reckoned she had earned £100,000 in America (over £1 million in today's money), and £20,000 since their return (about £220,000 today), but it all vanished, what with the cottage bills, and Mrs Ridgewell, and the gardener's wages of £10 a week. Books were an extravagance at £100 a year, but at least they could be set against income tax. So she really must produce a workable play. Her mind was never at peace. She could not remember looking back on a year with less pleasure: general dullness, voting Liberal in the general election, continual naggings of bad news about her work. A chill wind seemed to be blowing, when even Isherwood had had a story turned down by *Encounter*. She was 'harrowed' by reading Wilde's letters — 'he was so confident that the Ballad of Reading Gaol would earn large sums in America and it must have been an appalling blow to find they refused to publish it there. Bloody hypocrites! Even when we lived there, people would tell us there was no homosexuality there! And we knew there was a terrific amount; I bet there always has been.' Luckily she could write herself into a state of euphoria just by reflecting on daily blessings of food, books, baths, work 'and the constant but not encroaching presence of a very dear husband'. 'But God knows,' she added, 'I could do with a few dogs.'

Perhaps she needed a change of scene. The country roads were full of cars travelling at horrifying speeds, the skies full of American planes destroying the peace, the field paths vanished; she might as well be in London — but Alec looked stricken if she mentioned selling the cottage. The Rolls, however, was a disposable extravagance. It cost them £50 a year and was frankly unsuitable for Sudbury shopping. Alec advertised its mint condition in *The Times* as 'practically kept in the drawing room', adding jestingly, 'would make nice Christmas present'. A handsome doctor from Malvern snapped it up, and Dodie was relieved to find she had not grown too hard-hearted to feel a pang of sickly distress as it was driven away: 'One grows arid, and aridity of emotion represents age. Annoyingly, age does not lessen one's capacity for worry. Worry brings nothing of value, and tends to destroy one's capacity for emotion.'

The doctor from Malvern told Dodie: 'Again and again, I close the door of a house and know that I leave behind me a couple going through hell. And there is nothing I can do about it.' Dodie found this fascinating; there ought to be a play about it . . . but it was not for her to write. She was now going to plays again, but the only one she came near to enjoying was John Mortimer's *The Wrong Side of the Park*. After Enid Bagnold's *The Last Joke*, they went round to see John Gielgud (by whom Dodie longed to be liked, and never felt she was) and were greeted by Gielgud: 'Well, we've got ourselves a stinker, haven't we?' Yet Binkie had promised them it was wonderful. Dodie told him she kept finding herself longing for plays to end, longing for her supper. Gielgud said, 'Oh, I'm always doing that.'

What really galled her was that her old friend Gwen Ffrangcon-Davies managed to keep working, and gamely travelling: she was soon off to the United States with Binkie and Gielgud, to play Mrs Candour in *The School for Scandal*. Dodie disguised her resentment in her journals by constantly 'despairing' of Gwen's appearance. She had cut her hair into a 'skittish' fringe and it was 'so obviously dyed'. She dressed 'messily' in a dusty black wool dress with a bright pink headscarf and her throat wrapped round and round with pink and white beads. She could have become 'a pretty, elderly, white-haired lady', said Dodie (as if she herself would ever have liked to be white-haired or elderly-looking), but instead made 'this desperate attempt to reject age'. And since Dodie was increasingly reluctant to leave home for any reason — 'Oh dear, Gwen is determined we should go to Cambridge and see her at the Arts Theatre. It will mean driving there with Sybil Thorndike and Lewis Casson . . . If only we can get out of it' — she was furious when the irrepressible Gwen came home from America full of enthusiastic tales of visits to museums, theatres, and the new friends she had made.

One new friendship Dodie herself forged briefly that year was with a striking young woman named Jennifer Lash, known as Jini, who arrived in the village to stay in the barn of The Old Parsonage, where the writer Norman Lewis and his wife lived (and live today). Jini was a most extraordinary girl: aged twenty-two, unconventional, original and funny, 'almost too interesting to be true,' said Dodie. She had just published her first novel, *The Burial*, and though quite unable to punctuate or spell, was working on her second. One of her uncles was Bishop of Bombay, another was a master at Downside: 'Lock up your drinks if a Benedictine visits you,' Jini used to say. She would ride around on a motor-scooter in beatnik gear combined with upper-class twinsets and pearls. 'She is completely right-wing in her attitude to life. George Devine said there is no reason why there should not be a right-wing *A Taste of Honey*, so Jini wrote one in five days. She could easily turn out to be the most brilliant person I've ever written about, not excluding Christopher — I'm sure that at 22 he could not have shown the conversational form she did.'

When Jini came to lunch she stayed six hours, with never a moment's dullness. She told them that at sixteen she had loathed her parents so passionately that a psychiatrist made her leave home. Even now, she said, she seldom heard a telephone ring without hoping it would bring news of her parents' sudden deaths. 'We talked almost as much as she did — about literature, philosophy, religion, people — and she was never less-informed than we were, and sometimes very much better-informed. She is a courteous listener and has an admirable sense of humour. Why, then, am I faintly suspicious? Only because she seems too clever, and is satirically critical of people.'

However, this brief friendship abruptly ended when Jini, according to Dodie, simply 'vanished' from the village. Shortly after this, on the train at Audley End, Dodie met a Mrs Fiennes, owner of a Dalmatian, a Great Dane and six Chihuahuas, who turned out to be the mother of Jini's new husband Mark: she told Dodie that she could not have *invented* a daughter-in-law she loved more than the vivacious Jini, 'a pleasant thing to hear'.

Jennifer Lash was every bit as interesting as Dodie had supposed. She eventually published five novels altogether and had six talented children. Later she took up painting, and had several exhibitions before her death from breast cancer at fifty-nine in 1993. After her first cancer treatment, she had set off alone on foot on a pilgrimage to Santiago de Compostela, the subject of her last book, and three months before she died she was dancing at the wedding of her eldest son, the actor Ralph Fiennes. She did not live to see his starring performance in *Quiz Show*, or his memorable Hamlet at Hackney Empire and on Broadway, but she did see him play Amon Goetz in *Schindler's List*, and when Ralph received his BAFTA award he paid tribute to Jini, 'more of a friend than a mother'.

★ ★ ★

Cheeringly, the film of *101 Dalmatians*, which had cost four million dollars to make, and took three years of work by 300 artists under the art director Ken Anderson, opened on Christmas Day 1961. Dodie went to London to see a preview, where the delighted audience included a perfectly-mannered Dalmatian in the front row who never took his eyes off the screen. Dodie was peeved to discover that Bill Peet had given Mr Dearly a new name and a new identity as a songwriter, Roger Raddiff. But she started to enjoy the film during the scene when the puppies watched television. She was sorry to see that the sleek snide tabby had become an ordinary cartoon cat, and she disliked the car chase, but she had to admit that the characterisation of most of the animals was inspired, the Suffolk background exquisitely drawn, and the whole cartoon both inventively realised and beautifully animated in the old Disney tradition.

The movie was hailed by the trade paper *Variety* in its unmistakable prose: 'Blighty's four-legged population rescue 99 dog-napped pups from the clutches of one Cruella de Vil, a chic up-to-date personification of the classic witch . . . Cruella ends up in the doghouse, and for the syrupy-sweet pups, it's arf-arf ever after . . . ' The reviews were magnificent, headlined 'Disney Back On Top Form', 'Disney's Best Ever', etc. — and the cinema houses were packed, as they are to this day every time it is re-released. The royalty earnings on the books began to go up too — and there were Disney picture-books of the film, including one re-named *Lucky Puppy* at 25 cents.

This threw Dodie back into a winning frame of mind. After the preview, she had written to Walt, praising the film but lamenting in a postscript the puniness of her credit. Disney wrote back: 'If you write us another cute little story like *Dalmatians* I will see that your credit is plenty large,' and sent her several of the original cartoon drawings. Suddenly Dodie had an inspiration: *I Capture the Castle* (whose previous unfulfilled film options had now expired) would be the perfect vehicle for Disney's new acquisition, Hayley Mills, who would be seventeen in two years' time.

She had given Disney the book at their lunch, and told him that 'of everything I've written, books or plays, *Castle* is my favourite piece of work.' But knowing he would never read it, she now sent him an outline of the story and a flagrant sales pitch. Soon a Disney executive rang Laurence Fitch asking him to quote a price. Dodie had now grown wise: $100,000 was the sum she suggested.

Disney might offer $25,000, she said: so why not save time and settle for $50,000? There were delays, of course, but Disney eventually agreed, if they could first take a one-year option for $10,000. Alec said, 'Let them stew.' After 24 hours of suspense, Disney rang and agreed to $50,000. Dodie received the call and went out in a daze to tell Alec, who was in the greenhouse at the time. Eureka! To be sure of having $10,000 a year for the next five years! When Shirley Flack of the *Daily Mail* came down to interview her, she informed readers that Dodie had made so much money she would not have to work for the rest of her life. 'I jolly well do!' Dodie wrote to Shirley. 'Still, it doesn't do one any harm to sound rich — one's then liable to become richer.' She would buy Alec a lawnmower, and perhaps a television set for Henry, or a motorbike for Basil the gardener. She splashed out on getting Debenhams to dye her Canadian sable cape at 50 guineas, and making Alec buy a suit for 30 guineas, his first since 1938. Though they had little call for dressing up, it made them feel younger.

However, when she heard that Keith Waterhouse and Willis Hall were to write the screenplay she was appalled. She had read their play *Billy Liar* and found it 'vulgar and dull'. 'I can't believe they will turn out anything but a charmless, common script. Apparently they do not want to be type-cast as lower-class writers. Huh, — if they write about royalty they will still be lower-class writers.'

In the event, Disney commissioned an American script-writer named Sally Benson, who had written *Meet Me in St Louis*, was a staff writer on the *New Yorker*, and had 'a wonderful feeling for this type of story', wrote Disney. 'I am sending Sally over to England for a few weeks to see the country and meet the people, to assist her in capturing the true flavor of England.' He would pay Dodie $2000 to help Sally, who duly arrived: small, sixty, and wrinkled, with dyed hair and eyes heavily and smudgily made up. Alec found her 'repulsive'. Dodie instantly recoiled at the harsh St Louis accent and voluble conversation. Sally had never been to England before and erupted in rapturous praise for the antique shops of Bury St Edmunds. She had drafted an outline of the screenplay which, although clearly the work of a shrewd, amusing writer who loved the book, incorporated 'all sorts of things which could never happen in England'.

They took her to a 'rather poor' dinner at a local hotel, only to be told the next day that the unfortunate woman was 'indisposed'. Dodie and Alec nevertheless went to her hotel and found her 'giving an admirable performance of a cold'. They showed her Thetford Motte, and Wingfield, the original castle, now inhabited by the elderly eccentric Baron Ash, with a manservant who would not let anyone in. So they went to Wingfield Priory instead, where the octogenarian owner, living alone with her cat, showed them round. They showed her St Andrew's Church, South Lopham — 'suitable for the church in the film' — and together they mapped out a good story line, which neither could have accomplished on her own. When Sally left (to their relief: why must American women talk so much?) they sent flowers to welcome her home to California. They also sent Disney a gallery of photographs — of Castle Hedingham, Essex; Bodiam in Sussex; the Long Gallery at Haddon Hall, Derbyshire; Scotney Castle in Kent and Wingfield in Suffolk. But the wait for the film proved interminable. Within a few years Hayley Mills was no longer with Disney, and the film 'Cassandra Captures The Castle' had not been made. Dodie, hearing Hayley later on *Desert Island Discs*, was relieved, as she sounded like a giggly twelve-year-old, quite wrong for Cassandra.

The winning frame of mind persisted: the following year she delivered a plump novel, about a pampered family suddenly impoverished, as in *The Railway Children*. She named it *The New Moon With The Old*, from the old Scottish ballad 'Sir Patrick Spens', because it would lend itself to an attractive jacket:

I saw the new moon late yestre'en
Wi' the auld moon in her arm . . .

The narrative has the classic *Jane Eyre* reversal-of-fortune formula. Jane Minton arrives at a country house to work for a family of eerily old-fashioned, well-mannered young people whose circumstances are straitened when their father becomes a fugitive from justice. All go their separate ways: the jolliest episode involves Merrie (a little Dodie character, but possibly influenced by the lively Jini), an aspiring actress aged fourteen, who passes herself off as twenty-one and lands an earl with a stately pile in Suffolk within days of meeting him. But the novel has neither the flavour nor the tightly-worked prose style of *I Capture the Castle*. It is episodic and curiously immature; with an amateurish lack of discrimination about conversational banalities. Alec's approval was qualified; he wondered if she could get away with writing about rich people who lived a luxurious life with servants in the 1960s.

At Heinemann, A. Dwye Evans had now succeeded A. S. Frere: a slight, gentle man of fifty-four, a Catholic and a father of five. Dodie found Dwye formidably firm and tenacious. To her surprise she discovered that she could be receptive to his criticism, and changed characters as he advised ('I decided Jane *was* too sentimental and made other revisions on suggested lines . . . '). Ted Weeks at Little, Brown offered a £5000 advance for America too; and a *Woman's Own* serialisation brought £3000. Money was flowing in, but she could not feel that anyone really *liked* the book. And she found contracts, dust-jackets, blurbs and proof-correcting wearisome. Isherwood had told her that what authors should do is shut books up in drawers: the pain of publication and its aftermath was just too much of an ordeal.

Her ordeal was the greater since no detail escaped her attention. She had a very sure and lofty idea of her own skills. To Ted Weeks, her American publisher, she wrote: 'I've given a lot of very careful thought to some aspects of punctuation, such as the use of dots and dashes, the setting off of dialogue sometimes by colons and sometimes by commas according to mood (I was delighted to find that this is something I share with Katherine Anne Porter). And it would distress me very much if your House did the kind of thing Viking treated me to over *The Hundred and One Dalmatians*, quite without warning. They removed every colon in the book and sometimes changed the paragraphing . . . ' Weeks came to visit and bored them to distraction with his talk of fishing ('God help me!'). After he had left, Alec said gloomily, 'That was the Weeks, that was' (the BBC television satire programme *That Was The Week That Was* had arrived), 'and we laughed and laughed,' Dodie noted Pooterishly, 'with relief but also with despair, as the book will be mis-presented and mis-handled.'

As well as reading two pages of *Science and Health* every morning (a chore, since she had no time for God, but feared what might happen to her if she let 'Science' slip) she was still memorising her favourite poems, especially Eliot's *Four Quartets* — 'my bible'. The lines from 'Little Gidding' —

This is the use of memory:
For liberation — not less of love but
  expanding

Of love beyond desire, and so
   liberation
From the future as well as the past

had a perpetual resonance for her. But Dodie was never liberated from her past. Outside events like Kennedy's assassination barely intruded in her journal, though she did find the Profumo scandal fascinating because she had met John Profumo's wife, Valerie Hobson, ten years before. 'I have often thought of her as a happy woman, with her handsome rich husband, her children, her Regent's Park house . . . She had retired from the stage . . . and now this dreadful thing has hit her. Perhaps one should be ashamed of one's passionate interest in it but neither Alec nor I nor Henry are ashamed. I am more deeply sorry for Valerie than for her husband. It is the kind of subject novels ought to be written about; I wish I were capable of doing the job myself.' Dodie was struck by the chic outfits worn by Mandy Rice-Davies and Christine Keeler at the trial of Stephen Ward. It was almost a recommendation: 'Do put your daughter on the streets,

Mrs Worthington.'

In February 1964 Isherwood wrote cheerily from Santa Monica: 'Happy Carson McCullers Birthday!' His new book *A Single Man* had received universal praise: 'partly because it was short,' wrote Dodie privately. 'And it is very honest about homosexuality. Alec and I did not much like it; nor did Henry. We found it depressing: Christopher without his humour and charm.' (Alec's letter to Isherwood about *A Single Man*, terse, brisk and critical, contrasts with Dodie's mendaciously fulsome praise.) Dodie did add, however, that she longed for a fuller portrait of the whole Isherwood. 'Also, I'm a tiny bit fed up with drunk people and I don't damn well believe that George could go on getting drunker and drunker and yet do all the things he does. (But then, I can't make tuna fish sandwiches even when sober.) . . . You said the book was inspired by Virginia Woolf. I was more reminded of the drinking in *Who's Afraid of Virginia Woolf*.' Isherwood responded: 'You put your finger on the real weak spot — namely that George is me minus my work, Vedanta [i.e. the philosophy he had followed with the Swami in Hollywood] and Don — which is a pretty appalling subtraction!' She felt that she now wrote poor, self-conscious letters to Isherwood, and was infuriated that he used off-putting airmail letters, impossible to file away, just to save a few cents when he had no need to.

The distractions at home were zoological. Alec had bought two donkeys named Sugar and Spice, and although Spice was Sugar's son they achieved one foal effortlessly every year, 'incest,' Dodie explained, 'being highly thought of in the donkey world'. Sugar would go to the far end of the paddock and give birth when nobody was looking. Dodie's mistake was to fatten Spice with sweet biscuits until he contracted a hoof disease called laminitis, as donkeys cannot bear anything richer than arid stalks.

The donkeys were followed by pigeons. Alec started with a pair of white fantails, which fluttered prettily about the cottage eaves, but soon there were thirteen, and then thirty-five. They would bang on the windows with their beaks, and invaded the dining room and ate all that year's crop of peas, but Dodie indulged them, saying: 'After all, we can buy frozen peas, they can't.' Young squeakers fell out of nesting-boxes, half-fledged, and the cats got them. One favourite old and lame pigeon, whose mate had left him for a younger bird, would sit on Dodie's window ledge for hours, impervious to cold and rain, while she wrote.

Dodie also encouraged a fat, furry, large-eared mouse which visited her bedroom; it would sit beside her fearlessly eating an Energen roll and she would fall asleep each night to the sound of its crunching. The bedroom mouse soon acquired a mate, and Mrs Ridgewell found two babies sitting washing their faces. So there were four mice skipping about while Dodie worked. Within weeks, Mrs Ridgewell found the kitchen 'carpeted in mice' and insisted on laying traps. Dodie had to descend nightly after dark every time she heard the trap spring. The survivors migrated to her study where they ran squealing across the bed, and over her face at night, leaping on furniture and bumping into each other. The 'ironmongery of death' was removed, and each night she fed her mice. After all, she reasoned, she had once been a god-like creature, bringing Energen rolls; how could she now betray them?

Finally only one mouse remained, named Teapot Tail, and he ate out of Gwen Ffrangcon-Davies's hand. When the mouse population began to grow again, she got Alec to make them a cave in the compost heap with a tarpaulin tunnel to protect them from wind and rain, and a small exit for any mouse in need of fresh air; Dodie replenished the biscuits in the tunnel every evening, but Teapot Tail continued to come into the television room for biscuits, without Mrs Ridgewell ever knowing of its existence. One night, Mrs R appeared unexpectedly and Dodie seized the mouse — 'it felt soft as silk and surprisingly *hot*' — and pushed it through its hole whereupon it gave the smallest of squeaks.

In the snowy winter of 1963 Dodie had set down her main activity as bird feeding. When the rats arrived the following spring, she fed them too. They multiplied until the lawn was alive with great rats, small rats, lean rats, brawny rats, brown rats, black rats, grey rats, tawny rats, as in Browning's Hamelin. Car after car drew up, on a sort of rat safari. When neighbours complained, Alec succumbed and bought Warfarin, 'Said to be the kindest poison,' wrote Dodie bitterly, 'as it is supposed to take only two or three days, during which the rats painlessly bleed internally. But who knows that this is painless? Who's been a rat?' The very last rat, she noted, took its bread from her sadly, and slowly limped away, obviously ill. 'There is so much good in rats. They love their young, they have so much energy, patience, such a will to survive. The essential rattiness of rats is a fine thing.'

Plainly these animal obsessions were a replacement for lost dogs. So when Esmé and Joanna Robertson, who bred Dalmatians near Sudbury, told Dodie that their beautiful bitch, Ophelia, had produced a litter of ten, she and Alec went over to Redbraes cottage and fell in love with the most engaging pup in the play-pen, a liver-spotted one named Brutus. All the Redbraes dogs were named after Shakespearean characters since the sisters — who still live at Redbraes — were the daughters of the Revd Cornwell Robertson, chaplain and housemaster at Marlborough and some-time head of the grammar school at Stratford-upon-Avon, Shakespeare's school.

Dodie had been fixed on never having another dog; how could they tie themselves again, and be unable to go to the theatre or see a play through production? Then Alec said: 'But it seems a bit awful to think we shall *never* have another dog,' and Dodie realised he had been secretly hankering for a dog even more than she did. Anyway, she reasoned, they no longer enjoyed theatre-going. And she had earned plenty in the twenty-four years when they had dogs. Brutus it was to be. The Robertson sisters nobly did not tell Dodie that Brutus was the pup they had been hoping to keep for themselves. They charged £15 for him, but Alec said it was too little and gave them £20.

It was twenty years since they had coped with a puppy. In high excitement they shopped for a trousseau of toys and dog baskets in Braintree, and took Henry and Phyllis with them when they collected eight-week-old 'Brutus of Redbraes', re-naming him Disney after the beneficent Walt. Disney soon ceased to be a roly-poly creature and displayed the Dalmatian temperament at its best: he was prepared to love every human being on sight, and would greet all other dogs with a disarming optimism. He once stood by and allowed a visiting Jack Russell to consume his dinner, benevolently wagging his tail. They never regretted having him for an instant. It was a pleasure even to watch him sleep.

Dodie now felt she could begin *The Town in Bloom*, the novel about her twenties, its heroine a girl actress named 'Mouse' who seduces an actor-manager, Rex Crossway, a combination of Norman MacDermott and Ambrose Heal. She identified so closely with Mouse that it was more like remembering than inventing. The seduction scene is instantly recognisable: 'I can still see the whole occasion,' she recalled once more in her journal, 'lit by the lamps of the Outer Circle, the dim lights of a quiet road in Chalk Farm, Norman's studio light, an orange glow, a deathly dawn light through gaps in the curtains, the bright sunshine as I trudged the whole way down Tottenham Court Road hoping vainly for a bus and, far more important, for a lavatory . . . ' She read a bound volume of *Punch* for 1927, but found herself constantly drifting into nostalgia, which meant the depressing realisation, once again, that 'the shape of my life was *right* until 1939, when I went to America, and has been wrong ever since.'

Dodie was thankful for advances larger than most authors', but was wounded by the critics' consensus that *The Town in Bloom* was 'childish' and 'unreal'. Its readability was grudgingly mentioned. 'There *is* a certain childishness about my work,' said Dodie, 'but this has never mattered before.' Having started novel-writing in the guise of a seventeen-year-old in *I Capture the Castle*, she wrote habitually in a style without pretension or sophistication but also without any shred of the irony or wry humour she had achieved with Cassandra. Brigid Brophy's review in the *New Statesman* said: 'Miss Dodie Smith's new novel is an oddity about an oddity — a self-possessed, not un-engaging, freakish gamine who gets into an actor-manager's bed, though not very far on the stage. The story is told in clean prose, in first person and in flashback. To my sensibilities, the book has *no tone whatever* — which constitutes its oddity; but it is interesting, observant and unaffected.' This reliable summary accurately pinpointed Dodie's weakness. Tabloid reviews were 'full of cosy Dodie nonsense'. In the quality Sunday papers, the novel did not even merit a batch review — 'a mass grave'. Alec consoled her with his theory that serious critics 'preferred novels about homosexual blacksmiths in Zagreb to unpretentious tales of real English life'.

Having been a playwright, whose every production was noticed, she had discovered how selective literary editors were about novels: only serious, important novelists achieved serious, important reviews. Otherwise they looked only for newcomers, and she had already had her day as a newcomer with

I Capture the Castle. Then in July the *Evening Standard*'s fiction reviewer, Richard Lister (*nom-de-plume* of the critic T. C. Worsley), gave her a long solus review 'so savage that it probably did more good than harm'. 'Do you remember *Autumn Crocus* and *Dear Octopus*' he began. 'Those clean, sweet, middle-class family plays before the Theatre had discovered Cruelty? When plays were as mushy and soft as the chocolates you ate all through them?' It was almost incredible, he said, to find this kind of stuff still being written thirty years on, 'as if the war had never happened and the Bomb had never exploded and the North of England had never been discovered and Kingsley Amis had never written *Lucky Jim* and Mr Wilson had never been elected'. 'Mouse is tiny and 18 and innocent . . . she's a funny, engaging little Mouse and an indomitable Mouse, too, who knows what she wants: Rex himself, even if he is 40, and she seduces him in the most charming, innocent way one night . . . In short, it's a lovely little whiff of an ever so romantic yesterday that never was on land or sea, even in

Shaftesbury Avenue. And it will make you either brush away a tear, or throw up your dinner.'

'I am in a way rather flattered by such a *huge* insult,' said Dodie.

She looked up Richard Lister in the *Authors' Yearbook* and surmised that he must be a failed novelist like whom hell hath no fury. (In fact T. C. Worsley was a distinguished author as well as a critic, whose autobiography *Flannelled Fool* is a classic of the genre, later read and enjoyed, unwittingly, by Dodie.) *The Town in Bloom* went on to sell a creditable 14,000 copies in hardback, and made her £10,000. And the makers of Veda bread — she had mentioned the Veda bread feasts at midnight at the Three Arts — supplied her with two loaves a week for three months.

At sixty-nine she was long since entitled to her old age pension, but she had to battle with the Department of Social Security to be allowed her £7, since she was still officially working. 'If I work seven days a week and earn nothing, they will presumably let me starve.' She had just read in *The Author* magazine of the sad case of an aged lady writer whose royalties had dried up completely: she sent her twenty guineas, thinking 'there but for the grace of God . . . '

So it was with great interest that she and Alec watched a Rattigan play on television, *Heart to Heart*. Peter Black the next day in the *Daily Mail* said, somewhat prematurely, that it signalled a trend away from the sauce bottle and back to plays about well-to-do, articulate, professional people. If Rattigan could come back into fashion, why not Dodie?

The pages of her journal were more and more filled with nagging regret for her 'lost years'. There was no avoiding it: the 1930s would not come back, with or without a new Dodie Smith play. And she had to face the fact that her homesickness for the theatre was homesickness for her lost youth, and her vanished success. Her life had taken a wrong turning in 1939, and even after twelve years back in England, she had not managed to find the right road again. Perhaps, she rebuked herself, she need never have another play success, and should accept that both *Castle* and

Dalmatians would outlast any play. Was it not sheer egoism, to mind so much about the past, when her present life was so much happier than anyone's she knew? Except Alec, of course, who was God's happiest man, and Disney who was God's happiest dog. 'As usual,' wrote Dodie, 'I have written myself into a Pollyanna-ish mood.'

16

When The Party's Over

'**W**HAT a tiny list of friends I have! All my fault,' wrote Dodie in her journal in 1965. 'I less and less want to see people.' Dodie's social life increasingly had the flavour of 'My dear, the noise, the people!' She preferred 'the bliss of when the party's over'. If she had bought that house in Regent's Park, things might have been different; she would have been surrounded by fellow writers and artists, with the Vaughan Williamses, Harold Pinter and Feliks Topolski for neighbours. But Finchingfield's remoteness fed the 'hermititis' she cultivated. Bachardy's journal noted that the interior cottage life suited Dodie: 'When she steps outside, even just into the street, she suddenly seems older, much more lined and weary, lacking in strength and vitality. Noise and confusion worry her.' She dreaded leaving home at all, except on excursions into Sudbury. Sometimes on Sundays they would take Henry and Phyllis, Gwen and the dog-breeding family Robertson to the charming old Swan Hotel at Lavenham for lunch, which cost £12 for the seven of them — a gesture no longer chargeable against tax.

One day Alec and Dodie had visited Phyllis's room at Gosfield Hall in her absence and succumbed to the temptation to snoop, lingering to ponder on the paltriness of Phyllis's furniture: 'just battered bits of stuff, all needing repainting'. The only decent pieces were the Heal's things Dodie had given her thirty years ago, a little table from Alec's bachelor days and a good desk lent by Jean Batters. There was also a stool made for Dodie by Norman MacDermott in the 1920s that made her feel awash with tenderness, as she always did about inanimate objects which had shared her youth.

She stood in Phyllis's room, feeling 'sadness for her, sadness for the passing of the years . . . And I wondered if I might have done more for her, and somehow stopped our minds from getting out of touch.' She had always acted kindly enough towards Phyllis, but there was no longer any real contact, and the fault was Dodie's. She had stopped confiding about love affairs since Ambrose Heal, because Phyllis was so indiscreet. 'And of course, my having a perfect companion in Alec made a difference. One has to work at keeping friendship alive; I haven't worked hard enough and I don't now. I haven't really much talent for friendship.'

This is plainly not the case: Dodie clung tenaciously to a few very particular friendships. But she had become increasingly uncharitable about friends' failings; and Phyllis in particular, being prickly, argumentative and still ambitious, was a constant butt of Dodie's criticism. She was now 'talking all the time in a loud, arrogant voice, laying down the law about writing for television at £600 a time . . . Neither Alec nor Henry will have her around'. She had bought two hats which Dodie found 'utterly unsuitable' for the mad price of £10. As for her paintings, that had once seemed to have a naive Grandma Moses promise — Phyllis had by now had several solo exhibitions — Dodie found them 'utterly bad'. 'She says that when painting she is utterly absorbed and never lonely', but Dodie knew better: 'she is depressed that it costs a lot and earns her nothing.'

Dodie had once liked seeing people, and welcomed visitors — especially in the thirties, when flushed with the magnanimity that accompanied her success. Without anything to celebrate, she was less inclined to be a magnet to people who might once have flocked from London. But in contrast to unsatisfactory old friends, Dodie welcomed her cousin Ronnie's son, Christopher Reynolds-Jones, who had come to live with his wife Bridget only half an hour away at Matching Green. Dodie found Christopher immensely agreeable, despite the fact that, unlike Laurien's brilliant son Nicholas, he 'went to a minor public school, is not in the least intellectual and I gather never reads a book. [Christopher] is a wonderful companion, really alive, appreciative and eager; it's no wonder he makes friends; he even seemed a bit harassed by having so many invitations.' All the Reynolds-Joneses were 'the most unboring companions'. There was nothing boring either about Laurien's family, the Wades. Laurien was married and the mother of two children, Nicholas and Alison, but her family, Dodie felt, seemed to be in ever deeper trouble. Her marriage was difficult and she would sometimes confide in Dodie and Alec, coming to The Barretts for tea and sympathy. Dodie must have thought that books would cheer or distract Laurien: at one stage she paid Laurien's Harrods library subscriptions.

Dodie herself was spending more and more of her time reading. All her life she was proud to have managed to afford books, even when she hadn't enough food. 'One of my great moments was when I realised I could drop my Times Library subscription and buy and buy and buy books. And still do.' She sent for all her new books from F. J. Ward of the King's Road: in 1965 she was 'struggling through' Christopher Hassall's long life of Rupert Brooke, admiring Elizabeth Longford's *Victoria RI*, and reading Iris Murdoch,

Jacqueline Susann, Stephen Vizinczey, Simon Raven, Kingsley Amis (whose poems she preferred to his novels), Edna O'Brien, A. S. Byatt; Harold Nicolson, Nancy Mitford, Margaret Lane, Edith Wharton; Millicent Bell's biography of Henry James (and Edith Wharton), and Doris Langley Moore's biography of E. Nesbit (published in the 1930s).

Guests were invited to The Barretts only on Sundays: the Reynolds-Joneses, the Wynne-Tysons, the Grahame-Johnstone twins. The formula was always the same: they would arrive at twelve noon for drinks. Mrs Ridgewell cooked roast chicken with roast parsnips and excellent plum pudding, served in the dining room where the curtains, chair-cushions and table-cloth were all in a matching green and white print with blackbirds. While everyone had coffee in the barn Mrs Ridgewell washed up and went home. If visitors were slow to leave they were gently 'edged into the garden', or if they were invited to stay for tea, Alec would uncover the Gentleman's Relish sandwiches prepared by Mrs R. No hospitable gestures were ever expected of Dodie herself. Guests were invariably waved off down the road by Alec and Dodie with their arms around each other. And everything was so agreeable that no visitors ever guessed at Dodie's increasingly anguished self-doubt, or her obsessive sense of failure.

Journalists who came down to do interviews were also treated hospitably. Nancy Spain, who had accused *The Hundred and One Dalmatians* of 'nauseating sentimentality', arrived: 'a curious, rather masculine creature, whose TV personality and articles I have greatly disliked.' Her article, when it appeared, described Dodie as fascinating, with 'enormous' eyes. 'My own view is that my eyes are little more than Chinese slits,' retorted Dodie. Then a child named Hazel Burney, who wrote an article on Dodie for her school magazine, described Dodie coming to the door with her hair in curlers — 'I, who have dead straight hair, plaited into a bun!' But one must sympathise with any journalist who came into Dodie's orbit. Alec and Dodie by now met so few new people that any visitor was mercilessly scrutinised and interrogated, and pages of Dodie's journal were filled with the shortcomings, real and imagined, of journalists, especially if they had failed to do their homework, or (worse) did not declare their admiration for the furnishing style of the cottage.

In 1965, she was still working — at approaching seventy — on six projects: two novels, two plays, her autobiography and *The Starlight Barking*. This last was a less successful sequel to *The Hundred and One Dalmatians*, partly inspired by a film cartoon on the children's TV programme *Blue Peter* called 'Bleep and Booster'. In her story every creature on earth was mysteriously in the depths of sleep, except dogs, who were wide awake and endowed with magic powers. She knew Alec would hate the science-fantasy element. However, she roped in the willing Grahame-Johnstone twins — now living with their mother and their horses in a handsome old Suffolk farmhouse — to repeat their charming illustrations, this time paying them £250.

Alec spent almost all his time on the garden, its rambling clematises, its herbaceous borders brilliant with nicotiana and night-scented stock, its pots of fuchsia and bright begonias. He had the help of Basil Jervis, who had arrived at sixteen from a school for backward boys, and their garden was so spectacular that every Sunday cars drew up and occupants fell out with cameras. Alec's pride and pleasure in his work was slightly dented by the 'commonness' of the admirers; he had to dodge meeting them, and put up a sign: Please Do Not Pick The Flowers. Some locals, however, found The Barretts' garden too bright, loud and 'un-country'. Dodie herself, as all their friends remarked, was happy to have the garden there but never walked in it, or learnt the names of the roses. She was not really a countrywoman at all, and began to persuade herself that she hankered for London again; all she needed was a room to write in, and peace.

Their domestic life had fixed routines. Each morning while Alec had his bath, Dodie would do her face and hair in the bathroom, 'a pleasantly matey start to the day'. Then they fed the pigeons together, and Alec breakfasted in the dining room, while Dodie carried her tray back to bed. In the daytime Dodie wrote at her desk at the study window. Her ideal days were those when no letter came needing an answer (worst type of offender: 'Dear Miss Smith, I am a Library Science graduate from Southern Connecticut State College and I am writing a thesis on children's books . . . '). She preferred to have nothing to do but revise some piece of writing at her desk and play the gramophone. Each day ended cosily, when Alec fetched the supper Mrs R had prepared. Dodie had taken to having half a glass of Bristol Cream sherry before dinner: 'I feel rather vicious because it really does make me feel rather better, and I don't approve of letting anything in the way of drink do that, really.'

On the rare days when Dodie went to London, she would revisit Heal's, although the shop had been updated to become 'almost hysterically with-it'. She would still pat the tall cast bronze cat on the circular staircase, but all her wishes were tied up with the Heal's of forty years ago, and one could not wish in the past. On the train home she would be absorbed by other people's lives glimpsed through lighted windows as the train rushed past ramshackle back gardens. She had dinner on the train and always talked to fellow diners: once she chanced on a Cambridge professor who had read both *I Capture the Castle* and *Dalmatians*; once, a charming woman whose hair was the colour of a thunder cloud, who would appear as the wife in her next novel. And she would bask in the glow of knowing that Alec and Disney were waiting for her at Audley End station.

Newly addicted to television, in the evenings they watched *Maigret* and *Compact* (the 1960s soap about a women's magazine) and the news review programme *Tonight*, and any discussions featuring interesting characters like Muggeridge, A. J. Ayer, Archbishop Fisher, or the judge Christmas Humphreys. In a rare glimpse into their separate bedroom life, Dodie recorded that every night, before going to bed herself, she always tucked Alec into his own bed first. He appreciated this when it was cold, but even in summer it gave him, said Dodie, a sort of nursery pleasure — perhaps because he had lacked such attentions as a child. 'He never fails to *groan* with pleasure at the prospect of a night's sleep ahead of him, with dog Disney in his own proper bed alongside. I never cease to wonder how a man who so enjoys his days can be so glad when one is ended.'

Much later, she would take an hour getting to bed herself. She had what she called a 'neurotic compulsion' to touch and say goodnight to various inanimate objects before retiring. This, like feeding her rats, and saving squeaker pigeons from predators, made her feel 'ecstatic'. She perpetually fussed over the comforts of birds and insects, and could not close a window without making sure no spider would be inconvenienced. 'I must spend hours of each day,' she supposed, 'on nonsense of this description.' But she dared not stop, she said, because of her innate masochism: if she cured herself of the constant friction of her neuroses, she believed, she would award herself some genuine misery. So she clung onto them.

Only a miracle would now re-establish

her as a playwright. Binkie had flatly turned down her last play, *Between You and Me*. Binkie, John Gielgud and John Perry had all written what seemed to her *stupid* letters about it. It was then turned down by Peter Saunders, Michael Codron, Donald Albery and Geoffrey Russell. Instead, Dodie started a new novel centred on a famous actor who although married is in fact homosexual. The titles *Two Loves Have I* and *Shades of Grey* were rejected in favour of *It Ends With Revelations*: the line comes from Oscar Wilde's *A Woman Of No Importance*:

LORD ILLINGWORTH: The book of life begins with a man and a woman in a garden.
MRS ALLONBY: It ends with Revelations . . .

It was hard going, and she wrote with deep misgivings. She feared that it would shock what family she had left — but also that serious critics would find the book too innocuous for its controversial subject. She was right about this. Since Dodie had read so much about homosexual life, and had been close to her gay friends, the novel ought to have been more knowing and more daring. She copied out a passage from Brigid Brophy's article 'What's Wrong With Homosexuals?' in the *New Statesman* of 25 March 1966, an imagined answer to an imaginary correspondent: 'Dear Madam: It does not matter twopence if your son grows up a homosexual. Be thankful he can love anybody, and direct your anxiety to seeing he doesn't grow up a vivisector, a matador or a napalm bomb-dropper.'

Alec, to her surprise, liked this book better than the last two, and found the hero, Miles, charming and sympathetic. Dodie was vastly relieved: although Alec was tolerant about homosexuality he was also squeamish about it. Laurence Fitch too was enthusiastic, but Phyllis objected to the ending, when the wife Jill, who has had several lovers in her youth, but is no longer keen on sex, finds her libido restored by another man and leaves her kind, sweet homosexual husband Miles for him. Phyllis became unreasonable, shrill with rage. What did sex matter?

How could Jill leave a charming man who had plenty of money? 'I soon realised that Phyl (at 72) was seeing herself as Jill (aged 34); Phyl would *love* to have a kind man who would give her an expensive flat and lovely food and demand nothing more than companionship.'

In fact Dodie's résumé of Jill's sexual history closely mirrors her own. 'At 20 she had been alone in the world. "I was sex-mad and sex-starved. It's a repulsive combination — I was 22 before anyone obliged by seducing me. He was 50 and the occasion couldn't have been less glamorous".' Miles, having just lost his boy lover in a car crash, marries Jill out of kindness when she is pregnant and abandoned by her married lover. She then miscarries; Miles waits on her, bringing trays to her bed, and they come to depend on each other's kindness. Their marriage is happy, and telepathically close, but they are never lovers. Miles keeps his own gay sex life secret and generally conducts it abroad, unless invited to 'a gorgeous orgy'. The female characters discuss homosexuality at length, and the young girl Robin

607

probably reflects Dodie's view: 'It seems to me that homosexuality is neither a wrong thing nor a right thing. It's merely something that exists. Children should learn about it at the same time as they learn about normal sex — jolly early. And they shouldn't be told that normality is necessarily right.' Dodie at seventy was perceptive and open-minded about sexual matters — 'politically correct', twenty-five years before the expression came in.

Her American publisher Ted Weeks was bitterly shocked. How would Dodie's women readers react? he asked. In America homosexuality was simply not talked about ('disgusting, hypocritical Old Bostonian!' said Dodie) and he did not care for the precocious young sisters Kit and Robin — the Dodie Smiths of the book — who are indeed rather tiresome, with their 'mincing' voices and arch comments. (They wear white Courrèges boots, placing the novel very precisely in 1966; Dodie's First World War memory of wearing white lace-up boots re-emerges with an elderly actress saying 'My dear, when I'd me white boots on I could have kicked God's throne from under him.') Weeks sent a list of changes that amounted to a re-think of the whole book, and reduced the advance to £3,500. Dodie was incensed, but the prospect of starting all over with a new publisher at her age appalled her. She wrote to Weeks explaining that the law on homosexuality was about to be changed in Britain in 1967, but he was unmoved: his colleagues liked it even less than he did. There followed months of mealy-mouthed letters and long delays. Although furious, Dodie could see his point about women readers. When the novel was eventually published, the dust-jacket blurb claimed it was about 'a matinée idol who has flirtations' — two obsolete and entirely misleading terms. 'Well so much for *It Ends With Revelations*,' wrote Dodie. 'I only hope it won't on publication end in tears.'

Henry Warren had fallen ill. Alec, tolerant as always despite Henry's irascible temper, was still doing odd jobs and shopping for him and bringing him books. Then one day in 1966 he drove Henry fifty miles to Papworth Hospital. Lung cancer was diagnosed. It destroyed his voice, 'a most musical voice, deliberately modulated' as the poet Richard Church wrote of him. In great pain, Henry was a difficult invalid, hating hospital. His friends Joan and Elizabeth Gili from Oxford were almost his only visitors: Joan Gili ('John' to Dodie) was a soft-voiced Catalan bookseller and publisher from Barcelona, an ardent Anglophile, who had set up in bookselling with Henry in the 1930s in London. Dodie went to the hospital just once, and talked to Henry of poetry. She had spent three days writing a letter urging him to embark on the kind of contemplation that can lead to a mystical experience, quoting Wordsworth's 'Tintern Abbey', which she read aloud to him, whereupon Henry's eyes brightened. But he told Dodie that when he looked back on his past he could feel nothing but a desperate sadness and a bitter resentment.

Dodie pondered: 'Death takes everything . . . It's too much.' On the day the Royal Literary Fund sent Henry £200, the Gilis arrived with champagne and they all had a glass. But he died that night. Dodie refused to go to his funeral ('Funerals are bad for the living'). They had seen more of Henry than anyone else since they returned to England, and she would miss those drives into the countryside. 'We never shop in Sudbury,' wrote Dodie to the Gilis, 'without missing Henry. We used to store up little incidents, overheard snatches of conversation etc. to bring back to the car and tell each other. I still find myself planning the words in which I would tell him something, if only he were there.' Privately, she felt that Henry did not really care for her or Alec, and his bad temper had exhausted their affection. 'Alec's kindness to him was out of sheer goodness, though it was sometimes hard to go on loving one's next-door neighbour.'

The obituaries were fulsome in praise of Henry's charm ('He had a happy life because he had a happy nature' — *The Times*) and celebrated him as one of a fading breed, the man of letters. His last book of essays, *Content With What I Have*, was published posthumously with an introduction by Richard Church who said that Henry occupied a place in English letters alongside Gilbert White,

W. H. Hudson and Richard Jefferies, and described him as 'almost a hermit of Essex, content with local friendships and an almost mystical conversation with nature'. Henry's cottage, Timbers, cold and damp and primitive (Henry believed there was virtue in discomfort), was bequeathed to the Gilis and sold to a local farmer and his wife. The gold damask curtains from Dodie's Marylebone Road bedsitter, chosen by Norman MacDermott and handed on by Dodie to Henry, were carried off to Oxford by the Gilis where they still hang, in tatters, in their spare bedroom today. Henry's bank manager came along and dug up his polyanthus for his own garden, which scandalised the village. But Dodie considered he had the right, since he had been good to Henry, whose bank account stood at just £400.

At least Isherwood was still around. He arrived in London, pleased to be raking in royalties from *Cabaret* the musical, thanks to dead John and dear Dodie ('I send you a vibration of gratitude every time I collect my weekly cheque!') and she asked him to read *It Ends With*

Revelations. He read it at top speed and rang at once: he found it absorbing, and had only two criticisms. One, it was a bit of a cheat that Miles's homosexuality was not disclosed until the middle of the book; and two, surely Jill would have longed for sex during her years without it? Dodie doubted if 'any homosexual of Chris's temperament' could admire her book. But he was willing to give it a public seal of approval to be used on the dust-jacket, and Dodie longed to have this, to get some notice from serious critics; but for some reason the publishers were not enthusiastic. In fact the whole book, though perfectly readable, lacks conviction despite its bold theme. The most vivid passages are about the provincial theatre, about plays that are 'teeterers' (between success and failure) and dress rehearsals where scenery, lighting, cues are all a mess, and actors shout and weep and finish exhausted at 3 a.m. 'They lived in a lunatic world. But if the play succeeded one forgot about the nightmare, much as women were said to forget the agonies of childbirth.'

A new penfriend named Allan Turpin, author of four novels they had liked, began a correspondence of closely-typed, lengthy letters that made him potentially a candidate to replace van Druten; might he replace Henry too? They invited him to visit, and he came in May 1967, but they found him 'repellently self-absorbed'. 'His novels are a carefully worked rehash of his own life,' Dodie commented without any self-conscious irony, adding that it was a bit thick, considering what praise she and Alec had lavished on his work, that he had not even bothered to read a single line of her plays or books before he arrived. Instead, he praised 'a perfectly horrid book called *Rosemary's Baby*'. And she decided, after all, that she could not keep up with his colossal letters arriving by return of post. So Allan Turpin was deleted from the address-book. Alec would always cross names out when friends died; for good measure, he would write 'DEAD' alongside. But even without the aid of the grim reaper, they were quick to write people off. (Rather in the same way, Dodie kept an index of writers who had mistreated animals in their books — Boswell, Steinbeck — and she never read them again.)

That summer, she was reading Maragaret Drabble ('bitterly disappointing'), Isherwood's *A Meeting By the River*, Stoppard's new play *Rosencrantz and Guildenstern are Dead*, Muggeridge's autobiography, and T. C. Worsley's *Flannelled Fools*. But no book that year could match the impact on Dodie and Alec of the Beatles' *Sergeant Pepper* LP.

She had previously assumed that the Beatles were just another gang of long-haired youths who came from the Liverpool slums (she supposed) and made an unpleasant noise. But alerted by *The Times*' music critic and the *New Statesman*, she had bought their new LP and was 'bowled over flat'. Never had popular music affected her so. The songs were not only funny, moving, astoundingly original, but Lennon and McCartney were plainly in touch with the past, and with real life, particularly in 'When I'm Sixty-Four'. All their songs had a living quality, not necessarily based on sentimental or even sexual love: 'It seems to be a love of mankind'. (Dodie's reaction was entirely in tune with the general one: the *Times Literary Supplement* called the *Sergeant Pepper* lyrics 'a barometer of our times' and at least one critic saw echoes of Eliot's *The Waste Land*.) How absurd of the BBC to ban 'A Day in the Life' because of LSD connotations, Dodie thought. Drug-taking among the youth was nothing but a substitute for religion: 'and no intelligent young person could believe in conventional Christianity, surely.' Alec said he wished he could write a poem 'On Hearing the Beatles in North West Essex'. They bought more records, 'Eleanor Rigby', 'Penny Lane'; they read Michael Braun's biography of the Beatles, *Love Me Do* (and later Hunter Davies's), eager to find out more. 'Those Beatles,' Dodie said, 'have done more for me than any experience I've had in recent years . . .'

But a new excitement drew her back where she longed to be, even if she denied it, stoutly telling her journal that her desire for the theatrical life had now gone for ever. Peter Bridge, then forty-two and the most energetic and stage-struck impresario of his day, wanted to revive *Dear Octopus*. (At first she confused him with Peter Saunders, the *Mousetrap* man, and was quite put out at the idea.) It turned out that Bridge thought *Dear Octopus*, being about a golden wedding, would make the ideal fiftieth wedding anniversary celebration for Cicely Courtneidge and Jack Hulbert at Christmas in 1967. Dodie was frankly appalled: she could not imagine these 'musical comedy stars' in any straight play, let alone as Dora and Charles Randolph in her masterpiece.

However, in her green costume she took the train to London to meet Peter Bridge. Crowds were milling around Liverpool Street Station for the yachtsman Francis Chichester's arrival after his lone circumnavigation of the globe by yacht when Dodie arrived. At the Ivy, Kenneth More sat at the next table. The boyish-faced Bridge was the antithesis of what Dodie expected, continually joking and laughing — so unlike Binkie who was now, she decided, just paying her out for old scores. Why, Peter Bridge wanted to know, had Dodie given up writing plays? She retorted that a copy of *The Zing Thing* had been sitting in his office for a year. But Bridge had only just read *Dear Octopus* for the first time, and it was the Dodie of 1938 he wanted, flushed as he was with the success of another revival he had put on: Wilde's *An Ideal Husband*. In fact, he confessed, he had already booked *Dear Octopus*'s pre-London tour. Dodie cautioned him that this meant little: Vivien Leigh's tour of *I Capture the Castle* had also been 'booked'. (And now Vivien had just died, she noted, alone in the night . . .)

But it all went ahead. The director was to be Frith Banbury, whom Bridge had met by chance in the street, and who happened to be free. 'A very obvious homosexual. Terribly garrulous,' remarked Dodie, 'and tells interminable stories.' Child actors were auditioned for Bill, and all proved to have painful 1960s accents, except for Paul Ackland (son of the actor Joss) who at fourteen was too big to play ten. Once the company was assembled, Bridge introduced Dodie to the cast with a flourish: 'Look who I've got here!' and their expressions, said Dodie, suggested the response 'Who the hell *have* you got there?' But dear Joyce Carey, Ursula Howells and the Hulberts all greeted her warmly. She was back home.

As usual Dodie interfered, and as usual the producer and director had to conspire to keep her away from the set and later had to soothe her ruffled feelings. Frith Banbury says, today, that he did not mind Dodie's presence at all, and that she was far less interfering than some playwrights he could name, but in Dodie's version he told her 'authors upset companies' and begged her to remain invisible. He told her that she had a reputation for being difficult, and asked her to make any comments to him, not to the actors. On tour in Edinburgh, when Dodie pointed out that the fires on the set ought to be lit, Banbury erupted and said that either Dodie should leave the theatre or he would. He later apologised for his rudeness — the cut-price sets had arrived in all the wrong sizes, so tempers were frayed — but the situation remained uneasy. 'Frith has never known an author of my type and I can well believe he finds me exhausting.' (Not at all, he says: he became 'quite fond of the old girl'.)

She disliked the gloomy sets: the boy-faced designer had not been born when *Octopus* was first played, and seemed to think it took place in a decadent mansion, lit for some ancient melodrama. Of course, she told herself, she could no longer expect to be consulted, but people seemed determined to 'get away with things'. When a portrait of a young officer was required, they hoped to get away with a ludicrous portrait of a civilian youth c. 1880. There was also a problem with the boy engaged to play Bill instead of Paul Ackland. Dodie found him 'too Jewish looking and possibly a midget' and suggested to his mother that his hair should be lightened, 'but not too fair: he couldn't be fair with those dark eyes' — then realised that the mother had black, black eyes and brilliantly peroxided hair. Eventually the 'formidable' Cis Courtneidge herself went on the warpath and managed to have the cast changed to everyone's satisfaction.

Alec and Dodie took Dog Disney to Edinburgh for the opening, where they shared a room in the Royal Caledonian Hotel for one of the only times in their lives, and found to their surprise that they did not get on each other's nerves: Alec's snoring did not disturb her, though the bill (£114 for a week) did. On the tour, Jack Hulbert broke his ribs in a fall but managed not to miss a show; and the houses were full. Every theatre they played held memories for Dodie: from Ripon, where she had toured happily with Frank Vosper in 1920, to Brighton, where *Letter From Paris* had opened wretchedly in 1952. But *Dear Octopus* was once again a certain hit. At the first night party, Richard Todd, who took the Gielgud role of Nicholas, started the applause as Dodie walked in, an echo of her old acclaim. It all turned out to be a useful consolation for *Revelations*, which had totally flopped. 'No reviews, until the *Telegraph* obliged with four disparaging lines.'

Back at The Barretts, a revival of interest in Dodie Smith as a curiosity was taking place, as the London opening was imminent. Ion Trewin arrived from *The Times'* Diary to write a story beginning with a quote from Dodie: 'It's so nice to be revived before you're dead.' The BBC came to film her at home, and never had Dodie and Alec known such pandemonium. Sheridan Morley and his team from BBC-2's *Late Night Line-Up* got lost, turning up just as the light began to fade. They started in the barn, but had to move into the road and repeat all the questions. None of the planned filming — of cottage, donkeys, pigeons, Dog Disney — could take place. Dodie found the interview irritating, but never faltered, walking alongside the enormous Morley telling him how she had bought the cottage for £425 and had set *Dear Octopus* in north-west Essex because she was so fond of it. Afterwards the crew of eleven descended on Dodie's sandwiches like locusts, gave her a tenner to cover the electricity (and £15 for the interview) and departed to have a proper meal on the way home.

For the London opening Dodie and Alec took on a young driver and dog-minder named Peter Sterson to accompany them at five guineas a day. Dodie was captivated by his easy manners and charm: although young and out of work, he was a social asset, who got on well with all the celebrities at the first night supper. He was struggling along in a house in Islington, where the walls bulged and the whole structure needed underpinning.

By contrast they visited Frith Banbury at his 'fabulously luxurious' house on Prince Albert Road, overlooking Regent's Park. Dodie was more than ever convinced that Regency was the 'right' period for London houses, just as Tudor was 'right' for the country. In Frith's house (actually mid-Victorian), his parents' portraits hung on the stairs. Dodie imagined how furious Frith's father, painted in his Rear-Admiral's uniform, must have been that Frith had been a conscientious objector. And there was a Canadian friend (Christopher Taylor, the playwright) in a flat over the garage about whom Frith was 'very cagey, which is pretty silly, Frith being so plainly what he is'. Frith later sold his freehold to a developer and now lives on the eighth floor of the block of flats built on the site, with the best view in London. Christopher Taylor lives in another flat on the same floor; Frith says that the apparent cageyness was simply that Christopher did not wish to be introduced as an 'adjunct' to him.

And so to the first night in the West End — the flowers, the seats in the stalls, the party. W. A. Darlington (*Daily Telegraph*) gave the warmest, and B. A. Young (*Financial Times*) the fairest summary: 'It is not a great play. It is simply great entertainment.' Milton Shulman (*Evening Standard*) called it the antithesis of the dustbin play; 'It might be called a finger-bowl play: refined, genteel and shamelessly sentimental' with 'a middle-class aura of chintz, chrysanthemums and muffins'. Harold Hobson recoiled from it. But it was the *Spectator* notice that shocked Dodie most of all. 'We felt the writer must be a bit demented, especially as he or she — the name is Hilary Spurling — suggested that Frith should have altered the play or burlesqued it.' *The*

Critics discussed it on BBC Radio 3 and Julian Mitchell said he had come out 'shivering with horror'. Dilys Powell, who dared to say she had been impressed by the play's craftsmanship and character drawing, was practically howled down. Even Dodie's old friend W. A. Darlington had said that perhaps the Randolphs were too rich? Dodie wrote to him pointing out that one needed very little money to live as they did in the 1930s.

Afterwards Dodie watched herself on the *Line-Up* programme: 'I thought I looked as old as the witch of Endor — rather like her too — but God knows I sounded young! My voice seemed to me the voice of a very skittish musical comedy star of the nineteen-twenties, or earlier. But everyone said my voice is just like that. And I was a roaring success. I hadn't planned to be funny but what I said kept getting laughs. Except for my face, I really was pretty good.'

At a time when *Dalmatians* no longer brought in much money — the Japanese seemed able to bring out editions without any royalty 'under the peculiarity of Japanese law' — the income was welcome. But although Peter Bridge remained 'a dear', the wranglings over the play's production costs, takings, advertising, cuts, transfer theatres and cast changes, occupied Dodie for weeks. Frith made twenty minutes of cuts, including the exchange between Cynthia and Nicholas: 'Not married or anything?' 'I don't know what you mean by "or anything".' In Banbury's view this passage clearly suggested that Nicholas was homosexual and it did not accord with his suddenly falling in love with the family factotum Fenny: 'You have started up a hare which you do not follow,' he told Dodie. And Dodie approved this cut: it meant 'a hell of a lot' just to have a play on in London again. 'Having a play running in London feels right, it is natural for me. I always did love House Full boards. And it has driven away the frustration which has been constantly with me ever since *Dear Octopus* was on before.'

It is a testimony to *Dear Octopus*'s lasting appeal (and also to Frith's sure direction) that this archetypally pre-war play with its nursery tea and dated jokes, the singing of a sentimental song ('The Kerry Dancing') and the patriotic Grand Toast speech, should have been revived so successfully and run so long precisely when *les événements de mai* were erupting in Paris and the youth revolution was in full swing: 1968 was the summer of 'happenings', love-ins and pop festivals.

One summer day in 1969, Laurien Wade, Alec's half-sister and his one remaining link with his family, who at fifty-three was still in Dodie's view 'beautiful, vivacious, and good', arrived to visit them. Alec had felt guilty, when he first left home, about leaving Laurien to cope with the family. Dodie's version is that Laurien had always wanted Alec to 'remain sane and outside the family circle of horror, so she could always run to him'. She visited them often, and this time she brought with her a tall, good-looking, pleasant-voiced young man of twenty-two. 'His name is Julian Bond and we liked him extremely.' It was Julian Barnes.

The story of how Julian Barnes had met the Beesleys later became an episode in his novel *A History of the World in 10½ Chapters*. Into Lawrence Beesley's tutorial school, half a mile from Julian's parents' home in Northwood, in the more salubrious reaches of Betjeman's Metroland, Julian had arrived in 1965 at the age of eighteen, while waiting to take up his scholarship at Magdalen College, Oxford: a 'shuttered, self-conscious, untravelled, but sneering; violently educated, socially crass, emotionally blurting' youth. He was filling in his gap half-year by teaching at this undistinguished crammer. It was not quite Paul Pennyfeather country, he realised, but the Beesleys' household accoutrements fitted Julian's fancy: their mahogany banisters, their brass taps, the woodwormy old furniture and the college oar that hung impressively in the hall. Lawrence Beesley, then in his mid-eighties, no longer taught but would wander through the house in his cream linen jacket and his Gonville & Caius College tie, or sit outside on warm afternoons listening to his Roberts radio beneath the wisteria, when Julian would cruelly yell out to him invented and absurd cricket Test Match scores. Fifty-three years earlier, old Mr Beesley had been on the maiden voyage of the *Titanic*, and had escaped in lifeboat 13. He had written his account, *The Loss of the Titanic*, in six weeks, holed up at a Boston club courtesy of the publishers Houghton Mifflin, and was thereafter frequently consulted by historians and newsmen, and retained as a consultant on the film *A Night To Remember*.

While working at Beesley's, Julian Barnes became the confidant and companion of Laurien, who had taken over the running of the school from her father. When Laurien brought Julian to Finchingfield, he had finished his degree in modern languages but had remained, in Laurien's house, in Oxford as a lexicographer working on the supplement to the *Oxford English Dictionary*. But Julian had literary ambitions, and despite the fifty-year gap in their ages, he struck up a lasting friendship with Dodie. She was the first professional writer he had met, he explains; she possessed an impressive library of first editions, and a complete set of *Horizons*, she had lived in America and she knew Isherwood and other writers. 'She was also totally unshockable,' he says.

Laurien's life seemed to Dodie to be in a somewhat disordered state. The behaviour of everyone around her 'is apparently beyond the telling,' reported Dodie. Laurien's troubles and dramas became a running theme of her visits. Dodie had always hitherto lavished doting praise on Laurien. Now she found herself increasingly exasperated by her. Laurien's life had been afflicted since childhood by her father's refusal to let her have a proper education. He had wanted his daughter to become a champion golfer, and in Laurien's house today there hangs a charming photograph of old Beesley in plus-fours teaching four of his children — including his son Hugh, who died in the Second World War — to play golf at Moor Park. Laurien in turn depended on Dodie and Alec as a refuge, and says today that she still misses Dodie 'dreadfully'. But as time went on, Dodie began to wonder what was the truth about Laurien's life. (Laurien herself never guessed at the growing irritation: she felt warmly cocooned by the friendship of Dodie and Alec.) 'She likes to come here and *talk*, but never takes any notice of our advice . . . '

Dodie and Alec, who had originally made Laurien the chief beneficiary of their wills, made new wills, reducing Laurien's bequest and adding sums for Basil the gardener, and money in trust to look after Dog Disney. With van Druten gone, and Isherwood fading from view, they thought that Dodie's voluminous papers should be left to Essex University, so that they would stay in England. (In the end, they were sold to Boston University.)

The London run of *Dear Octopus* had made Dodie think longingly of moving to London again. Alec did not want to move one bit, but she managed to persuade him to come and look at houses. Peter Sterson drove them around Islington, near where he lived, and dog-sat Disney while they inspected, and fell in love with, two bow-fronted houses in Canonbury at £19,300 each. Everyone advised them that the thing to do nowadays was to get a mortgage 'as one didn't ever have to pay it off'. However, after several visits they discovered that there was a children's school playground just below what would have become Dodie's study window. The relief of not having to move, after all, was 'fantastic'.

Instead, she worked on her new novel, *A Tale of Two Families*, lyrical in its reflection of the pleasures of country life: a rather sub-Joanna Trollope tale of two sisters married to two brothers, all sharing an old house in East Anglia, one sister secretly in love with the other's husband. The elderly characters are amusing. Baggy, the sisters' father, is an engaging old cove who, like Ambrose Heal, refers to his daughter's dog as 'the creature'. Granny Fran quotes Rossetti, shares Dodie's permissive views and tolerance of drugs, as well as her opinion of marriage: 'She never did consider marriage romantic; just, at best, reasonably comfortable, as her own had been.' Fran takes a nostalgic trip to London, filled with memories of her Bloomsbury bedsitter, the white lilac brought by her lover, and the scent he gave her, Temps du Lilas — all very reminiscent of Ambrose Heal. 'She hadn't been surprised that the affair ended; the miracle was that it had ever begun. Such a well-known man, famous really. How much had that counted with her? Quite a lot. She'd worn the affair like a feather in her cap.' Another character is skittish old Aunt Mildred who wears nursery-rhyme frocks and hats and carries as a handbag a little wicker basket 'that looked as if it might house a dove'. She holds her faded blue eyes very wide: 'At their best they looked starry; at their worst, just a little mad.' The young are precocious and golden. Corinna is at drama school, where she is told by Sir Henry Tremayne (in an echo of Dodie's own RADA experience): 'Dear child, you are invincibly a sweet, old-fashioned girl who will make a devoted wife and mother, but I more and more doubt if you will ever make an actress.' After finishing this lively tale filled with memories of her own past, Dodie felt flat and depleted.

It was incredible to be seventy-three. She still felt like a child trying on her grandmother's funny hat. As for death, she had long ago decided to plan her life on the premise that she would never die. She watched her friends succumbing to age. Phyllis at seventy-seven seemed to her 'self-obsessed and complaining' — though she was in *Uncle Vanya* touring Oxford, Cambridge and Bath, and later that year played at the Royal Court Theatre in London, so she was not doing badly for a seventy-seven-year-old in the swinging sixties, even if she did draw the line at being asked to appear 'in the buff'. Madge Compton seemed quite dotty: 'She is an old, ailing woman and sillier than ever; it is heartbreaking to think of her as she was forty years ago in the gay twenties.' (A few weeks later she was dead.) There was an uncomfortable Christmas night at Gwen Ffrangcon-Davies's when Marda was embarrassingly drunk — maudlin, lugubrious, and coughing viscerally — while Gwen combined extreme patience with obvious fury. 'My poor Gwen', Dodie repeated, hated age more than anyone: with her dressing up and her false hair, she looked like a fortune teller in a tent, yet despite her deafness she continued to get film and television work. Don Bachardy, who had arrived for a show of his work in London, reported that Charlie Brackett had had two strokes; Charlie too was soon dead. Now only Isherwood remained of their former little gang. And because they never socialised, they rarely met new people: so anyone they did meet, especially a striking young man like Julian Barnes, became an object of intense fascination.

There is something almost gloatingly smug about Dodie's periodic résumés of her friends' lives, all seemingly unsatisfactory, as lives so often are. Why did she write these updates on people's shortcomings? she asked herself. 'What is the point of remarking on the foibles of Phyl, Gwen, Marda etc?' The reason, it seems to me, is that her tiny circle of friends were Dodie's 'family' now that most of the Manchester relations had gone, and while most people at her age might cogitate on their family's fortunes and misdemeanours, Dodie's thoughts (when not mulling over her own writing) were firmly fixed on the lives of a few elderly people, none with children of their own. And it gave her 'some sense of inner virtue', she guiltily realised, to conclude that since she believed everyone was responsible for their own lives, and she was better off than her friends, she must be a better person. Her deepest pleasures now were: reading over breakfast; reading over coffee after lunch with Alec; getting into a warm pre-supper bath with a book; and reading in bed. But in clear-sighted moments she wondered how she herself would fare, if left alone. If Alec were to be ill, how would she manage the dogs (they had now acquired, from an American serviceman, another Dalmatian, named Jason, so energetic that he once ran into a tree and knocked himself out), not to mention the garden, the donkeys, the multitudinous pigeons, all made far more complicated by the fact that they lived miles from shops, and she was unable to drive? She would be entirely dependent on Mrs Ridgewell and Basil.

Again she ran through her unproduced plays. Frith Banbury, who read them, and had seen all her early plays in youth, speaks with insight and understanding of the Dodie he now came to know. It was he who told her she must move

636

back to London, to discover how much England had really changed, and why it was not 'at her service' any more. 'She had become essentially different from the writer she had been in her heyday. What she wrote in the 1930s exactly suited her audience, and it went to her head a bit. It was that sense of appropriateness that she had lost. I felt a great deal of sympathy for her: she had become wiser and sadder; and it takes courage to acknowledge that one's life has taken a wrong turning. But although there was nothing very wrong with the plots of her later plays, the observation was faulty: she was apt to go for the comfortable.

'There is a conversation in *Dear Octopus* between Dora and Charles about whether they believe in an after-life, and Dora says: "Of course I do wish you believed, because you'd feel much more comfortable, wouldn't you?" which was exactly what her audience in 1938 wanted to hear. Dodie belonged essentially to the theatre of comfort and reassurance. After the war, the world had moved on, and her audience's experience had been very different from hers. There was a deadness about her later plays. They were not even rescuable. She had lost touch with the way English people think and behave. She was marooned.'

One day at Gwen's they met Victor Pemberton, writer of television scripts, and his friend David Spenser, formerly an actor. They had taken a cottage named Craig's End situated between The Barretts and Gwen's house, and theirs was just the kind of company Dodie liked best. David had played Player Queen to Ken Tynan's King in Alec Guinness's *Hamlet*, and in 1947 he had been Just William on the wireless. Dodie soon asked Victor to adapt *I Capture the Castle* for television serialisation, but they could not wrest the rights from the Disney Corporation.

Alec, possibly to keep out of the way while Dodie was writing, would sometimes leave his gardening and shopping and just sit talking at the kitchen table of David and Vic's cottage at Stambourne. He would bring a seedling — several trees in their garden today are the results of Alec's propagation — and they found him good company: interesting, generous, fascinated by the theatre. He had many feminine qualities, they thought, but like Don Bachardy they emphatically believe that Alec was not gay. He was perfectly happy to run around after the 'manipulative and tricky' Dodie, who struck them as a complete contrast to their friend Gwen. 'Everyone had to do things her way, so that she could get on with her writing. She would appear to boss Alec about: "Alec, go and fetch another plate." But she did love him, and he was happy to look after her. There was no doubt about that.'

17

Looking Back

TO undertake a five-volume project entirely about oneself is unquestionably egotistical. Even biographies of the great rarely aspire to such a quantity. But then, as is already clear, Dodie was immoderately interested in her own life, and when she re-read her journals she was generally impressed. Reading 'An Eye on Posterity' she found it bad, but oh, how she longed to be once more the self she was then, just for a few hours. 'I have such a vivid memory I can see myself in the clothes I wore, and remember complete incidents — but what an enormous difference in mentality there must be, between me now, and me when young.' For ten years from 1970, Dodie worked almost exclusively on her autobiographies.

She started on 23 April that year and kept at it for 22 months. It was a reclusive existence, interrupted only for Phyllis's visits or trips to the dentist, and for Alec's period in hospital with pneumonia — when Dodie travelled thirty miles a day by taxi to see him, and had for the first time a jolting glimpse of what life might be like without him, alone in the cottage at night. His homecoming was like a holiday. Pneumonia, she reflected, had been good for him. Before, he had seemed jaded. Afterwards, he gave up smoking, with no fuss, and worked harder than ever in the garden: that spring and summer The Barretts erupted in daffodils and hyacinths, tubs of fuchsia, dozens of different species of clematis.

She did not tell Alec what she was working on. In the early days, she had always discussed new projects with him and shown him what she had written. He was such a good critic she sometimes felt guilty that he had no outlet for what might be a dormant creative ability. But this time she kept on until she had the whole of Volume One — *Look Back With Love*, about her childhood, the best of the five — to show him, pausing only to note items in her commonplace book. She copied out, for instance, a little verse called 'Home Thoughts' from the 'Look!' pages of the *Sunday Times* in January 1972, which — allowing for a style somewhat reminiscent of E. Jarvis Thribb, the parodic modern poet of *Private Eye* magazine — must have struck an ironical, or perhaps semi-ironical, chord:

I am glad I am not
Penelope Mortimer
Edna O'Brien
Muriel Spark, Margaret Drabble,
    Doris Lessing, Iris Murdoch and
    Mary McCarthy and all;
I would rather
Have the pleasure
Of peeling a hard-boiled egg under
    the cold tap,
I would rather
Make all this jam
Than be them.
How sour are your grapes?
But really,
Failing being Jane Austen, I would
    rather look out of the kitchen
    window
At our field.

Dodie had hardly ever peeled a boiled egg and never made jam in her life, but she *was* struck by her own incapacity to make the kind of impact on the fiction scene enjoyed by Spark, Drabble, Lessing, Murdoch. She thought so little of these contemporary novelists (she had started by liking them, but they were all now on her Index of Writers to Avoid) she would sympathise with the view that if you could not be Jane Austen, you might just as well stare out of the kitchen window at your field.

On her seventy-seventh birthday, 3 May 1973 — just six cards arrived, as usual — she recorded that she no longer had the time or the urge to keep up her journal (though she did so for another six years). Alec had read Volume One of her autobiography and given it the kind of exacting critical scrutiny he had applied to her first novel. Much tightening was needed, and Alec set about tightening. In fact she dedicated *Look Back With Love* 'To my husband whom, in spite of the great critical help he gave me with this book, I don't really dislike'. But who, she did wonder, would publish a book of memoirs that proceeded only as far as the author's fourteenth year?

Thoughts of moving back to London had now vanished. Whenever she went there she was dismayed by the modern buildings, the incivility of shop assistants, and by the sight of the clodhopping platform-soled shoes then in fashion. Only on one occasion a young man held her hand to help her down from the train and sweetly smiled, 'and it was strangely pleasant to hold his warm ungloved hand in mine'.

What had taken her to London that year was another television revival of *Dear Octopus*, broadcast on Boxing Day 1972. Joan Kemp-Welch, who had directed all the early Pinter plays on television, was doing a series of classic favourites for Yorkshire TV, including Ibsen, Chekhov, *Lady Windermere's Fan*, and *A Midsummer Night's Dream*. Joan invited Dodie to attend rehearsals in London before the recording in Leeds, and to Dodie's delight she found that Peter Barkworth was perfect as Nicholas. At last, by the whirligig of fortune, he had become a West End star — he had lately shone as Edward VIII in *Crown Matrimonial* — and now, in her view (and in Joan Kemp-Welch's too), he was even better than Gielgud in the role. Anna Massey, who played Cynthia, recalls Dodie as 'a little wizened prune in a mink coat', at rehearsals; but she no longer tried to interfere or take over the director's role.

One day in March 1973 Gwen telephoned to tell her that Binkie had been found dead in bed that morning. Dodie was surprised to find how distressed she felt; she had not seen him for twelve years, but, after all, she was writing her journal in what had been *his* bedroom. Nine days later, a pseudonymous article in *The Spectator* — 'Will Waspe on a world suddenly less gay' — shocked her as it shocked many others at the time. At last it could be revealed to what extent Binkie's 'iron fist wrapped in fifteen pastel-shaded velvet gloves' (as Tyrone Guthrie put it) had ruled the West End theatre, and how far his whim depended on the sexual proclivities of male actors, the camper the better. 'There is ineffable sadness this week in the twee coteries,' wrote Waspe (pseudonym of the bearded theatre critic Kenneth Hurren, who died in 1993). 'Elsewhere in the theatre there are audible sighs of relief.' It was 'a bloodcurdling piece of writing about a man only a few days dead,' Dodie declared. 'It was also about Noël Coward, who died only a few days after Binkie, another death that saddened me.' *The Spectator* received an avalanche of letters and printed some: from Francis King, from Brian Masters, and from Sheridan Morley lamenting 'a vicious post-mortem' for its tastelessness. An editorial note in the Letters column, however, stated that most of the letters they had received endorsed Will Waspe's view, but 'cannot, for legal reasons, be printed'.

So her acquaintance dwindled further. Isherwood and Bachardy came that February but she could not hope to set the friendship back on its old footing. Phyllis had moved into Denville Hall, the actors' retirement home at Northwood, at £30 a week — everyone there seemed to 'dodder on until their nineties', Phyllis said — and was bickering with the inhabitants, reporting that Austin Trevor had just got married, in his seventies, and Fay Compton had to leave because she insisted on smoking in bed, even though one of her sisters had burned to death there while smoking in bed. 'Poor Fay!' wrote Dodie. 'When I think of her as young and beautiful, and how good she was in *Autumn Crocus* and *Call It A Day*!'

She was far less charitable about Gwen, who was at eighty-two as energetic and adventurous as ever. That Christmas she had her usual fork supper for fourteen before going off to Marrakesh, despite waning eyesight and hearing. (She was still giving her Christmas parties at the age of 100, and reciting, from prodigious memory, on the radio.) By contrast, Dodie went nowhere, and fed nobody except her pigeons: 'Oh, the pigeons, the pigeons!' These still consumed well over half an hour, in all weathers, early morning and late afternoon. Then there were the dogs, and the donkeys, and the ducks, and the feral cats.

But she also carried on writing. 'I must work at something or I feel ill. I suppose for nearly eighty I am a blooming miracle in some ways: I eat well, digest well, sleep well, weight stable at seven stone four. It is true my heart beats rather loudly at night but it's been doing that for 35 years. When I go to bed I am glad to go — never before 12.30 a.m. after feeding my cats, which takes an hour. I used to say I hated the day to end. I still try to lengthen it, and read till I fall asleep over my book, about 1.30 a.m. I think one reason so many old people sleep so badly is they go to bed too early and allow themselves too much time for sleep. I keep myself a little short.'

She still had ideas for plays, though it was sixteen years since any management had accepted a new play by her. One was to be called *Virgins Anonymous*, set in an old house in Wapping, the heroine a bestselling author whose sales were declining. When Laurence Fitch told her that plays nowadays had to have a nude girl, Dodie said in jest that she would write one with lots of nudes, and write it she did: it was about witches, called *Down In The Forest*, but Michael Codron said it just wasn't his kind of play. It joined the others in Laurence's drawer.

Of her old plays only *Dear Octopus* regularly resurfaced. Richard Digby Day revived it in 1975 at the Theatre Royal in York, with Evelyn Laye as Dora: Boo's first ever appearance in a Dodie play. Dodie wrote a programme note reminiscing about their first meeting: 'Long before the first performance of *Dear Octopus* in 1938,' she wrote, 'two girls were on tour in a play called *Mr Wu*, and shared a dressing-room. Their names were Evelyn and Dodie. True, Evelyn had a few more lines than Dodie had, but Dodie's were all in Chinese, all four of them. And Evelyn earned only thirty shillings a week, while Dodie earned thirty-five. Dodie notices that when Evelyn tells this story, she is apt to reverse these salaries . . . The tour of *Mr Wu* was in 1915. So now, dear Boo, as you like to be called, you and I can celebrate the Diamond Jubilee of our first meeting. I know you will be a perfect Dora.' She was, and looked exquisite.

But when Laurence sent *Look Back With Love* to Roland Gant at Heinemann,

Gant offered only £800. He said it would cost twice the price of a novel to print (with photographs) and would sell less well. This left Dodie and Alec beset with anxiety. Inflation was mounting, while their investment income did not. Alec tried to keep from Dodie their straitened financial circumstances, while Dodie persisted in her Micawberesque faith in windfalls, which had always come along if she 'treated for glut', i.e. spent money in the confident hope of making money. The cottage was a drain, even with Mrs Ridgewell charging less than the market rate. (She had started working for Binkie in 1939 at sixpence an hour, and she was now paid £15 a week by Dodie. But in thirty years she had only one week off.) Basil was paid full agricultural wages, £20 a week plus insurance. Dodie had had no new clothes since Georgie Roberts died; Alec, she said, looked like a scarecrow. She had persuaded him to buy, by mail order, two Shetland wool dressing-gowns and two brightly coloured Norwegian lumber coats, which they both wore.

Alec had an additional sense of

grievance because he had wanted to use half their capital to buy annuities the previous year, but Dodie hated annuities. While they dithered, the bottom dropped out of the stock market and inflation soared. Alec would lie awake wishing they had bought the annuities. Dodie kept telling him she had always managed to pull rabbits out of the hat — just as she did with *Autumn Crocus* forty-two years ago. But now she needed a giant rabbit. If she died, she consoled herself, Alec would be all right: their assets plus the sale of the cottage and land would buy him a handsome annuity.

The rabbit looked as if it might appear when the reviews for *Look Back With Love*, published in 1974, were outstandingly enthusiastic. Interviewers flocked to see her, and Dodie put on a good, chatty performance as a quaint old character, a voice from the past. The book's newspaper serialisation meant the arrival of long letters from people who had been at school with her, and a shoal of letters from people named Smith who wondered if they might be related. A beautiful girl called Gay

Search arrived to interview her for *The Times* and Dodie thought it the best representation of herself ever. By careless mismanagement, Dodie's interviews on the *Today* programme, *Woman's Hour* and *Kaleidoscope* with Sarah Dunant all came out on the same day: by the time *Kaleidoscope* was aired the announcer said in a weary voice: 'As anyone who listens to the BBC will know, Dodie Smith's autobiography came out today . . .'

In August that year the BBC asked her again to choose her Desert Island Discs. She had originally been asked in 1967, but had backed out because they would not let her play the Beatles' 'A Day in the Life', banned for its alleged reference to drugs. This time she decided not to insist: the Beatles had never been the same since the group broke up. She made a rare excursion to London for lunch with Roy Plomley and back to Broadcasting House to listen to records for an hour, and to make the recording 'peacefully and with no snags'. Her selection consisted of Tchaikovsky's 'June Barcarolle' (for her childhood in Kingston House);

Schumann's '*Im Wunderschönen Monat Mai*' (reminiscent of the Three Arts Club and *Autumn Crocus*); two Beethoven quartets; Brahms's Clarinet Quintet, to link with *Lovers and Friends*; a Fauré song to represent a specially loved composer; the Beatles' 'For the Benefit of Mr Kite', from *Sergeant Pepper*; and Scott Joplin's 'The Entertainer' to please Alec. She had not told Alec she was including the Scott Joplin, and when they listened to the broadcast together, tears of pleased surprise came into his eyes.

She had not realised how many letters would arrive for 'Dodie Smith, Finchingfield' as she had mentioned the village by name. Many were dreary, 'from people who just wanted to write about themselves'. (Dodie, who so loved to write about herself, was always annoyed if others indulged themselves in the same way.) The only interesting one came from Evelyn Herring, now a retired sculptor living in St Ives, whose giving up her job at Heal's in 1923 opened up that momentous window of opportunity to Dodie. And the writer Michael De-la-Noy wrote to tell Dodie that *I Capture the Castle*, which he had first read at school, had pulled him through a nervous breakdown once, while he was in the army in Egypt; he had even called his Sealyham dog Dodie. (From the ensuing interview he did for the *Illustrated London News* developed a penfriendship, and every year he rang Dodie on 3 May.)

Only the sales of her memoirs — barely 3000 — were depressing. But she got another £3000 from Pan for the paperback of *The Hundred and One Dalmatians* which had now sold 150,000 copies. She was grateful to Disney because it was through his film that the hardcover of *The Hundred and One Dalmatians* still sold so well after twenty years — at £6.95 now instead of ten-and-sixpence. Batches of letters came from schoolchildren encouraged by their teachers, and it was a blessed relief when Viking released a handout entitled 'About the Author' for schools — although 'Dalmatians' was incorrectly spelled eight times.

In September that year came a blow. Heinemann turned down Volume Two of her memoirs — *Look Back With*

Mixed Feelings, about her twenties, the Three Arts, and Heal's — saying it was 'much too long and dull'. They suggested cutting it by half and sticking it together with Volume Three. Dodie was outraged — what a suggestion 'to an author who has been with Heinemann for forty years, and never lost them a penny'. 'And despite the fact that *Look Back With Love* got the best reviews I have ever had, was reprinted and still brings in letters asking for a continuation,' she wrote to Michael De-la-Noy. He had gone down to The Barretts on a Saturday of wind and rain, and was treated with the usual courtesy: a letter beforehand asking if he had any special likes or dislikes in food, sherry in the barn before lunch, waving goodbye at the gate afterwards. Before he left the cottage, he was earnestly asked, 'What do you think about people like us? How do we come across?' De-la-Noy felt strangely drawn to Dodie, 'a little gnome of a woman with a squeaky voice' whom one could not imagine ever having been pretty, or able to act. She had told him: 'I think I'm rather an oddity, really. But I do my very very best to write well.'

When his interview appeared, apart from the fact that it announced 'Dodie Smith is 80 this year' and that 'Dalmatians' was again spelt 'Dalmations', she liked it very well, especially the photograph in which an enormous seven-year-old Jason appeared to be bursting out of the picture. 'But I now like no photograph of myself.' Dodie had always privately referred to the two photographs newspapers used of her as 'The Corpse' and 'The Horse' but now she hated her elderly physique. Her legs and feet were no longer pretty; her hands, which had remained a child's hands for so long, were gnarled; her stomach stuck out, possibly making up for her behind which had disappeared altogether; and she was sure she had lost height — as indeed she had.

Winter gales removed part of the thatch from the back barn, in which Dodie's adopted wild kittens were living, and the thatch needed expensive repairs. The cottage itself earned £100 for a two-day shoot as Betsey Trotwood's cottage in a televised *David Copperfield*. Alec, so proud of the cottage and garden, welcomed the disruption and the hurly-burly of the television world: a crew of thirty, two enormous trucks and a mobile canteen arrived. Dodie found it huge fun, and declared that 'all BBC people are nice.'

A month after her eightieth birthday, inspired by the kittens in the barn, she embarked on a new children's book, *The Midnight Kittens*, about a pair of orphaned and preternaturally bright twins who live with their grandmother in a cottage in Suffolk and put out saucers of milk for some kittens that appear each midnight. Their investigation into where the kittens come from leads them to Freke Hall and a 100–year-old lady, Miss Freke (reminiscent of Grandima), who keeps them rapt with her reminiscences, and to a commune of hippies in kaftans and headbands named Gary, Sandra, Kevin, Marlene and their babies, Lance and Maureen. It is lively, funny, full of well-observed characters and quite charming.

But as Dodie had told Gay Search, quoting Shaw: 'The bucket still goes down into the well, but less and less water comes up each time.' A period of miserable frustration set in after the letter from Heinemann. Frith Banbury tried to help, as did Isherwood and Bachardy, who professed themselves 'horrified' by this treatment of her. Other publishers were approached while Dodie spiritedly polished off her first thriller, *The Girl From the Candlelit Bath*. Livia Gollancz turned this down, saying she could not quite believe the story. One can only say this is hardly surprising: it is a preposterous story, even for a thriller. The heroine is a dim young actress known as 'the girl from the candlelit bath' since she once appeared, tastefully naked, in a soap commercial filmed in a candlelit bathroom. She is now married to a Tory MP. But the plot is fantastical: the villains, a mad brother and sister named Cyprian and Celina Slepe, live in a crumbling Suffolk manor, and the solution involves an organisation pledged to fight the threat of Marxism which will dominate the entire world if left unchecked. It is all so absurd that one cannot imagine Alec allowing it past his blue pencil.

Dodie had decided to finish *The Midnight Kittens* for the sheer pleasure of *not* sending it to Heinemann. Publishers, she said, were just not keen on elderly authors. She was therefore cheered that Ben Travers — author of pre-war Aldwych farces, whose plays had been refused by London managements for longer than Dodie's — was having, at the age of ninety-two, a spectacular success with *The Bed Before Yesterday* — 'at the National Theatre, forsooth! And now managements jump on the bandwagon to revive his old farces, and he has just been awarded the OBE. Hooray!'

Before *Look Back With Mixed Feelings* found a publisher, she discovered that Norman MacDermott was still alive — and he figured prominently in this manuscript. She had assumed he was dead, but just in case, she had disguised him as 'Arlington'. Now she heard that he was publishing his own memoir of the Everyman years, called *Everymania*. Before her ordered copy arrived, a gift copy arrived from MacDermott himself, inscribed 'To Dodie, one of the maniacs'. Dodie found it 'perfunctory' about herself, which it is, but wrote to thank him, praising it highly. In a stiff and courteous reply that gave no hint of their long-ago intimacy, he said he was now approaching ninety, lived in Argyllshire overlooking a magnificent seascape, had survived nineteen operations (in 1922 he had said he had five years to live) and still regretted that in 1931 he had been unable to raise the money to present *Autumn Crocus* himself. Dodie decided to tone down all her references to 'Arlington'.

She felt no emotion for him, but memories of her own young self still moved her deeply. She went one day, while in London, to Regent's Park and found it almost unrecognisable. The young may trees, so pretty that Easter when she first went to Heal's, were now colossal. She realised that *fifty* years had passed. 'I felt like a ghost revisiting, I cannot recapture how strange I found it. But it is still beautiful, and soothing to have such an oasis in changing London. I have tried to like some of the changes: tried to admire the great glass boxes towering over a fast-vanishing elegance. But the shops get commoner and commoner, and the people in the streets look unbelievably shoddy. Surely there will never come a time when the clothes of the present day acquire a period charm?' On the site of the bedsitter in the Marylebone Road where she wrote *Autumn Crocus*, there now stood an office block, Castrol House.

Dodie and Alec had become useful sources for biographers of Isherwood. Brian Finney, a bearded young Open University teacher, arrived and took away the Isherwood correspondence. They liked him, though his wife's style ('no makeup except eyes outlined with black; a long with-it dress and thin black stockings with mauve suede shoes') was not to their ossified taste. They were even more fascinated by the next biographer, Jonathan Fryer, an attractive young man of twenty-six. He had been adopted as a child and brought up a few miles from Old Trafford. After Manchester Grammar School and Oxford, he had become a Quaker, and was now living in Brussels 'with a nice friend. He doesn't give the impression of being a homosexual but he probably is,' wrote Dodie, adding, 'We are always faintly astonished to realise how famous Christopher is.' Isherwood himself came in June 1976 with Bachardy, bringing David Hockney; they had all been to Aldeburgh to call on Benjamin Britten, who was now terminally ill. But these brief visitations were no substitute for the friendship of a quarter of a century before.

In the tremendous heatwave that June Alec went regularly to bathe in the pool belonging to the neighbours, the Mortiboys, nostalgic for the bathing days in California which Dodie, of course, did not share. Victor Pemberton has an abiding memory that whenever he drove past The Barretts on his way to Stambourne from London after midnight, he would see Dodie's small figure silhouetted in the upstairs window crouched over her typewriter, the rest of the cottage in darkness, as she wrote into the night.

They had by now acquired the seventh Dalmatian, Charley, to join Jason after Disney died. Charley — 'Charles on

Sundays' — was by far the roughest and most destructive and mischievous of their dogs. He was pink-eyed and volatile, and would bare his teeth and snarl. He knocked Dodie down with ease, bit people's feet, broke things, stole food, pushed people off their chairs by getting up behind them, and barked continuously. 'He was vociferous and nearly always violent,' Julian Barnes says. When he was still a puppy they had to construct a fireplace bed with a heavy cage to keep him in, which some thought made him more savage. But if let loose, he would break up the house. When Alec was in hospital with a hiatus hernia, Dodie had to enlist the saintly Mrs Ridgewell to come back at night to help get Charley in and out. But Mrs Ridgewell loved Charley: he would put his head in her lap and lick her hands.

The fate of Dodie's next four volumes of autobiography was a constant nagging worry. Despite her extraordinary flair for autobiography, it shows an unrealistic conceit about her life and her work, that she still insisted on five volumes, and could not understand that people might be less interested in the latter half of her life. W. H. Allen, then owned by the theatre group Howard and Wyndham, came to the rescue; they would pay £1000 for Volume Two, and would also publish her thriller *and* her new children's book — and all on the same day: 24 April 1978.

Victoria Huxley, whom W. H. Allen deemed their most suitable editor, discovered that dealing with Dodie and Alec meant 'receiving Alec's meticulously typed instructions, being summoned to the cottage, having to guarantee full consultation with Dodie at every stage of the book's production, and no mucking about with the text.' She arrived at Finchingfield: 'small, beautiful in an odd way,' wrote Dodie, 'dressed in antique clothes from second hand shops.' She was met by Alec at Audley End, and greeted at the cottage by the two bounding dogs, one of which knocked Dodie right over. After lunch at a pub on the village green, Victoria was ushered into the barn to talk. When Dodie turned frosty at her suggestion of cuts, Victoria at once responded: 'Oh, we'll publish the book even if you don't change a line.' 'Since the prose was beautiful and clear, not a comma needed altering anyway, but it was obvious that Dodie would be hard to convince that anything needed reworking or revising. She was a hard taskmistress, but the kind you wanted to please.' Dodie presented Victoria with one of her mother's fine Victorian shawls.

'She was amused by the Huxley connection,' Victoria says, 'and said she thought there was too much sex in my great-uncle Aldous's books. But Alec told me that what fascinated Dodie was that I had been living with someone for ten years without marrying him. She wanted to know all about that.' Victoria's life, and subsequent fling with a rock musician, occupied pages of speculation in Dodie's journal. 'I have no objection to people living together without being married and I think the lack of secrecy is a good thing. But I don't think it is a good idea from the woman's point of view. I have the feeling that such permissive sex makes sex a little dull.' As a woman who, ever since she saw Houghton's *Hindle Wakes*, had prized sexual liberation for women and celebrated it in her own writings, Dodie recognised that her own youthful sexual activities had thrived only when forbidden.

Victoria in turn was rather fascinated by Dodie and Alec. 'Alec was so good-looking, even at seventy-seven, and seemed to be there wholly to act on Dodie's wishes. I found it slightly embarrassing that the book we were discussing in his presence was all about Dodie's past lovers.' What Dodie was never told was that W. H. Allen had to reprint the dust-jacket at the eleventh hour the day before publication, which cost them £1000, because 'Dalmatians' — yet again — was spelt 'Dalmations'.

For the publication of *Look Back With Mixed Feelings*, *The Girl From the Candlelit Bath* and *The Midnight Kittens*, Dodie went to London and was put up at the Churchill Hotel. Her room was too hot, and the windows would not open. But it was a relief not to have Alec there: he made her nervous in interviews. W. H. Allen gave her dinner at the Savoy. She thought the food poor and the prices 'fantastic'. The whole

London experience seemed strange, 'like glimpsing the moon'. She was interviewed for the *Today* programme by Jack de Manio, who loved to talk about the past: just after ten in the morning she found him 'slightly affected by drink'. Interviewers noted her 'almost Cowardesque diction.' Then came the reviews: Hilary Spurling, the critic who had flayed the revived *Dear Octopus*, said *Mixed Feelings* was a classic to rank with *The Diary of a Nobody* and James Thurber's *My Life and Hard Times*. Arthur Marshall praised her to the skies on *Kaleidoscope*. Even *The Girl From the Candlelit Bath*, mercifully ignored by critics, was reprinting by May.

Julian Barnes, who was still invited twice a year to The Barretts with Laurien, was now deputy literary editor of the *New Statesman*, and wrote Dodie a 'treasurable' letter about *Mixed Feelings*, especially appreciative of the bizarre tale of the dwarfs in the Tottenham Court Road café on the morning after her deflowering. 'I once thought of putting them in a novel,' she told Julian, 'but realised that, as fiction, they wouldn't be believable.' A month later Dodie wrote to thank him for the *New Statesman* review by Jonathan Keates, who had written: 'This is autobiography at its most refined, a triumph of self-deprecating amusement, modesty and common sense' — Dodie evidently being convinced that 'Jonathan Keates' was one of Julian's many aliases. (Since he did write for the *Statesman* under several different in-house pseudonyms, including Spiro Keats and Edward Pygge, and later for the *Tatler* as Basil Seal, this was not necessarily a foolish assumption.)

Isherwood had by now published *Christopher and His Kind*, warning Dodie that this book 'tells all' and was perhaps over-aggressive. She enjoyed it, but found it embarrassing. 'And Alec, much as he cares for Christopher, has come to find homosexuality distasteful. It is so fully out in the open now, yet not fully enough to be taken for granted: it retains an exhibitionist streak. A few nights ago there was a television play about it, reasonably good but fairly distasteful. Mrs Ridgewell said, "Men kissing each other — so soppy!" and turned it off.' The very last entry of Dodie's forty-year journal notes that Noël Coward's friend Cole Lesley was now living happily with Graham Payn. It was 1979 and she decided she no longer had the will for journal-writing. Then she numbered the pages (3,653) and lamented that the journals 'gave little impression' of those last years. 'And' (after a million words) 'there is so much left out.'

18

'My Companion Is Gone . . . '

SINCE there was nothing she enjoyed more than remembering her success, Dodie looked forward to writing Volume Three, about 'the whole welter of excitement of the years 1931 to 1938 — the people, parties, first nights, restaurants, clothes: the joy of the cottage, the car drives, the never-ending astonishment of being able to *buy* freely.' She did not look forward to Volumes Four (America) or Five (the return from exile) — and who would want to read them anyway? It would take all her efforts to get Volume Three published at all.

She began to despair of 'time's tricks'. As her own celebrity faded, so had the reputations of people she had known. Who cared now about Binkie Beaumont? And even the recent obituaries for Basil Dean had hardly made anything of 'his formidable character'. (Amusingly, the

Times obituary had claimed: 'Dean held that it was a director's duty faithfully to interpret an author's intentions . . . ') Still, she persevered. She wrote in September 1979 to Anne Harvey, the BBC poetry producer, 'How I envy Edward Thomas's feeling "Nothing undone remains"; I doubt if you or I will ever feel that. Always, always, jobs, especially letters, remain undone. And I must somehow get back to my Volume Four, before the impetus dies.'

Look Back With Astonishment came out in September 1979, again dedicated to Alec. When Julian Barnes congratulated her, he was able to tell Dodie about the forthcoming publication of his first novel *Metroland*. Even more intriguingly, his letter was written from Romania, from 'a village with an unprintably rude name' where he had gone with the literary agent, Pat Kavanagh, whom he had just married. Dodie and Alec were naturally curious to meet her. But they could not bring themselves to attend the wedding party in London. Thirty-five years before, Isherwood had given them an ashtray with a drawing of a cringeing figure saying 'Who are all those others?' which represented their attitude to all parties. And they were much worse now, said Dodie: the very thought of a party made her legs wobble. So they did not meet Julian's wife until 1981, by which time *Metroland* had been published with some *éclat*. Dodie read it, was 'amazed by his economy of style' and admired the writing about the loss of virginity, but said she rather hankered for some of the soul-searching he had mentioned in a letter to her.

Julian's second novel, *Before She Met Me*, did not please her nearly so well. Its theme, retrospective sexual jealousy, was a subject Dodie knew something about: 'I think the theme is good. I have often wondered why people are not more jealous of the past of those they love,' she wrote. About the novel itself she was ambivalent. She wished she could say she liked it but she could not. 'It has many virtues; it is unusual, beautifully written, the use of words is so often clever and, again and again, the book is really funny. But I don't like it or the people in it, or really feel interested in them.

672

'I realise that I am at fault. I am too old. Novels have changed, life has changed. I don't find myself shocked by the language — indeed. I am rather shocked at myself for minding it so little and not finding words that are new to me. But I am shocked that characters in such a well-written book, by an author whose work I so much respect, mean so little to me. *It must be due to my age.*' Alec too wrote to Julian asking: 'Is there a danger that you may become regarded as "too clever"?'

Dodie's social life now depended on what Daphne du Maurier called paper friendships, conducted by letter. She saw only selected people for very restricted visits. She told Paul Mortimer, a PhD student who wanted to gather her reminiscences of the Manchester playwright Stanley Houghton: 'At eighty-five I find it something of a strain to meet people, and I am trying to save all my energy for my autobiography.' On Dodie's behalf, Alec struck up a penfriendship with Diana, Lady Barry, widow of Sir Gerald Barry 'the Festival of Britain chap'. Diana had written from her old watermill in the Dordogne, where she had heard *Look Back With Mixed Feelings* read on *Woman's Hour*, and she had many connections that entranced Dodie, who loved 'links'. Diana, née Brewer, had been to Newnham and lived in Bloomsbury in the 1920s. Her father, Maurice Brewer, was a first cousin of Sir Ambrose Heal (her uncle Cecil Brewer was architect of the 1916 Heal's building) and a backer of Norman MacDermott at the Everyman.

'Would it be fun for us to meet — or would it not? you choose,' Diana wrote. When next in London, having her hip replaced, she asked them to visit: 'Thank you for inviting us to your Mayfair pad,' wrote Alec, 'but at 84 Dodie is not up to it. She finds it harder and harder to work. At the moment one page a day is all she can hope for; two pages is marvellous.' He said he was 'proud of her being, at over eighty, able to recreate our fifteen years in America' and told Diana she ought to write her own memoirs. Charmed by his interest, she began sending reminiscences of her childhood and youthful travels, her friendships with the actress Martita Hunt and the educational pioneer A. S. Neill.

Alec would take the mail into Dodie's bedroom while she had her breakfast, and they cursed the bad handwriting of which most people seemed so proud. 'Dear Diana,' he wrote to Lady Barry, whose hand was large, round and clear, 'I do declare that yours are the nicest letters that I ever did see.' By 1981 he was writing at almost van Druten-like length to Diana, exchanging advice on reading (Raymond Asquith's letters; Michael Holroyd's biography of Lytton Strachey) and bringing her up to date about Dodie's Volume Four: 'a headache, much too long, with too many journals to draw from, needs drastic cutting.' He had offered to help: 'Fatal! Authors need praise and praise, not what seems to them silly and interfering suggestions from people who can't write.'

There is no record of Dodie's last thoughts on Phyllis, who had died at Denville Hall in February 1982, eighteen months after a stroke. Phyllis merited a handsome *Times* obituary which lauded her early plays and her success as a character actress of 'quick and intelligent observation', particularly in Dodie's plays. In her eighties, Phyllis had been amused to observe that she figured on almost every page of Dodie's autobiography, but made no other comment when she wrote about it to Jon Wynne-Tyson. She had left her books and pictures to him, instructing him to bonfire anything he did not want.

Dodie and Alec became even more home-bound when Mrs Ridgewell had to look after her husband Percy, who had Parkinson's Disease. No longer could Mrs Ridgewell bicycle up to the cottage at 8 a.m. to prepare Dodie's breakfast tray and take it to her in bed, or flit back and forth during the day to do their housework, prepare their lunch and supper as well as getting her husband's meals. In her last weeks at The Barretts, she had been thrown off her bicycle, and was carried into the cottage and given brandy. Without her, they could have no visitors at all. Alec had lumbago, 'and Dodie is completely undomesticated,' he wrote to Lady Barry. 'She says, "I write; I don't cook." So I do some meagre male cooking — scrambled eggs — and house tending.' That year Dodie told Michael De-la-Noy she had only been able to work on eight days during the past three months 'owing to domestic difficulties'. She seemed to get slower and slower, and wondered if she would ever finish the autobiography: 'But perhaps three volumes is enough!' 'Dodie got so that she didn't want to see anyone at all, other than me and Basil,' Mrs Ridgewell says. 'She wouldn't make friends with anyone in the village, saying she had to write for her living and must have leisure and peace. She just loved her work.'

Dodie galvanised herself to write a letter of protest to the *Observer* about a galling injustice over the new Public Lending Right, under which *Dalmatians*, despite being a much-borrowed book, could earn no PLR royalties, because one of the Grahame-Johnstone twins, Janet, had died tragically in 1979 in a fire in their kitchen; and the scheme curiously did not then apply to any book where one of the authors or illustrators had since died.

The reading lists continued as before:

Barbara Pym's *Crampton Hodnet*; Julian Barnes's *Flaubert's Parrot*; *Adrian Mole*; *The Private Eye Story*; Iris Murdoch; Kingsley Amis; John Gielgud's autobiography *Distinguished Company*, which she thought 'negligible'. The fiction was usually 'deplorable'; Murdoch she now found so 'deadly' she would give up reading her; and among thrillers she thought only P. D. James worth hearing about. She was mystified that Antonia Fraser's thriller heroine Jemima Shore 'gets frightfully excited because a man is undoing her suspenders. I've never been able to see what is exciting about suspenders.' She enjoyed Nigel Nicolson's *Portrait of a Marriage* but it made her admire Vita Sackville-West the less, not that she had admired her much before. She also read *The Heyday*, a 'promising and gifted' novel by Bamber Gascoigne which suddenly became 'unreadable'. Dodie's books are all annotated with the pencilled dates on which she read and re-read them. (In 1994 I asked Sir Peter Saunders, producer of *The Mousetrap*, if I could borrow a copy of his autobiography. To my astonishment he replied, 'Does the name of Dodie Smith mean anything to you?' and produced a copy he had found in a second-hand bookshop, annotated in the familiar pencilled script: 'DS read on publication 1972; re-read January 1979; Alec read January 1979, probably for 2nd time.') Alec and Dodie always read in tandem, often disagreeing. As she once wrote to van Druten, 'Alec has tried the new Elizabeth Bowen, and handed it back to me grimly — with his "fetch me a shovel" look.'

Julian Barnes eventually brought his wife Pat — plus a picnic lunch of lobster and wine. It amused Dodie that, in a way, the Barneses were like them, but fifty years younger: a writer married to agent/business manager. She liked the fact that Pat Kavanagh had made her own way in the world, and she was fascinated by her clothes. She wrote to her: 'I've made very few women friends since I got older and when I first knew you I felt, "That's someone I could really like if I got the chance." Well, I now feel I am getting it and I hope it goes on.' Dodie carefully did not mention a thriller of Julian's, one of a series about a bisexual private detective named Duffy, written under the pseudonym of Dan Kavanagh, because a cat was spit-roasted in the first chapter. It vanished from the shelf of Julian's books at The Barretts, he noticed. But they still took his advice about which new authors to read, and when he recommended Paul Theroux, Alec read *The Great Railway Bazaar* twice within two months.

Finally a publisher was found for Volume Four, *Look Back With Gratitude*, covering the years in America and the publication of *I Capture the Castle*. It was over-long, too detailed and diffuse, exactly as Dodie feared it would be, and inside her Christmas card to Julian that year was a brief bitter note about her publisher (Anthony Blond) and about the lack of national reviews. Alec reported that life at The Barretts was now 'pretty dire'. The next year's Christmas card to Julian had a brief, shakily handwritten note from Dodie about his fourth novel, *Staring At The Sun*. 'I admire it very greatly. But I'm a bit more puzzled than Alec is, and I can't *write* about this. I need to be talked to.' But Julian should have had the Booker Prize, Alec added, for *Flaubert's Parrot*.

In brief cards and letters to correspondents Dodie would confess: 'My legs are a bit wobbly. Not keen to be walked on,' and, 'As I get older (I'm 89 and a half) I do seem to, well, *notice* age.' The house was now kept for them by Winnie Amos from the village; but Alec did not get on with Winnie. Christmas arrived, with its 'tyranny' of cards. 'Dodie is having to say no even to her oldest friends because after half an hour she feels utterly exhausted,' wrote Jon Wynne-Tyson in his journal. 'She is writing nothing and can do little but move about from one piece of furniture to another.'

Alec gave Mrs Ridgewell no peace in his appeals to her to come back. Why not put Percy in a home, which they would pay for, and help them out instead? Mrs Ridgewell was deeply upset by this suggestion. 'I loved my husband and felt terrible to be asked to send him away. Alec sat and looked at me, and I said "I must look after my husband for as long as he needs me". I couldn't leave him, in case he fell and I wasn't there.'

Yet the BBC Radio 4 profile 'Dodie at Ninety' broadcast for her birthday in May 1986 (along with a Saturday Night Theatre production of *Dear Octopus* with Martin Jarvis in the Gielgud role) showed how lively Dodie still sounded. As always when a new young woman came into her life, Dodie was fascinated by Frances Donnelly, an intelligent and observant broadcaster, and later novelist, who did the interviewing. Dodie questioned her in turn about her private life and was disturbed that Frances seemed to be in a doomed relationship ('I'm worried about you, Frances'), and Frances says Dodie was quite right.

What struck Frances was that though Dodie was a frankly plain woman (and at ninety 'dwarfish, bent, witch-like and hairy') she had early in life recognised that people take you at your own estimation of yourself, and had created her own innate sense of style. She achieved this fifty years before all those how-to manuals about improving your lot in life, fifty years before Helen Gurley Brown's book *Sex and the Single Girl* which told *Cosmopolitan* readers how even if you are plain, poor, and provincial, with no natural advantages, you can ensnare a rich film producer (as she did) by determination and self-presentation. Dodie, orphaned at the age of eighteen, knew that half the battle is getting one's clothes right, and the interior decoration of one's bedsitter right, if you want to collect a prize like Ambrose Heal.

Dodie liked the radio programme. Both Boo Laye and John Gielgud had spoken admiringly of her, and she was most grateful to the critic J. C. Trewin, who spoke of her plays 'in a way that would bring joy to any author'. 'She was a professional of professionals,' he had said. 'In those days there were a great many skimble-skamble, one-play dramatists, but nobody could have been less skimble-skamble than Dodie. Her work really was so good that she was the woman playwright of her decade.

'In a peculiarly difficult time, at the end of an economic slump, she made people escape to their own households and domesticities, and to people that they knew: she really was just what was needed. I have the feeling that her plays in time will become pieces of social history, and it's wrong to undervalue them. I think they meant far more, in retrospect, than other West End successes of their day.'

The programme provoked a small avalanche of letters to The Barretts, including one from Virginia McKenna, now running her wildlife foundation with Bill Travers. Most letter-writers had been struck by Alec's contribution to the programme. Asked by Frances about the success of their marriage, he replied: 'My belief is that kindness is almost more important than what is usually called love. The trouble with the world nowadays is that kindness is dying, and what has made our marriage so successful is that we both try to be kind all the time. It may sound rather priggish, perhaps, these days, but I'm very emphatic about the fact that kindness should govern all.' 'So it seems,' said Dodie, commenting on the response to Alec's words, 'that most of the world is longing for some kind of reassurance.'

Old age, Dodie told one correspondent, 'isn't exactly easy, and I'm lucky to spend mine with someone like Alec.' She added: 'But I'm indeed lucky to have had him with me ever since our late twenties.'

Christopher Isherwood, the last of their little circle, died later that year. He had telephoned them during his last visit to London, but did not call: and although he had cabled on the publication of Dodie's last books, and Alec had sent press cuttings of reviews for *Christopher and His Kind,* no acknowledgement had arrived. Alec wrote to say they were anxious for news, since there had been floods in California, but silence had fallen. They did not hear from Bachardy until 12 February 1987, when he wrote apologising for the long delay: he had had such a mountain of mail, as well as his own work. 'For many months after Chris's death, I read the volumes of journals he left behind, twelve thick volumes . . . There was a complete record of our nearly thirty-three years together, much of it addressed directly to me. I think these journals may be his very best work . . . at the very least they made those first months without him bearable for me.'

That spring, just before her ninety-first birthday, Dodie was interviewed in the *Observer* about *I Capture the Castle*, which was reissued by The Bodley Head. This was Dodie's last published comment on her life and work. She said: 'I never did much like publicity. I only like to have all my own way! Of all my books and plays I think I like *Castle* best. I wrote myself into Cassandra.'

She was now very frail, barely able to walk, totally dependent on Alec. Clearly anxious about the fate of Dodie's huge archive of papers, Alec wrote to Julian Barnes in July 1987, asking him to be Dodie's literary executor after both their deaths — and setting out his duties as the disposer of Dodie's works. 'Neither Dodie nor I have any grandiose ideas of vast sums accruing, or much work entailed,' he said. Julian would be willed £500 — 'a comparatively paltry sum,' wrote Alec, 'but wait. You are left in the wills every single movable thing on and in this property: from frying pan to motor mowers to beds to books to Blüthner piano, car, etc. etc., which would certainly amount to several thousands' worth.' He would also be given first refusal on purchasing The Barretts.

Mrs Ridgewell vividly recalls the last visit she had from Alec. He came down to her cottage to beg her once more to come back and work for them. 'He was so desperate. He said he couldn't eat what Winnie cooked. I'd had to alter his trouser buttons, he had got so thin.' This time he brought his dressing-gown for her to hem the cuffs — just an excuse to call, she thought — and threw it down on a chair in angry frustration when she refused once again to abandon her husband. Alec at eighty-three was probably, by this time, more ill himself than anyone realised. In a local shop he had broken down and said, 'Is there no one who can help me?' Dodie, although no longer keeping her journals, still kept a little pocket diary for 1987, with perfunctory thoughts. On 3 May that year, her ninety-first birthday, she had written, 'My birthday. We're lucky to be together — and in many ways. Letters weighing on me.' The diary stops abruptly on Thursday 20 August; there are no more entries.

What is certain is that it was Dodie who

found Alec dead on his bedroom floor one morning five weeks after that last diary entry, on 27 September. She was quite stunned. She rang her neighbour Mrs Clark at Timbers, who found her seated on the sofa; Basil the gardener and Winnie Amos stayed with her all day. Julian was told by Dodie, on the telephone, that everything was under control; and that she did not want him or Laurence Fitch to come to Alec's funeral. She was, he says, very 'cut and dried' about it all: Alec was to be removed and cremated without Dodie's ever leaving the house. As Christopher Reynolds-Jones tells, Dodie telephoned him and he asked her how she was. 'Oh, I've had a terrible morning,' said Dodie. 'My breakfast didn't arrive, so I went along to see what was happening and found Alec dead.' Christopher too was rather surprised by her apparent lack of emotion. (But indignation had always been Dodie's first reaction to death. 'I really cannot be philosophical about death,' she had noted when T. S. Eliot died, having so recently found happiness with a young wife. 'It is too much to ask of the living. If one is allowed to live, it seems to me utterly outrageous that one should face extinction.')

Gwen Ffrangcon-Davies arrived at The Barretts in a voluminous cloak; Dodie reluctantly let her in, whereupon Gwen put her arms around Dodie and told her Alec was in heaven. Cousin Ronnie Reynolds-Jones and his wife Frances also arrived, expecting to attend Alec's funeral, only to be told by Dodie that they were not to go to the cremation, and not to buy any flowers. Did she mean it? they asked, horrified. Dodie said yes she did. She and Alec did not believe in funerals. They had talked it over and agreed that this was how it was to be. Could they not pick some of Alec's own flowers out of the garden, and take them? No, said Dodie. 'We don't believe in it. When we moved in here, we said we'd be carried out. And you're not to come to my funeral either.' She was insistent that the hearse should not come to the house. It was said that only the village butcher attended Alec's cremation. In Alec and Dodie's wills it was always specified that they should be cremated without ceremony and their ashes 'scattered to the four winds'.

Mrs Ridgewell was astonished by Dodie's reaction: it seemed to her principally one of annoyance. 'Alec wasn't supposed to die first. And she didn't want anyone to know; it was Mrs Clark who told me. When I went up to see Mrs Beesley she said she didn't want me or anyone to go to the funeral. Well, he didn't deserve that. He was a nice man.'

Everyone agrees on that: Alec was a good man, Dodie's life support system. She had been cocooned by his dedication. Having him in her life — 'my greatest blessing' — enabled her to write. When he died, Laurence Fitch said, she was scarcely able to write a cheque. Paul Mortimer, the Rochdale teacher researching Stanley Houghton for his PhD thesis, received an apologetic card from Dodie: his request for information had arrived only days after 'my dear husband, Alec Beesley, died in the night, most unexpectedly, and I have never come to feel normal about it.' She implored him not to feel that he had to write with condolences.

Michael De-la-Noy telephoned Dodie as usual on her ninety-second birthday in 1988, and asked how Alec was. 'And she replied, in her squeaky voice, "He's dead! Yes, I went in one morning and there he was, quite dead, on the floor!" There was something quite hilarious about her manner of telling it.'

'My dear husband has recently died,' she wrote to Dr Gotlieb at Boston who had corresponded with her for years. 'A complete shock to me. Please do not write to me about this. My companion is gone. Forgive this note — Dodie.' The line 'My companion is gone' succinctly reflects how she felt. No writer could have wished for a more slavishly devoted helpmeet. Typically, one day in 1944 when she had to go to MGM studios, she came home to find Alec had put violets and narcissi on her bedside table, with chocolates, the mail from England, a new detective novel, and a glass of sherry, and had set out towels and bath oil in the bathroom. 'And all this presumably because the little woman had been out to work on a wet day!' she wrote. Not only had he relished waiting on her, he was an inexhaustible adviser. 'Even Alec seldom *praises* my work much,' she noted at one point. 'He is too busy trying to help me to improve it. Alec has served my work for so many years, at the cost of making a career of his own.' In 1965, while writing about her earlier affairs, when she regarded her lovers as 'collectable status symbols', she concluded: 'Ironically, Alec has over the years become the greatest status symbol of my lifetime. I have not one friend who has a devoted husband, let alone a handsome and intelligent one. I barely know of one woman in my world of the theatre (I can only think of Sybil Thorndike) who has had a happy, lasting marriage. Our marriage has been a joint creation and we deserve credit for it — fifty-fifty.'

There is no question but that Alec too regarded his marriage as an entirely happy one. Julian Barnes remembers him pausing during lunch, heaving a deep sigh and saying: 'I've been happy for forty-five years . . .' Julian believes Alec's attitude to happiness was entirely practical: he would draw a line under certain things, and decide not to think about them any more. He was entirely unself-pitying about looking after Dodie. He had written to Diana Barry that after forty years they were 'happy beyond the dreams of matrimony'. And when Dodie sat down to count her blessings, as she did every year, first among them was always Alec. They would say to each other, in the evening, 'Oh I do like being us.' 'So do I.'

After her own husband Percy eventually died, at the age of eighty-five, Mrs Ridgewell went up to The Barretts. To her dismay, Dodie said: 'There's only you and me left now. If you come up here we will help one another.' Mrs Ridgewell wondered what help Dodie could be to her, since Dodie was by now quite helpless herself. She had fallen and injured her hip, and after August 1987 needed daily visits from a district nurse.

In the next three years she became increasingly frail, immobile and forgetful, barely able to enjoy the revivals of her work. Just after Christmas that year, in December 1987, Jonathan James-Moore produced a lively radio version of *The*

Hundred and One Dalmatians, with music and lyrics, narrated by Dorothy Tutin and with a superb cast, including Patricia Hodge as Cruella de Vil. And in May the next year, *Dear Octopus* was revived at the Theatre Royal, Windsor. Dodie's handwriting was shaky when she wrote to Anthony Heal to say she was not well enough, at ninety-two, to go to see it with him. 'But I find myself thinking of you in the old days, when you were little more than a boy. Your father sent us to Leipzig together — I should have been lost without your German, and without your help and companionship . . . I often think of the old days at Heal's. How much your father did for me! He would be shocked at my terrible writing of these days.' After the Windsor *Dear Octopus*, a letter arrived from Clarence House, from the Queen Mother's secretary: 'I am commanded by Her Majesty to tell you how much she enjoyed seeing *Dear Octopus* again'. But Dodie asked Laurence to acknowledge this letter for her, and the following Christmas her cards were signed on her behalf.

She was now cared for by Winnie Amos

who came daily, and by a district nurse whose notes give an indication of Dodie's distressing decline. 'Full general care given (to patient's disgust).' Confronted by the catheter and the commode, Dodie was 'confused'. Julian Barnes's 1990 diary records (shortly before she went into a nursing home): 'Went to visit Dodie. She's 94, incredibly frail, bedridden. She falls out of bed occasionally giving the dog a biscuit in the middle of the night. She is in no pain. Most of the time she sleeps or watches television; she reads a little. Laurence Fitch and I stayed about eight minutes, in the course of which she kept trying to get rid of us, saying she was sure we wanted our lunch, we mustn't waste our time with her, hadn't we better be going, and so on. Presumably her sense of time has slipped, and she thinks we've been there ages and she's afraid of getting tired — or *is* tired. What's it like, what's it like? Even if one retains health and cheerfulness, it can't be much fun.'

Winnie Amos would leave The Barretts at two o'clock; Basil would remain till five, go home for his tea, and return at 9 p.m. to give Dodie her supper, fill her hot water bottle, make her a cup of coffee, and leave her in the care of Charley, the faithful last Dalmatian. Dodie now slept downstairs, with Charley beside her on the floor on guard. But before long Dr Ambross the GP decided she must have full-time nursing, in a home. Basil reported that she screamed out when she reached the gate of The Barretts: 'I don't want to go, I don't want to go.'

Dodie died in November 1990. Against her express wishes, people did come to her funeral, because as Basil said, 'She won't know.' Dr Paul Mortimer, now a headmaster, drove down from Rochdale; cousin Ronnie and his wife Frances came from Devon, their son Christopher and his wife Bridget from Cheshire. From Stambourne came Gwen, Victor and David. And from London came Alec's half-sister Laurien, Julian Barnes and Laurence Fitch. There were no baked meats; everyone simply dispersed afterwards.

Julian's diary records: 'To Dodie's cremation. The vicar says at one point in his *oraison funèbre*: "I do myself have a connection with the world of show business. I shared a house with Cliff Richard for ten years."'

The British Dalmatian Society, in eternal gratitude towards Dodie for so helping to popularise the breed, sent a wreath in the Club's colours of blue and yellow.

'There were only three things in life that really interested Dodie,' Laurence Fitch says. 'Her writing, her husband and her dogs. She had once been interested in other people — but she increasingly found that people took her away from her writing.'

One of the last friends left, Don Bachardy, heard about Dodie's death while staying with the writer Armistead Maupin in New Zealand. Maupin had specifically asked Bachardy to bring with him Isherwood's copy of *It Ends With Revelations*. (Though he grew up in the southern United States, Maupin had been introduced to *I Capture the Castle* by his English grandmother, and divided his own enchanting 1993 novel, *Maybe the Moon*, into 'The Spiral Notebook', 'The Leatherette Journal' etc., with thanks to

Dodie.) Bachardy told me: 'She was so funny, so sharp and acerbic: such a witty conversationalist. We always howled. That was the attraction of Dodie.'

At The Barretts, Julian Barnes and the Reynolds-Jones family found the tidily annotated archive of writings ('with about fifty million mouse-droppings') and files and boxes containing every bill and letter Dodie and Alec had ever had, for building alterations, decorating (£2 10s per room), letters protesting when charged five shillings too much. Nothing had ever been thrown away. There were several hundred half-used lipstick cases and face cream bottles in the cupboards. Some of her furs still hung in her tiny wardrobe, and jewellery, and delicate handmade silk slips and nightdresses. There were thousands of books, and about fifty jigsaws, including two of The Barretts. A sale of Dodie's possessions was held at Bonhams. I wonder who bought the gold witch's ball.

Christopher Reynolds-Jones bought The Barretts (valued at £160,000) as his wife Bridget had always regarded it as her dream home. There was wet rot and dry rot, woodworm and other inevitable house ailments, fifty-six years on from Dodie's and Alec's 1934 renovations. Christopher decided to link the barn to the cottage with a new conservatory: otherwise The Barretts still looks, essentially, like Dodie's picture-postcard white cottage.

Of the six plays and six novels that Dodie published between 1931 and 1967, at least one play and one novel will stand in a class of their own. Her life was essentially limited and, to a degree, pampered. Though she had to struggle in her actress days, even at her poorest she never cooked herself a meal, and even as a 'shopgirl' there was always someone to wake her and fetch her breakfast. After her mother's death, she never had to look after anyone — husband, children or aged parents; and she was nannied by her husband for fifty years. A writer who has no family, no responsibility for other people, nobody to consider but himself and his own work (and there have been legions of such writers, most of them men) lives a peculiarly privileged and self-indulgent life. But however self-absorbed, she was always curious about others, perceptive, incisive, extravagant, obsessively hard-working and oddly vulnerable. One cannot help liking Dodie for her spirit and her humour.

John Gielgud recalls: 'She did love her white Rolls-Royce and those first nights, and being on equal terms with the stars. She fussed terribly over her clothes, because she really was rather ugly. But she was a great perfectionist. Fussed, on the set, about knives and forks and door-handles; it was the same at home.' Laurence Fitch says: 'She would fight like a cat to get things done her way.' Was she vain? 'For a writer,' said Julian Barnes, 'no more than usual.' She had a compelling presence; she talked precisely, listened intently; and her indomitable determination and diligence in the face of her own fading appeal were quite remarkable. It was the cruellest of torments for her to live through the age of kitchen sink drama, even if Coward, Rattigan, Lonsdale and Priestley all suffered in much the same way. So it was a kind of blessing to have a preternatural belief in herself, a sense of her own worth that was bred in childhood.

'What fascinates me,' Dodie wrote during one of her long delvings into the past, 'is how long I have been obsessed with getting my own life down on paper. I had thought that I only began attempting that when I started this journal in 1939. Now I see that I have been obsessed with the idea since I was a girl. Why? Has it always been a kind of compulsion neurosis? Or do I need to write my woes out of my system? Or does it all stem from something deeper? I am constantly trying to possess life, to save it up, to bring the then into now, and make it available for ever.

'The strange thing is, that I should hate anyone to read most of this self-exploration while I was living, and I have no great desire for my journals to be read after my death. And yet I feel they ought to be there, available. I am always trying to make things clear to some — utterly unimagined — reader. I do not fancy reading through these millions of words in extreme old age.

Nor do I care to think of Alec reading them after my death. And yet I have the desire — though it feels more like an obligation — to make these notebooks understood by — God knows who.

'Perhaps I have, after all, thought of someone, some far distant day, wading through the millions of words in this journal, my letters, notebooks etc. But the words would only be of interest if I had become a far more considerable writer than I ever have been or shall become. And I have little desire for posthumous fame.' But I feel she would have loved to know that people do still remember her most famous and lasting works, and quote lines from them, such as the 'District Nurse' joke from *Dear Octopus*, which Dodie had fought like a tigress to keep in.

* * *

In the last chapter of the typescript of Volume Five of her autobiography — which never did find a publisher — there are many references to 'the traitor within'. 'I have for many years believed that, in life, one awards oneself everything that happens to one, no one else is to blame. It is one's own choice. But one rarely, in retrospect, recognises this. It is as if there is some traitor within who makes the decision — and frequently wrecks one's happiness. I can see now that many of my miseries *were* for the best (for instance, I would have made three absolutely fatal marriages) but I see the traitor as my bitter enemy. Suppose I admit that my loss of the whole world of the theatre has been worth while? Why have I been allowed so little pleasure out of my books? I was miserable over the publication of *I Capture the Castle*, and able to find little joy in its eventual success. The same applies to *Dalmatians*.' In her notebook of 'Fragments Shored Against My Ruin' Dodie copied out a quotation from Henry James's *The Middle Years*, in which Denscombe speaks shortly before he dies: 'A second chance — that's the delusion. There never was to be but one. We work in the dark — we do what we can — we give what we have. Our doubt is our passion, and our passion is our task. The rest is the madness of art.'

Dodie did have a second chance, with novels, and a third, with children's books. Yet her later journals' most persistent theme is chronic regret for lack of appreciation. She regarded the playwright's craft as different from, and technically harder than, any other form of writing; and having once practised its mysterious alchemy with such success, she never reconciled herself to having lost the magic touch. The success of her first novel and her first children's book just did not count for her. So she became Grandima's Discontented Elf all over again. But many playwrights seem to share this obsession with critics: unlike novelists and poets (who can toil for years without being reviewed at all) every dramatist expects solus attention — and once you have that first-night success, nothing can quite match it.

'Critically, she was probably undervalued. Dodie Smith had her own decided gift,' wrote *The Times* in her obituary. 'She could heighten the humours of daily life without being merely glib. She knew what would register in performance.' J. C. Trewin wrote: 'Half a dozen plays stay in the memory as several brimming cups of milky tea, suitably sugared. In Dodie Smith's home-from-home, you know precisely where you are. This is the familiarity that breeds content.'

In the last year of her life Dodie's writings had earned her about £18,000, so she was not hard up, but Laurence Fitch and Julian Barnes, who had power of attorney and paid the nursing home bills, were slightly anxious. On her death her estate was valued at £472,571 net (£473,833 gross). Since her death, her estate continued to earn the kind of money she would have enjoyed: Walt Disney's re-release of *The 101 Dalmatians* in the United States in 1991 grossed $66 million and Dodie's small percentage royalty rose accordingly (her cousin Ronnie and his son Christopher being the beneficiaries). She would have been entranced by the idea of a Disney re-make of the film, with human characters and live puppies, in 1995.

Dodie belonged to an honourable tradition of women writers who have been the sole breadwinner for their husbands and families: Harriet Beecher

Stowe, Louisa May Alcott, Frances Hodgson Burnett, Elizabeth Gaskell. But her real legacy is incalculable, as is that of anyone who creates characters which pass into common childhood lore. There are Dalmatians everywhere named 'Pongo'. And I have my Mr Beesley, Dodie's unimagined legacy.

Dodie's own last Dalmatian, Charley, proved to be more sensitive than anyone had supposed. In the end he took care of her like J. M. Barrie's Nana. Mrs Ridgewell is convinced that Charley's heart was broken, after Dodie was taken away from The Barretts. 'He was left alone in the cottage, and he fretted. There was nobody there — only Basil coming in to feed him.' (Remember, 'Dalmatians need people'.) Dodie had left £2000 in her will for 'the utmost care and protection of Charley', but three weeks after her departure, Charley died — having bitten the postman as a final angry gesture. Basil buried him alongside Dodie's other Dalmatians, among Alec's flowers, under the mulberry tree in the garden of The Barretts.

Acknowledgements
& Notes on Sources

My chief source for Dodie's life story was Dodie's own journals and letters, stored in Dr Howard Gotlieb's Twentieth Century Archive at the Mugar Memorial Library, Boston University, Boston, Massachusetts. These reinforced and sometimes contradicted the accounts given in her four published volumes of autobiography: *Look Back With Love* (Heinemann, 1974), *Look Back With Mixed Feelings* (W. H. Allen, 1978), *Look Back With Astonishment* (W. H. Allen, 1979) and *Look Back With Gratitude* (Muller Blond & White, 1985) which took Dodie's life story to 1951, providing the framework for Parts One and Two of this biography. The fifth volume, covering the 1950s and the return to England, was unpublished, but remains in typescript in Boston. From 1939 to 1979, Dodie's journal runs to millions of words and, as if to aid the biographer, Dodie also kept, from 1956, a detailed index to the subjects covered on each page of the journal, which itself ran to fifty pages. The earlier years of Dodie's life were not recorded so minutely, but her 100,000–word fictionalised version, 'An Eye on Posterity', written in pencil when she was thirty, gave a full account of her life from fourteen to twenty. In the Red Notebook and the Black Notebook she wrote occasional thoughts and observations.

It would have been unwieldy to give an exact reference for all the many quotations from letters: Dodie was a prolific letter-writer and kept copies of almost all of them, repeating to many different friends the same observations and recollections. Essentially the letters reinforced her journals.

Jon Wynne-Tyson, son of Dodie's former secretary Esmé Wynne-Tyson, was particularly helpful in letting me see letters and cuttings from before 1939. Dodie figures in comparatively few memoirs, but among my sources were Basil Dean's two-volume autobiography,

709

Brian Finney's biography of Christopher Isherwood, Richard Huggett's biography of Binkie Beaumont, and the autobiography of Raymond Massey, *A Hundred Different Lives*.

Many of those who knew Dodie talked to me about her: in particular Julian Barnes, Dodie's literary executor, and Laurence Fitch, her theatrical agent. For their help with reminiscences, suggesting sources and finding references, I also thank Don Bachardy, Frith Banbury, Peter Barkworth, Jo Brandt, Brenda Bruce, Carole Burnes, Eileen Clark, Joan Curtis of the British Dalmatian Club, Paul and Meredith Daneman, Honey de Lacy, Michael De-la-Noy, Frances Donnelly, Vivian Ellis, Mark Fiennes, Sir John Gielgud, Joan and Elizabeth Gili, Dr Howard Gotlieb and his librarian, Margaret Goostray, Anne Grahame-Johnstone, Patsy Grigg, Doris Harris, Anne Harvey, the late Anthony Heal, Doë Howard, Sheila Huftel, Victoria Huxley, Jonathan James-Moore, Joan Kemp-Welch, Quentin Letts, Norman Lewis, Virginia McKenna, Pippin Markandya, Dr Paul Mortimer, Jenny

Naipaul, John Julius Norwich, Peter Parker, Victor Pemberton, George Pownall, Janet Rance, Lois Rathbone, Christopher Reynolds-Jones, Ronnie and Frances Reynolds-Jones, Constance Ridgewell, Esmé and Joanna Robertson, James Roose-Evans, Roger Smith, David Spenser, John Stride, Hilary Thomas, Ann Thwaite, Ion Trewin, Wendy Trewin, Ursula Vaughan Williams, John Vulliamy, Laurien Wade, and Jon Wynne-Tyson.

I am especially grateful to Julian Barnes and the Estate of Dodie Smith for permission to quote from Dodie Smith's published and unpublished works; to Don Bachardy for allowing me to quote at length from his own diaries and letters about Dodie; and to the omniscient Frith Banbury for checking the manuscript.

And I give special thanks to Alison Samuel, my editor, and to the 'Cassandra Club' — the aficionados who came in straw hats to Peg's Club in Covent Garden one April day to talk about *I Capture the Castle*: Xandra Bingley, Carmen Callil (begetter of this book), Maureen Cleave, Frances Donnelly,

Antonia Fraser, Caroline Seitz and Joanna Trollope.

Thanks, too, to the entire Grove family — Trevor, Peter, Colin, Lesley, Aurora, Avril, Lucy, Emma, Victoria, Oliver, Lara, Diana, Nicola, Edward and Alexandra — who took part in a family performance of *Dear Octopus* at Dané, St-Jean-Poutge, Gascony, in the summer of 1992 — especially Lesley Grove (Lesley Burton, RADA class of 1933) who played Dora incomparably.

Acknowledgements are also due to the following for permission to quote lines of poetry: *The New Yorker* for 'Denise' by Robert Beverly Hale © 1958, 1986 The New Yorker Magazine, Inc.; and Faber & Faber for the lines from 'Little Gidding', *Collected Poems 1909 – 1962* by T. S. Eliot.

FATAL RING OF LIGHT
Helen Eastwood

Katy's brother was supposed to have died in 1897 but a scrawled note in his handwriting showed July 1899. What had happened to him in those two years? Katy was determined to help him.

NIGHT ACTION
Alan Evans

Captain David Brent sails at dead of night to the German occupied Normandy town of St. Jean on a mission which will stretch loyalty and ingenuity to its limits, and beyond.

A MURDER TOO MANY
Elizabeth Ferrars

Many, including the murdered man's widow, believed the wrong man had been convicted. The further murder of a key witness in the earlier case convinced Basnett that the seemingly unrelated deaths were linked.

THE WILDERNESS WALK
Sheila Bishop

Stifling unpleasant memories of a misbegotten romance in Cleave with Lord Francis Aubrey, Lavinia goes on holiday there with her sister. The two women are thrust into a romantic intrigue involving none other than Lord Francis.

THE RELUCTANT GUEST
Rosalind Brett

Ann Calvert went to spend a month on a South African farm with Theo Borland and his sister. They both proved to be different from her first idea of them, and there was Storr Peterson — the most disturbing man she had ever met.

ONE ENCHANTED SUMMER
Anne Tedlock Brooks

A tale of mystery and romance and a girl who found both during one enchanted summer.

CLOUD OVER MALVERTON
Nancy Buckingham

Dulcie soon realises that something is seriously wrong at Malverton, and when violence strikes she is horrified to find herself under suspicion of murder.

AFTER THOUGHTS
Max Bygraves

The Cockney entertainer tells stories of his East End childhood, of his RAF days, and his post-war showbusiness successes and friendships with fellow comedians.

MOONLIGHT
AND MARCH ROSES
D. Y. Cameron

Lynn's search to trace a missing girl takes her to Spain, where she meets Clive Hendon. While untangling the situation, she untangles her emotions and decides on her own future.

NURSE ALICE IN LOVE
Theresa Charles

Accepting the post of nurse to little Fernie Sherrod, Alice Everton could not guess at the romance, suspense and danger which lay ahead at the Sherrod's isolated estate.

POIROT INVESTIGATES
Agatha Christie

Two things bind these eleven stories together — the brilliance and uncanny skill of the diminutive Belgian detective, and the stupidity of his Watson-like partner, Captain Hastings.

LET LOOSE THE TIGERS
Josephine Cox

Queenie promised to find the long-lost son of the frail, elderly murderess, Hannah Jason. But her enquiries threatened to unlock the cage where crucial secrets had long been held captive.

THE TWILIGHT MAN
Frank Gruber

Jim Rand lives alone in the California desert awaiting death. Into his hermit existence comes a teenage girl who blows both his past and his brief future wide open.

DOG IN THE DARK
Gerald Hammond

Jim Cunningham breeds and trains gun dogs, and his antagonism towards the devotees of show spaniels earns him many enemies. So when one of them is found murdered, the police are on his doorstep within hours.

THE RED KNIGHT
Geoffrey Moxon

When he finds himself a pawn on the chessboard of international espionage with his family in constant danger, Guy Trent becomes embroiled in moves and countermoves which may mean life or death for Western scientists.

TIGER TIGER
Frank Ryan

A young man involved in drugs is found murdered. This is the first event which will draw Detective Inspector Sandy Woodings into a whirlpool of murder and deceit.

CAROLINE MINUSCULE
Andrew Taylor

Caroline Minuscule, a medieval script, is the first clue to the whereabouts of a cache of diamonds. The search becomes a deadly kind of fairy story in which several murders have an other-worldly quality.

LONG CHAIN OF DEATH
Sarah Wolf

During the Second World War four American teenagers from the same town join the Army together. Forty-two years later, the son of one of the soldiers realises that someone is systematically wiping out the families of the four men.

THE LISTERDALE MYSTERY
Agatha Christie

Twelve short stories ranging from the light-hearted to the macabre, diverse mysteries ingeniously and plausibly contrived and convincingly unravelled.

TO BE LOVED
Lynne Collins

Andrew married the woman he had always loved despite the knowledge that Sarah married him for reasons of her own. So much heartache could have been avoided if only he had known how vital it was to be loved.

ACCUSED NURSE
Jane Converse

Paula found herself accused of a crime which could cost her her job, her nurse's reputation, and even the man she loved, unless the truth came to light.

BUTTERFLY MONTANE
Dorothy Cork

Parma had come to New Guinea to marry Alec Rivers, but she found him completely disinterested and that overbearing Pierce Adams getting entirely the wrong idea about her.

HONOURABLE FRIENDS
Janet Daley

Priscilla Burford is happily married when she meets Junior Environment Minister Alistair Thurston. Inevitably, sexual obsession and political necessity collide.

WANDERING MINSTRELS
Mary Delorme

Stella Wade's career as a concert pianist might have been ruined by the rudeness of a famous conductor, so it seemed to her agent and benefactor. Even Sir Nicholas fails to see the possibilities when John Tallis falls deeply in love with Stella.

CHATEAU OF FLOWERS
Margaret Rome

Alain, Comte de Treville needed a wife to look after him, and Fleur went into marriage on a business basis only, hoping that eventually he would come to trust and care for her.

CRISS-CROSS
Alan Scholefield

As her ex-husband had succeeded in kidnapping their young daughter once, Jane was determined to take her safely back to England. But all too soon Jane is caught up in a new web of intrigue.

DEAD BY MORNING
Dorothy Simpson

Leo Martindale's body was discovered outside the gates of his ancestral home. Is it, as Inspector Thanet begins to suspect, murder?